Painted Words
Kangra Paintings of Matiram's Rasraj

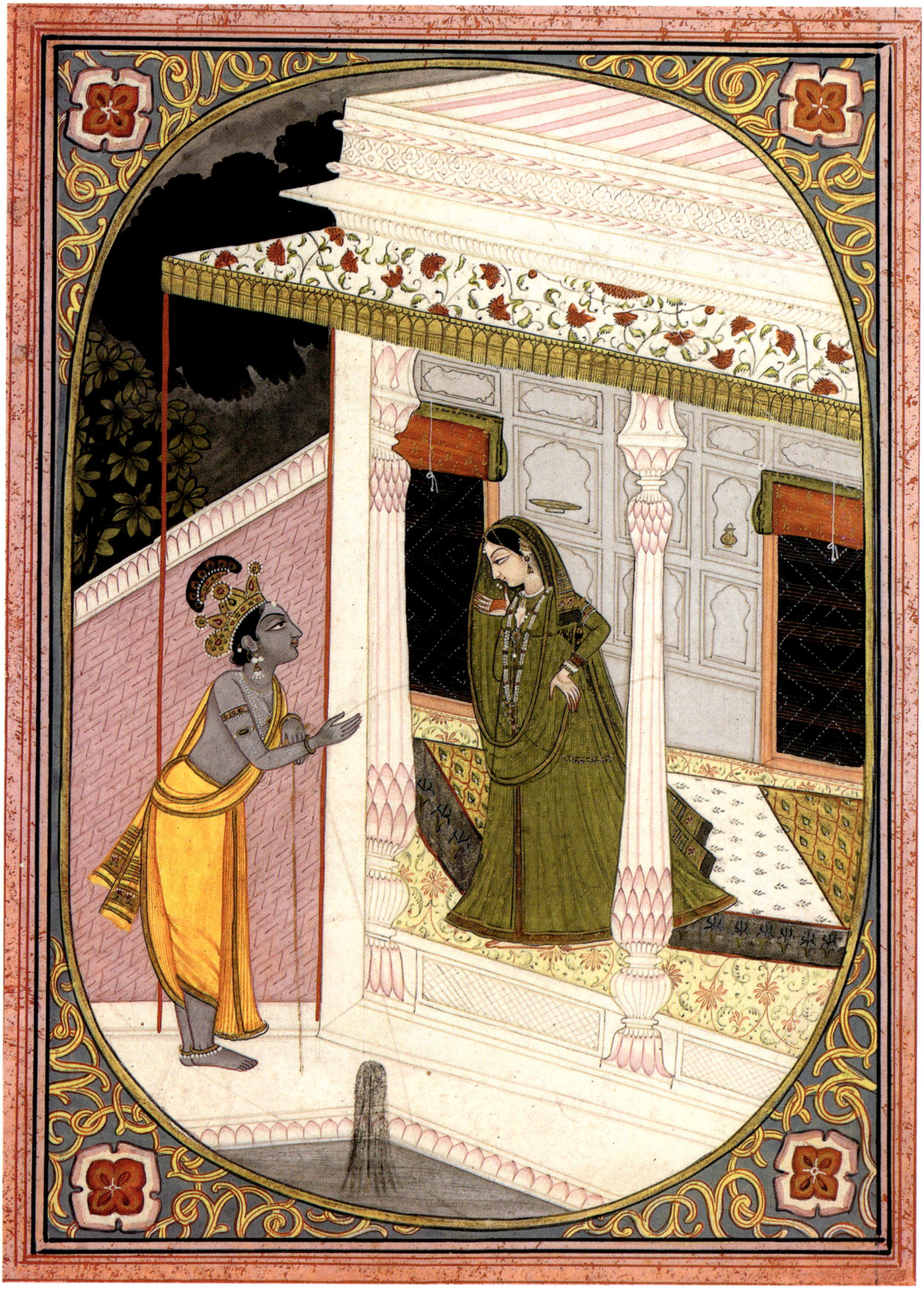

Madhya Dhira-Adhira Nayika, school of Purkhu, Kangra CE 1785-90, Dehejia collection

Contours of Indian Art & Architecture, no. 7

Painted Words

Kangra Paintings of Matiram's Rasraj

Harsha V. Dehejia
Vijay Sharma

DK
PRINTWORLD
Publishers of Indian Traditions

Cataloging in Publication Data — DK
[Courtesy: D.K. Agencies (P) Ltd. <docinfo@dkagencies.com>]

Dehejia, Harsha V.
Painted words : Kangra paintings of Matiram's Rasraj / Harsha V. Dehejia, Vijay Sharma.
p. cm. — (Contours of Indian art & architecture ; no. 7)
Includes text of Rasarāja in Braj; with English translation.
Includes bibliographical references.
ISBN 13: 9788124606124

1. Matirāma, 17th cent. Rasarāja — Illustrations. 2. Purkhu, fl. 18th cent. — Criticism and interpretation. 3. Pahari painting — India — Kangra (Princely State) 4. Miniature painting, Indic — India — Kangra (Princely State) I. Sharma, Vijay, 1962-, joint author. II. Matirāma, 17th cent. Rasarāja. English & Braj. III. Title. IV. Series: Contours of Indian art & architecture ; no. 7.

DDC 759.954 23

Designed by : Graeme Bruce, Alex Wagstaff, and Ryan Krieg, Ottawa, ON, Canada

Grateful thanks to Prof. Krishan Lal Sharma for his help and guidance in reading *Rasraj* and who made this text come alive.

We gratefully acknowledge Art of the Past, Harish Patel and Dr. Daljeet for lending their images

ISBN 13: 978-81-246-0612-4 ISBN 10: 81-246-0612-9
Year of Publication: 2012

Published & Printed by:
D.K. Printworld (P) Ltd.
Regd. Office : *'Vedaśrī'*, F-395, Sudarshan Park, New Delhi – 110 015
e-mail : indology@dkprintworld.com; *Web* : www.dkprintworld.com

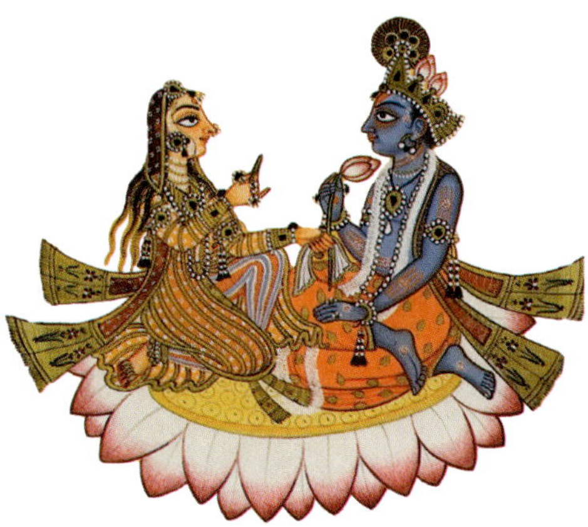

No celebration of *ritikavya* can be complete until we have enjoyed
the sonorous poetry of Matiram.

With well-sculpted words and lyrical rhythms Matiram takes us into the rarefied world of the *nayak* and the *nayika*, their amorous exchanges, the sensuality of loving glances, the charged moments of romantic feelings, the heart-throb of belonging, the poignancy of longing and above all the fulfilment of desire.
Line by line and *doha* after *doha* Matiram leads us into the emotionally charged world of *shringara rasa* and for those of us who are chastened by *harishringara* we go from one level to another till we hear the flute of Krishna.

And when we find that these sonorous words of Matiram have been brought alive by none other than Purkhu and his school of painting under the patronage of Sansar Chand of Kangra, our joy is doubled and Matiram's words become visual poetry.

In the hands of Purkhu words become lines, emotions take on a colour and desire becomes palpable through the magic of his *kalam*.

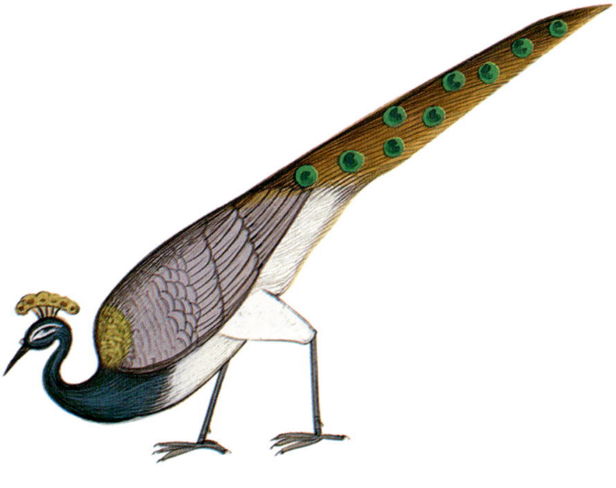

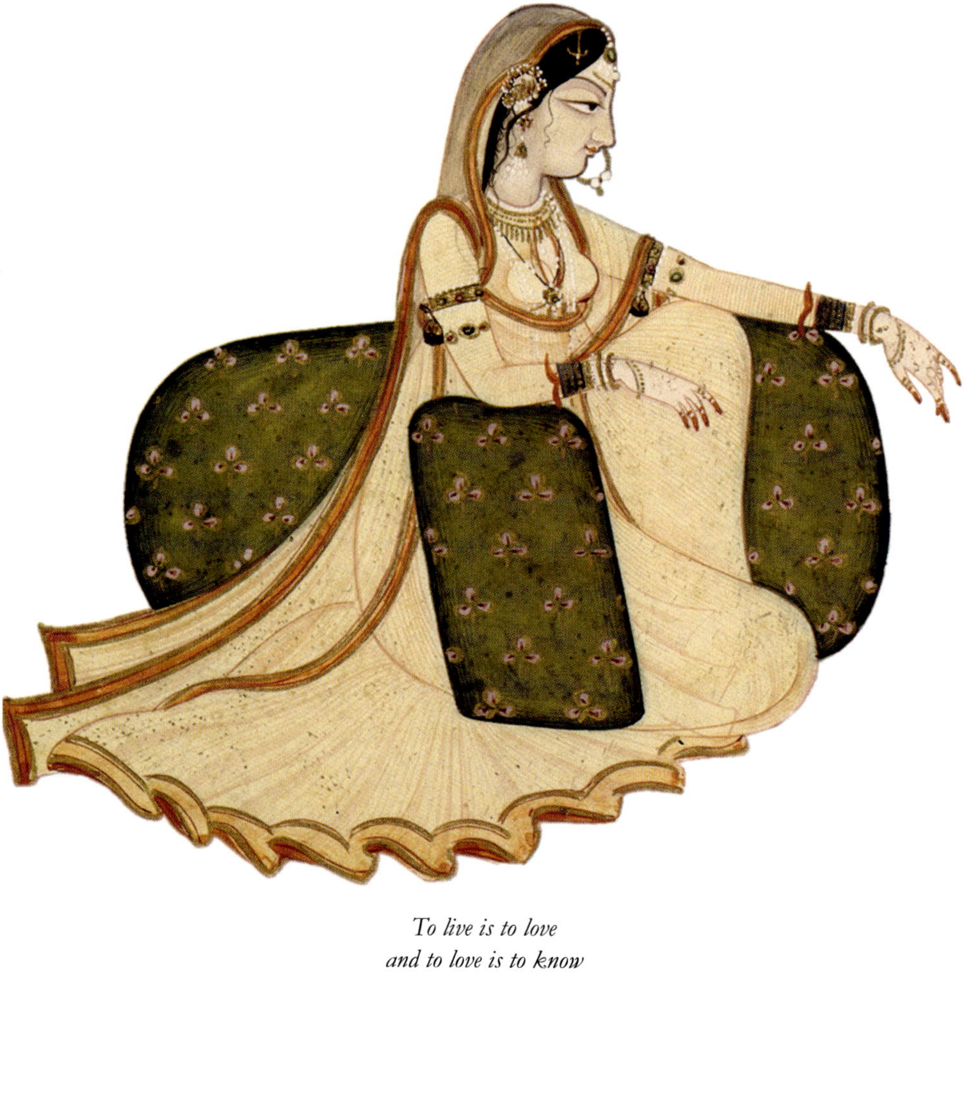

To live is to love
and to love is to know

CONTENTS

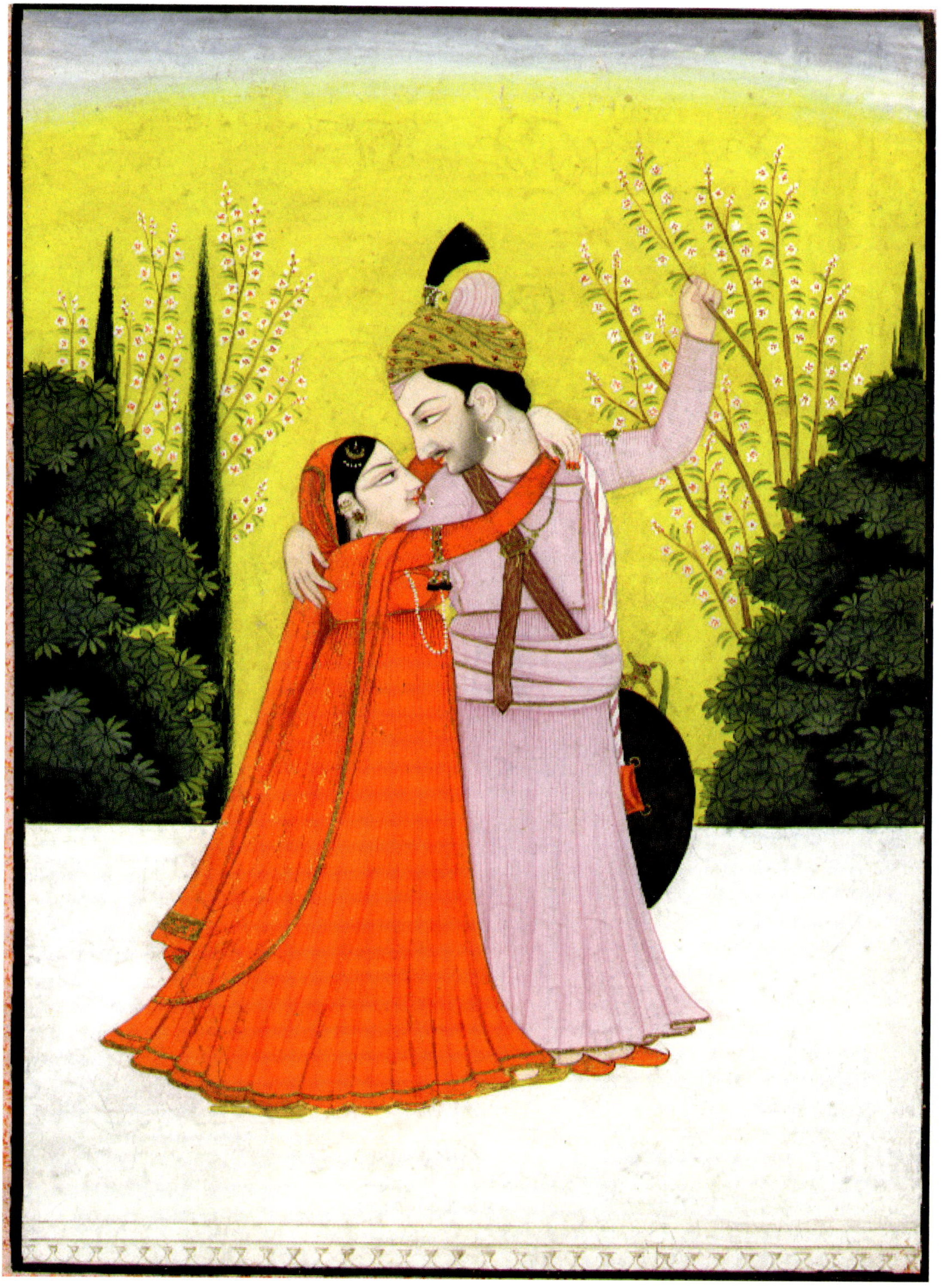

A young hill prince dallies with his wife, Guler, CE 1800, Kapoor Galleries, New York

The Patron and the Painter: Sansar Chand and Purkhu

In the lap of the river Beas with its limpid waters and surrounded by idyllic meadows and verdant rolling hills lies the valley of Kangra. The ancient name of Kangra was Trigarta or the valley of three pits and it was ruled by Katoch chiefs who claimed their descent from the moon and called themselves Chandravamshi. Historically, the Katoch clan traced their pedigree to Raja Susarma Chandra, who fought in the favour of Kauravas in the great war of Mahabharata. Panini categorises the people of Kangra as *ayudhajivi* or those who earn their livelihood through weapons. The people of Kangra have a martial history and about the Kangra fort there was a popular saying in the hills that 'one who holds the fort could rule the hills'.

It was Raja Trilok Chand, a contemporary of Akbar and a deputy to his father Jai Chand, who looked after the affairs of the Kangra state. It was during the reign of Hari Chand Katoch (r. 1612-27) that Jahangir invaded Kangra and took the Kangra fort in his possession. The fort of Kangra remained under Mughal possession until 1783 until the rule of the last Mughal Governor Saif Ali Khan. Kangra rulers constantly waged guerrilla wars against the Mughal garrison stationed in the fort to regain possession of it. Eventually, it was during Aurangzeb's rule that peace prevailed when Raja Vijay Ram Chand of Kangra was granted a *jagir*. This

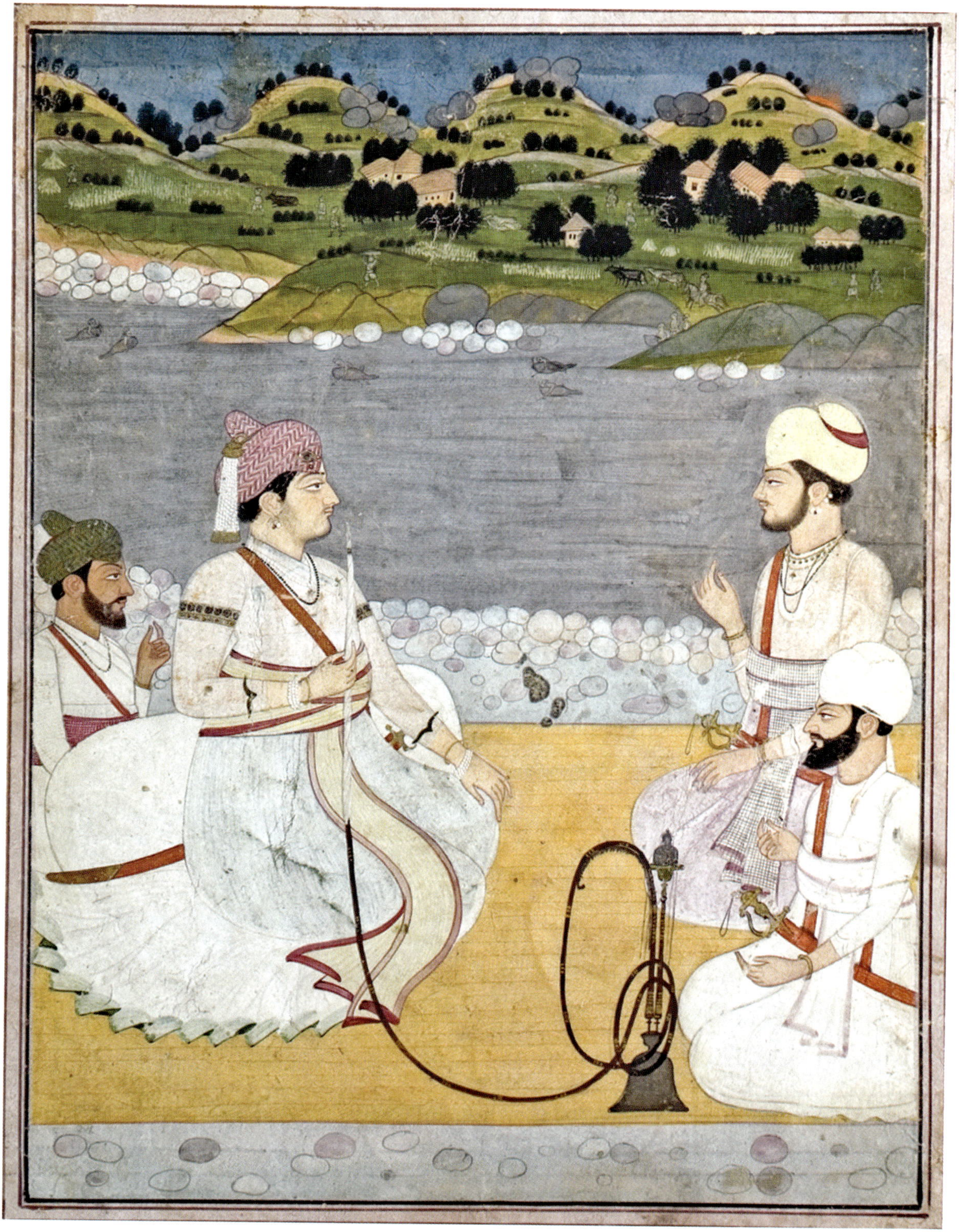

Young Raja Sansar Chand camping beside river Beas at Nadaun, school of Purkhu, 1785.
Jagdish and Kamla Mittal Museum of Indian Art, Hyderabad

ruler established the town of Bijapur, which remained the abode of Katoch chiefs till the regime of Raja Ghamand Chand. It was Raja Alam Chand (r. 1697-1700) of Kangra who established a township at Alampur at the bank of the Beas River.

In medieval India, Kangra was home to the cult of the Devi. Devi temples in the Kangra Valley are well known and millions of pilgrims from various parts of India throng to these temples in Kangra Valley every year even today. While murals may have had an ancient presence in this part of the world, the earliest evidence of the painting in the Kangra Valley comes in the form of an illustrated manuscript of the *Devimahatmya.*

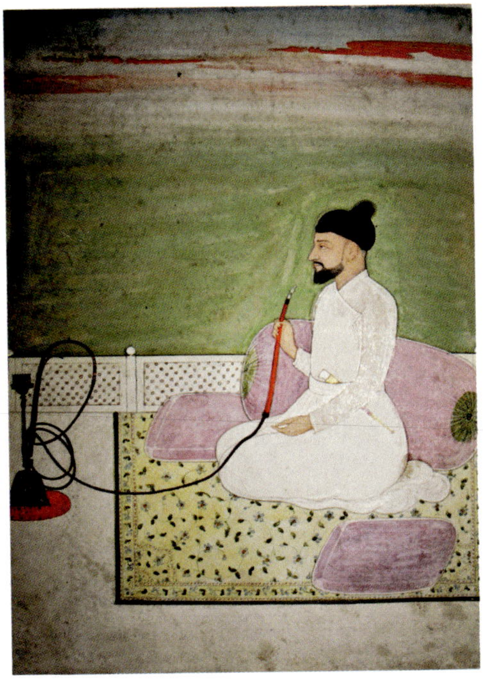

Raja Ghamand Chand of Kangra, Guler, 1775, Bhuri Singh Museum, Chamba

The colophon of the manuscript of *Devimahatmya* records that it was written in 1575 at the town of Jaisimhapur near Kangra. Stylistically the pictures painted in this manuscript bear strong affinities with that of the Chaurapanchashika paintings. This early style of Rajput painting was prevalent in the sixteenth century in northern India from Delhi to Jaunpur. It is possible that a painter accomplished in the Chaurapanchashika style may have come to Kangra and presumably settled there. The hot palette of pigments used in the illustrations of this manuscript suggests the continuity of the Rajput painting tradition, which one notices again in the early Pahari paintings of the seventeenth century. The female figures with large wide open eyes seen in the *Devimahatmya* may have been a precursor of Nurpur and Basohli paintings in the late seventeenth century.

Another illustrated manuscript that was painted at Nagarkot in Kangra in 1695 is done in the Kashmiri style. This manuscript entitled *Shahnama* was commissioned by one Mirza Rustam, a Mughal functionary perhaps stationed at Kangra. Painted against a monochromatic background, the *Shahnama* paintings bear strong Mughal influences, although in certain elements like architecture,

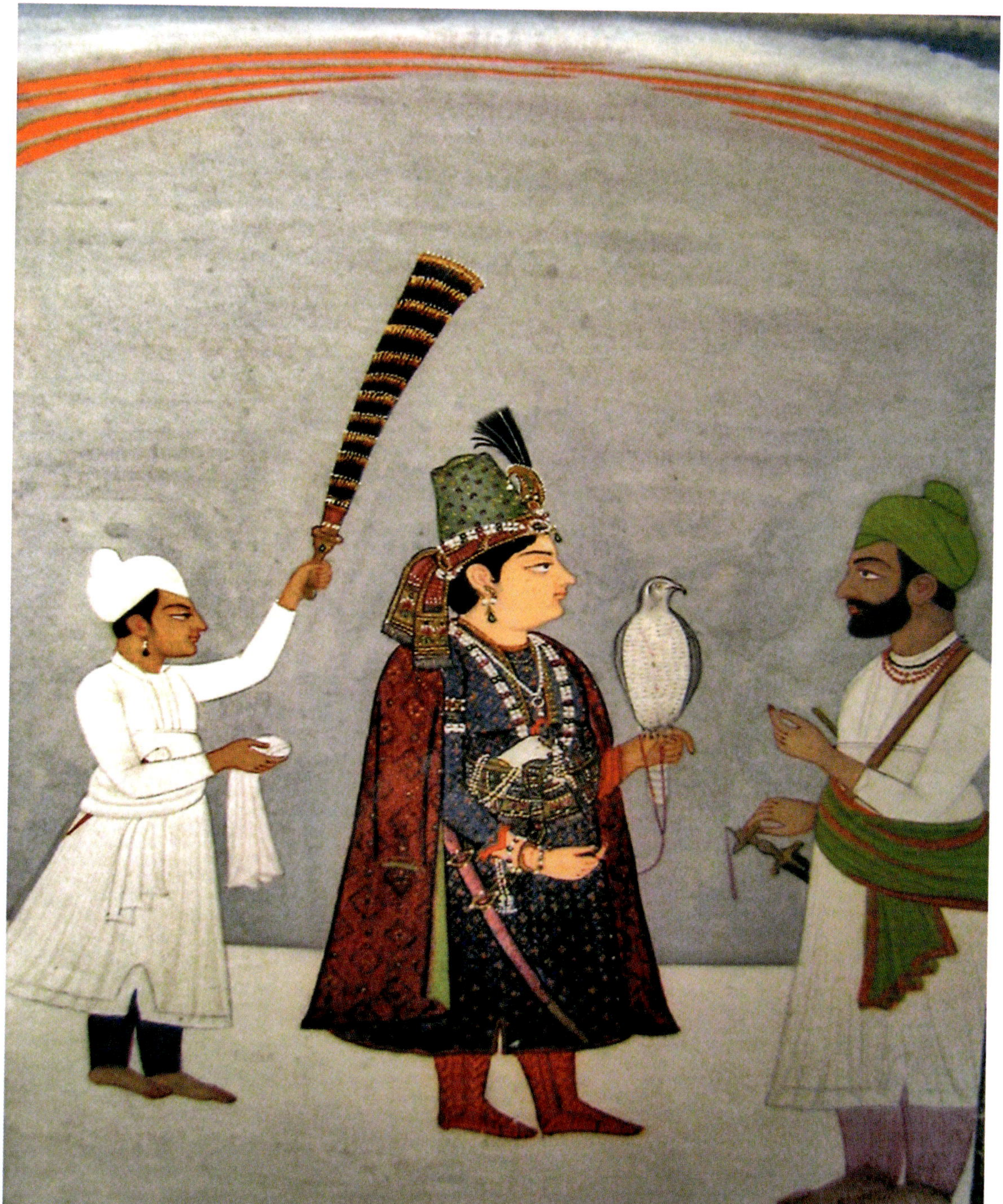

Young Sansar Chand holding a falcon, Kangra, CE 1770-80, private collection

vegetation, division of space and the horizon broken with white streaks are to be seen in the early Pahari paintings of the late seventeenth century.

During the period of Jahangir and Shahjahan Mughal painting had reached its zenith and Pahari kingdoms did not lag behind in patronising the art of painting. This was particularly true of states like Nurpur, Chamba, Basohli and Mandi. However, one does not hear of such artistic activities in Kangra. It is possible that the rulers of Kangra at that time were more interested in building palaces and forts rather than establishing ateliers of painters.

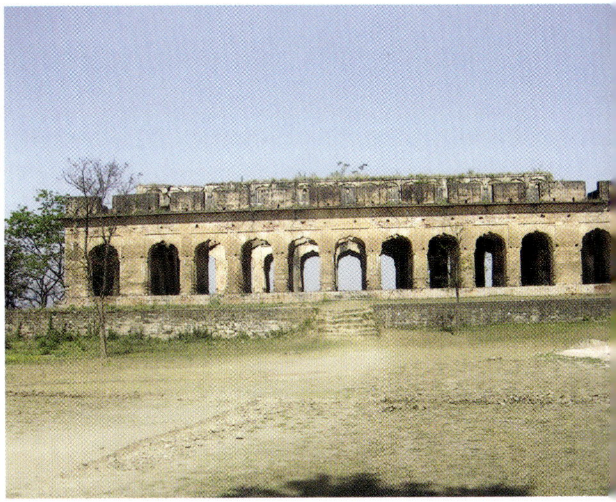

Baradari at the palace of Tira-Sujanpur, Kangra

After the death of the Mughal emperor Aurangzeb, the Mughal empire rapidly began to decline. Numerous incursions by Nadir Shah and Ahmad Shah Durrani further weakened the empire.

As a result, the Punjab Hill states were able to free themselves of their Mughal overlords. While Nadir Shah looted and took away the booty to his country, Ahmad Shah Durrani established his suzerainty in Punjab and made all Hill states his vassals. He proved to be more merciless than Nadir Shah and a common saying in the hills went thus — *khada pita lahe da, reha se ahmad sahe da* meaning 'only what we eat and drink is ours, what remains belongs to Ahmad Shah'. Ahmad Shah Durrani had appointed Raja Ghamand Chand of Kangra (1758-74) as Governor of the entire hill region. During this period, Kangra emerged as a powerful state both politically and economically. During the regime of Ghamand Chand Kangra experienced a new era of prosperity. This sudden affluence enabled Raja Ghamand Chand to embellish his kingdom by constructing palaces, forts and temples. For this, he engaged several artisans trained in the Mughal style of architecture, especially in the style prevailing in Awadh, which is seen in the palaces of Tira-Sujanpur. Raja

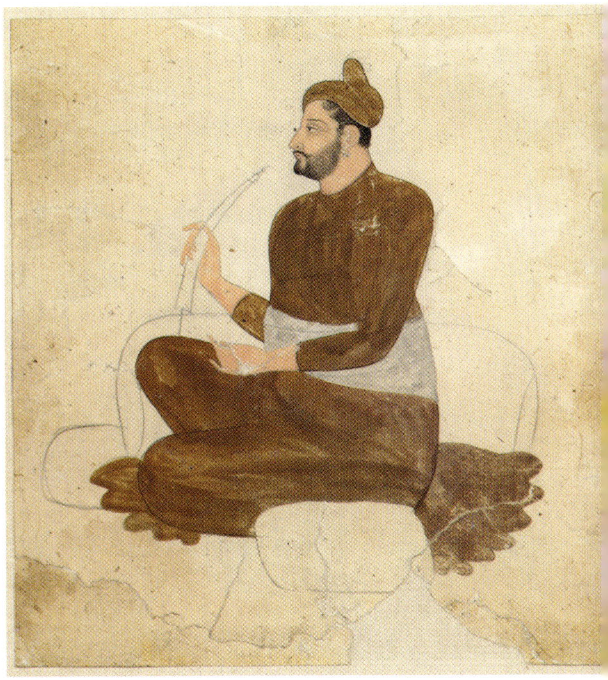

Sansar Chand smoking huqqa, ascribed to Purkhu, Kangra, CE 1800, Museum of Fine Arts, Boston

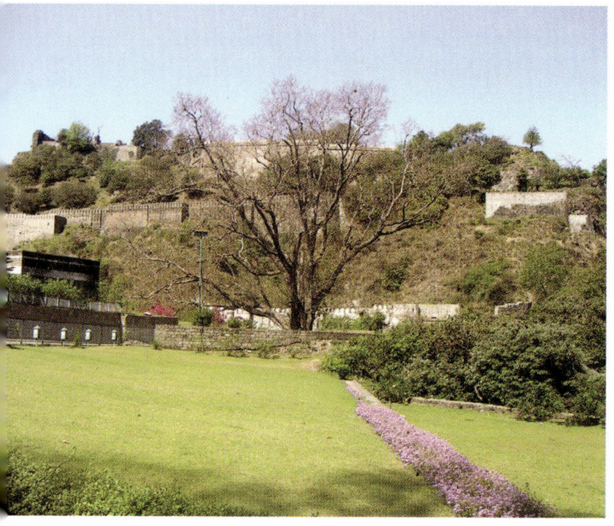

The fortress of Kangra

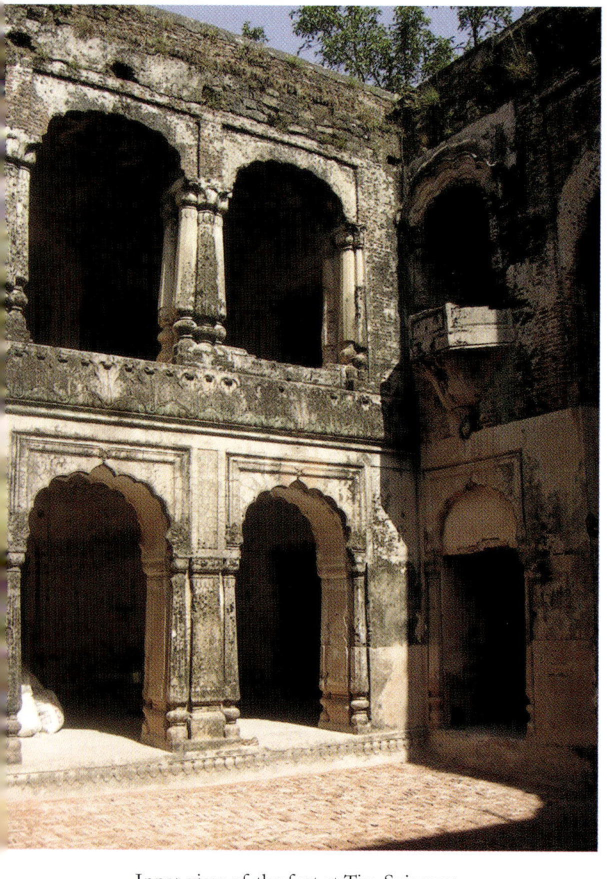

Inner view of the fort at Tira-Sujanpur

Ghamand Chand Katoch died in 1774 and was succeeded by his son Tegh Bahadur, who ruled for a short period of one year.

Tegh Bahadur's son Sansar Chand II ascended the throne in 1776 at the tender age of ten. Sansar Chand, like his grandfather, was also an ambitious ruler who further consolidated his kingdom following the footsteps of his grandfather. It was Sansar Chand who completed the construction of palaces and temples at Tira-Sujanpur and later at Nadaun. He also embellished with splendid wall paintings the temples of Gauri-Shankar and Narbadeshwar at Sujanpur, the capital town of Kangra state. A marked influence of Awadh architecture can be noticed in the buildings and palaces of Sujanpur. The noted art historian Hermann Goetz rightly remarks on the Awadh influence:

> The splendid political succession and cultural achievements of Sansar Chand II were, in fact, the results of ideas, ideals and techniques imported from outside. His treacherous diplomacy, his exactions, his Rohilla Afghan mercenary army, his plan to organise battalions drilled in the European manner, his palaces, temples, the costumes and style of life at his court, and finally his painting studies, were imports from outside, from Oudh. The new court dresses were those of Faizabad and Lucknow under Shuja and Asaf-ud-Daula. His palaces at Tira and Nadaun are purest Lucknow architecture. The Baradari at Tira is a smaller imitation of the great Imambara of Asaf-ud-Daula; the garden house at Nadaun resembles the Badshah Bagh. The walls of both the Sita Ram and the Narbadeshwar temple are covered with miniature paintings arranged in cartouches between the other wall ornaments. Hardly any of these wall paintings is in the Mughal taste, just because the transition from the latter to an indigenous Kangra style had already been achieved in the preceding reign of Ghamand Chand (1758-74). Even then the influence of the Oudh school can be traced in many minor details.[1]

By the end of eighteenth century Sansar Chand had become a powerful and affluent prince in the entire hill region and a new era in Kangra was ushered in. His political stature, connoisseurship for the arts and magnanimity attracted several artists, poets, musicians and learned scholars to his court. Tira-Sujanpur and Nadaun had become the

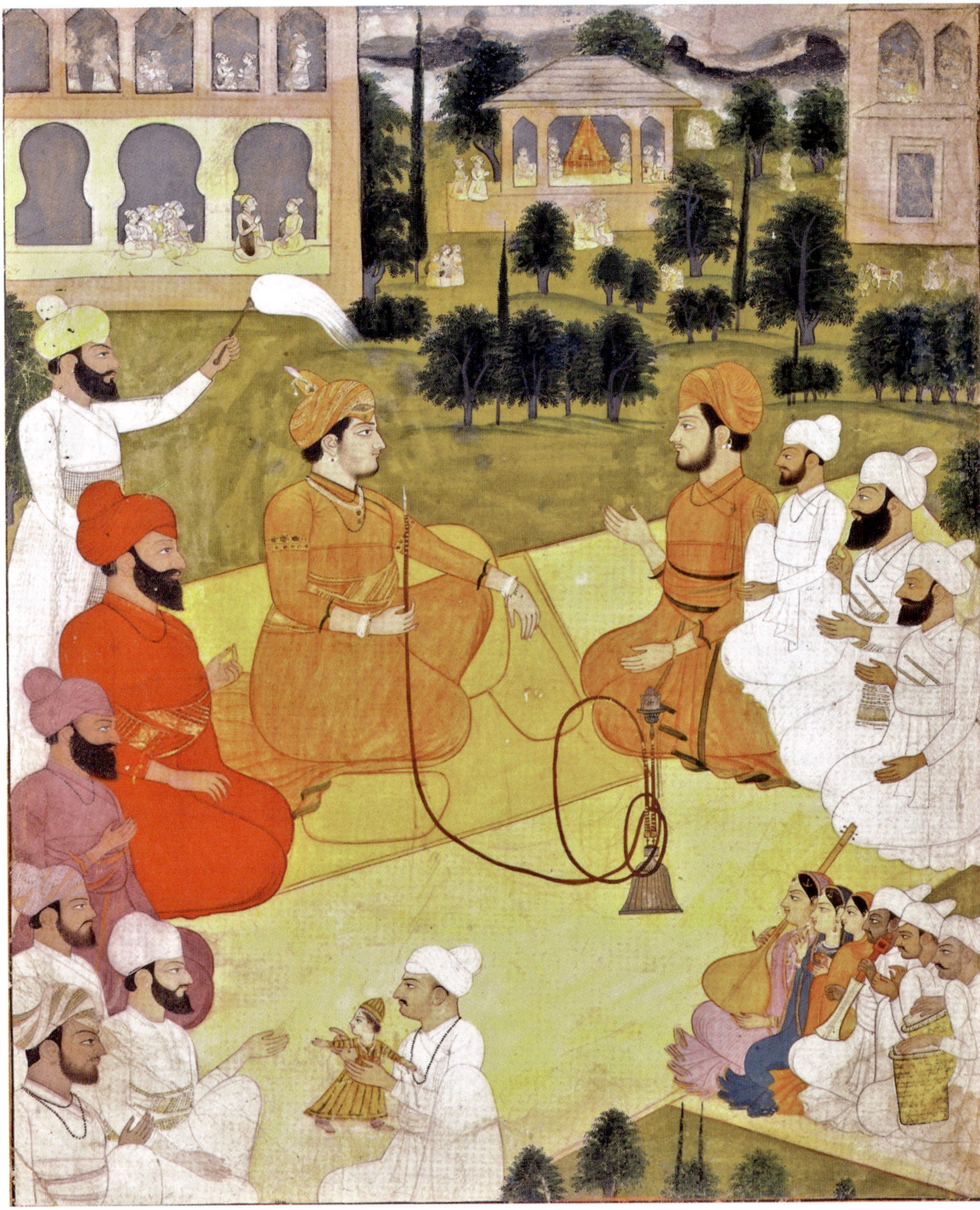

Sansar Chand with courtiers and musicians, school of Purkhu, Kangra, CE 1790, private collection

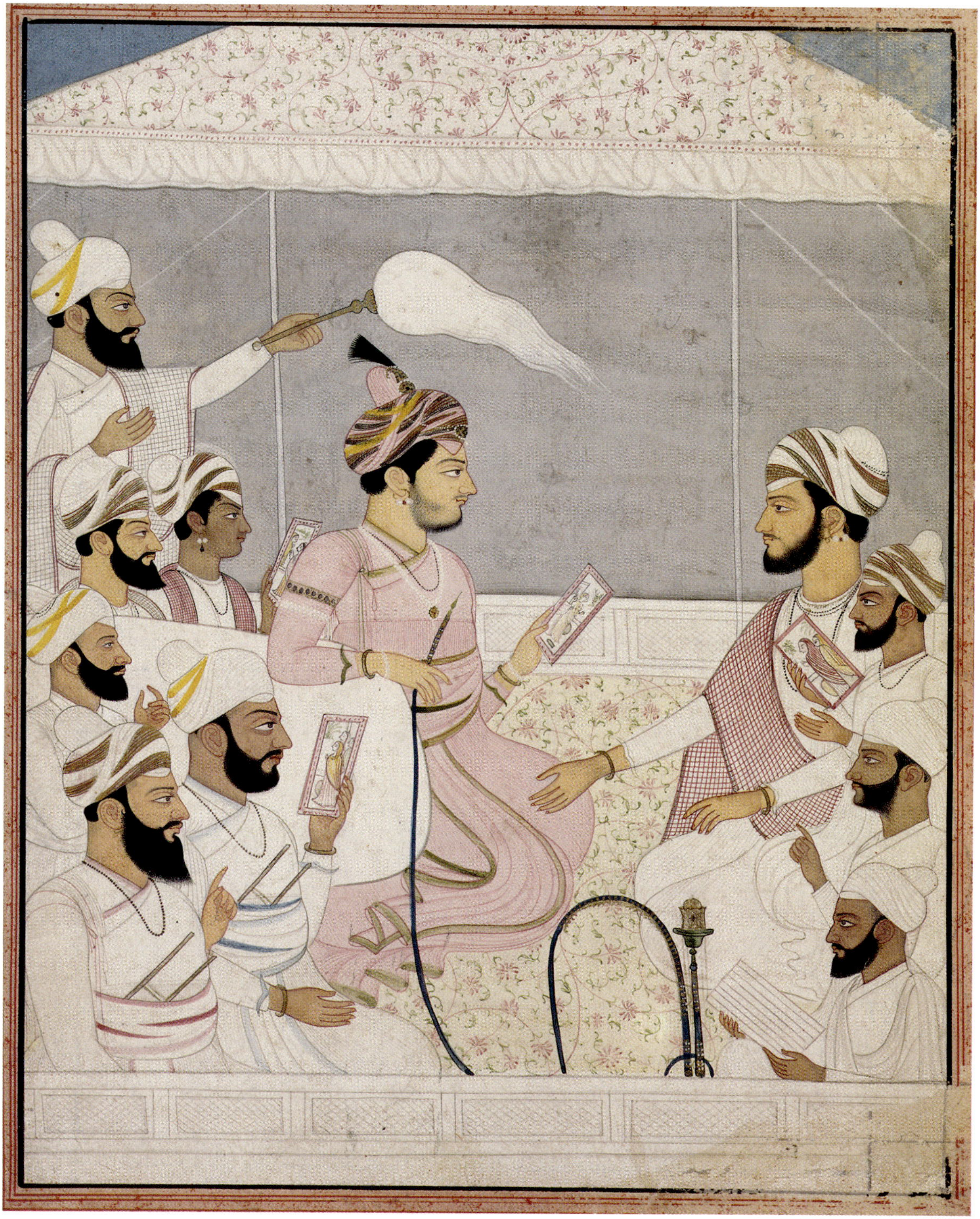

Sansar Chand appreciating pictures, school of Purkhu, CE 1790.
Museum Rietberg, Zurich

hub of artistic activities and creativity. This was the golden period of Kangra when fine arts flourished and achieved new heights. In his *Tarikh-i-Punjab*, the noted historian Ghulam Muhai-ud-din writes about Sansar Chand's passion for the arts:

. . . For many years, he passed his days in great felicity. He was generous in conduct, kind to his subjects, just as Nushirvan and a second Akbar in his recognition of men's good qualities. Crowds of people of skill and talent, professional soldiers and others, resorted to Kangra and gained happiness from his gifts and favours. Those addicted to pleasure, who live for the gratification of others, flocked from all quarters and profited exceedingly by his liberality. Performers and story-tellers collected in such numbers and received such gifts and favours at his hands that he was regarded as the Hatim of that age and in generosity, the Rustam of the time.[2]

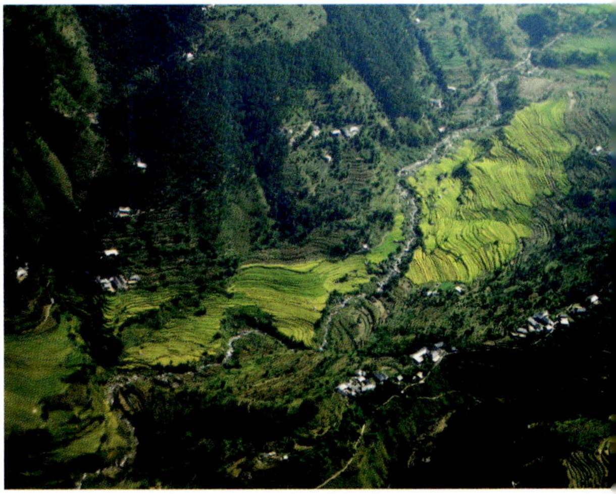

The Kangra Valley

During Sansar Chand's regime, Kangra had reached the height of its prosperity and artistic excellence. Its annual revenue had surpassed Rs. 36 lakh. This sudden affluence was solely responsible for establishing a larger atelier of painters. Sansar Chand liberally extended patronage also to painters of neighbouring states who sought patronage in his court. Khushala, the son of Manak and Godhu, the son of Nainsukh, among others also worked at Sansar Chand's atelier. His was a star-studded atelier with a prolific output of paintings. While Khushala and Godhu painted in the characteristic style of the Seu family, Purkhu had his own individual style. About Sansar Chand's taste and inclination towards the art of painting, a European traveller William Moorcroft and guest of Sansar Chand, who visited Kangra in July 1820, wrote thus:

. . . Sansar Chand has a taste for the arts, (which) would have been magnificent had he possessed the means and is now more generous than suits his finances although his liberality is occasionally shaded by efforts of parsimony.[3]

Sansar Chand, even as a child, was fond of looking at paintings and had a special fondness for romantic paintings and especially that of Krishna. On coming of age, when he emerged as a paramount power

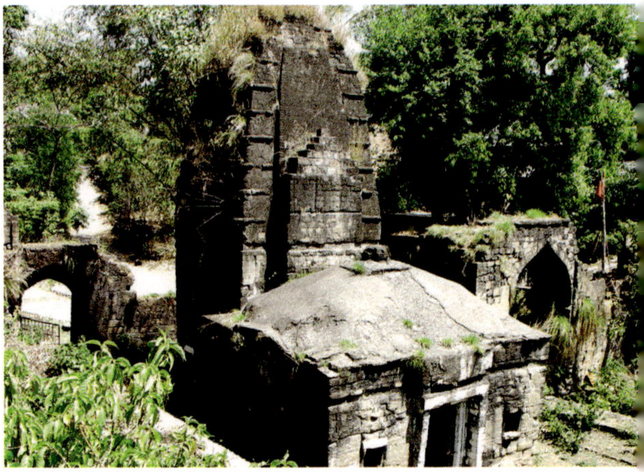

Temples, Guler, seventeenth century

in the hills and established himself as a great ruler and administrator, he turned his attention to the arts and became a respected patron and connoisseur. Sansar Chand had attained political power and success at a very young age and had developed an impressive atelier in his court. In some of his court paintings he is shown examining paintings with his courtiers. Besides pictorial arts, he was equally interested in romantic poetry, classical music and dance.

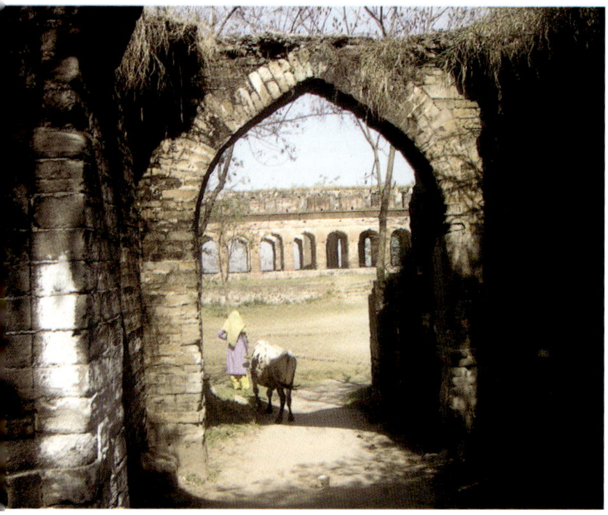

Ruins of the fort at Tira-Sujanpur

We are privy to a large number of paintings from the Sansar Chand period that emerged from his atelier. There are number of paintings which show him in his daily courtly activities. There are paintings where he is shown parading his troops, giving audience to his court musicians, enjoying dance performances, celebrating the festival of Holi, Ramanavami, Krishna-Janmashtami and Diwali or in audience with other hill chiefs.

In 1820 an English traveller Moorcroft paid a visit to Sansar Chand at Alampur. During his visit the Maharaja's younger brother Mian Fateh Chand developed a serious illness. Moorcroft was able to cure Mian Fateh Chand. To express his gratitude Sansar Chand presented a robe of honour to Moorcroft. In addition, he conferred a piece of land on him. Thus, by exchanging Fateh Chand's turban with the hat of Moorcroft the former became his "turban brother".

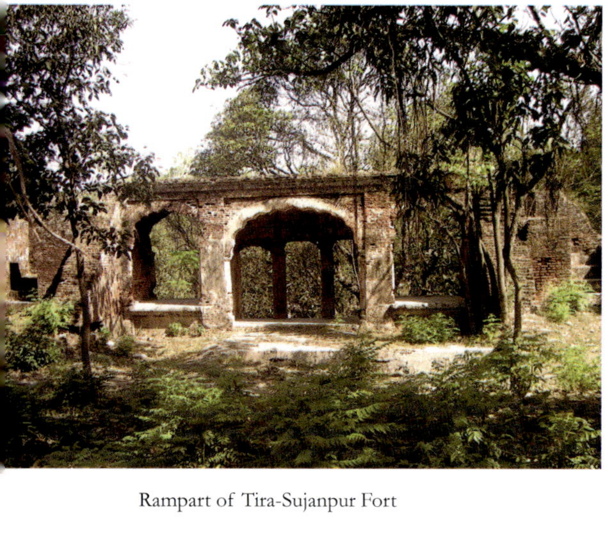

Rampart of Tira-Sujanpur Fort

Moorcroft, writing about the routine life of Sansar Chand, states:

> Raja Sansar Chand spends the early part of the day in the ceremonies of his religion, and from ten till noon in communication with his officers and courtiers. For several days prior to my departure, he passed this period at a small bungala, which he had given up for my accommodation, on the outside of the garden. At noon the Raja retires for two or three hours, after which he ordinarily plays at chess for some time, and the evening is devoted to song and dance. Sansar Chand

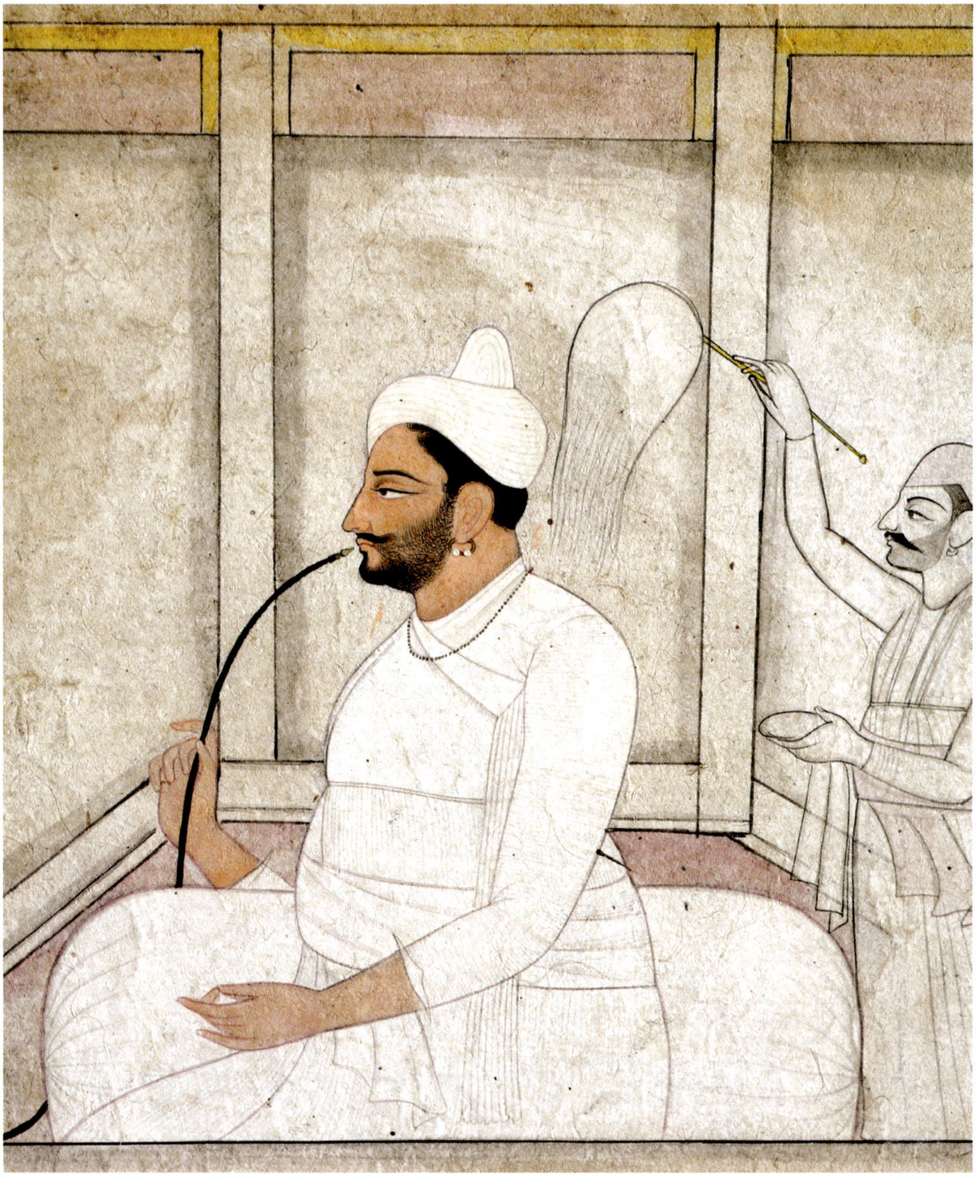

Sansar Chand smoking, school of Purkhu, Kangra, CE 1800, Bhuri Singh Museum, Chamba

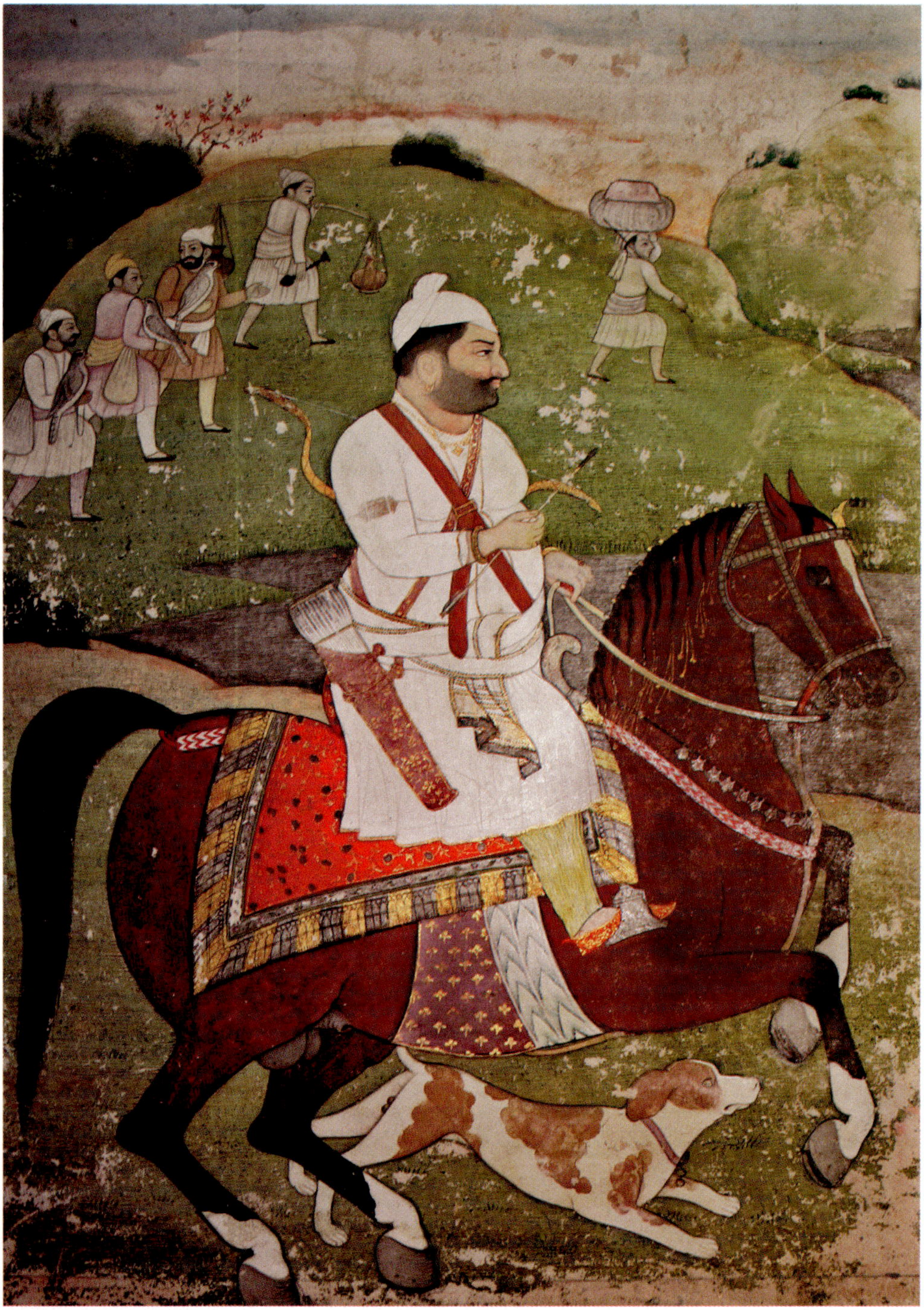

Sansar Chand, early Guler, CE 1810-20, Bhuri Singh Museum, Chamba

was particularly fond of *shringara rasa* and the soirees in his court resounded with the songs in Brajbhasha. . . . Sansar Chand is fond of drawing and has many artists in his employ; he has a large collection of pictures, but the greater part represents the feats of Krishna and Balarama, the adventures of Arjuna and subjects from Mahabharata. He [Sansar Chand] is fond of drawings, keeps several artists who execute the minute parts with great fidelity, but are almost wholly ignorant of perspective.[4]

Being an epicurean, Sansar Chand established a large and active court by extending lavish patronage to painters. His fame as a liberal connoisseur of the arts encouraged several painters from other hill states and the plains to join the royal atelier of Kangra. One of the painter families that had migrated to Ustehad in the Kangra Valley was that of Purkhu, who was to become one of the foremost painters at the court of Sansar Chand. This family had earlier migrated from the neighbouring state of Guler. Records available from priests at Hardwar and Pehowa state:

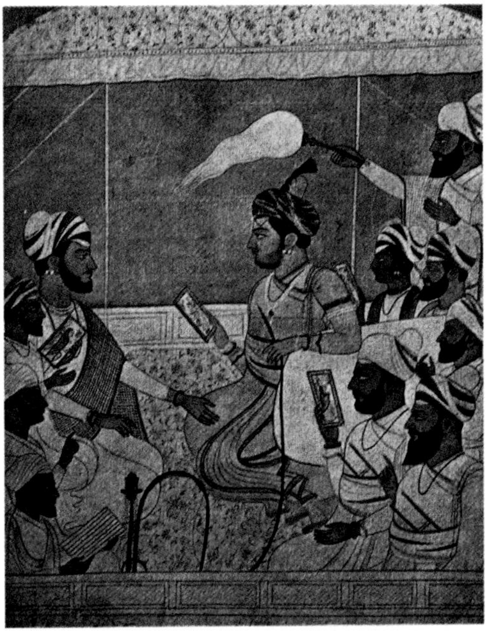

Sansar Chand appreciating paintings with courtiers, school of Purkhu, Kangra, CE 1790. Present whereabouts unknown

The painters of Samloti: Jwala, son of Buddhu and grandson of Dhumman; Chandanu, Ramdayal, Ramkishan and Ruldu, all sons of Purkhu; Sukhanand, son of Jwala; Inder Mohan, son of Ramdyal; Jwala brought the mortal remains of his mother. . . . Beli, son of Ramdyal; together with mother, Ramdyal came [Pehowa] and brought the ashes of his father [Purkhu].[5]

From this and other accounts, one can reconstruct Purkhu's genealogy thus:

Dharu: grandfather
Dhumman: father
Buddhu: elder brother
Purkhu
Purkhu's sons: Chandanu, Ramdayal,
Ramkishan, Ruldu

Equally problematic is to ascribe paintings to Purkhu or his workshop. Since there are no signed works by Purkhu, any assessment of his extensive oeuvre has to be done by careful examination and intelligent inference of the pictorial styles and conventions, motifs and designs in

Kangra paintings. Purkhu was first and foremost an accomplished portrait painter; this was his forte. The many portraits of his patron attest to that. However, Purkhu is remembered and celebrated most for his large narrative paintings like those from the *Bhagavata Purana*, *Harivamsha Purana*, *Shiva Purana*, *Parijata Harana* and the *Gita-Govinda*. Even in these large paintings populated with so many figures, Purkhu pays attention to each figure and makes it almost a portrait. It is almost certain that either Purkhu or his atelier also produced *chitravali*s from *ritikavya* notably from *Rasikapriya*, *Satsai* and *Rasraj*. It is obvious that this amount of artistic output must have required a large atelier where all his sons, collaterals and cousins worked together in the family workshop.

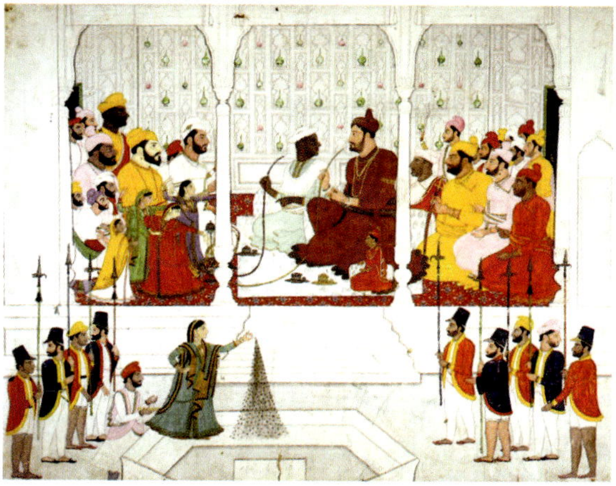

Sansar Chand holding court, school of Purkhu, Kangra, CE 1800

The name of Purkhu finds reference in the Handbook of the Manufacturers and Arts of the Punjab written by Baden Powell in 1872. Purkhu's paintings were displayed in an exhibition in Lahore in 1864, in which the jury's report made the following comment:

> Collection of Pundit Manphul. The collection commences with an interesting series of the emperors of Delhi. Most of these were painted by Purkhu, an artist in the service of Raja Sansar Chand of Katoch, who was a great patron of art and prepared a fine collection of paintings. There is a remarkable clearness of tone and delicacy of handling in most of Purkhu's works but he was not so great a master of colour as many other artists inferior to him in other respects. His son, Ramdayal, who is still living, inherits much of his father's talents. Number 76 is a clever portrait of Gulab Singh, said to be one of the best likeness ever taken of that prince. The next painting to it, 77, is an interesting portrait of Raja Sansar Chand by Purkhu.[6]

Purkhu's style of painting seems to have been influenced by both the Guler and Awadh school of paintings. It would not be wrong to assume that the family of Purkhu, which had migrated from Guler to Kangra in the first half of the eighteenth century must have been influenced by pictorial conventions from the Guler Gharana of the celebrated painter Seu and his illustrious sons. This

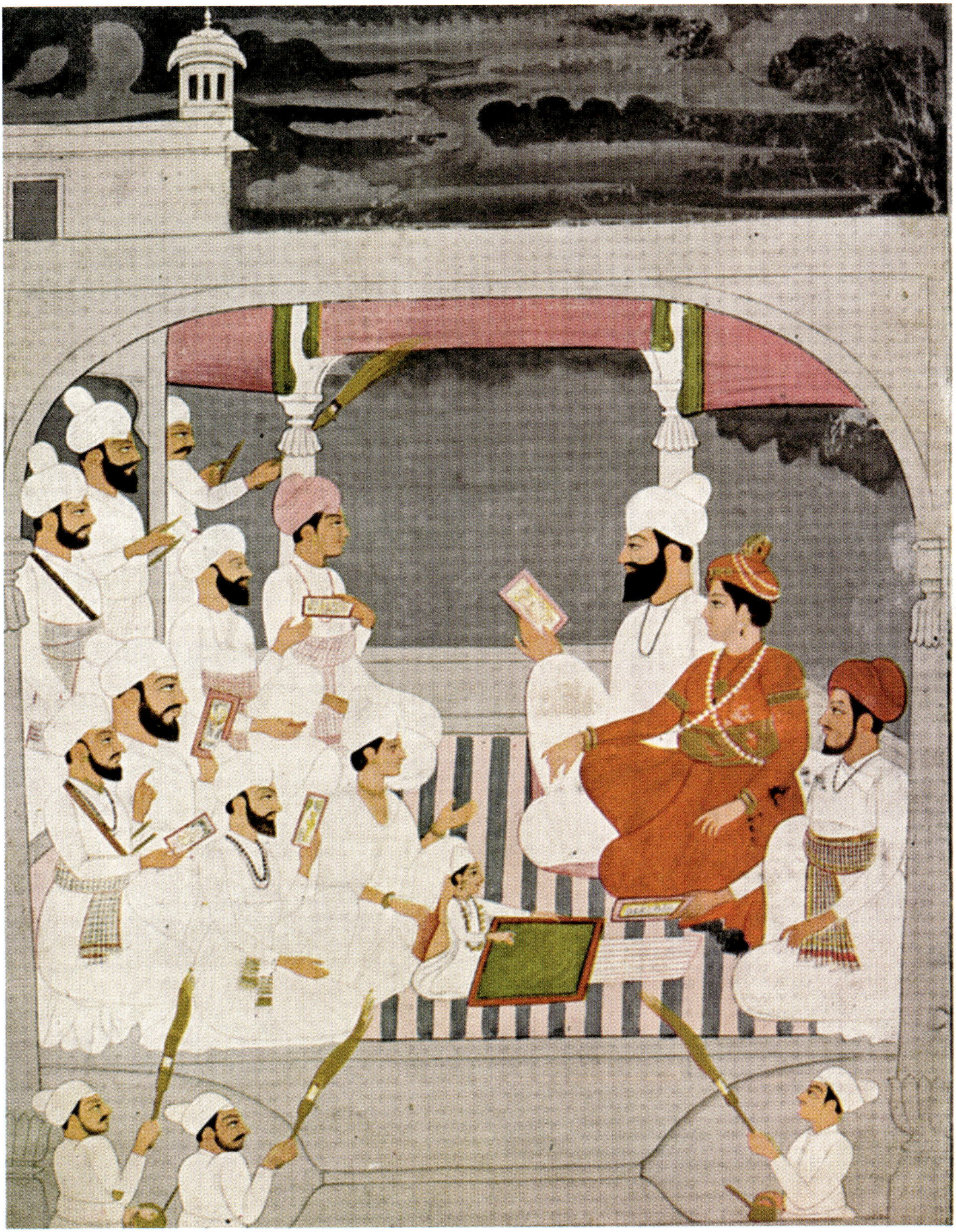

Sansar Chand in his atelier, school of Purkhu, Kangra, CE 1780, Government Museum and Art Gallery, Chandigarh

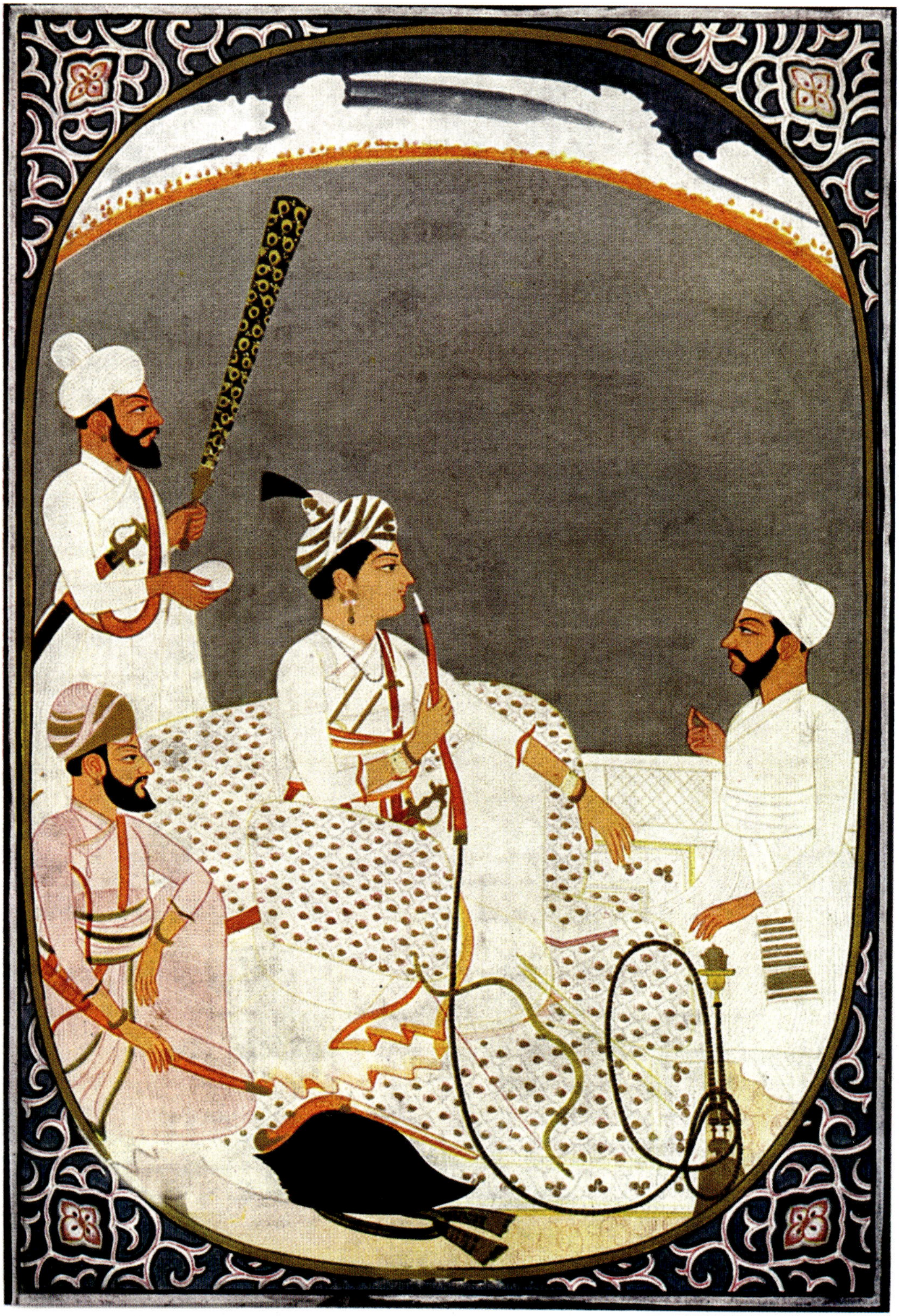

Young Sansar Chand smoking, school of Purkhu, Kangra, CE 1782. Government Museum and Art Gallery, Chandigarh

is seen particularly in the treatment of the landscape and the female figures of Purkhu which carries the characteristic Kangra stamp of soft and sensual beauty. However, Purkhu also seems to be influenced by Awadh painting when it comes to the multi-tiered and lively architecture that dominate his paintings.

Purkhu excelled in painting large size horizontal *wasli* pasteboards. Typically, his compositions are packed by many people in processions or in an ambience of royal grandeur or festive spirit. His signature style is of countless figures against monochromatic backgrounds of soft muted colours. In depictions of episodes from the epics like *Ramayana*, *Bhagavata* or *Harivamsha Purana*, his compositions are dominated by resplendent architectural edifices of glowing marble or golden walls. From *jharokha*s and doors, people in his paintings are in a state of movement and move in and out. At times, the important mythological figures are labelled above their head with brief inscriptions in the Devanagari script. Purkhu's figures are never generic as one sees in a painting that he has successfully captured the individual facial characteristics of each Pahari chieftain. At times, their heads appear somewhat larger than the torsos. A special feature of Purkhu's female figures are tender hands with tapering fingers. Most of the male figures seen in his works wear a *jama*, a long *kamaraband* and sport a *kuledar turban,* while female figures are shown clad in a *peshwaz* as well as in a *choli* and *ghaghra.* He prefers to draw one-eyed faces in profile (*ekchashmi*) rather than one and a half (*dedha-chashmi*) faces.

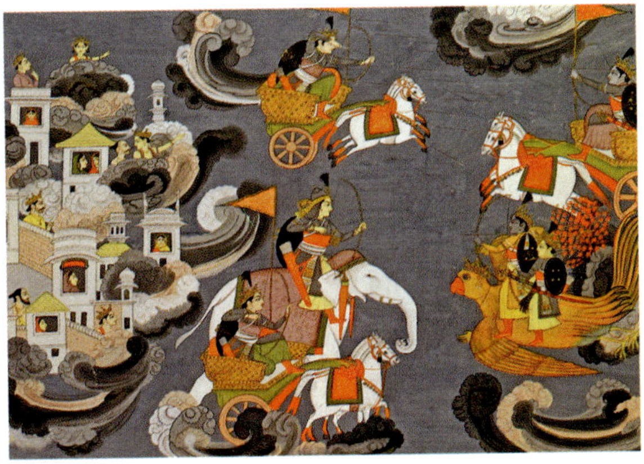

Illustration to *Harivamsha Purana.* School of Purkhu, Kangra, CE 1820-25

Writing about the Shiva-Parvati painting, Pal states:

> The proportion of the figures, the decorative exuberance of the flowering plants and trees, the smooth tonality of the vivid yellows and oranges, the subtle variation of the greens and the orange glow of the setting sun on

the curving horizon under the streaked blue canopy are features that be associated with works ascribed to Purkhu's workshop.[7]

Commenting on the Rukmini Haran series, Pal writes:

> In the panoramic procession and marriage pictures we encounter complex renderings of architecture, with multiple perspectives, as if each artist were observing the scene from an exalted vantage point on a rooftop or balcony. Such deft and idiosyncratic manipulations of architectural forms to enliven a composition was a peculiarity of Purkhu.[8]

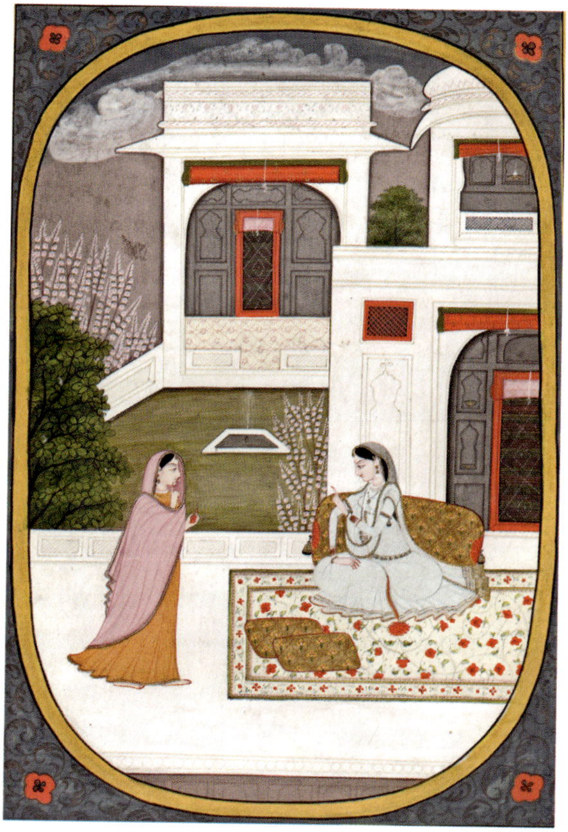

Illustration to *Rasikapriya*, school of Purkhu, Kangra, CE 1820-25, private collection

Purkhu's genius lay not only in creating beautiful paintings, but where form and feeling, architecture and people, life and landscape, blended into a seamless whole. While his human figures were alive with movement and feeling, his architecture was imaginatively created at multiple levels with cupolas and turrets, balconies and terraces, teeming with activity at different levels. When one moves one's eye across his canvas at no point does the eye blink as one is privy to a panoramic vista of colour and form and it participates in the life that unfolds. All this leaves one spellbound in the richness of the spectacle and the energy and radiance of the composition where line and colour, texture and movement add up to make a picture that is radiantly alive. If Purkhu's painting of *haveli*s and people shows the control of his *kalam*, Purkhu's *nayikas* are suffused with grace and elegance and are driven by his adoration of sensuality. The depiction of her hands has an artistic finesses and beauty unmatched in Indian painting. The hands of the *nayikas* with tapering fingers are painted so delicately that they seem like those of a dancer performing a *hasta-mudra*. Purkhu fills the entire body of the *nayika* from the tresses to the toes with an elegant sensuousness and feeling, which makes the beautiful figure almost palpable. It seems to tremble with every emotion of love, every feeling of romance, every pang of longing and every thrill of belonging. Purkhu's treatment of the landscape shows an equal sensitivity and equally he imbues his trees and blossoms with buoyancy and feeling, where one almost

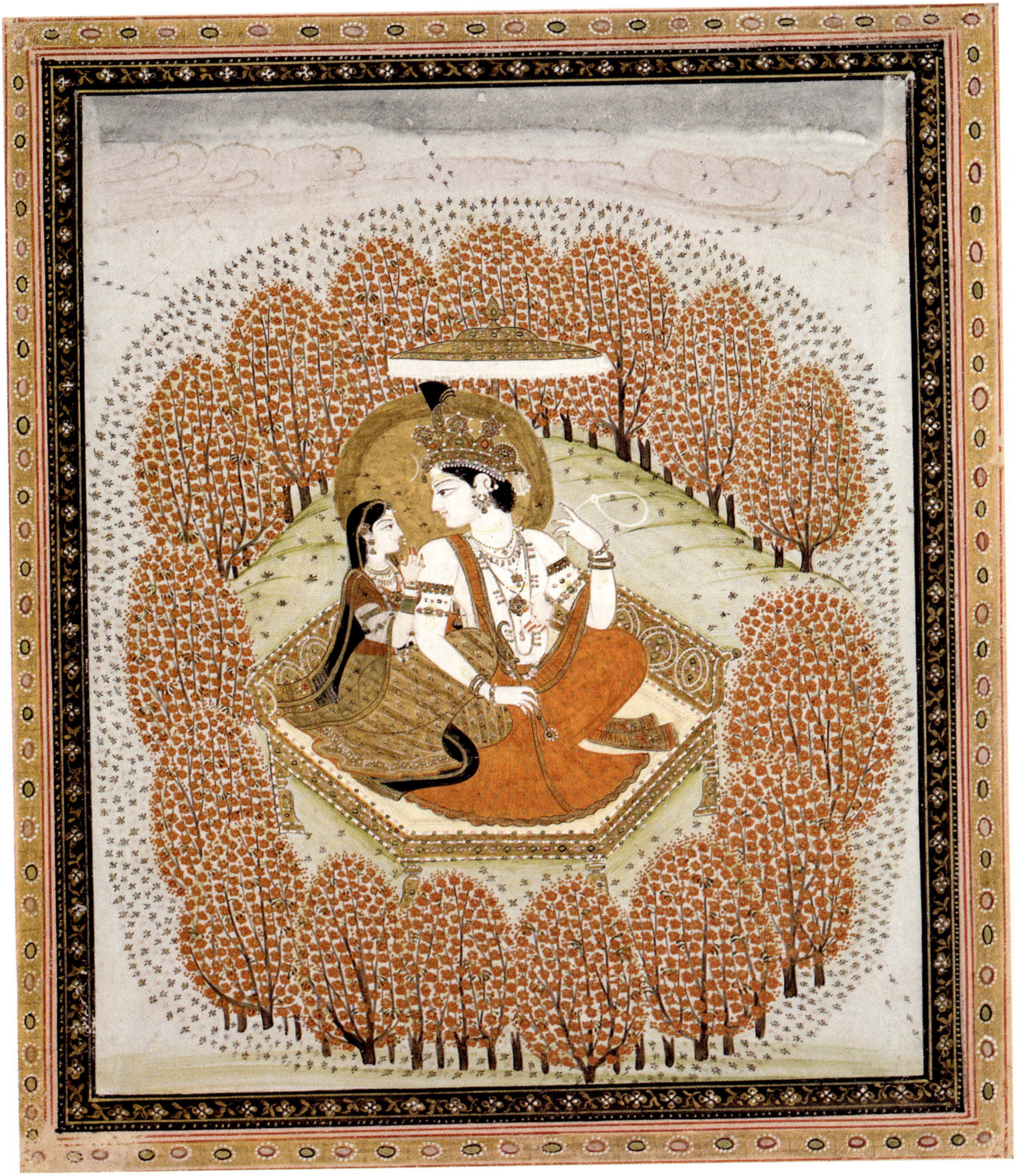

Crowned Shiva with his consort Parvati, school of Purkhu, Kangra, CE 1800, Dehejia collection

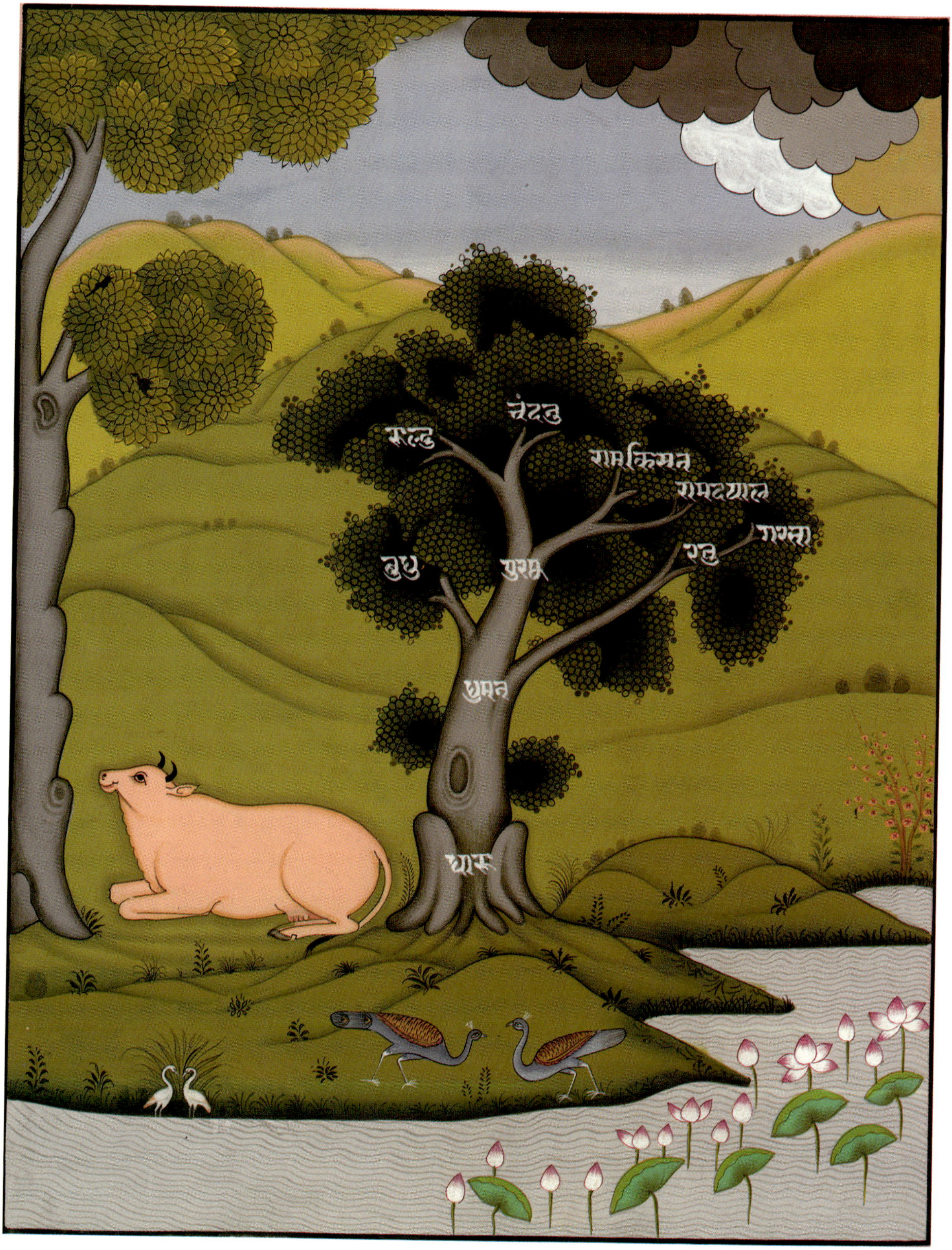

Family Tree of Purkhu, painting by Trilok Soni

smells the fragrance and appreciates the lushness and it becomes difficult to decipher where the painting ends and feelings begin. Purkhu handles the pictorial space more like a poet rather than a painter and to him, time seems to flow majestically rather than being frozen in a moment. Purkhu stands out as an artist who masters both time and space with his *kalam* and gives another visual dimension to the painted narrative.

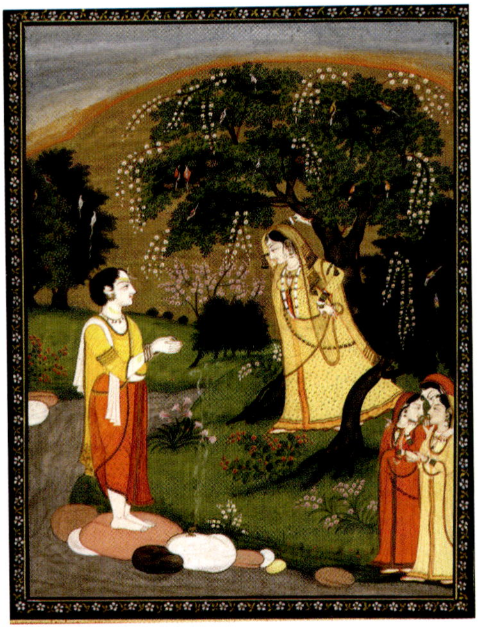

Shiva performs the sandhya rite, school of Purkhu, Kangra, CE 1800, Kapoor Galleries, New York

It has rightly been said that Kangra painting is the superb lyricism and the melody of the sweet love of Krishna made visual. The landscape in the paintings which is inspired by the bucolic and luxuriant Pahari terrain is assimilated to the mood of the personages through a symbolism that is very transparent in its poetic suggestion. While the Kangra *kalam* exudes a refined sensuousness and lyrical grace, drawing its inspiration not only from its idyllic landscape but equally by the living presence of the Krishna of love in the courts, it is in the depiction of the graceful and elegantly sensuous *shringara rasa nayika* that it reaches its greatest heights of artistic finesse and mastery. The paintings of the *Harivamsha Purana* and the Lambagraon *Gita Govinda* rank as the highest watermark of the magnificent Kangra *kalam*. The Kangra *nayika* of painting not only has an elegant and sensuous charm, a luminous elegance and unsurpassed beauty but a refined romantic sensibility, whether she was experiencing the pain of pathos of the pleasures of love, and in the genre of romantic figures that Indian artists have produced she represents the most beautiful and the most exalted. There is in her, not only the charm of romantic sensuality but the serenity of a woman in love, who is also aware that her sensuality is the doorway to spirituality. As Coomaraswamy has said

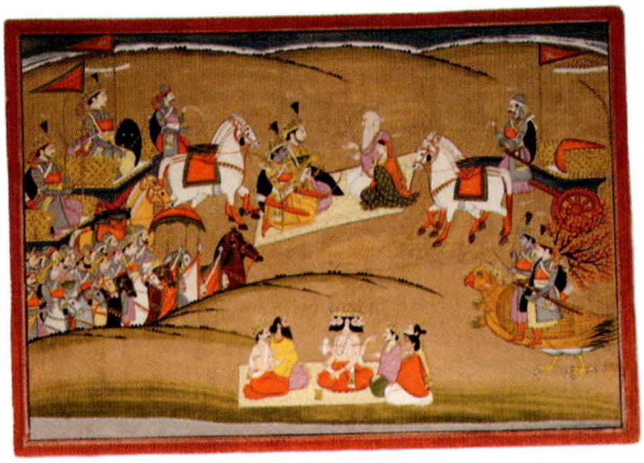

Parijat Haran, Harivamsha Purana, school of Purkhu, Kangra, CE 1820-30, Harish Patel, New York

> The Kangra *kalam* is indeed a feminine art, intrinsically an art of sentiment rather than of passion.[9]

While painting the beauty of Kangra *nayikas*, he also writes:

> The heroine's eyes are large as any lotus, her tresses fall

in heavy plaits, her breasts are firm, her thighs are full and smooth, her hands are like rosy flowers, her gait as dignified as any elephant and her demeanour bemused.[10]

Such praise of Kangra art can be attributed also to Purkhu's *kalam* who along with the Seu family raised that art to a high art form.

When one thinks of the glorious tradition of Kangra painting many images pass through the mind's eye: idyllic landscapes, verdant meadows, limpid waters, graceful women with beautiful eyes, splendid architecture, the majesty of royal courts, evocative portraits and with all this the names of Sansar Chand, the extraordinary patron of the arts and Purkhu a master painter of his court will always echo. Both together have left behind a legacy of paintings that will be counted as some of the most beautiful artistic expressions of the late eighteenth and the nineteenth centuries, where form and feeling, the patron and the painter, regal splendour and tender emotions, blend seamlessly into a charmed universe, where *shringara rasa* was a *rajaras* and the celebration of love in word and image was a cultivated and cherished activity.

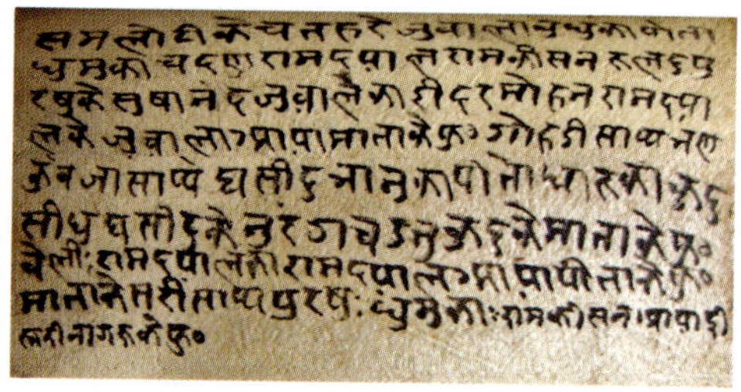

Bahi entry containing the pedigree of Purkhu, from the archival record of a priest at Pehowa.

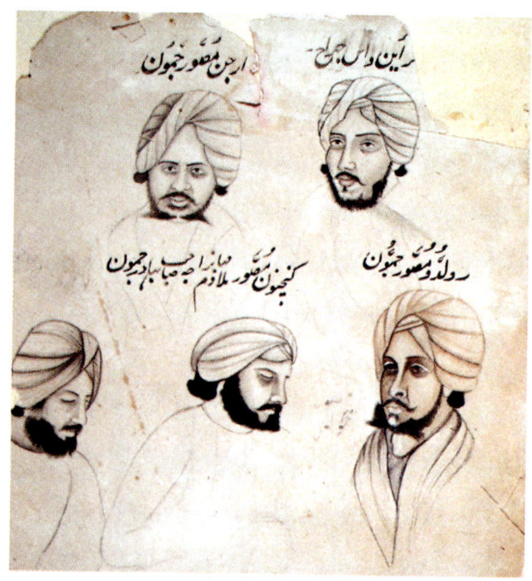

Sketch portraits of Kangra painters working at Jammu court, 19th century Government Museum and Art Gallery, Chandigarh

Endnotes

1. Hermann Goetz, *The Coming of Muslim Cultural Influence in the Punjab Himalaya* (reproduced from Indian Antiqua, A volume of oriental studies presented J. Ph. Vogel), Leiden, 1947, pp. 155-56.
2. Ghulam Mohiuddin, *Tarikh-i-Punjab*. See, M.S. Randhawa, "Maharaja Sansar Chand the Patron of Kangra Painting", *Roopa-Lekha*, volume XXXII, no. 2, December 1961, p. 13.
3. W. Moorcroft and G. Trebeck, *Travels in the Himalayan Provinces of Hindustan and the Punjab*; in Ladakh, Kashmir, Peshawar, Kabul, Kunduz and Bokhara, from 1819 to 1825, London, 1841. p. 66.
4. Ibid.
5. Researched by Vijay Sharma.
6. Baden Powell, *Handbook of Manufacturers and Arts of the Punjab*, Lahore, London, 1872, p. 355.
7. Pratapaditya Pal, *Painted Poems*, Rajput Paintings ftom the Ramesh and Urmil Kapoor Collection, Norton Simon Museum, Mapin Publishing, Ahmedabad, 2004, p. 24.
8. Ibid.
9. A.K. Coomaraswamy, *History of Indian and Indonesian Art*, 1927 Dover, New York, p. 132.
10. Ibid.

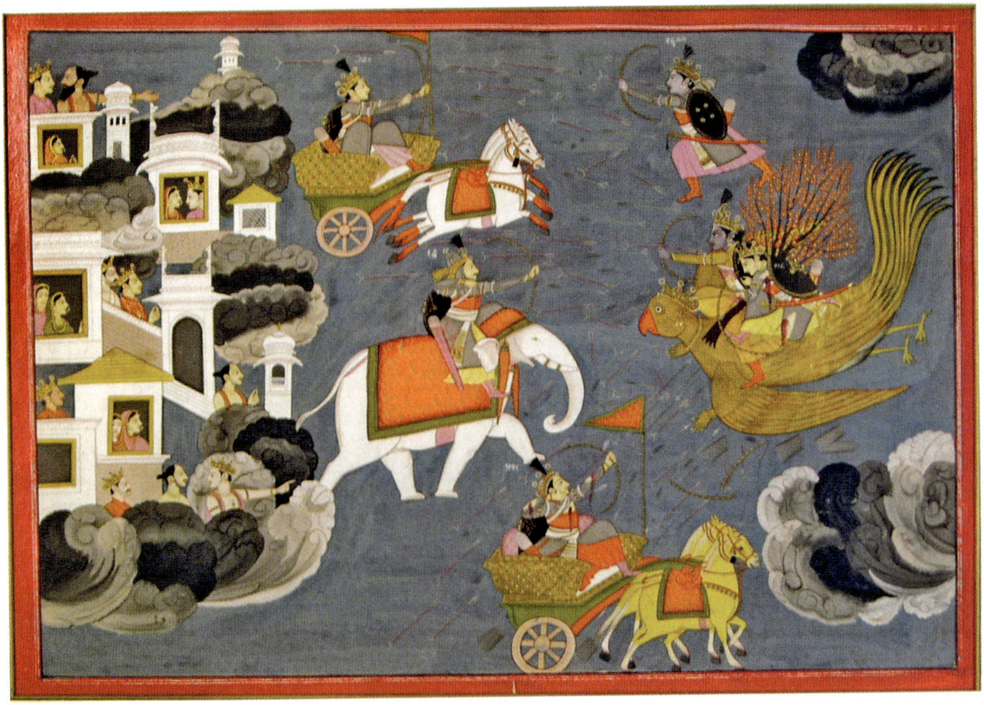

Parijata-Harana, illustration to Harivamsha, school of Purkhu, Kangra, CE 1820, Harish Patel Collection

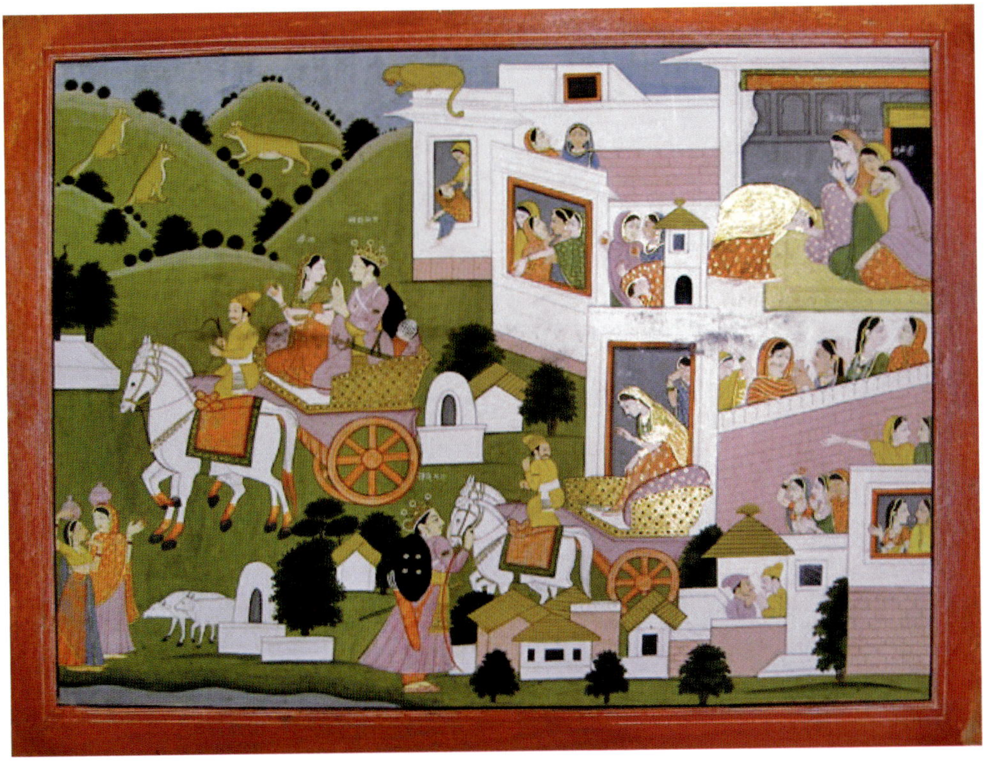

Illustration to Ramayana, school of Purkhu, Kangra, CE 1825, Honolulu Academy of Arts.

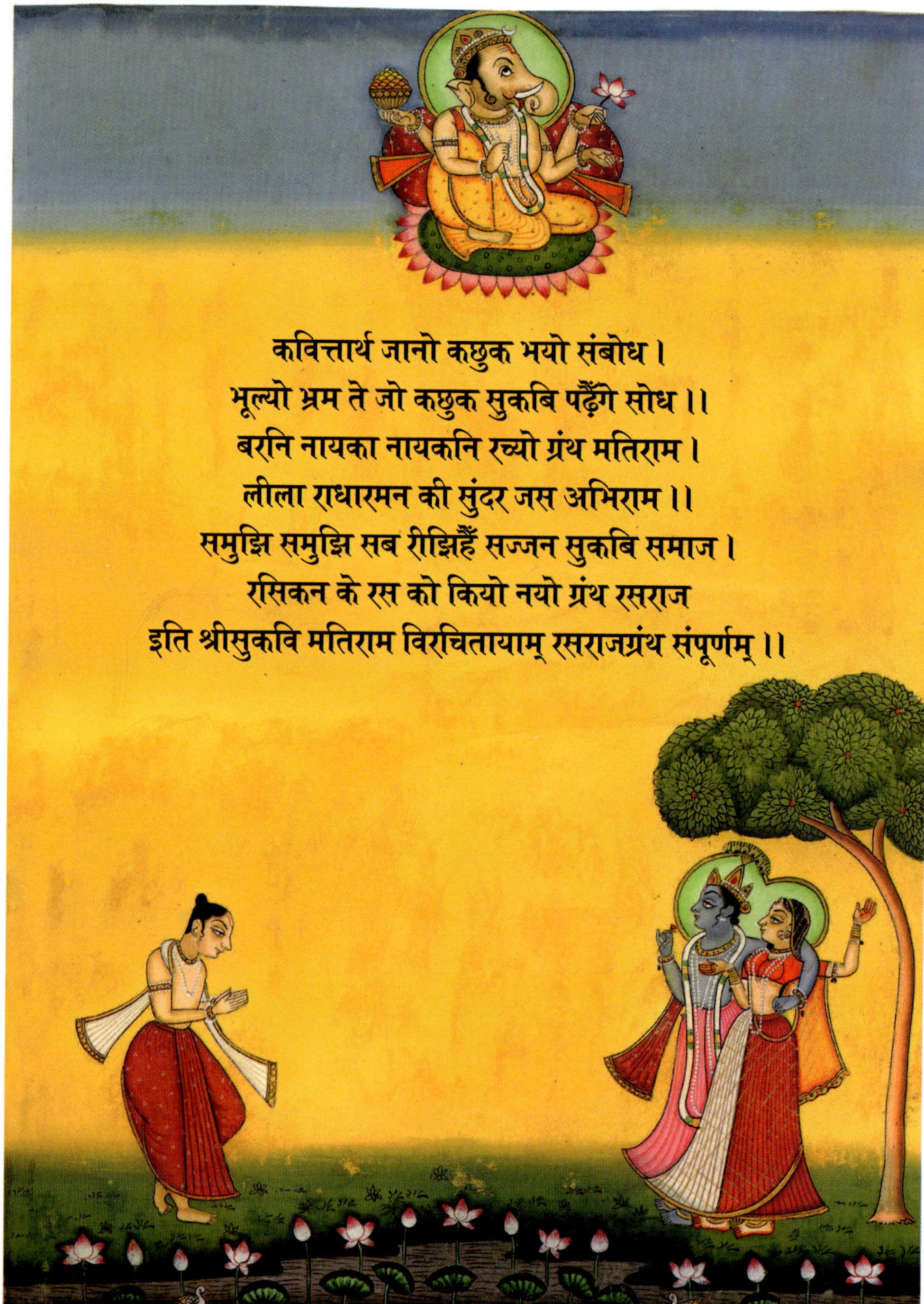
कवित्तार्थ जानो कछुक भयो संबोध ।
भूल्यो भ्रम ते जो कछुक सुकबि पढ़ैंगे सोध ।।
बरनि नायका नायकनि रच्यो ग्रंथ मतिराम ।
लीला राधारमन की सुंदर जस अभिराम ।।
समुझि समुझि सब रीझिहैं सज्जन सुकबि समाज ।
रसिकन के रस को कियो नयो ग्रंथ रसराज
इति श्रीसुकवि मतिराम विरचितायाम् रसराजग्रंथ संपूर्णम् ।।

Rasraj
in Braj and English

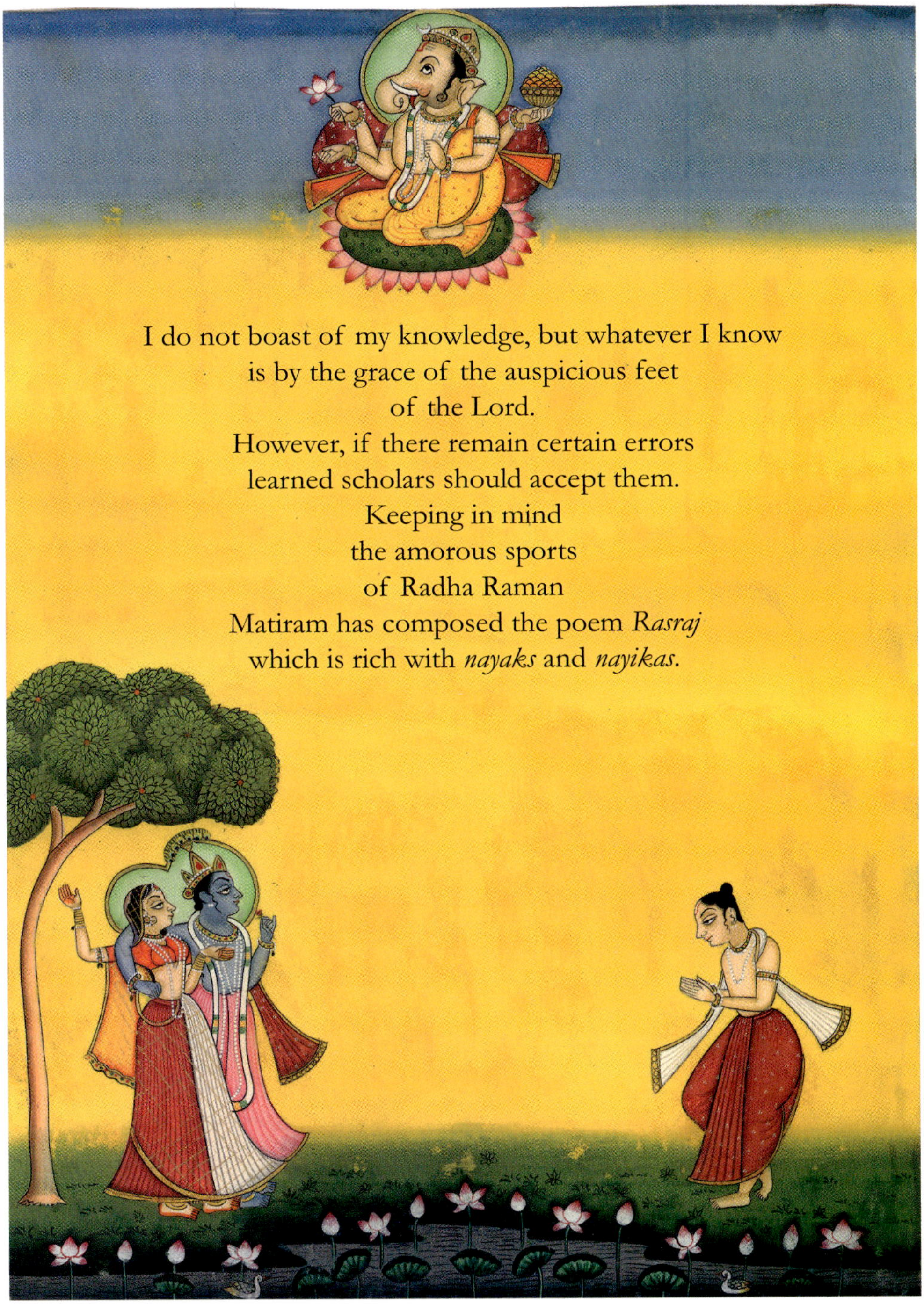

I do not boast of my knowledge, but whatever I know
is by the grace of the auspicious feet
of the Lord.
However, if there remain certain errors
learned scholars should accept them.
Keeping in mind
the amorous sports
of Radha Raman
Matiram has composed the poem *Rasraj*
which is rich with *nayaks* and *nayikas*.

नायक-नायिका

होत नायका नायकहि आलंबित सिंगार।
तातैं बरनौं नायका नायक मति अनुसार।।
उपजत जाहि बिलोकिकै चित्त-बीच रसभाव।
ताहि बखानत नायका जे प्रबीन कबिराव।।५।।

A *nayika* is someone who excites romantic feelings in the onlooker. [5]

उदाहरण (सवैया)

कुंदन को रँगु फीको लगै
झलकै अति अंगन चारु गुराई।
आँखिन मैं अलसानि चितौन मैं मंजु
बिलासन की सरसाई।
को बिन मोल बिकात नहीं
मतिराम लहै मुसकानि मिठाई।
ज्यों ज्यों निहारिये नेरे ह्वै नैननि
त्यों त्यों खरी निकरै सी निकाई।।६।।

Her body has a radiant glow and in front of it even gold pales. Her languid eyes radiate love. Her sweet smile is enough to capture anyone. The more you look at her the more beautiful she appears. [6]

मुग्धा

A *mugdha* is a young *nayika* who has passed her childhood and has entered youth. She is full of bashfulness and modesty and because of her
timid nature, turns away from erotic activity with her beloved.

नवोढ़ा

A *navodha* is a newly-wedded *nayika* who appears to be full of romance but is fearful of erotic activity.

प्रौढ़ा

A *praudha* is one who is mature in the various arts of love.

मध्या

A *madhya* is a *nayika* who is neither shy nor yet mature in the arts of love.

परकीया

A *parakiya* is another's wife.

सामान्या

A *samanya* is the ordinary *nayika*.

गणिका

A *ganika* is a courtesan.

दोहा

जाल रंध्र भग ह्वै कढ़ै तियतनु दीपति पुंज।
झिझिया कैसो घट भयो दिन ही मैं बन कुंज।।७।।

The *nayika* sits in a grove. The radiance of her body shines through the trees and it seems that one can see the light of a lamp within a pot even in daylight. [7]

तरुनि अरुन एँड़ीन की किरनी-समूह-उदोत।
बैनी मंडन मुकुत के पुंज गुंज दुति होत।।८।।

The reflection of her red heel falls on the pearls on her hair and it seems as if there is arch of pearls. [8]

नायिका भेद

कही नायका तीन बिधि प्रथम स्वकीया मान।
परकीया पुनि दूसरी गनिका तीजी जान।।९।।

There are three kinds of *nayikas*: *svakiya*, *parakiya* and *ganika*. [9]

स्वकीया लक्षण

लाजवती, निसदिन पगी निज पति के अनुराग ।
कहत स्वकीया सीलमय, ताको पति बड़ भाग ।। १०।।

A *svakiya nayika* is one who is committed to her husband and is bashful. The husband of such a *nayika* is indeed fortunate. [10]

उदाहरण

संचि बिरंचि निकाई मनोहर
लाजति मूरतिवंत बनाई ;
तापर तो परभाग बड़े,
'मतिराम' लसै पति प्रीति सुहाई ।
तेरे सुसील सुभाव भटू,
कुलनारिन को कुलकानि सिखाई ;

तैं ही जनो पतिदेवत के गुन
गौरि सबै गुन गौरि पढ़ाई ।।११।।

A *sakhi* speaks to a *nayika* :
O *sakhi* ! Brahma has distilled beauty into your form and made you into an icon of beauty and bashfulness. Your are fortunate that you loved your husband and this increases your beauty. You are good natured and it seems as if Goddess Gauri teaches other women to be like you. [11]

जानति सौति अनीति है, जानति सखी सुनीति।
गुरुजन जानत लाज है, प्रीतम जानत प्रीति।।१२।।

The *svakiya nayika* looks at her co-wives with displeasure and to her friends with affection. She is bashful towards her elders and loves her husband. [12]

स्वकीया भेद

त्रिबिध स्वकीया जानियो प्रथमहि मुग्धा नाम।
मध्या पुनि प्रौढ़ा गनौं बरनत कबि मतिराम।।१३।।

There are three types of *svakiya nayikas*, *mugdha*, *madhya* and *praudha*. [13]

मुग्धा लक्षण

अभिनव जौबन-आगमन जाके तन मैं होय।
तासौं मुग्धा कहत हैं कबि कोबिद सब कोय।। १४।।

Mugdha is she who shows signs of approaching youth.[14]

उदाहरण (कवित्त)

नैक मंद मधुर कपोल मुसक्यान लगे
नैक मंद गमन गयंदन की चाल भौ।
रंचक न ऊँचो लगो अंचल उरोजन के
अंकुरनि बंक दीठि नैक सो बिसाल भौ।
मतिराम सुकबि रसीले कछु बैन भए
बदन सिंगाररस बेलि-आलबाल भौ।
बालतनु-जोबन-रसाल उलहत सब
सौतिन कै साल भौ निहाल नंदलाल भौ।। १५।।

She has a smiling face and her gait is slow like that of an elephant. The *odhni* on her chest is flat but her eyes are large and her glance is inviting. Matiram says that her speech is sweet and it seems as if her entire body is like a creeper of love. Her body is full of enchanting youth and this hurts her co-wives but Nandlal is joyous. [15]

दोहा

अभिनव जौबनजोति सौं जगमग होत बिलास।
तिय के तनु पानिप बढ़ै पिय के नैननि प्यास।।१६।।

Her gestures seem to sparkle in the light of her youth and even as her splendour increases so does desire in his eyes. [16]

मुग्धा भेद

मुग्धा के द्वै भेद बर भाषत सुकबि सुजान।
एक अज्ञातहि जौबना ज्ञातजौबना आन।।१७।।

There are two types of *mugdha*, *ajnatyauvana* and *jnatyauvana*. [17]

अज्ञातयौवना लक्षण

निज तनु जौबन-आगमन जो नहिं जानति नारि।
सो अज्ञात सु जौबना बरनत कबि निरधारि।।१८।।

Mugdha ajnatyauvana is one who is ignorant of the signs of youth.[18]

उदाहरण (सवैया)

खेलन चोर-मिहीचनि आजु
गई हुती पाछिले द्यौस की नाई।
आली कहा कहौं एक भई
मतिराम नई यह बात तहाँई।
एकहि भौन दुरे इकसंग ही
अंग सौं अंग छुवायो कन्हाई।
कंप छुट्यो घनस्वेद बढ्यो
तनु रोम उठ्यो अँखियाँ भरि आई।।१९।।

Talking to her *sakhi* she says that I went to play hide and seek as I used to when I was young. There something unusual happened. Krishna and I hid in the same room and Krishna sat close to me and because of his touch my body started trembling and I began to sweat, my hair stood on end and my eyes were filled with tears. [19]

दोहा

लाल तिहारे संग मैं खेलै खेल बलाइ।
मूँदत मेरे नयन हो करन कपूर लगाइ।।२०।।

The *nayika* while playing hide and seek with her beloved is touched by him and she gets excited and tears of joy start streaming from her eyes. She feels that this is due to camphor from his body and she therefore tells him not to apply camphor. [20]

ज्ञातयौवना लक्षण

निज तनु जोबन-आगमन जानि परत है जाहि।
कबि कोबिद सब कहत हैं ज्ञातजौबना ताहि।।२१।।

Jnantyauvana is one who is aware of her approaching youth. [21]

उदाहरण (कवित्त)

कानन लौं लागे मुसकान प्रेमपागे लौने
लाजभरे लागे लोल लोचन अनंग ते।
भारु धरि भुजनि डुलावति चलति मंद
औरैं ओप उलहत उरज उतंग ते।
मतिराम जोबन-पवन की झकोर आय
बढ़िकै सरस रस तरल तरंग ते।
पानिप अमल की झलक झलकन लागी
काई-सी गई है लरिकाई कढ़ि अंग ते।।२२।।

Her beautiful eyes are elongated and seem to reach her ears and touched by love they appear to smile. And afflicted by the pangs of love, she is bashful. When she walks her hands move rhythmically. Her full breasts are attractive. The beauty of her emerging youth is like a breeze that creates ripples of love in her heart. Childhood has vanished from her body and her body has a shining glow. [22]

दोहा

इतै उतै सचकित चितै चलत डुलावत बाँह।
दीठि बचाइ सखीन की छिनक निहारति छाँह।।२३।।

The *nayika* is aware of the onset of youth and she walks with flair and while avoiding her friends she discreetly sees her own breasts through the corner of her eyes. [23]

नवोढ़ा लक्षण

मुग्धा जो भय लाज युत रति न चहै पतिसंग।
ताहि नवोढ़ा कहत हैं जे प्रबीन रसरंग।।२४।।

Navodha is one who out of fear and shame does not want to engage in love sports with her husband. [24]

उदाहरण (सवैया)

साथ सखी के नई दुलही को
भयो हरि को हियो हेरि हिमंचल।
आय गए मतिराम तहाँ
घरु जानि इकंत अनंद ते चंचल।
देखत ही नँदलाल को बाल के
पूरि रहे अँसुवानि दृगंचल।
बात कही न गई सु रही गहि
हाथ दुहू सौं सहेली को अंचल ।।२५।।

Seeing his new bride with her *sakhi* Krishna's heart froze and missed a beat. Seeing that the house was empty he was excited and came near her. On seeing Krishna her eyes were filled with tears. She did not say a word to him but held on to her *sakhi*'s *odhni* with both her hands. [25]

दोहा

ज्यौं ज्यौं परसत लाल तनु त्यौं त्यौं राखै गोय।
नवल बधू डर लाज तें इंद्रबधू सी होय।।२६।।

Even as the *nayak* touches her she withdraws her body like the *indrabadhu* (a small insect in the monsoon which withdraws its limbs and freezes). [26]

विश्रब्धनवोढ़ा लक्षण

होय नवोढ़ा कै कछू प्रीतम सौं परतीति।
सो बिश्रब्धनवोढ़ यौं बरनत कबि रसरीति।।२७।।

Vishrabdha navodha is a *nayika* who trusts the *nayak*. [27]

उदाहरण (सवैया)

केलि कै राति अघाने नहीं
दिन ही मैं लला पुनि घात लगाई।
प्यास लगी कोउ पानी दै जाइयो
भीतर बैठिकै बात सुनाई।
जेठी पठाई गई दुलही हँसि
हेरि हरे मतिराम बुलाई।
कान्ह के बोल मैं कान न दीनो
सो गेह की देहरी पै धरि आई।।२८।।

Not satisfied with a whole night of making

love the *nayak* devises a plan to continue with love sports. Sitting inside he says aloud that he is thirsty and wants water. The sister-in-law understood his plan and asked the *nayika* to take water for him. When the *nayika* came to the door the *nayak* smiled and invited her in. But the *nayika* keeping in mind the respect for the elders in the family ignored him and placed the water on the threshold of the room. [28]

दोहा

प्रीतम तुम्हरी सेज पर हौं आऊँ नँदलाल।
दया गहो बात न कहो दुख न दीजिए लाल।।२९।।

Vishrabhda navodha

A *nayika* tells her beloved that I am prepared to sleep on the bed but please do not speak sweet words and be hard on me. [29]

मध्या लक्षण

जाके तन मैं होत है लाज मनोज समान।
ताकौं मध्या कहत हैं कबि मतिराम सुजान।।३०।।

She is one in who romance and bashfulness are in equal measure. [30]

उदाहरण

चित्र मैं बिलोकत ही लाल को बदन बाल
जीते जिहि कोटि चंद सरद-पुनीन के।
मुसकानि अमल कपोलन मैं रुचिबृंद
चमकै तख्योननि की रुचिर चुनीन के।
प्रीतम निहार्यो बाँह गहत अचानक ही
जामैं मतिराम मन सकल मुनीन के।
गाढ़े गही लाज मैन कंठ ह्वै फिरत बैन
मूल छ्वै फिरत नैनबारि बरुनीन के।।३१।।

A *nayika* as looking at a picture of her beloved and the rubies in her earring cast a shadow on her cheek. Her beloved suddenly appeared and caught her arm and she stared at him. She saw a *rishi* in the picture she was holding and tears of joy appeared but she controlled them. [31]

दोहा

केलिभवन की देहरी
खरी बाल छबि नौल।
कामकलित हिय को लहै
लाजकलित दृगकौल।।३२।।

After coming to the threshold of the love pavilion she was in two minds. On the one hand, her romantic feelings were encouraging her to advance but at the same time her sense of bashfulness caused her lotus-like eyes to wilt. [32]

प्रौढ़ा लक्षण

निज पति सौं रति-केलि की सकल कलानि प्रबीन।
तासौं प्रौढ़ा कहत हैं, जे कबिता-रस-लीन।।३३।।

A *praudha* is a *nayika* who is proficient in the arts of love. [33]

उदाहरण (सवैया)

प्रानप्रिया मनभावन संग अनंग-तरंगनि रंग पसारे।
सारी निसा मतिराम मनोहर केलि के पुंज हजार उघारे।
होत प्रभात चल्यो चहै प्रीतम सुंदरि के हिय मैं दुख भारे।
चंद-सो आनन दीप-सी दीपति
स्याम सरोज-से नैन निहारे।।३४।।

The *nayika* performed a variety of love sports with the *nayika* all night to please him and in the process created a number of different love games. When at dawn the *nayak* began to leave she was heartbroken. Her face at that time looked like the faded moon and her body was like a flickering lamp. Her eyes were like the blue lotus that folds with the first rays of the sun, they were filled with tears and in order to con-ceal them from ber beloved, she had shut them. [34]

दोहा

लपटानी अति प्रेम सौं दै उर उरज उतंग।
घरी एक लौं छुटेहु पर रही लगी-सी अंग।।३५।।

The *nayika* who was so full of love that with her heaving breasts she clung to her beloved all night. Even though she would lose her grip from time to time her body would remain entwined with his. [35]

मध्या-प्रौढ़ा भेद

मध्या प्रौढ़ा मान तैं तीन भाँति पुनि जानि।
धीरा बहुरि अधीर तिय धीराधीरा मानि।।३६।।

Madhya and *praudha nayikas* are of three types: *dhira*, *adhira* and *dhiradhira*. [36]

मध्या-धीरा-प्रौढ़ा लक्षण

बचननि की रचनानि सौं पियहि जनावत कोप।
मध्या धीरा कहत हैं ताहि सुमति-रस-चोप।।३७।।

A *madhya dhira* is one who expresses her anger through words. [37]

कवित्त

तुम कहा करो कान काम तें अटकि रहे
तुमकों न दोस सो तो आपनोई भाग है।
आय मेरे भौन बड़े भोर उठि प्यार ही तें
अति हरबरन बनाय बाँधी पाग है।
मेरे ही बियोग रहे जागत सकल राति
गात अलसात मेरो परम सुहाग है।
मनहु की जानी प्रानप्यारे मतिराम यहै
नैननिहूँ माहिं पाइयतु अनुराग है।।३८।।

A *nayika* addresses a *nayak* who has returned at dawn after spending the night with another woman.

O Krishna ! you got tied up with some unexpected business and that is none of your fault but just my bad luck that you could not be with me. But since you have come to me at the crack of dawn it speaks of your love for me. You were in a rush to come here and your turban has been tied in a hurry. Your body shows signs of fatigue since you spent the whole night without me and this really is my good fortune. The redness of your eye speaks of your love for me. [38]

दोहा

अजौं उड़ावत हौ नहीं पीर न होत सभाग।
ठौर ठौर या भौंर के डसे अधरदल-दाग।।३९।।

The *nayika* was expressing her anger through clever words. When she saw bites on his lip she said that he was probably bitten by a bee. Could you not brush it off? [39]

मध्या-अधीरा लक्षण

मध्या कही अधीर तिय बोलै बोल कठोर।
पियहिं जनावति कोप सो बरनत कबि सिरमौर।।४०।।

Madhya adhira is one who expresses her anger with strong words. [40]

सवैया

कोऊ नहीं बरजै मतिराम
रहो तितही जितही मन भायो।
काहे कों सौंहैं हजार करौ तुम
तौ कबहूँ अपराध न ठायो।
सोवन दीजै न दीजै हमैं दुख
यौं ही कहा रसबाद बढ़ायो।
मान रहोई नहीं मनमोहन
मानिनी होय सो मानै मनायो।।४१।।

Who is stopping you? You can go where you want to. If you have not done anything wrong why do you ask for forgiveness? I do not respect you so you do not need to win me over to you. There is no need to prolong this argument. I am sleepy. [41]

दोहा

बलय पीठि तरिवन भुजन उर कुच कुंकुम-छाप।
तितैं जाहु मनभावते जितैं बिकाने आप।।४२।।

Why do you go to a place where you are not respected? On your back there are marks of bangles, on your arms there are signs of earrings and on your chest there are signs of saffron rubbed off from her breasts. It is evident that you have embraced some other woman. [42]

मध्या-धीराधीरा लक्षण

मध्या धीराधीर तिय ताहि कहत सब कोय।
पिय सौं कहिकै बचन कछु रोस जतावै रोय।।४३।।

Madhya dhira adhira is one who speaks words of admonition but when she cries it expresses anger. [43]

सवैया

आजु कहा तजि बैठी हो भूषन
ऐसे हीं अंग कछू अरसीले।
बोलती बोल रुखाई लिये
मतिराम सनेह सने न रसीले।
क्यों न कहौं दुख प्रानप्रिया
अँसुवानि रहे भरि नैन लजीले।
कौन तिन्हैं दुख है जिनके
तुम-से मनभावन छैल छबीले।।४४।।

Nayak : Why have you abandoned your ornaments today?
Nayika : I feel tired and had no desire of wearing them.
Nayak : Why is your speech so dry today? There is neither love nor sweetness in your speech. O dear! why don't you confide your pain with me? Your bashful eyes are full of tears.
Nayika : Those women who have you as their beloved, what pain can they have? [44]

दोहा

तुमसौं कीजै मान क्यौं बहु नायक मनरंज।
बात कहत यौं बाल के भरि आए दृगकंज।।४५।।

How can I be offended with you as you are capable of pleasing so many women? Saying this, the lotus eyes of the *nayika* were filled with tears. [45]

प्रौढ़ा-धीरा लक्षण

पिय सौं प्रगट न रिस करै रति ते रहै उदास।
प्रौढ़ा-धीरा जानिये सो निज सुमति बिकास।।४६।।

A *praudha dhira* is a *nayika* who does not express anger outwardly but does not enjoy romantic pleasures. [46]

उदाहरण (कवित्त)

वैसे ही चितैकै मेरे चित्त को चुरावति हौ
बोलती हौ वैसे ही मधुर मृदु बानि सौं
कबि मतिराम अंक भरत मयंकमुखी
वैसे ही रहत गहि भुज-लतिकानि सौं।
चूमती कपोल पान करत अधररस
वैसे ही निहारियत सकल कलानि सौं।
कहा चतुराई ठानियत प्रानप्यारी तेरो
मान जानियत रूखी मुख-मुसकानि सौं।।४७।।

Praudha Dhira expresses her anger by showing indifference towards the sports of love.
Nayak addresses her beloved, "O moon-faced ! You win my heart and speak eloquently. Also you place a garland around my neck, embrace and kiss me as usual. All your actions are quite usual, yet your cheerless smile reveals your annoyance." [47]

दोहा

ढीली बाँहन सौं मिली बोली कछू न बोल।
सुंदरि मान जनाय यौं लियो प्रानपति मोल।।४८।।

When the *nayak* arrived the *nayika* greeted him but her arms were stiff and she did not say a word. Showing her anger this way, she was able to win over the *nayak*. [48]

प्रौढ़ा-अधीरा लक्षण

डरु दैकै प्रिय को प्रिया देय सुमन की मारु।
प्रौढ़-अधीरा कहत हैं ताहि सुकबि मति चारु।।४९।।

Praudha adhira is one who frightens her *nayak* and then hits him with flowers. [49]

उदाहरण (कवित्त)

जाके अंग अंग की निकाई निरखत आली
वारनैं अनंग की निकाई कीजियतु है।
कबि मतिराम जाकी चाह ब्रजनारिन को
देह अँसुवान के प्रबाह भीजियतु है।
जाके बिनु देखे न परत कल तुमहूँ कौं
जाके बैन सुनत सुधा-सी पीजियतु है।
ऐसे सुकुमार प्रिय नंद के कुमार को यौं
फूलन के मालन की मारु दीजियतु है।।५०।।

His body is more beautiful than that of Kama and which causes the maidens of Braj to have tears in their eyes. They are restless if they do not see him even for a minute and whose words are as sweet as nectar. O *sakhi* ! please place a garland around his neck. [50]

दोहा

जहाँ तहाँ सखि देत तू फूलमाल की मारु।
तहाँ तहाँ नँदलाल के उठैं रोम तन चारु।।५१।।

O *sakhi* wherever you have struck Krishna with flowers his body has reacted with goosebumps. [51]

प्रौढ़ा-धीरा-अधीरा लक्षण

रति उदास ह्वै नाह कौं डर दिखरावै बाम।
प्रौढ़-अधीरा-धीर तिय बरनत कबि मतिराम।।५२।।

Praudha dhira adhira is one who frightens the *nayak* by showing indifference to the sports of love. [52]

सवैया

प्रीतम आए प्रभात प्रियाघर
राति रमैं रतिचिह्न लिये हीं।
बैठि रही पलका पर सुंदरि
नैन नवायकै धीर धरैं हीं।
बाँह गहैं मतिराम कहैं न
रही रिस मानिनी के हठ कैं हीं।
बोली न बोल कछू सतरायकै
भौंह चढ़ाय तकी तिरछौंहीं।।५३।।

The *nayak* reaches the home of the *nayika* at dawn and on his body marks of love sports with another woman are clearly visible. Having seen this, the *nayika* covered her eyes and sat courageously on the bed and did not welcome the *nayak*. The *nayak* held her hands and spoke words of love but the angry *nayika* kept a straight face and with cross eyes and did not relent. [53]

दोहा

आवत उठि आदर कियो बोली बोल रसाल।
बाँह गही नँदलाल जब भए बालदृग लाल।।५४।।

When Krishna came the *nayika* welcomed him respectfully but when Krishna held her arms, her eyes became bloodshot with anger. [54]

ज्येष्ठा-कनिष्ठा लक्षण

बरनत ज्येष्ठ-कनिष्ठका जहँ द्वै ब्याही नारि।
प्रथम पियारी दूसरी घटि प्यारी निरधारि।।५५।।

Jyeshtha kanishtha is a *nayak* who has two wives and he prefers one over the other. [55]

कवित्त

बैठी एक सेज पै सलोनी मृगनैनी दोऊ
आय तहाँ प्रीतम सुधारसमूह बरसै।
कबि मतिराम ढिग बैठे मनभावनजू
दुहुँन के हिय-अरबिंद मोद सरसै।
आरसी दै एक सौं कह्यो यों निज मुख
देखौ जामे बिधु-बारिज-बिलास बर दरसै।
दरप-सौं भरी वह दरपन देख्यो जौलौं
तौलौं प्रानप्यारी के उरोज हरि परसै।।५६।।

Both the wives with lotus eyes were sitting on the same bed. Just then their husband came there and it was as if there was a shower of nectar and when he came and sat next to them it was as if their lotus-like hearts bloomed. Then the *nayak* gave a mirror to one and said, "look at your face which has the beauty of both the moon and the lotus." On hearing that, the *nayika* was pleased and felt reassured and while she was looking at herself in the mirror the *nayak* touched her breasts indicating his preference. [56]

दोहा

बेनी गूँथत एक की नंदलाल चित लोल।
चूमत प्यारी के मधुर बिहँसत गोल कपोल।।५७।।

Krishna was braiding the *jyeshtha nayika*'s hair and at that time he kissed the *kanishtha*. [57]

परकीया लक्षण

प्रेम करै पर-पुरुष सौं, परकीया सो जान।
दोय भेद ऊढ़ा कहत, बहुरि अनूढ़ा मान।।५८।।

A *parakiya* is a *nayika* who is in love with a man other than her husband. She is further divided into two types: *udha* and *anudha*. [58]

ऊढ़ा-लक्षण

ब्याही औरै पुरुष सौं, औरै सों रस-लीन।
ऊढ़ा तासों कहत हैं, कबि-पंडित-परबीन।।५९।।

An *udha* is married but loves another man. [59]

उदाहरण

क्यों इन आँखिन सों निरसंक
ह्वै मोहन को तन-पानिप पीजै;
नेकु निहारैं कलंक लगै,
इहि गाँव बसे कहौ कैसे के जीजै।
होत रहै मन यों 'मतिराम'
कहूँ बन जाय बड़ी तप कीजै;
ह्वै बनमाल हिए लगिए,
अरु ह्वै मुरली अधरा-रस लीजै।। ६०।।

How can one see with one's eyes Krishna's beauty? In this town people are quick to criticise. How can one live here? I wish I could go to a forest, meditate and return by becoming Krishna's garland to be on his neck, or become his flute and drink the nectar of his lips. [60]

कत चौक सीमंत की बैठी गाँठि जुराय ।
पेखि परोसिनी कौं प्रिया घूँघट मैं मुसकाय ।।६१।।

The *nayika* is sitting on a seat along with her husband for a ritual and her garment is tied to that of her husband. At that time, she surreptitiously sees through her *odhni* another couple in the audience and smiles. [61]

अनूढ़ा लक्षण

अनब्याही केहु पुरुष सों अनुरागिनि जो होय ।
ताहि अनूढ़ा कहत हैं कबि-कोबिद सब कोय ।।६२।।

Anudha is one who is not married but loves a man. [62]

उदाहरण

गोप-सुता कहै, गौरि गुसाइँन !
पायँ परौं, बिनती सुनि लीजै;
दीन-दया-निधि दासी के ऊपर
नेक सुचित्त दया-रस भीजे ।
देहि जो ब्याहि उछाह सों मोहनै,
मात-पिता हू को सो मन कीजै;
सुंदर साँवरो नंदकुमार,
बसै उर जो वह, सो बर दीजै ।।६३।।

Praying to a Devi a maiden says, O Goddess! I fall at your feet. Please listen to my prayer. You are compassionate towards the oppressed and the distressed. Please have pity on me as well. Please tell my parents to get me married to Krishna. Bless me so that the handsome Krishna is always in my heart. [63]

दोहा

मैं सुन आई नंद-घर, अब तू होहु निसंक ।
राधे-मोहन-ब्याह सौं जैहै धोव कलंक ।।६४।।

A *sakhi* speaks with Radha:
O *sakhi!* stop worrying. I was in Nand's home and I heard that they have decided to get Krishna married to you. The stain of courting Krishna will forever be removed from you. [64]

परकीया भेद

परकीया के भेद षट गुप्ता प्रथम बखान।
बहुरि बिदग्धा लच्छिता मुदिता कुलटा मान।।६५।।

और जु अनुसयना कही तिनके बिमल बिबेक।
बरनत कबि मतिराम यह रस सिँगार को सेक।।६६।।

There are six types of *parakiya nayikas* : *gupta*, *vidagdha*, *lakshita*, *mudita*, *kulata* and *anushayana*. [65, 66]

गुप्ता लक्षण

सुरति छिपावै जो तिया सो गुप्ता, उरआनि।
बरनतकबि 'मतिराम' यह, चतुराई की खानि।।६७।।

A *gupta* is one who skilfully hides her love games. [67]

सवैया

लेन गई हुती बागन फूल
अँध्यारी लखें डर बाढ्यो महाई।
रोम उठै तन कंप छुटै
मतिराम भई श्रम की सरसाई।
बेलिन में उरझी अँगिया
छतिया अति कंटक के छतछाई।
देह मैं नैक सँभार रह्यो न
यहाँ लगि भाजि मरू करि आई।।६८।।

O *sakhi* ! I had gone to the garden to pick some flowers and finding that it was dark I was frightened. My body began to tremble and I felt tired. When I was returning my *odhni* got caught in a creeper and my chest was scratched and I could not save myself. With great difficulty I have escaped from there. [68]

विदग्धा लक्षण

भलो नहीं यह केवरो, सजनी गेह अराम।
वसन फटै कंटक लगै, निसि दिन आठौं जाम।।६९।।

The *Gupta nayika* cleverly conceals the nail marks on her bosom made by her lover during love making. She speaks to her *sakhi* that thorns of *kewara* plants tear her garments and made scratches on her bosom. [69]

विदग्धा भेद

द्विबिध बिदग्धा कहत हैं कबि करि बिमल बिबेक।
बचनबिदग्धा एक है क्रियाबिदग्धा एक।।७०।।

There are two types of *vidagdha nayikas*: *vachan vidagdha* and *kriya vidagdha*. [70]

वचनविदग्धा लक्षण

करै बचन सों चातुरी बचन बिदग्धा जान।
करै क्रिया सों चातुरी क्रिया बिदग्धा मान।।७१।।

A *vachan vidagdha* is one who arranges her meetings with clever words and who arranges her meetings with actions, is known as *Kriya Vidagdha.* [71]

कवित्त

आई है निपट साँझ गैयाँ गईं घरमाँझ
ह्वाँ सो दौरि आई मेरो कह्यो कान्ह कीजिए।
हौं तो हौं अकेली और दूसरो न देखियत
बन की अँधेरी में अधिक भय भीजिए।
कबि मतिराम मनमोहन सौं पुनि पुनि
राधिका कहति बात साँचो ये पतीजिए।
कब की हौ हेरति न हेरे हरि पावति हौं
बछरा हिरान्यो सो हिराय नैक दीजिए।।७२।।

O Krishna ! it is evening and the cows have returned home. But one calf is missing and I have come running here. Please help me, for I am alone and am frightened to go alone in this dark forest. Matiram says that she kept on pleading for help saying that her calf was lost and she need help in finding it. [72]

क्रियाविदग्धा उदाहरण

खेत निहारै धान को यों बूझो मुसकाय।
इहो हमारो है कह्यो सघन ज्वार दरसाय।।७३।।

Nayika shows to *nayak* the paddy-crop of her fields with a suggestions that it can be an ideal spot for love making. [73]

सवैया

बैठी तिया गुरु लोगन में
रति तें अति सुंदर रूप बिसेखी।
आयो तहाँ मतिराम सुजान
मनोभव सों बढ़ि कांति उरेखी।
लोचन रूप पियो ही चहैं
अरु लाजनि जात नहीं छबि पेखी।
नैन नमाय रही हियमाल में
लाल की मूरति लाल में देखी।।७४।।

A *nayika* prettier than Rati was sitting in the midst of elderly people. As it happened, a *nayak* more handsome than Kama came there. She wanted to enjoy his good looks but was bashful and could not stare at him. With downcast eyes she looked at the beads that were swinging on his chest and caught a glimpse of him in those beads. [74]

दोहा

चढ़ी अटारी बाम वह कियौ प्रनाम अखोट।
तरनिकिरन तें दृगन कौं करसरोज की ओट।।७५।।

A *sakhi* talks to another *sakhi.*
A *nayika* climbed on the threshold, protected her eyes from the rays of the sun and venerated it. Actually she saluted her beloved but made it look like she was worshipping the sun. This way she felt secure. [75]

लक्षिता लक्षण

होत लखाय सखीन कौं पिय सौं जाको प्रेम।
ताहि लच्छिता कहत हैं कबि-कोबिद करि नेम।।७६।।

A *lakshita* is one who expresses her love on the *sakhis.* [76]

सवैया

आई हौ पायँ दिवाय महावर
कुंजन तें करिकै सुखसैनी।
साँवरे आजु सँवारयो है अंजन
नैनन को लखि लाजति ऐनी।
बात के बूझत ही मतिराम
कहा करियै यह भौंह तनैनी।
मूँदि न राखत प्रीति भटू यह
गूँदी गुपाल के हाथ की बैनी।।७७।।

O *sakhi* ! I know that you have enjoyed love sports in the grove and that is he who has applied the red dye to your feet. He has applied corrylium to your eyes and it makes the deer bashful. When I ask you something you make a cross face and get angry. But you cannot hide your love and your braid done by Krishna shows that the two of you are in love. [77]

दोहा

सतरौंहीं भौंहन नहीं दुरै दुरायो नेह।
होत नाम नँदलाल के नीपमाल सी देह।।७८।।

The *nayika* hides her love marks from her friend. The *sakhi* tells her that she cannot hide her love for Krishna from her because even on hearing the name of Krishna you get goosebumps. [78]

कुलटा लक्षण

जो चाहत बहु नायकन, सरस सुरति पर-प्रीति ।
तासौं कुलटा कहत हैं, लखि ग्रंथन की रीति ।।७९।।

A *kulata* is a *nayika* who wishes to engage romantically with many men. [79]

उदाहरण

अंजन दै निकसै नित नैनन,
मंजन कै अति अंग सँवारै;
रूप-गुमान-भरी मग मैं
पग ही के अँगूठा-अनौट सुधारै ।
जोबन के मद सौं 'मतिराम'
भई मतवारिनि लोग निहारै ;
जति चलि यहि भाँति गली,
बिथुरी अलकैं अँचरा न सँभारै ।। ८०।।

A *nayika* has finished her bath and having adorned herself has left home. She has worn a toe ring and she walks feeling proud of her beauty. She is vain and aware of her own youth and looks at everyone with intoxicated eyes. Her hair is dishevelled and her *odhni* is out of place and she walks down the street. [80]

दोहा

मोह मधुर मुसकानि सौं सबै गाम के छैल।
सकल सैल बन कुज मैं तरुनि सुरति की सैल।।८१।।

All the young and romantic people of this village are attracted by her sweet smile. And all the mountains, forests and groves are her rendezvous. [81]

मुदिता लक्षण

चित चाही सुन बात लखि मुदित होय जो बाल।
तासौं मुदिता कहत हैं कबि मतिराम रसाल।।८२।।

Mudita is a *nayika* who is happy anticipating the future prospect of romance. [82]

उदाहरण (सवैया)

मोहन तैं कछु द्योसन मैं
मतिराम बढ्यो अनुराग सुहायो।
बैठी हुती तिय मायके मैं
ससुरारि को काहू सँदेसो सुनायो।
नाह के ब्याह की चाह सुनी
हिय माँहि उछाह छबीली के छायो।
पौढ़ि रही पट ओढ़ि अटा
दुख को मिस कै सुख बाल छिपायो।।८३।।

Lately the *nayika* is increasingly in love with Krishna. One day when she came to her mother's home and is sitting with the ladies when her father-in-law sent a message that her husband was getting married a second time. She was happy on hearing that news, for she could now really meet her beloved. But she put on a sad face and slept on the threshold. This way she was able to hide her joy and at the same time express her anger. [83]

दोहा

बिछुरत रोवत दुहुँन को सखि यह रूप लखै न।
दुख-अँसुवा पियनैन हैं सुख-अँसुवा तियनैन।।८४।।

Her husband is about to leave on a journey and he is sad because he will be separated from his wife. There are tears in their eyes. While the husband is sad, the wife is happy as she can meet her beloved. [84]

पहली अनुसयना लक्षण

केलि करे जहँ कंत सौं, सो थल मिट्यो निहारि।
कहि अनुसयना तासु सौं, सोच करे बरनारि।।८५।।

Anusayana is a *nayika* who is sad on seeing the rendezvous destroyed. [85]

कवित्त

आई ऋतु पावस अकास आठौं दिसन मैं
सोहत स्वरूप जलधरन की भीर को।
मतिराम सुकबि कदंबन की बासजुत
सरस बढ़ावैं रस परस समीर को।
भौन तैं निकसि वृषभानु की कुमारि देख्यो
ता समै सहेट को निकुंज गिर्यो तीर को।
नागरि के नैननि तैं नीर को प्रबाह बढ़्यो
निरखि प्रबाह बढ़्यो जमुना के नीर को।।८६।।

With the onset of the monsoon season clouds gathered in all eight directions. Matiram says that fragrant winds touched the body and increased her happiness. When Vrishbhanu's daughter (Radha) stepped out of her home she saw that the grove where she and Krishna used to meet is covered with water of the Yamuna. When she saw that the waters of the Yamuna were rising, her eyes were filled with tears. [86]

दोहा

ग्रीषम ऋतु में देखिकै बन में लगी दवारि।
एक अपूरब बात यह जरत हिये बर नारि।।८७।।

It is summer and there is a fire in the forest and at the same time there is a fire in her heart as she anticipates meeting her beloved in that forest. Now their meeting place was destroyed. [87]

द्वितीय अनुसयना लक्षण

होनहार संकेत को जहँ अभाव उर आनि।
अनुसयना कहिये यहौ हिये दुखनि की खानि।।८८।।

An *anusayana* is one who has become unhappy on account of the romantic rendezvous being destroyed. [88]

सवैया

बेलिन सौं लपटाय रही है
तमालन की अवली अति कारी।
कोकिल केकी कपोतन के कुल
केलि करैं जहँ आनँद भारी।
सोच करौ जिन होहु सुखी
मतिराम प्रबीन सबै नर नारी।
मंजुल बंजुल-कुंजन में
घनपुंज सखी ससुरारि तिहारी।।८९।।

O *sakhi* ! do not be unhappy as even here there are a number of meeting places. Look, these creepers are clinging to the leaves of the black *tamal* tree. And there groups of cuckoos, peacocks and pigeons are playing and making merry. Clever romantic couples can go there and find happiness. In the yonder dense *ashoka* grove was your mother-in-law's meeting place. [89]

दोहा

केलि करैं मधुमत्त जहँ घन मधुपन के पुंज।
सोच न कर तुव सासुरे सखी सघन बनकुंज।।९०।।

The *nayika* was preparing to leave for her husband's home and she was sad and her friend said, O *sakhi* ! There will be no difficulty in engaging in amorous sports with her husband in his home as there are dense grooves where bees buzz. [90]

तृतीय अनुसयना लक्षण

प्रीतम गए सहेट कों जानै हेतुहि पाय।
तृतिया अनुसयना कही हौं न गई पछिताय।।९१।।

An *anusayana* is one who is distressed at not being able to go to the appointed rendezvous. [91]

कवित्त

साँझ समै मतिराम कामबस बंसीधर
बंसीबट तट पै बजाई जाय बाँसुरी।
सुमिरि सहेट बृषभानु की कुमारि-उर
दुख अधिकानो भयो सुख की बिनासु री।
सर-सौं समीर लाग्यो सूल-सी सहेली सब
बिष-सौं बिनोद लाग्यो बन-सो निवासु री।
ताप चढ़ि आयो तन पीरी परि आई मुख
आँखिन के ऊपर उमँगि आए आँसु री।।९२।।

Matiram says that Krishna goes to the banks of the Yamuna in the evening and plays the flute to invite Radha. On hearing that, Radha remembered the tryst but because of circumstances was unable to go there and felt sad. The wind seemed to her like arrows and her *sakhis* were like thorns, merriment was like poison and her home was like a jungle, her longing caused her body to burn, her face turned pale and her eyes were full of tears. [92]

दोहा

छरी सपल्लव लाल कर लखि तमाल की हाल।
कुम्हिलानी उरसाल धरि फूलमाल ज्यौं बाल।।९३।।

The *nayak* holds a branch freshy cut from a *tamal* tree. Seeing this, the *nayika* realised that her beloved had waited for her at the tryst and was returning disappointed. She was very sad and the pain made her distressed and she was like wilted flowers. [93]

गणिका-लक्षण

धन दै जाके संग मैं रमें पुरुष सब कोइ।
ग्रंथन को मत देखि कैं गणिका जानहु सोइ।।९४।।

A *ganika* is a *nayika* who is prepared to engage in love sports if she is paid.[94]

कवित्त

लाल कर चरन रदनछद नख लाल
मोतिन की रदन रही है छबि छाइकै।
कबि मतिराम मुख सुबरन रूप रहि
रूपखानि मुसकानि सोभा सरसाइकै।
आनन को इंदु जान आँखैं अरबिंद मानि
इंदिरा रजनि-दिन रहति सिहाइकै।
नायक नवल क्यों न देय धन-मन ऐसे
सुतनु कौं सुतनु अतनु-धन पाइकै।।९५।।

Her hands are coloured with *mehendi* and her feet with *mahavar*. Her lips and nails are also red. Her teeth shine like pearls. Her face has a golden glow and her appearance is a mine of beauty. Her smile is bright as the stars. Her face is like the moon and her eyes like a lotus. She is endowed with both beauty and wealth that even Goddess Lakshmi is envious of her. Is there any doubt that a young man will not be willing to make love and offer wealth to such a beautiful and young *ganika*? [95]

दोहा

लसत गूजरी ऊजरी बिलसत लाल ईजार।
हिये हजारनि के हरै बैठी बाल बजार।।९६।।

A fair maiden *gujari* had adorned herself and was sitting in the market and her red drawstring was hanging. Such a maiden is able to capture many a heart. [96]

अन्य-संभोगदुःखितादि-भेद

अनसौं रति हुय दुःखिता, प्रेमगरबिता जान।
रूपगरबिता और पुनि मानवती उर आन।।९७।।

When a *nayika* sees signs on the person of her husband made by love-making with another woman, that *nayika* becomes sorrowful. Thus she is known as *anya sambhoga dukhita*. Another *nayika* who is proud of her faithful lover is *prema-garvita* and one who is proud of her beauty is known as *rupa-garvita*. Manavati is the fourth type of *nayika* who is displeased even with her inimical lover. [97]

अन्य-संभोगदुःखिता लक्षण

निजपति के रतिचिह्न जो लखे और तिय-देह।
अन्य सुरतिदुखिता कहौ, करै पेच-रिस-तेह।।९८।।

Anya sambhog duhkhita nayika is one who becomes distressed upon seeing lovemarks made by her husband on the person of another woman, *duti* or *sakhi*. [98]

कवित्त

याही कौं पठाई भलो काम करि आई बड़ी
तेरी ये बड़ाई लखे लोचन लजीले सौं।
साँची क्यों न कहै कछु मोकौं किधौं आपही कौं
पाई बकसीस लाई बसन छबीले सौं।
मतिराम सुकबि सँदेसा अनुमानियत
तेरे नखसिख अंग हरष कटीले सौं।
तू तो है रसीली रसबातन बनाय जानै
मेरे जान आई रस राखिकै रसीले सौं।।९९।।

A *nayika* sent her *sakhi* to the *nayak* with a message but when the *sakhi* returned there were signs of lovemaking on her body and she concluded that she was erotically involved with the *nayak*. She was unhappy and she confronted the *sakhi*. "Did I send you to the *nayak* for this reason? Your eyes show your guilt. If you are not able to confess to me you should be honest to yourself. You have brought his *uttariya* with you." Matiram says that "signs on your entire body reveal the time you spent with the *nayak*. You are adept in the speech of love and it seems to me that you have fallen in love with him". [99]

दोहा

कहत तिहारो रूप यह सखी पैंड को खेद।
ऊँची लेत उसास है कलित सकल तन स्वेद।।१००।।

The *nayika* has realised that her *sakhi* has returned after a romantic involvement with her beloved. She says, O *sakhi* ! Your face shows that you have come from a long distance. That is why you are tired and are taking deep breaths. The drops of sweat on your body tell your story. And I have come to know everything. [100]

प्रेमगर्विता लक्षण

निज नायक के प्रेम कौं गरब जानवै बाल।
प्रेम-गरबिता कहत हैं तासौं सुमति-रसाल।।१०१।।

She is convinced that the *nayak* loves her and she declares this to her *sakhis*. [101]

कवित्त

मेरे हँसे हँसत हैं मेरे बोले बोलत हैं
मोही कौं जानत तन मन धन प्रान री।
कबि मतिराम भौंह टेढ़ी किये हाँसीहू में
छोड़ देत भूषन बसन खान पान री।
मोतें प्रानप्यारी प्रानप्यारे के न और कोऊ
तासों रिस कीजै कहौ कहाँ की सयान री।
मैनकामिनी के मैनकाहू के न रूप रीझे
मैं न काहू के सिखाएँ आनो मन मान री।।१०२।।

O *sakhi* ! My lover laughs when I laugh, and talks at my command. For him I am everything. If even in jest I pretend to be angry he gives up eating. There is no one dear to him than me. It would be foolish of me to be angry with him. He is not the one to be attracted by the beauty of Menaka and Rati, so why should I demand anything more from him? [102]

दोहा

औरन के पाइन दियो नायनि जावक लाल।
प्रानपियारी रावरी परखति तुम्हैं रसाल।।१०३।।

A *sakhi* speaks to the *nayak*. O *nayak* ! The *nayika* is proud of her love for you. That is why she did not ask the barber's wife to apply red dye to her feet. [103]

रूपगर्विता लक्षण

जाकें अपने रूप को अति ही होय गुमान।
रूप-गरबिता कहत हैं तासौं परम सुजान।।१०४।।

Rupa garvita is one who is proud of her beauty. [104]

सवैया

सोय रही रति अंत रसीली
अनंत बढ़ाय अनंग-तरंगनि।
केसरि खौरि रची तिय के तन
प्रीतम और सुबास के संगनि।
जागि परी मतिराम सरूप
गुमान जनावत भौंह के भंगनि।
लाल सौं बोलति नाहिन बाल
सु पोंछति आँखि अँगोछति अंगनि।।१०५।।

Having enjoyed romantic pleasures the *nayika* is resting. Desiring romantic activity with her the *nayak* applies a saffron unguent to her body. She woke up and with upturned eyebrows expressed resentment as she felt that her body was very beautiful and fragrant than sandalwood. She kept on rubbing off the saffron paste from her body. [105]

दोहा

कैसे आऊँ हूँ वहाँ है जित नंदकिसोर।
दिनहूँ मैं मुखचंद को लखि ललचात चकोर।।१०६।।

A *nayika* speaks to her *sakhi*. O *sakhi* ! How can I go to meet Krishna? For if I go during the day the *chakor* bird would be attracted to my moon-like face. [106]

मानवती लक्षण

करै ईरषा सों जु तिय मनभावन सों मान।
मानवती तासों कहत कबि 'मतिराम' सुजान।।१०७।।

A *manvati* is a *nayika* who is jealous and sulks. [107]

उदाहरण

सो मनमोहन होत लटू मुख जाके भटू !
बिधु की छबि छाजै;
खोल कै नैनन देखैं जो नेक
तो स्याम सरोज-पराजय साजै।

जो बिहँसे मुख सुंदर तो
'मतिराम' विहान को बारिज लाजै;
बोले अली मृदु मंजुल बोल तो
कोकिल-बोलनि को मद भाजै ।।१०८।।

O *sakhi*! When Krishna is infatuated by the moon-faced *nayika*, then when the *nayika* opens her eyes then the blue lotus accepts defeat, when she laughs then the even the morning lotus is bashful, when that *nayika* speaks sweet words then the cuckoo considers its voice to be inferior to hers. [108]

दोहा

सुन चित दै मनमानिनी बिन अपराध रिसानि।
नेह जरावन को महा दीपजोति जिय जानि।।१०९।।

O Manini! Please listen to me carefully. The *nayak* has not committed any offence yet you sulk with him. The fire of your sulking will destroy your love. So stop sulking. [109]

दशनायिका

प्रोषितपतिका खंडिता कलहंतरिता जान।
बिप्रलुब्ध उतकंठिता बासकसज्जा मान।।
स्वाधिनपतिका कहत कबि अभिसारिका सुनाम।
कही प्रबच्छतिप्रेयसी आगतपतिका बाम।।
दसौं अवस्थाभेद सौं दसौं नायका जानि।
तिनके लच्छन लच्छ अब आछे कहौं बखानि।।११०।।

The ten *nayikas* that poets celebrate are: *proshitapatika, khandita, kalahantarita, vipralabdha, utkanthita, vasaksajja, svadhinapatika, abhisarika, pravatsyapatika* and *agatapatika*. [110]

मुग्धा-प्रोषितपतिका-लक्षण

जाको पिय परदेश मैं बिरह-बिकल तिय होय।
प्रोषितपतिका-नायका ताहि कहत सब कोय।।१११।।

Mugdha proshitapatika is one who is in despair on account of her beloved being abroad. [111]

सवैया

बार कितेक सहेलिन के कहैं
कैसेहूँ लेत न बीरी सँवारी।
राखति रोकि कहै मतिराम
चलैं अँसुवा अँखियानि तें भारी।
प्रानपियारो चल्यो जबतें
तबतें कछु और ही रीति निहारी।
पीरी जनावति अंगन में कहि
पीर जनावति काहे न प्यारी।।११२।।

Despite loving persuasion of your *sakhis* you refuse to eat betel. You control the flow of tears from your eyes. Your entire behaviour has changed since our beloved has gone abroad. Your body has become pale. [112]

दोहा

पियबियोग तियदृग जलधि जलतरंग अधिकाय।
बरुनि-मूल-बेला परसि बहुरयो जात बिलाय।।११३।।

On account of longing, a sea of tears flows from her eyes but her eyelashes are like the shore of the ocean which the waves cannot cross. [113]

मध्या-प्रोषितपतिका

उदाहरण (कवित्त)

चंद के उदोत होत नैनकंज तपे कंत
छायो परदेस देह दाहनि दगतु है।
उसिर गुलाबनीर करपूरपरसत
बिरहअनल-ज्वाल-जालन जगतु है।
लाजनि ते कछू न जनावै काहू सखीहूँ सौं
उर को उदार अनुराग उमगतु है।
कहा करौं मेरी बीर उठी है अधिक पीर
सुरभी-समीर सीरो तीर सौं लगतु है।।११४।।

As soon as the moon rises her lotus-like eyes begin to burn and the whole body is on fire and does not respond to the cooling effects of rose water, poppy seeds and camphor. Her heart has pangs of love and on account of her bashfulness she is unable to speak about this even to her *sakhis*. All she can say is that my heart is afflicted and my body hurts as if touched by arrows. [114]

दोहा

बहू दूबरी होत क्यौं यौं जब बूझो सास।
ऊतर कढ्यो न बालमुख ऊँचे लेत उसास।।११५।।

When the mother-in-law asks the *nayika* why she is losing weight the *nayika* is unable to answer and takes long sighing breaths. [115]

प्रौढ़ा-प्रोषितपतिका

A *praudha proshitapatika* is a *nayika* who is mature even in longing.

कवित्त

बिरह तिहारे लाल बिकल भई है बाल
नींद भूख प्यास सिगरी बिसारियतु है।
चोरी कैसी बात चंद्रमाहूँ ते चुराइयति
बसननि तानिकै बयारि बारियतु है।
कहै मतिराम कलाधर कैसी कला छीन
जीवनबिहीन मीन सी निहारियतु है।
बार बार सुकुमार फूलन की मार ऐसी
मार के मरोरन मरोरि मारियतु है।।११६।।

In your absence the *nayika* is distressed. She has given up sleep, hunger and thirst. She tries to conceal her pain. She protects herself from the wind by covering her body. Matiram says that she has wasted like the second day of the moon and trembles like a fish out of water. Kama has assaulted her body with his arrows and is taking her life. [116]

परकीया-प्रोषितपतिका

चंद्रकिरन लगि बालतन उठति आँच यों जागि।
दुपहर-दिनकरकर परसि ज्यों दरपन मैं आगि।।११७।।

When moonlight falls on her body a fire radiates from it and it seems as if sunlight falls on a lens and creates fire. [117]

सवैया

ह्वाँ मिलि मोहन सों मतिराम
सुकेलि करी अति आनँदवारी।
तेई लता द्रुम देखत दुःख
चलै अँसुवा अँखियान तैं भारी।
आवति हौं जमुनातट कों
नहिं जानि परै बिछुरे गिरिधारी।
जानति हौं सखि आवत चाहत
कुंजन तें कढ़ि कुंजबिहारी।।११८।।

O *sakhi* I used to enjoy the sports of love with Mohan in that grove but now looking at those trees and creepers my eyes are filled with tears. When I come to the banks of the Yamuna I cannot accept that Giridhari is away from me, for it seems that he will come out of the grove any minute. [118]

दोहा

लाज छुटि गेहौ छुट्यो सुख सों छुट्यो सनेह।
सखि कहियो वा निठुर सों रही छूटिबे देह।।११९।।

O *sakhi* ! in the absence of my beloved I have lost my honour and my home, and I have no happiness left. Tell that heartless *nayak* that I am about to die. [119]

सामान्य-प्रोषितपतिका

सवैया

आली सिँगारति है हठ सों पर
लागत अंग सिँगार अँगारो।
पीरी परी तनमैं मतिराम
चले अँखियान तैं नीर पनारो।
सोउ नहीं मनभावन नायक
आवत जो बहुतै धनवारो।
बार बिलासिनि कों बिसरै न
बिदेस गयो पिय प्रानपियारो।।१२०।।

When her *sakhis* forcibly adorn her body those adornments burn her body. Her body has become pale and streams of tears flow from her eyes. A number of wealthy clients visit her but her beloved, who is very generous, is in a distant land. She remembers him constantly and suffers. [120]

दोहा

धन के हेतु बिलासिनी रही सँवारे बेस।
जो तिय के हिय मैं बसे सो पिय बसे बिदेस।।१२१।।

A *ganika nayika* is adorning herself with the expectation of earning money. But the man she is thinking about is in another place and she is therefore unhappy. [121]

खंडिता लक्षण

पिय-तन औरै नारि के
रति के चिह्न निहारि।

दुखित होत सो खंडिता,
बरनत सुकबि बिचारि॥१२२॥

A *khandita* is one who is saddened to see marks of love sports on her beloved caused by other women. [122]

सवैया

लाल तुम्हैं कहुँ और तिया की
लख्यो अँगिया मैं लगावत चोवै।
ता छिन तें मतिराम न खेलत
बूझैं सखीनहुँ सों दुख गोवै।
लिखै कर के नख सों पग को नख
सीस नवायकै नीचे ही जोवै।
बाल नवेली न रूसनो जानति
भीतर भौन मसूसनि रोवे ॥१२३॥

A *sakhi* tells the *nayak* that ever since the *nayika* has seen you applying fragrant unguents to another woman, she has lost all interest and even though we question her she refuses to speak and hides her pain. She stares with her head downcast and scratches her toes with her finger nails. She is very innocent and all she can do is to hide in the house and cry. [123]

दोहा

बाल सखिन की सीख तें मान न जानति ठानि।
पिय बिन आगम भौन में बैठी भौंहैं तानि॥१२४॥

The *nayika* does not sulk even though she has been instructed. She sits in the *haveli* with raised eyebrows even though the *nayak* has not arrived. [124]

मध्या-खंडिता

कवित्त

जावक लिलार ओठ अंजन की लीक सोहै
खैये न अलीक लोकलीक न बिसारिये।
कबि मतिराम छाती नखछत जगमगै
डगमगै पग सूधे मग मैं न धारिये।
कसकै उघारत हौ पलक पलक यातें
पलका पै पौढ़ि श्रम राति को निवारिये।
अटपटे बैन मुख बात न कहत बनै
लटपटे पेंच सिरपाग के सुधारिये॥१२५॥

A *nayika* tells her *nayak*. There are red marks on your forehead as you have prostrated yourself before another woman. There are marks of corrylium on your lips as you have kissed the eyes of another woman. So do not speak words of deceit. Matiram says that nail marks are clearly visible on your chest and you can barely walk straight and your eyes are drooping. So please lie down on the bed and recover from the fatigue of the night. Your speech is indistinct and your turban is dishevelled. [125]

दोहा

कोऊ करो कितेक यह तजो न टेव गुपाल।
निसि औरनि के पग परो दिन औरनि के लाल॥१२६॥

Despite all attempts, you do not change. At night you fall at another woman's feet and in the morning you bow before me. [126]

सवैया

प्रीतम आए प्रभात प्रिया
मुसकाय उठी दृग सों दृग जोरै।
आगें ह्वै आदर सों मतिराम
कहै मृदु बैन सुधारस बोरै।
ऐसे सयान सुभायन हीं सों
मिली मनभावन सों मन भोरै।
मान गो जानि सुजान तबै
अँगिया की तनी न छुटी जब छोरै॥१२७॥

When the *nayak* returned after spending the night with another woman the *nayika* looked at his eyes and started to laugh. Then she respectfully greeted him and spoke sweet words to him and won over the *nayak*. But the *nayak* realised that the *nayika* is offended when he was unable to untie the laces of her *kanchuki* (bodice). [127]

प्रौढ़ा-खंडिता

दोहा

आदर करि पिय सों मिली तिय हिय राखि सयान।
दृग कसि बाँधी कुंचुकी समुझायो मन-मान॥१२८॥

When the *nayak* arrived in the morning after spending a night with another woman he was respectfully received by the *nayika*. She tied her *choli* so tight that the *nayak* was not about to open it. In this way she was able to express her anger. [128]

परकीया-खंडिता

सवैया

रावरे नेह को लाज तजी अरु
गेह के काज सबै बिसराए।
डारि दिये गुरु लोगन को डर
गाम चवाय में नाम धराए।
हेत कियो हम जो तो कहा
तुमतो मतिराम सबै बहराए।
कोऊ कितेक उपाय करो
कहुँ होत हैं आपने पीउ पराए।।१२९।।

A *nayika* tells the *nayak*. I have given up my honour on account of my love for you and have left all my household duties. I have ignored the elders and in this gossipy town I have been called various names. I have loved you but you have forgotten my many acts of love. Truly, has it been said that you can never win over a stranger with love. [129]

दोहा

हमसौं तुमसौं लाल इत नैनन ही सौं नेह।
उत प्यारी के दृगन के सलिल सींचियत देह।।१३०।।

A *duti* speaks to the *nayak*. O Krishna ! Your love for the *nayika* is only in your eyes. Radha has smeared her body with a stream of tears in your absence. [130]

गणिका-खंडिता

ह्याँ हमसों मिलिबो ठहराय कैं
सैन कहूँ अनतैं ही करीजै;
भोरहिं आय बनाय कें बातनि
चातुर ह्वै बिनती बहु कीजै ।
ऐसीहि रीति सदा 'मतिराम' सु
कैसे पियारे जु प्रेम पतीजै ;
सौहैं न खाइए जाइए ह्याँ ते
न मानहु जो धन लाखन दीजै ।।१३१।।

My beloved you promised to meet me but you spent the night somewhere else. You come at dawn and make excuses. You are trying to win me over. Do you consider yourself very clever? How can I trust you anymore? Do not swear allegiance to me, just leave. Even if you give me a lot of money I will not listen. [131]

दोहा

कंत कहा सौंहन करौ जानि पर्‍यो अब नेह।
देन कह्यो सो बिन दियैं जान न पैहो गेह।।१३२।।

A *ganika* speaks to a *nayak*. Why do you take an oath? I am not concerned that you are involved with another woman. You had promised to pay me. Until you pay me I will not let you go home. [132]

कलहांतरिता लक्षण

कह्यो न मानै कंत को पुनि पीछे पछिताय।
कलहंतरिता नायका ताहि कहत कविराय।।१३३।।

Kalahantarita nayika is one who disobeys her *nayak* but then repents. [133]

सवैया

गौने की चूनरी वैसिय है
दुलही अबही ते ढिठाई बगारी।
वेऊ मनावन आए हैं
आपन हाथ सौं जात न पाग सँवारी।
पाँइ परे मतिराम लला
मनुहारि करी कर जोरि हहारी।
आप ही मान्यो मनायो न कान्ह को
आप ही खात न पान पियारी।।१३४।।

Her special *odhni* on the occasion of *gauna* is untouched but she still holds it bashfully. Her beloved came to win her over and asked her to straighten his turban saying he was unable to do it. But she did not relent. With folded hands he entreated her and fell at her feet but even then she did not pay any attention. Now she repents and has given up eating betel. [134]

दोहा

आई गौने कालि ही सीखी कहा सयान।
अबहीं तें रूसन लगी अबहीं तें पछितान।।१३५।।

A *sakhi* speaks to a *kalahantarita nayika* :
O *sakhi* ! You have just returned from the *gauna* and already you have started being clever. You fought with the *nayak* and now you repent. From where have you learnt this art? [135]

मध्या-कलहांतरिता

सवैया

पाँयन आनि परे तो परे रहे
केती करी मनुहारि न झेली।
मान्यो मनायो न मैं मतिराम
गुमान मैं ऐसी भई अलबेली।
प्यारो गयो दुख मान कहूँ अब
कैसे रहूँ यहि राति अकेली।
आप ते ल्याउ मनाय कन्हाई को
मेरो न लीजियो नाम सहेली।।१३६।।

A *nayika* tells her *sakhi*. He fell at my feet and stayed there for a long time and even though he tried to appease me I did not relent. I was so arrogant that I did not listen to him one bit. Now that my beloved has gone, to whom shall I express my remorse and how shall I spend the night all alone? My dear *sakhi*, please go and win over Krishna but do not let him know that I have sent you. [136]

दोहा

जो तू कहै तो राधिका पियहि मनावन जाउँ।
वहाँ कहौंगी जायकै सखी तिहारो नाउँ।।१३७।।

I will go and assuage the *nayak* if you want me to. But I will make it clear that it is you who have sent me. [137]

प्रौढ़ा-कलहांतरिता

सवैया

ठाढ़े भए कर जोरिकै आगे
अधीन हवै पाँयन सीस नवायो।
केती करी बिनती मतिराम पै
मैं न कियो हठ तें मन भायो।
देखत ही सिगरी सजनी तुम
मेरो तो मान महा मद छायो।
रूठि गयो उठि प्रानपियारो
कहा कहिये तुमहूँ न मनायो।।१३८।।

A *nayika* tells her *sakhi*. My beloved stood in front of me with folded hands and then placed his head on my feet. He entreated me several times but I was obstinate and did not listen to his pleadings. You know how arrogant I was and that is why my beloved was displeased and left. But even you did not try to win him over. [138]

दोहा

पीतम जब पाँयन पर्‌यो तब अति भई सरोस।
कह्यो न मान्यो कंत को हमें दीजियतु दोस।।१३९।।

O *sakhi* ! Even though the *nayak* fell at your feet you continue to be angry and sulk. You now repent and are blaming me. [139]

परकीया-कलहांतरिता

सवैया

जाके लिये गृहकाज तज्यो
न सिखी सखियान की सीख सिखाई।
बैर कियो सिगरे ब्रजगाम सौं
जाके लिये कुलकानि गँमाई।
जाके लिये घर बाहरहूँ
मतिराम रहे हँसि लोग लुगाई।
ता हरि सौं हित एकहि बार
गँवारि मैं तोरत बार न लाई।।१४०।।

I left my household duties and did not listen to my *sakhis*, created enemies with the people of Braj, I left the honour of my family and was ridiculed by people everywhere. In spite of this, it was my stupidity that I broke away from Krishna. [140]

दोहा

जोरतहू सजनी बिपति
तोरत बिपति समाज।
नेह कियो बिन काज पुनि
तोहि कियो बिन काज।।१४१।।

A *sakhi* speaks to a *nayika* :
When there is a problem it can bring two people in difficulty together. But it can

equally be destructive. To be unreasonably angry would break our relationship. [141]

गणिका-कलहांतरिता

सवैया

जाते लही जगबीच बड़ाई मैं
मेरे बियोग जो होत है छीनो।
मोहि गिने मतिराम जो प्रान सो
मेरे सदा हीं रहे जो अधीनो।
मेरे लिये नित ही उठिकै
गहनौं जु गढ़ायकै लावे नवीनो।
प्रानपियारो सो पाइन लाग्यो री
मैं हँसि कंठ लगाई न लीनो।।१४२।।

O *sakhi* ! because of whose association I got recognition in the world, who becomes powerless in my absence, who loves me more than himself, who is always dependent on me, who gives me new ornaments everyday, he fell at my feet but I rejected him. [142]

दोहा

जासौं कियो सनेह मन रही न एको साध।
तासौं भई सरोस हौं सजनी बिन अपराध।।१४३।।

A *nayika* speaks to a *sakhi* :
O *sakhi* ! I loved him and he fulfilled all my wishes and yet I have been displeased with him and that too without any fault of his. What shall I do now? [143]

विप्रलब्धा-लक्षण

मिलन आस करि जाय तिय,
मिले न पिय संकेत।
बिप्रलब्ध सो जानिए,
बिरह-बिकल बिन चेत।।१४४।।

A *vipralabdha* is one who reaches the appointed tryst in anticipation of romantic pleasures but her beloved does not come. [144]

मुग्धा विप्रलब्धा

उदाहरण (सवैया)

आलिन को सुख मानिबे कौं
पियप्यारे की सेज गई चलि बागै।
छाय रह्यो हियरा दुख सौं
जब देख न हवाँ नँदलाल सभागै।
काहू सौं बोल कछू न कह्यो
मतिराम न चित्त कहूँ अनुरागै।
खेलति खेल सहेलिन मैं
पर खेल नबेली कौं जेल सौं लागै।।१४५।।

At the encouragement of her *sakhis* the *nayika* went to the rendezvous where a bed was kept but Krishna did not keep the appointment and she was saddened. She was not able to speak to anyone and nothing would please her. She kept on playing with her *sakhis* but this was more an irritation rather than pleasure. [145]

दोहा

लख्यो न कंत सहेट मैं
लख्यो नखत को राय।
नवल बाल को कमल सौं
गयो बदन कुँभिलाय।।१४६।।

The *nayika* reached the appointed spot but the *nayak* was nowhere to be seen. The moon had risen; it was night-time and the chances of his coming were remote. On looking at the moon her face wilted like the lotus at night-time. [146]

सवैया

केलि के मंदिर देखो न लाल को
बाल के दाहन अंग दहे हैं।
भौंह चढ़ाय सखी सो लख्यो
मतिराम कछू न कुबोल कहे हैं।
भूलि हुलास बिलास गए
दुख तैं भरिके अँसुवा उमहे हैं।
ईछन छोरन तैं न गिरे
मनौं तीछन छोरन छेद रहे हैं।।१४७।।

On not seeing her beloved at the romantic tryst the *nayika*'s body began to burn. She got angry and looked at her *sakhis* with a cross face, for she had come here at their behest but she was not able to speak. She forgot her happiness and her eyes were filled with tears. But her tears were held back and it seemed as if her angry gaze controlled the tears from flowing. [147]

दोहा

तिय को मिलो न प्रानप्रिय सजल जलद तन मैन।
सजल जलद लखिकै भए सजल जलद-से नैन।।१४८।।

At the meeting place, the *nayika* did not find her lover. The dark clouds reminded her of Krishna and Kamadev. The clo ud-laden sky caused her much pain, so tears rolled down from her eyes. [148]

प्रौढ़ा-विप्रलब्धा

उदाहरण (कवित्त)

सकल ही सिँगार साजि संग लै सहेलिन कौं
सुंदरि मिलन चली आनँद के कंद कौं।
कबि मतिराम यग करति मनोरथनि
पेख्यो परजंक पै न प्यारे नँदनंद कौं।
नेह ते लगी है देह दाहन दहत गेह
बाग कौं बिलोकि द्रुम बेलिन के बृंद कौं।
चंद को हँसत तब आयो मुखचंद अब
चंद लाग्यो हँसन तिया के मुखचंद कौं।।१४९।।

Having adorned herself and accompanied by her *sakhis* the *nayika* set out to meet Krishna. On her way her mind was excited with anticipation. However, on seeing the empty bed and not finding Krishna at the appointed place she was saddened and her body began to burn. This increased when she saw the trees and the creepers in the grove. And as she returned, it seemed as if the moon was making fun of the moon-faced *nayika*. [149]

दोहा

लख्यो न मंदिर केलि के पिय रुचि-बिजित अनंग।।
नैनकरण तैं जल-बलय गिरे एक ही संग।।१५०।।

When driven by the passion of love the *nayika* went to the love pavilion. When she did not see her beloved there, her eyes were filled with tears and her bangles dropped from her arms. [150]

परकीया-विप्रलब्धा

उदाहरण (कवित्त)

चली मतिराम प्रानप्यारे को मिलन घात
नैसुक निहारिकै बिसारि काज घर को।
पियरो बदन दुख हियरे समाय रह्यो
कुंजन में भयो न मिलापु गिरिधर को।
बिसरे बिलासु वे बिलाय गयो हासु छायो
सुंदरि के तन में प्रताप पंचसर को।
तीछन जुन्हाई भई ग्रीषम को घाम भयो
भीसम पियूषभानु भानु दुपहर को।।१५१।।

The *nayika* saw that the time was right and leaving behind her house chores, set out to meet her beloved. When she did not see Krishna in the grove, her face turned pale and her heart was filled with sorrow. She forgot all the love sports and the smile on her face vanished. Kama's five arrows created a state of longing in her heart so that moonlight seemed to her like summer and the moon appeared to her like the afternoon sun. [151]

दोहा

सचि भूमि अति जोन्ह सौं झरे कुंज तैं फूल।
तुम बिन वाको बन भयो खडगपत्र के तूल।।१५२।।

The earth bathed in moonlight was useless for her and the flowers blooming in the bower appear burning hot for her. But without you the creepers seem like swords for her and it seems as if she is in the city of Yama. [152]

दोहा

साहस करि कुंजनि गई लख्यो न नंदकिसोर।
दीपसिखा सी थरहरी लगी बयारि झकोर।।१५३।।

With great effort the *nayika* went to the grove but on not seeing Krishna there, she began to tremble and looked like the windswept flame of a lamp. [153]

गणिका-विप्रलब्धा

उदाहरण (सवैया)

बारबिलासिनि कोटि हुलास
बढ़ायकै अंग सिँगार बनायो।
प्रीतमगेह गई चलिकै
मतिराम तहाँ न मिल्यो मनभायो।
संग सहेली सौं रोस कियो नहीं
आपुन को यह दोस लगायो।
हाय मैं कीनो मतो यह कौन जु
आपने भौन न बोलि पठायो।।१५४।।

The *nayika* adorned herself and with great excitement went to her beloved's home but he was not there. She did not blame her *sakhis* but blamed herself as it was her decision to come here. It would have been better if she had invited the beloved to her home. [154]

दोहा

मोहि पठाई कुंज मैं सठ आयो नहि आप।
आली औरै मित्त को मेरो मिट्यो मिलाप।।१५५।।

That *shatha nayak* invited me to the bower but did not come. Having done that he went to another woman and I was left alone. [155]

उत्कंठिता लक्षण

आप जाय संकेत में पीव न आयो होय।
ताकी मन चिंता करै उत्का कहिए सोय।।१५६।।

Utkanthita is one a *nayika* who goes to the appointed tryst and when the *nayak* fails to appear is anxious about him. [156]

मुग्धा उत्कंठिता

उदाहरण (सवैया)

बीत गई जुग जाम निसा
मतिराम मिटी तम की सरसाई।
जानति हौं कहुँ और तिया से
रहे रस मे रमिकै रसराई।
सोचति सेज परीयौं नबेली
सहेली सौं जाति न बात सुनाई।
चंद चढ़ो उदयाचल पै
मुखचंद पै आनि चढ़ी पियराई।।१५७।।

The *nayika* said to herself that half the night is over and darkness is receding. She was convinced that Krishna was spending time in romantic sports with another woman. She was too shy to talk about this to her *sakhis*. Just then the moon rose and the moon-faced *nayika* turned pale. [157]

दोहा

कत न कंत आयो अली लाजन बूझि सकै न।
नवल बाल पलिका परी पलक न लागत नैन।।१५८।।

The *nayika*, sitting on the bed, was too shy to ask why the *nayak* had not come and without batting her eyelids she kept on waiting. [158]

मध्या-उत्कंठिता

उदाहरण (सवैया)

बारहि बार बिलोकति द्वारहि
चौंकि परै तिनके खरके हूँ।
सेज परी मतिराम बिसूरति
आई अहो अबही लखि मैं हूँ।
संग सखान के खेलत हो
अजहूँ रजनीपति के अथए हूँ।
लालन बेगि न जाहु घरै
पुनि बाल न मानिहै पाँय परे हूँ।।१५९।।

A *sakhi* talks to a *nayak*. The moon is about to set and you are still playing with your friends. Your beloved awaits you and looks longingly at the door and she is startled even when a leaf moves. I have just returned from seeing her and she is lying on the bed and crying silently. Please go there speedily, otherwise she will be offended and even if you fall at her feet she will not rescind. [159]

दोहा

कहाँ रहो आयो सखी पीय पहर जुग मैन।
अधनिकरे अखरानि सौं बालबदन तें बैन।।१६०।।

The *nayika* asks her *sakhi* that why the *nayak* had not come, even though it is the middle of the night. Her words had both anxiety and romance. [160]

प्रौढ़ा-उत्कंठिता

उदाहरण (सवैया)

कैयो घरी निसि बीति गई अरु
मेह चहूँ दिसि आयो उनैहै।
अंग सिँगार कै बैठी है साँवरे
रावरी बाट बिलोकति ह्वैहै।
बैठे कहा मतिराम रसाल हो
राति मनावत ही पुनि जैहै।
जाहु न बेगि तिहारी पियारी सु
दोसु बिहारी हमैं पुनि दैहै।।१६१।।

A *sakhi* talks to a *nayak*. O *nayak* ! the night

is advancing and there are dark clouds everywhere. Your beloved must be adorning herself and must await your arrival yet you are still here. What if she is offended and the whole night would be spent in winning her over? Hasten and go to her, otherwise she might think that we were at fault in not sending you there. [161]

दोहा

पीव न आयो ध्यानकै मूँदे लोचन बाल।
पलक उघारी पलक मैं आयो होय न लाल।।१६२।।

The *utkanthita* was sitting in the grove waiting for her beloved. Thinking of him, she closed her eyes but then she quickly opened them in case he had just arrived. [162]

परकीया-उत्कंठिता

उदाहरण (कवित्त)

जमुना के तीर बहै सीतल समीर जहाँ
मधुकर करत मधुर मंद सोर हैं।
कबि मतिराम तहाँ छबि सौं छबीली बैठी
अंगन तें फैलत सुगंध के झकोर हैं।
पीतम बिहारी की निहारिबे को बाट ऐसी
चहूँ ओर दीरघ दृगन करि दौर हैं।
एक ओर मीन मनौं एक ओर कंजपुंज
एक ओर खंजन चकोर एक ओर हैं।।१६३।।

The adorned *nayika* sits in a grove in anticipation of her beloved as cold winds waft. Attracted by her fragrance, swarms of bees dance all around her. She gazes in every direction and it seems that her eyes are like that of a fish, a bunch of lotuses, a dagger or that of a *chakor*. [163]

दोहा

कंत बाट लखि गेह कौं कुंज देहरी आय ।
ऐहैं पीव बिचारि यों, नारि फेरि फिरि जाय ।।१६४।।

The *nayika* left her home and looking for beloved reached the grove. Not finding him there she turned back to go home. Having reached home she wondered if he had gone to the grove so she went back to go the grove again. In this way she kept on wandering between home and grove. [164]

गणिका-उत्कंठिता

उदाहरण (सवैया)

पीतम को धरि ध्यान घरीक
करे मन ही मन काम किलोलैं।
पातहु के खरकें मतिराम
अचानक ही अँखियाँ पुनि खोलैं।
पीतम ऐहैं अजो सजनी
अँगराय जँभाय घरीक यों बोलैं।
गावे घरीक गरे ही हरे हरे
गेह के बाग हरे हरे डोलैं।।१६५।।

The *nayika* thinks of her beloved and imagines romantic pleasures with him. Just then, on account of the flutter of the leaves she opens her eyes and tells her friends that her beloved will come very soon and so saying, she stretches her arms and yawns. After that, she begins to sing softly and wanders in her garden. [165]

दोहा

बारबधू पियपंथ लखि अँगरानी अँग मोरि।
पौढ़ि रही परजंक जनु डारी मदन मरोरि।।१६६।।

The *ganika nayika* got tired waiting for the *nayak*. She raised her arms and lay down on the bed and she looked as Kama had twisted her body. [166]

बासकसज्जा लक्षण

ऐहैंप्रीतमआजु यों, निश्चय जानेबाम।
साजेसेजसिंगारसुख बासक-सज्जानाम।।१६७।।

Vasakasajja is one who is certain that her beloved will come and adorns the bed chamber. [167]

मुग्धा वासकसज्जा

उदाहरण (कवित्त)

भई है सयानी तरुनाई सरसानी प्रीति
प्रीतम पत्यानी दूरि लाज उर नाखियो।
कबि मतिराम काम केलि की कलानि करि
मोहन लला को बास कीबो अभिलाखियो।
मृदु मुसकाय परजंक मैं निसंक जाय
अंक भरि आनँद अधरसुधा चाखियो।
नेवर की झनक भनक राखि प्यारी आजु
रसना की झनक तनक रस राखियो।।१६८।।

A *sakhi* talks to the *nayika*. You have now matured and both youth and love have spread within you. You must now trust your beloved and get rid of your bashfulness during your romantic encounter with him. Matiram says that you should bring Krishna under your influence through various love sports. Smiling softly, you should go to the pleasure pavilion, embrace him and kiss him. Silence your ankle bells but make sure that the bells on the waist band are loud. The poet here seems to suggest that the *nayika* should engage in reverse erotic play. [168]

दोहा

डीठि बचाय सखीन की केलिभवन मैं जाय।
पौढ़ि रहे छिन सेज मैं तिय आनँद अधिकाय।।१६९।।

Avoiding the gaze of her *sakhis* the *nayika* enters the love pavilion and delights herself by lying on the bed. [169]

मध्या-बासकसज्जा

उदाहरण (कवित्त)

केसरि कनक कहा चंपक बनक कहा
दामिनी यौं दुरि जात देह की दमक तैं।
कबि मतिराम लोने लोचन लपेट लाज
अरुन कपोल काम तेज की तमक तैं।
पग के धरत कल किंकिनी नूपुर बजे
बिछिया भनक उठै एक ही झमक तैं।
नाहसुख चाहि चित औचक हँसति चौंक
परै चंदमुखी निज चौका की चमक तैं।।१७०।।

What to talk of saffron and gold, or of the beauty of *champa* flowers, even lightning dims in front of the glow of her body. Matiram says that her beautiful eyes are shut on account of her bashfulness. And her red cheeks are radiant with the feelings of love. When she walks, the bells in her waistband ring and when she steps ahead, the toe ornaments also sound. With the anticipation of romantic pleasures she breaks into smile and the moon-like radiance of her teeth surprises her. [170]

दोहा

निसि नियराति निहारयति सौतिबदन अरबिंदु।
सखी एक यह देखिये तेरो आनन इंदु।।१७१।।

A *sakhi* speaks, to a *nayika*, O *sakhi* ! As night sets in your co-wives faces wither like the lotus. But you are the one whose face shines like the moon. [171]

प्रौढ़ा-बासकसज्जा

उदाहरण (सवैया)

बारनि धूपि अँगारनि धूप कै
धूम अँध्यारी पसारी महा है।
आननचंद समान उगो मृदु
मंद हँसी जनो जोन्हछटा है।
फैलि रही मतिराम जहाँ तहाँ
दीपति दीपनि की परभा है।
लाल तिहारे मिलाप को बाल ने
आजु करी दिन मैं ही निसा है।।१७२।।

A *sakhi* talks to the *nayak*. The *nayika* dried her hair in the sun and then made it fragrant by blowing incense in it. However, the incense created darkness in the room and her face appeared like the moon and when she smiles softly it is like moonshine. The jewels in her adornments and her clothes shine like stars. In this way, the *nayika* has turned day into night for her rendezvous. [172]

दोहा

सब सिँगार सुंदरि सजै बैठी सेज बिछाय।
भयो द्रौपदी को बसनु बासर नाहिँ बिहाय।।१७३।।

Adorning herself she sits on the bed. She is so keen on meeting her beloved, that the day has become unending as long as Draupadi's *sari*. [173]

परकीया-बासकसज्जा

उदाहरण (सवैया)

साँझ ही तैं करि राखे सबै
करिबे के जे काज हुते रजनी के।
पौढ़ि रही उमगी अति ही
मतिराम अनंद अमात न जी के।

सोवत जानिके लोग सबै
अधिकाने मिलाप मनोरथ पी को।
सेज ते बाल उठी हरुए हरुए
पट खोल दिये खिरकी को।।१७४।।

In the evening, the *nayika* took care of all her chores that she would normally do at night and with great expectation, lay on the bed. She could not contain her anticipation. When she found out that everyone in the household had fallen off to sleep, her desire to meet her beloved increased even more. She slowly got up from her bed and gently opened the window. [174]

दोहा

मनमोहन के मिलन को करै मनोरथ नारि।
धरै पौन के सामुहैं दियो भौन को बारि।।१७५।।

A *nayika* was very keen on meeting Krishna so she hatched a plot. When night came she lit the lamp but kept it in such a place that it would be exposed to the wind so that it would be extinguished soon and Krishna could easily enter her home. [175]

सामान्य-वासकसज्जा

उदाहरण (कवित्त)

सेत सारी सोहत उजारी मुखचंद की सी
महलनि मंद मुसक्यान की महमही।
अँगिया के ऊपर ह्वै उलही उरोज-ओप
उर मतिराम माल मालती डहडही।
माँजे मंजु मुकुर-से मंजुल कपोल गोल
गोरी की गुराई गोरे गातन गहगही।
फूलनि की सेज बैठी दीपति फैलाय लाय
बेला को फुलेल फूली बेलि-सी लहलही।।१७६।।

The *nayika* has worn a white *sari* and it radiates a glow all around as if it were moonlight. Her sweet smile spreads its fragrance in the entire room. Her *odhni* is so placed that the beauty of her breasts is seen. On her chest, she has worn a garland of *malti* flowers. Her cheeks are clean and radiant and her body is fair. Sitting on the bed covered with flowers her beauty spreads everywhere. She has applied the perfume of *bel* flowers. The *nayak* looks as beautiful like a creeper of *bel* flowers. [176]

दोहा

सुंदरि सेज सँवारिकै साजे सकल सिँगार।
दृगकमलन के द्वार पै बाँधे बंदनवार।।१७७।।

The *nayika* has decorated the bed and then adorned herself and then with her gaze fixed on the door, awaits the arrival of the *nayak*. The poet says that it is as if she has made a festoon for the door with her lotus-like eyes. [177]

स्वाधीनपतिका लक्षण

सदा रूप-गुनरीझि पिय जाके रहे अधीन।
स्वाधीनपतिका तियै, बरनत कबि परबीन।।१७८।।

Svadhinapatika is one who has her beloved under her command on account of her attributes and looks. [178]

सवैया

आपने हाथ सौं देत महावर
आप ही बार सँवारत नीके।
आपुन ही पहिरावत आनिकै
हार सँवारिकै मोर सिरी के।
हौं सखि लाजनि जात मरी
मतिराम सुभाव कहा कहौं पी के।
लोग मिलैं घर घेरु करैं
अबही ते ये चेरे भए दुलही के।।१७९।।

A *nayika* talks to her *sakhi*. My beloved loves me a lot. He applies red paint to my feet. He dresses my tresses. Then he makes a garland of *maulasiri* flowers and presents it to me. What can I say about his amiable disposition towards me? He makes me bashful. People speak ill of him and say that he has already become my slave. [179]

दोहा

अंग अंग अवलोकि कै तिय जोबन की जोति।
सुधासिंधु अवगाह जुत डीठ नाह की होति।।१८०।।

A *nayak* looks at the *nayika* and admires her emerging youth. He is so pleased that it seems that his sight is bathing in a sea of nectar. [180]

मध्या-स्वाधीनपतिका

उदाहरण (कवित्त)

जगमगे जोबन अनूप तेरो रूप चाहि
रति ऐसी रंभा-सी रमा-सी बिसराइये।
देखिबे को प्रानप्यारी पास खरो प्रानप्यारो
घूँघट उघारि नैक बदन दिखाइये।
तेरे अंग अंग मैं मिठाई औ लुनाई भरी
मतिराम सुकबि प्रगट यह पाइये।
नायक के नैनन मैं नाइये सुधा-सी सब
सौतिन के लोचनन लोन-सो लगाइये।।१८१।।

A *sakhi* talks to the *nayika* : Your exquisite and youthful beauty surpasses that of Rati, Rama and Lakshmi. Your beloved stands near you to admire your beauty. Do remove your veil and let him see your beauty in every limb and part of your body. Your beauty and grace is like nectar to his eyes but like salt to your co-wives. [181]

दोहा

बड़े आपने दृगन कौं तुम कहि सकौ सु मैन।
प्रियनैनन भीतर सदा बसत तिहारे नैन।।१८२।।

A *sakhi* speaks to the *nayika*, O *sakhi*! Your eyes are large and you can call them Kama because they reside in your beloved's eyes. [182]

प्रौढ़ा-स्वाधीनपतिका

उदाहरण (सवैया)

लालन मैं रतिनायक तैं
सुभ सुंदरता रुचि कुंजन पेखी।
बाल मैं त्यौं मतिराम कहै
रति तैं अति रूपकला अवरेखी।
सामुहि बैठि लखै इक सेज मैं
बोल अली सुख प्रीति बिसेखी।
भाल मैं तेरे लिखि बिधि सो यह
लाल की मूरति लाल मैं देखी।।१८३।।

The *nayika* considers her beloved more handsome than Kama and he considers her more beautiful than Rati. Seated on a bed, she stares at him. At that time her friend said, the ruby in your hair ornament reflects the image of your beloved and it seems as if Brahma has chosen this person for you. [183]

दोहा

सुधा-मधुर तेरे अधर सुंदर सुमन सुगंध।
पीय जीव को बंध यह बंधुजीव को बंध।।१८४।।

Your lips are sweeter than nectar and more fragrant than flowers. Your redness is enough to capture your beloved. It looks as if it is related to *dupahariya* flowers. [184]

परकीया-स्वाधीनपतिका

उदाहरण (सवैया)

मो जुग नैन चकोरन कौं यह
रावरो रूप सुधा ही को नैबो।
कीजै कहा कुलकानि तैं आनि
पर्‍यो अब आपनो प्रेम छिपैबो।
कुंजनि मैं मतिराम कहूँ
निसि द्योसहू घात परैं मिलि जैबो।
लाल सयानी सखीन के बीच
निवारिये ह्याँ की गलीन को ऐबो।।१८५।।

A *nayika* speaks to her *nayak*. Your handsome looks are like a sea of nectar for my eyes which are thirsty like the *chakor* birds. But I am helpless because of my family honour and that is why I have to keep your love secret. Do come and visit me in the love grove either at night or during the day. But please do not come in front of my *sakhis* in my street. [185]

दोहा

बिषम लोग ब्रजगाम के लाल बिलोको बास।
बढ़ि जैहै इन दृगन के हाँसहि ते उपहास।।१८६।।

O Krishna ! the inhabitants of Braj are truly unpredictable. That is why it is difficult to continue living here. Looking at the love in our eyes people will make fun of us and create trouble. [186]

सामान्या-स्वाधीनपतिका

उदाहरण (सवैया)

बारन बार सँवारि सिँगारत मोतिन हार धरैं तन गोरैं।
पाँई महावर देत बनाय यौं बेनी बनावत नेह निहोरैं।
यौं रसलीन रहै नित ही बस औरन सौं दृग नाहन जोरैं।
लाज गिनै नहिं लोगन की पिय
पाँइ परे धन देत करोरैं।।१८७।।

A *nayika* talks to her *sakhi*. My beloved dresses my tresses and then places a pearl necklace on my body and adorns me. He applies the red dye on my feet and braids my hair. He loves me and is always under my control and does not look at another woman and promises me a lot of money. [187]

दोहा

छाँडि सबै सुधि सदन की रहत मदनबस लीन।
मोही कौं धन देत हैं पिय सुजान परबीन।।१८८।।

My beloved has forgotten his home and stays under the spell of my love and it is to me that he gives all his wealth. [188]

मोहि लगो सजनी भलो जाको धन मन प्रान।
सपनेहू ता पिय सौं मान भलो न सयान।।१८९।।

If you are committed to the wealth, love and life to your beloved then it is not wise to quarrel with him. [189]

अभिसारिका लक्षण

पियहि बुलावै आप कै आपहि पिय पै जाय।
ताहि कहत अभिसारिका जे प्रबीन कबिराय।।१९०।।

Abhisarika is one who goes out to meet her beloved. [190]

मुग्धा-अभिसारिका

उदाहरण (सवैया)

बातन जाय लगाय लई रस
ही रस के मन हाथ के लीनो।
लाल तिहारे बुलावने को
मतिराम मैं बोल कह्यो परबीनो।
बेग चलौ न बिलंब करौ
लखि बाल नबेली को नेह नबीनो।
लाजभरी अँखियाँ बिहँसीं
चली बोल कह्यो बिन ऊतरु दीनो।।१९१।।

A *sakhi* talks to her *nayak*. O Krishna ! Hasten look at the fresh love of this young *nayika*, do not delay. When I met her I spoke to her cleverly about matters of love and suggested that you call for him. At that she did not respond but the twinkle in her eyes told me that she agreed. [191]

दोहा

चली अली नवलाहिं लै पिय पै साजि सिँगार।
ज्यौं मतंग अँड़दार को लिये जात गँडदार।।१९२।।

When the *sakhi* took the adorned *nayika* to the *nayak* her slow gait looked as if the *mahout* is leading an intoxicated elephant. [192]

मध्या-अभिसारिका

उदाहरण (सवैया)

बैठि रहे मतिराम लला घर
भीतर साँझहि तैं अनुरागी।
बानिक सौं बनि चारु सिँगारनि
आई सुहागिनि प्रेम सौं पागी।
प्यारे कह्यो हँसि आइहि सेजहि
प्यारी की जोति बिलासनि जागी।
नैन नवाय रही मुसकायकै
हार किये को सँवारन लागी।।१९३।।

The *nayak* sat in the home ever since the evening. Then the *nayika*, adorned with ornaments and clothes and full of love, went there. When the *nayak* smiled and invited her to sit on the bed, the anticipation of love sports arose in her but on account of bashfulness she did not advance but with downcast eyes played with her necklace. [193]

दोहा

जोबन-मदगज मंद गति चली बाल पिय गेह।
पगनि लाज आँदू परी चढ्यो महावत नेह।।१९४।।

When the young *nayika* was going towards her beloved's home she had the gait of an intoxicated elephant whose feet were chained but whose *mahout* was goading him onwards. [194]

प्रौढ़ा-अभिसारिका

उदाहरण (कवित्त)

सहज सुबासजतु देह की दुगुनि दुति
दामिनी दमक दीप केसरि कनक तैं।
मतिराम सुकब सरस सुकुमार अंग
सोहत सिँगार चारु जोबन-बनक तैं।

सोइबे को सेज चली प्रानपति प्यारे पास
जगत जुन्हाई जोति हँसन तनक तें।
चढ़त अटारी गुरु लोगन की लाज प्यारी
रसना दसन दाबै रसना-झनक तें।।१९५।।

When the *nayika* went towards the bed chamber, the fragrance of her body increased her beauty and her radiance was greater than lightning, lamp and saffron. Her love-afflicted beloved looked attractive on account of his handsome looks and the paraphernalia of love. Even if she smiled softly, it seemed as if moonlight was spreading everywhere. When she was climbing the stairs to go to the bed chamber, the bells on her waistband began to tinkle and in order to protect the honour of the elders in the house, felt bashful and bit her tongue. [195]

दोहा

सजि सिँगार सेजहि चली बाल प्रानपति प्रान।
चढ़त अटारी की सिढ़ी भई कोस परमान।।१९६।।

The adorned *nayika* went towards her beloved. When she was climbing the stairs of the bed chamber, she was bashful and this slowed her gait and the stairs seemed like several miles long. [196]

परकीया-कृष्णाभिसारिका

कवित्त

उमड़ि घुमड़ि दिगमंडल मंडि रहे
झूमि झूमि बादर कुहू की निसि कारी में।
अंगनि में कीनो मृगमद अंगराग तैसो
आनन ओढ़ाय लीनो स्याम रंग सारी में।
मतिराम सुकबि मेचक रुचि राजि रही
आभरन राजी मरकत मनिवारी में।
मोहन छबीले को मिलन चली ऐसी छबि
छाँह लौं छबीली छबि छाजत अँध्यारी में।।१९७।।

On the dark new moon night there were dark clouds everywhere. The *nayika* applied an unguent of musk and placed the *pallu* of her dark *sari* on her face. The *nayika* wore ornaments of green beads, which looked beautiful but on account of the *sari* they looked dark. She looked like a shadow in the darkness. [197]

दोहा

स्याम बसन मैं स्याम निसि दुरी न तिय की देह।
पहुँचाई चहुँ ओर घिरि भौंरभीर पियगेह।।१९८।।

The *nayika* in a dark *sari* and in the darkness of the night could not hide herself because of the radiance of her body. But she was a *padmini* and her body was full of the fragrance of lotuses and on account of this bumble-bees surrounded her and this helped her to reach her beloved's home in secrecy. [198]

चंद्राभिसारिका

उदाहरण (कवित्त)

अंगन मैं चंदन चढ़ाय घनसार सेत
सारी छीरफेन की सी आभा उफनाती है।
राजत रुचिर रुचि मोतिन के आभरन
कुसुमकलित केस सोभा सरसाति है।
कबि मतिराम प्रानप्यारे सौं मिलन जात
करिकै मनोरथनि मृदु मुसकाति है।
होति न लखाई निसिचंद की उज्यारी
मुख-चंद की उज्यारी तन छाँहौं छिपि जाति है।।१९९।।

The *nayika* applied an unguent of sandalwood and camphor and wore a white *sari* to blend with the light of the moon. Pearl ornaments and flowers in hair adorned her body. Matiram says that she is walking towards her beloved with a sweet smile and expectations of romantic pleasures that will follow. Even in the moonlight, which has spread everywhere she remains hidden because of her moon-like face her body does not cast a shadow. [199]

दोहा

मलिन करी छबि जोन्ह की तन छबि सौं बलि जाउँ।
क्यौं जैहौं पिय पै सखी लखि जैहै सब गाउँ।।२००।।

A *nayika* talks to a *sakhi*. The light of the moon fades in comparison to the radiance of my body. O *sakhi* ! How will I go to meet my beloved in this light as the whole town will see me? [200]

परकीया-दिवाभिसारिका

उदाहरण (कवित्त)

सारी जरतारी की झलक झलकति तैसी
केसरि को अंगराग कीनो सब तन मैं।
तीखन तरनि के किरन तें दुगुन जोति
जगत जवाहर-जटित आभरन मैं।
कबि मतिराम आभा अंगनि अँगरानि की
धूम की सी धार छबि छाजति कचन मैं।
ग्रीष्म-दुपहरी मैं हरि कौं मिलन जात
जानी जात नारि न दवारिजुत बन मैं।।२०१।।

The *nayika* has worn a glittering brocade *sari* and has applied an unguent of saffron. Her ornaments of bright stones shine brightly in the sun. Matiram says that her body is radiant like glowing embers and her black hair look like smoke. In the summer heat, the entire forest seems to be on fire and in this atmosphere the *nayika* is not seen as her own glow and the bright sun seem to mingle. [201]

दोहा

ग्रीषम ऋतु की दुपहरी चली बाल बनकुंज।
अंग लपटि तीछन लुएँ मलय पवन के पुंज।।२०२।।

In the heat of the afternoon, the *nayika* is going to the pleasure grove to meet her beloved. The burning heat seems to her like the cold breeze of the Malaya mountain. [202]

सामान्य-अभिसारिका

उदाहरण (कवित्त)

साँझि ही सिँगार साजि प्रानप्यारे पास जाति
बनिता बनिक बनी बेलि-सी अनंद की।
कबि मतिराम कलकिंकिनी की धुनि बाजै
मंद मंद चलनि बिराजति गयंद की।
केसरि रँग्यो दुकूल हाँसी मैं झरति फूल
केसनि मैं छाई छबि फूलन के बृंद की।
पीछे पीछे आवति अँधेरी-सी भँवरभीर
आगे आगे फैलति उजारी मुखचंद की।।२०३।।

When evening came, the *nayika* adorned herself and left to meet her beloved. She appeared like a happy, beautiful creeper. As she walked, the bells on her waistband were tinkling and it seemed as if an elephant was walking majestically. Her clothes were saffron coloured. When she smiled, it was as if flowers were spreading all around and her hair was full of flowers as well. The light from her moon-like face lit her path, but behind her there was a group of bumble-bees as they were attracted by the fragrance of lotuses from her body and there was darkness behind her. [203]

दोहा

नागरि सकल सिँगार सजि चली प्रानपति पास।
बाढ़ि चली बिहसनि मनौ सोभा सहज बिलास।।२०४।।

The *nayika* adorned herself and left to meet her beloved. She was smiling softly and it seemed as if her smile was adding to her adornments. [204]

प्रवत्स्यत्प्रेयसी लक्षण

होनहार पिय के बिरह बिकल होय जो बाल।
ताहि प्रवच्छतिप्रेयसी, बरनत बुद्धि-बिसाल।।२०५।।

Pravatsyatpreyasi is one who is saddened at the prospect of being separated from her beloved. [205]

मुग्धा प्रवत्स्यत्प्रेयसी

उदाहरण (कवित्त)

जा दिन तें चलिबे की चरचा चलाई तुम
ता दिन तें वाके पियराई तन छाई है।
कहै मतिराम छोड़े भूषन बसन पान
सखिन सौं खेलनि हँसनि बिसराई है।
आई ऋतु सुरभि सुहाई प्रीति वाके चित्त
ऐसे मैं चलो तो लाल रावरी बड़ाई है।
सोवत न रैन दिन रोवत रहति बाल
बूझे तें कहति मायके की सुधि आई है।।२०६।।

Ever since you have indicated that you will be going abroad her body has become pale. She has discarded her ornaments and good clothes. She has forgotten to eat betel and play and laugh with her friends. It is the spring season and love surges within her and if you go near her you will seem old.

She does not sleep by day or night. She cries incessantly and when she is asked about her state she says that she longs for her parent's home. [206]

दोहा

क्यौं सहिहै सुकुमारि वह पहलो बिरह गुपाल।
जब वाके चित हित भयो चलन लगे तब लाल।।२०७।।

A *sakhi* speaks to a *nayak*, O Gopal! The *nayika* is recently married and she is now in love with you. You have decided to go abroad and this will cause longing in her for you. Please cancel your plans. [207]

मध्या-प्रवत्स्यत्प्रेयसी

उदाहरण (सवैया)

गौने के द्योस छः सातक बीते न
चौथी कहा अबहीं चलि आई।
लालन बाल कैं ता हिन मैं
मतिराम परी मुख पै पियराई।
तू न बहू को पठाय अली
यह देख दुहूँन की प्रीति सुहाई।
रोए-से लोचन रोचन मोए-से
लोचन सोए न सोचन रैन बिताई ।।२०८।।

The *nayika* has come to her husband's home for the first time after the *gauna*, but according to tradition she has to return to her mother's home on the fourth day. The thought of this separation causes anxiety to the couple. Only a few days have passed since the *gauna* but the fourth day is already here and thinking of this, both the *nayak* and the *nayika* have turned pale. So please do not send the newly wed home. See how much they love each other. They have been crying with the thought of the impending separation. Their eyes have become a sea of tears. They have lost their sleep and have stayed up all night talking to each other. [208]

दोहा

अबहीं लै मिलि मोहि सखि चलत आज ब्रजराज।
अँसुवन राखति रोकिकै जियहि निकासति लाज।।२०९।।

O *sakhi* ! Hasten, take me to Krishna. I learn that he is about to set out to a distant land. My bashfulness controls my tears but allows releasing my soul. [209]

प्रौढ़ा-प्रवत्स्यत्प्रेयसी

उदाहरण (कवित्त)

मलय समीर लागो चलन सुगंध सीरो
पथिकन कीने परदेसन तैं आवने।
मतिराम सुकबि समूहनि सुमन फूले
कोकिल मधुप लागे बोलन सुहावने।
आयो है बसंत भए पल्लवित जलजात
तुम लागे चलिबे की चरचा चलावने।
रावरी तिया को तरवर सरवरन के
किसलै कमल ह्वैहैं बारक बिछावने।।२१०।।

Spring has arrived. Fragrant and soothing Malaya winds waft and travellers have started turning homewards. Matiram says that bunches of flowers have appeared and the cuckoo and the bumble-bees sing. New lotus petals have appeared. How can you talk of going away at this time when spring has blossomed? Do you think that delicate leaves and petals will cover my bed to help me in my separation when instead of cooling they will burn my body? [210]

दोहा

कौंपनि तैं किसलैं जबै होय कलिन तैं कौल।
तबहीं चलियो चलन की चरचा नायक नौल।।२११।।

O ignorant *nayak* ! New leaves have sprouted and buds have blossomed into flowers. Is this the time to announce your departure? [211]

परकीया-प्रवत्स्यत्प्रेयसी

उदाहरण (कवित्त)

मोहन लला को सुन्यो चलनि बिदेस भयो
बाल मोहनी को चित निपट उचाट मैं।
परी तलाबेली तनमन मैं छबीली राखै
छिति पर छिनकु छिनकु पाँव खाट मैं।
प्रीतम नयन-कुबलयन को चंद घरी
एक मैं चलेगो मतिराम जिहि बाट मैं।
नागरी नबेली रूप आगरी अकेली रीती
गागरी लै ठाढ़ी भई बाट ही के घाट मैं।।२१२।।

When she heard that her beloved is leaving for a journey, she felt depressed. Her body became restless but she concealed her pain. She would place her foot on the ground and then lift it up. She wondered on which road her handsome moon-faced beloved, who causes happiness to her lotus eyes, would appear. That clever and beautiful *nayika* stood on that path with an empty pot so that considering it an inauspicious sign, his journey would be cancelled. [212]

दोहा

चलत सुन्यो परदेस कौं हियरा रह्यो न ठौर।
लै मालिनि मीतहिं दयो नव रसाल को मौर।।२१३।।

No sooner she heard that her friend was leaving town her mind became restless. She asked the gardener to give her some mango blossoms. With that gesture she not only reminded him that spring was here but also she expressed her love, for the bow of Kama is made of mango blossoms. [213]

सामान्या-प्रवत्स्यत्प्रेयसी

उदाहरण (कवित्त)

मंजन कियो न तन अंजन दियो न नैन
जावक दियो न पाइ रही मनु मारिकै।
मतिराम सुकबि तमोल छोड़ि बैठी बाल
पहिरे बसन डारे भूषन उतारिकै।
ऐहैं आजु पीय बिदा माँगन बिदेस कौं यों
नेह के जनाइबे की चातुरी बिचारिकै।
गारि राख्यो चंदन बगारि राख्यो घनसार
आँगन मैं सेज सरसिजनि सँवारिकै।।२१४।।

The *nayika* has learnt that her beloved is going abroad. She was sure that he would come to bid her farewell. Knowing this, she hatched a plot. She did not bathe nor did she apply corrylium to her eyes or red paint to her feet, neither did she eat betel, removed her ornaments, washed off the sandalwood paste and rubbed off the camphor and spread lotus leaves on the bed in the courtyard to let him know that as soon as she heard that he was leaving her body began to burn and the lotus leaves, camphor and sandalwood were kept in readiness. [214]

दोहा

चलत पीव परदेस कौं बरज सकौं नहिं तोहि।
लै ऐहौ आभरन जो जियत पायहौ मोहि।।२१५।।

A *nayika* tells her beloved that I cannot stop you from going abroad. But I am not sure that I will be alive when you come back on account of my separation. But if I am still alive, get an ornament for me. [215]

आगतपतिका

उदाहरण (दोहा)

जा तिय को परदेस तैं
आयो प्यौ मतिराम।
ताहि कहत कबि लोग हैं
आगतपतिका बाम।।२१६।।

Agatapatika is one whose beloved has just returned from abroad. [216]

मुग्धा आगतपतिका

उदाहरण (सवैया)

आए बिदेस तें प्रानप्रिया
मतिराम अनंद बढ़ाय अलेखै।
लोगन सौं मिलि आँगन बैठि
घरी ही घरी सिगरो घर पेखै।
भीतर भौन के द्वार खरी
सुकुमारि तिया तनकंप बिसेखै।
घूँघट को पट ओट दिये
पट ओट किये पिय को मुख देखै ।।२१७।।

The *nayika*'s beloved has returned from abroad and she is beside herself with happiness. He is sitting in the courtyard meeting people. From time to time, he looks at the house hoping to catch a glimpse of his beloved. The *nayika* is standing at the door of her room with a trembling heart. Her shyness prevented her from coming out and all she could do was to peer through her veil. [217]

दोहा

पिय आयो नवबाल-तन बाढ्यो हरष बिलास।
प्रथम बारि बूँन उठै ज्यों बसुमती सुबास।।२१८।।

When her beloved returned from abroad the innocent *nayika* was filled with happiness. Her happiness spread all over her like the fragrant smell of the parched earth after the first rain. [218]

मध्या-आगतपतिका

उदाहरण (सवैया)

चंदमुखी सजनीन के संग हुती पिय अंगन में मनु फेरत।
ताहि समै पिय प्यारे को आवन प्यारी सखी कह्यो द्वार तें टेरत।
आए गए मतिराम जबै तबै देखत नैन अनंद भए रत।
भौन के भीतर भाजि गई
हँसिकै हरुवै हरि को फिरि हेरत ।।२१९।।

The moon-faced *nayika* was sitting with her *sakhis* in the courtyard and was lost in her thoughts. At that point a *sakhi* standing at the door announced that her beloved had returned from abroad. And when the *nayak* stood in front of her she kept on gazing at him. She felt bashful and she ran into the house but before entering her room she turned back and took one more look at him. [219]

दोहा

पियआगम सरदागमन बिमल बालमुख इंदु।
अंग अमल पानिप भयो फूले दृग अरबिंदु।।२२०।।

When she heard that her beloved had returned from abroad her face became as radiant as the moon, her body was an ocean of happiness and her lotus-like eyes opened. [220]

प्रौढ़ा-आगतपतिका

उदाहरण (सवैया)

प्रानपियारो मिल्यो सपने में परी जब नैसुक नींद निहोरैं।
कंत को आगत त्यों ही जगाय कह्यो सखी बैन पियूष निचोरैं।
यौं मतिराम बढ्यो हिय में सुख बाल के बालम सौं दृग जोरैं।
जैसे मिहीं पट में चटकीलो
चढ़ै रंग तीसरी बार के बोरैं।।२२१।।

After a lot of effort when the *nayika* finally fell asleep, she dreamt that her beloved is standing in front of him. Her *sakhi* woke her up and told her that her beloved had indeed returned. The *nayika* was happy beyond measure and the *sakhi*'s words were like nectar in her ears. Matiram says that when their eyes met she was thrilled. Comparing this experience to that of dyeing a fabric the poet says that it was as if a third coat of dye was applied and the fabric began to sparkle. In the same way, the body of the *nayika* became radiant. [221]

दोहा

पिय आयो परदेस तें हिय हुलसी अति बाम।
टूक टूक कंचुकि करी करि कमनैती काम।।२२२।।

When she heard that her beloved had returned from abroad, the *nayika* was so happy that her breasts swelled and her *choli* broke apart. The poet says that it was as Kama had discharged his arrows and tore open her *choli*. [222]

परकीया-आगतपतिका

उदाहरण (सवैया)

आयो बिलंब बिदेस तें बालम
बाल बियोग बिथा बिसराई।
आई तहाँ तिनके संग हवै
सब गाँव की जे जुवती मिलि आई।
देखत ही मतिराम कहै
अँखियान में आनँद की छबि छाई।
लाजन क्यौंकर बैन कहै सु
कह्यो दुख देहँहि की दुबराई।।२२३।।

The *nayak* has returned after a long absence from abroad and the *nayika* forgot her pain of longing. She came to meet him along with other people from the village and on seeing him, her eyes were filled with happiness. Overcome by shyness, she was not able to say anything but her lean body spoke of her pain in his absence. [223]

भावते को सुनि आगम
आनँद अंगन अंगन में उलह्यो है।
सो हमहूँ सी सखी सो दुराइये
आली कह्यो यह कौने कह्यो है।

खैंच लिये सुख के अँसुआ
यह क्यों दुरिहै जु हियो उमह्यो है।
गढ़ी भई कर की मुँदरी
अँगिया की तनीन तनाव गह्यो है।।२२४।।

The news of her *nayak*'s return filled her mind and body with happiness but she wanted to hide this from her *sakhis*. The *sakhis* asked her how could she hide her happiness from them? You may have pulled back your tears of happiness but how can you hide the happiness that is in your heart? Your body has swollen with happiness, your ring has tightened on your finger, and your *choli* has been stretched. [224]

दोहा

सुन्यो मायके तें वहै आयो बाम्हनु कंत।
कुसल बूझिबे के लिये लीनो बोलि इकंत।।२२५।।

The *nayika* heard that a brahmin from her mother's village was visiting her beloved. She called the brahmin to ask him about the welfare of her family. Actually, the brahmin was her lover. [225]

सामान्या-आगतपतिका

उदाहरण (कवित्त)

नागर बिदेस मैं बिताय बहु द्यौस आयो
नागरी के हिय मैं हुलासन की खान की।
कबि मतिराम अंक भरत मयंकमुखी
नेह सरसाय मोही मति सुखदान की।
सुबरन बोलिकै बतावति है सुबरन
हीरन जनावति है छबि मुसकान की।
आँखिन तें आनँद के आँसू उमगाय प्यारी
प्यारे को दिखावति सुरति मुकतान की।।२२६।।

Her lover has come back after a long absence and she was happy. She embraced him in her arms and won him over. With sweet speech she hinted at gold, with her smile she suggested diamonds and with her ears she was referring to pearls. [226]

दोहा

फूली नागरि-कमलिनी उड़िगे मित्र-मलिंद।
आयो मित्र बिदेस तें भयो सुदिन आनंद।।२२७।।

A *ganika nayika* was sitting with her male friends when she heard that her beloved was returning from abroad. At that time, she blossomed like a lotus and asked all her friends to leave as this was an important day for her. [227]

उत्तमा-नायिका लक्षण

पिय हित कैं अनहित करै, आप करै हित नारि।
तहि उत्तमा नायका, कबिजन कहत बिचारि।।२२८।।

Uttama is one who is always full of love for her beloved whether or not he loves her. [228]

सवैया

राति कहूँ रमिकै मनभावन आवन प्रात प्रियाघर कीनो।
देखत ही मुसकाय उठी चली आगे ह्वै आदर कै पुनि लीनो।
मोहन के तन मैं मतिराम दुकूल सु नील निहारि नवीनो।
केसरि के रँग सौं रँगिकै
पट पीत यों प्रीतम के कर दीनो।।२२९।।

The *nayak* has spent the night with another woman and has returned to the *nayika*'s home at dawn. She welcomed him with a smile. Krishna had forgotten his *pitambar* (yellow *dhoti*) in the other woman's home and had worn her blue *odhni* instead. The *nayika* did not admonish him, instead she took the blue *odhni* and dyed it with saffron and returned it to him. [229]

दोहा

पिय अपराध अनेकहूँ आँखिनहूँ लखि जाय।
तिय इकंतहू कंत सौं मानो करत लजाय।।२३०।।

The *nayika* continues to love her beloved even though she has seen all his transgressions. [230]

मध्यमा-नायिका लक्षण

पिय सौं हित तैं हित करै अनहित कीने मान।
ताहि मध्यमा कहत हैं कबि मतिराम सुजान।।२३१।।

Madhyama is one who responds with love when her *nayak* expresses love. But when he is cold to her, she is offended. [231]

उदाहरण (कवित्त)

आयो प्रानपति राति अनतैं बिताय बैठी
भौंहन चढ़ाय रँगी सुंदरि सुहाग की।
बातन बनाय पर्यो प्यारी के चरन आय
छल सौं छिपाई छैल छबि रतिदाग की।
छूटि गयो मान लगी आपु ही सँवारन कौं
खिरकी सुकबि मतिराम पिय पाग की।
रिस ही के आँसू रस-आँसू भए आँखिन मैं
रोस की ललाई सो ललाई अनुराग की।।२३२।।

The *nayak* has returned after spending the night with another woman and the *nayika* was sitting with a cross face. The *nayak* skilfully hid marks of love-making on his body and tired to win over the *nayika* and feel at her feet. At this behaviour the *nayika* rescinded and restored his badly tied turban. Tears of anger in her eyes turned to tears of love and the redness of anger in her eyes turned to redness of love. [232]

दोहा

मेरे तन के रोम ये मेरे नहीं निदान।
उठि आदरु आगम करैं करौं कौन बिधि मान।।२३३।।

How can I be offended with you? Even before I got up to welcome you I developed goosebumps on my body. It seems that these goosebumps are under your control, not mine. [233]

अधमा-नायिका लक्षण

पिय सौं हितहू के किये, करे मान जो बाल।
तासौं अधमा कहत हैं, कबि 'मतिराम' रसाल ।।२३४।।

If a *nayika* bitterly insults her faithful and devoted lover Matiram terms her as *adhama nayika*. [234]

उदाहरण (कवित्त)

आयो है सयानपन गयो है अयान मन
नित उठि मान करबे की टेव पकरी।
घर घर मानिनी हैं मानितीं मनाए तें वै
तेरी ऐसी रीति और काहू मैं न जकरी।
कबि मतिराम कामरूप घनस्याम
लाल तेरी नैनकोर ओर चाहैं इकटक री।
हा हा कै निहारेहूँ न हेरति हरिननैनी
काहे को करत हठ हारिल की लकरी।।२३५।।

The *nayika* has become so obstinate that she is sulks everyday and does not listen to anyone in the house. There are such women in every home, but then they give in to the requests of other members of the family. Krishna is more handsome than Kama and keeps on staring at the *nayika*, sincerely implores her to give up her anger, but even then she refuses. But this doe-eyed *nayika* continues to be offended and she appears like a Harila bird that strongly holds on to a stick. [235]

दोहा

कहा लियो गुरुमान को अति ताती ह्वै नेम।
पारद सौं उड़ि जायगो अलि चंचल यह प्रेम।।२३६।।

When the *nayika* refused to give in even after many requests from her beloved he went away. The *sakhi* asked her why she was so obstinate? Love is like mercury and will evaporate when heated. [236]

नायक लक्षण

तरुन सुघर सुंदर सकल
कामकलानि प्रबीन।
नायक सो मतिराम कहि
कबित गीत रसलीन।।२३७।।

Matiram says that a youthful *nayak* should be handsome and proficient in all the arts of love. [237]

सवैया

गुच्छनि के अवतंस लसै सिर पच्छन अच्छ किरीट बनायो।
पल्लव लाल समेत छरी करपल्लव सौं मतिराम सुहायो।
गुंजनि के उर मुंजल हार सुकुंजनि तें कढ़ि बाहर आयो।
आजु को रूप लखै नँदलाल को
आजुहि नैनन को फल पायो।।२३८।।

The *nayak* who has put flowers and feathers in his turban, holds a stick in his pink hands with red flowers and has a garland around his neck, steps out of the grove. My eyes are indeed fortunate to have seen such beauty of Krishna. [238]

दोहा

भरी भाँवरे साँवरै रास रसिक रस जान।
उनहीं में मति भ्रमति है हवै बौंडर को पान।।२३९।।

Just as a leaf keeps on turning round and round in a whirlwind, in the same way the *nayika*'s mind remains in the whirlwind of emotion ever since she has seen Krishna in amorous play of *Rasa*. [239]

पति आदि त्रिविध नायक भेद वर्णन

पति उपपति बैसिक त्रिबिध नायकभेद बखान।
बिधि सौं ब्याह्यौ पति कह्यो कबि मतिराम सुजान।।२४०।।

There are three types of husbands, husband, a paramour and *vaishik*. [240]

पति उदाहरण (सवैया)

पाँव धरे दुलही जिहिं
ठौर रहे मतिराम तहाँ द्रग दीने।
छोड़ि सखान के साथ को खेलिबो
बैठ रहे घर ही रस भीने।
साँझहि तें ललकैं मन ही मन
लालन यौं रस के बस लीने।
लोनी सलोनी के अंगनि नाह सु
गौने की चूनरी टोने-से कीने।।२४१।।

That young bride walks expectantly (as if her eyes follow her footsteps). The young bridegroom stopped playing with his friends and stayed mostly at home. As evening falls he becomes eager for romantic sports. It seems that the *odhni* of the bride has cast a spell on him. [241]

दोहा

जा दिन तें गौनो भयो आई बाल रसाल।
ता दिन तें बिरहिन भई हरि-उर तें बनमाल।।२४२।।

Ever since she has returned after the *gauna*, Krishna has stopped wearing the *vanamala* and puts it away. It seems that it has become like that of a *virahini*. [242]

चतुर्विध पति

चारि भाँति सौं बरनिये प्रथम कहत अनुकूल।
दच्छिन गन सठ धृष्ट पुनि रस सिँगार को मूल।।२४३।।

A *nayak* is of four types: *anukul*, *dakshin*, *shatha* and *dhrishta*. [243]

अनुकूल-नायक लक्षण

सदा आपनी नारि सौं राखै अति ही प्रीति।
परनारी तैं बिमुख जो, सो अनुकूल सुरीति।।२४४।।

Anukul is one who loves his wife and turns his face away from other women. [244]

उदाहरण (सवैया)

क्यौंहू नहीं बिसरैं निसि बासर
मंद हँसी मुखचंद उज्यारी।
त्यौं ही दीपै अति नेह सौं देह की
दीपकला सम दीपति न्यारी।
तेरिय जोति जगै हिय भीतर
आवत और न नारि-अँध्यारी।
नैननहूँ अरु बैननहूँ तनहूँ
मनहूँ को तुही अति प्यारी।।२४५।।

A *nayak* speaks to a *nayika*, O beloved! Day and night your moon-like face and your sweet smile is my thoughts, your body radiant with love is always in my eyes and heart. Other women are like darkness to me and never enter my heart. My eyes and words are only for you. [245]

दोहा

सपनेहूँ मनभावतो करत नहीं अपराध।
मेरे मन ही में रही सखी मान की साध।।२४६।।

O *sakhi* ! My beloved does not commit a crime even in his dream. How can I be offended with him? I have not had any occasion to be cross with him. [246]

दक्षिण नायक लक्षण

एक भाँति सब तियन सौं जाको होय सनेह।
सो दच्छिन 'मतिराम' कहि बरनत हैं मतिगेह।।२४७।।

Dakshin nayak is one who has equal love for many women. [247]

सवैया

साँझ-समय ललना मिलि आई
खरो जहाँ नंदलला अलबेलो।
खेलन कौं निसि चाँदनी माँहि
बनै न मतो मतिराम सुहेलो।

आपनि आपनि पौरि बतायकै
बोलि कह्यो सिगरिन नबेलो।
त्यौं हँसिकै ब्रजराज कह्यो अब
आज हमारिहि पौरि में खेलो।।२४८।।

At evening all the *gopis* went to meet Krishna but could not come up with a plan to meet under moonlight. Then each *gopi* invited Krishna to come to her home. Krishna was confused and did not know whose invitation to accept and whose to decline. At that, Krishna smiled and said, "Why don't you all come to my home where we will play on the terrace?" [248]

दोहा

दच्छिन नायक एक तुम मनमोहन ब्रजचंद।
फुलाए ब्रजबनितान के दृग इंदीबर बृंद।।२४९।।

A *sakhi* talks to Krishna. In the entire Braj you are the only *dakshin nayak*. You are like the moon and when the maidens look at you their blue lotus-like eyes bloom. [249]

शठ नायक लक्षण

डरै करत अपराध नहिं,
करै कपट की प्रीति।
बचन-क्रिया मैं अति चतुर,
सठ-नायक की रीति।।२५०।।

Shatha is one who is not afraid of dallying with many women, who fakes love and who is clever both in his speech and acts. [250]

कवित्त

मोतैं तो कछु न अपराध पर्यो प्रानप्यारी
मान करि रही यौं ही काहे को अरस तैं।
लोचन-चकोर मेरे सीतल हैं होत तेरे
अरुन कपोल मुखचंद के दरस तैं।
कहैं मतिराम उठि लागु उर मेरे किन
करत कठोर मन अँसुवा बरस तैं।
कोप तैं कटुक बोल बोलत हैं तऊ मोकौं
मीठे होत अधर-सुधारस परस तैं।।२५१।।

O my dear! Have I committed any crime that you are indifferent towards me? Your red cheeks and your moon-like face give my thirsty eyes comfort. Matiram says why don't you embrace me? You have put on a cross face, shed tears and speak harsh words. But when the bitter words come out of your nectar-dipped mouth they seem sweet. [251]

दोहा

पियत रहैं अधरान को रस अति मधुर अमोल।
तातैं मीठे कढ़त हैं लालबदन तैं बोल।।२५२।।

The *nayak* is cleverly trying to win over the *nayika* and says, "My dear! Your lips drink sweet nectar from my lips. That is why whatever words you speak are sweeter." [252]

धृष्ट नायक लक्षण

करै दोष निरसंक जो, डरे न तिय के मान।
लाज धरै मन मैं नहीं, नायक-धृष्ट निदान।।२५३।।

Dhrishta nayak is one who has no shame and does not care if the *nayika* is offended. [253]

कवित्त

बरज्यो न मानत हौ बार बार बरज्यो मैं
कौन काम मेरे इत भौन मैं न आइये।
लाज को न लेस जगहाँसी को न डर मन
हँसत हँसत आन बात न बनाइये।
कबि मतिराम नित उठी कलकानि करौ
नित झूँठी सौंहैं करो नित बिसराइये।
ताके पग लागो निस जागि जाके उर लागे
मेरे पग लागि उर आगि न लगाइये।।२५४।।

A *nayika* speaks to a *nayak*. You do not listen to me despite my telling you many times. There is no need for you to come to my room so please do not come here. You have no shame left, you are not concerned that the whole world is laughing, so do not make excuses. Matiram says that you make false promises and swear to be good every morning and then forget. Go and fall at her feet where you are all night. Do not fall at my feet and light a fire in my heart. [254]

दोहा

निलज नैन कुलटानि के आनि बसे ब्रजराज।
हिये तिहारे तें सकल मारि निकारी लाज।।२५५।।

The offended Radha speaks to Krishna. O Krishna ! The shameless eyes of wanton women reside in your heart, which has dislodged shame from it. [255]

उपपति और वैशिक नायक लक्षण

जो परनारिन को रसिक, उपपति ताहि बखानि।
प्रीति करै गनिकान सौ, बैसिक ताकौं जानि।।२५६।।

Upapati nayak is a *nayak* who loves other wives and *vaishik* is one who loves courtesans only. [256]

उपपति उदाहरण (कवित्त)

सुंदरि सरस सब अंगन सिँगार साजे
सहज सुभाव निसि नेह कछु कै गई।
कीने मतिराम बिहसौंहैं से कपोल गोल
बोलन अमोल इतनोई दुख दै गई।
मेरे ललचौंहैं मुख फेरिके लजौंहैं
ललचौंहैं चारू चखनि चितैकै सो चली गई।
निपट निकट ह्वै कै कपट छुवाय अंग
लाय की सी लपटि लपेटि मनु लै गई।।२५७।।

The *nayika* had adorned every part of her body and was very seductive, her cheeks were smiling and she had uttered sweet words. I was looking at her greedily. She coyly walked past me and touched her body to mine. It seemed as if she burned my body and stole my mind. [257]

दोहा

नैन जोरि मुख मोरि हँसि नैसुक नेह जनाय।
आगि लेन आई हियै मेरे गई लगाय ।।२५८।।

Locking her gaze with mine and turning her face, smiling and showing some affection she had come to take embers but ignited a fire in my heart. [258]

मंद हँसनि दृगकोर लखि बस कर लेत प्रबीन।
छिन बिछुरैं गति होत यों ज्यों जल बिछुरत मीन।।२५९।।

With a sweet smile and a loving gaze, the *nayika* is able to get anyone under her influence. Even if she looks at you for a brief moment it makes you like a fish out of water. [259]

वैशिक उदाहरण

आगमन चाहि चकचौंधि रहवौ जब तब,
जगर-मगर आभरन के नगन भौ;
जोबन के मद, रूप-मद वाके मैन-मद,
छकि मतवारो ह्वै कैं थकित पगन भौ।
कहै 'मतिराम' लोल लोचन बिसाल बंक,
तीछन कटाछन सौं छिदि कै लगन भौ;
बार-बार भ्रमि बारिबधु-बार-भौरन मैं,
माँग की मुकतमाल-गंग मैं मगन भौ ।।२६०।।

Vaishik is one who loves courtesans. The *vaishik nayak* passionately waits for the courtesan. The reflection of sparkling jewels of that courtesan dazzles the eyes of a *vaishik*. His heart fills with romantic feelings on seeing the ravishing beauty of the courtesan. The desire for sexual union with that *nayika* further enhances the passion of that *vaishik*. Pierced by the arrows of her elongated eyes the *vaishik nayak* becomes standstill. Eventually his heart is drowned in the swirls of her curly tresses. [260]

दोहा

लोचन-पानिप ढिग सजी लट-बंसी परबीन।
मो मन बारिबिलासिनी फाँसि लियो मनु मीन।।२६१।।

Looking like a fishing rod and next to the radiant eyes of a *ganika* is a strand of her hair, which has trapped my mind as if it were a fish. [261]

अभिमानी आदि त्रिविध नायक-भेद लक्षण

मानी बचनचतुर कह्यो
क्रियाचतुर पुनि जानि।
तीन भाँति औरैं कहत
नायक सुकबि बखानि।।२६२।।

There are three other types of *nayaks*, *mani*, *vachan chatur* and *kriya chatur*. [262]

अभिमानी लक्षण

करत नायका सौं कछू नायक मन अभिमान।
तासौं मानी कहत हैं कबि मतिराम सुजान।।२६३।।

That erring *nayak* who is arrogant and is offended is called *mani*. [263]

उदाहरण (कवित्त)

वह सुधि करौ क्यों न नैननलिनी के दल
सेज सारे सीरे सरसिजन बिछाइये।
अमल उसीर इंदु चंदन गुलाब नीर
कहाँ लगि और उपचारन गिनाइये।
छल बल छलि बलि बाको मैं मिलाइयत
कबि मतिराम अब साहबी जनाइये।
ऐसैं मनभावन गुमान है जु मन भायो
प्यारी के मनाइगे कौं तुमको मनाइये।।२६४।।

A *sakhi* speaks with a *mani nayak*. O Krishna ! You have spread cool lotuses on your bed while you await the lotus-eyed beloved. You also use cooling agents like the moon, sandalwood, rose water to allay the heat of your longing. What other remedies can I suggest? I used to bring her to meet you but now you have become arrogant. It seems to me that even before I reconcile the *nayika* I will have to assuage your feelings first. [264]

दोहा

यामैं कौन सयानु है मोहनलाल सुजान।
आपु करत अपराध हौ आपुहि पुनि अभिमान।।२६५।।

O Krishna ! This is not an intelligent thing to do. You make a mistake and then you get offended. [265]

वचनचतुर नायक लक्षण

बचनन मैं जो करत है चतुराई मतिराम।
बचनचतुर नायक सरस लीजै जानि सकाम।।२६६।।

A *nayak* who has clever in speech is called a *vachan chatur nayak*. [266]

उदाहरण (कवित्त)

दूसरे की बात सुनि परत न ऐसी जहाँ
कोकिल कपोतन की धुनि सरसाति है।
छाई रहे जहाँ द्रुम बेलिन सौं मिलि
मतिराम अलिकुलन अँध्यारी अधिकाति है।
नखत से फूलि रहैं फूलन के पुंज घन
कुंजन मैं होति जहाँ दिन ही मैं राति है।
ता बन की बाट कोऊ संग न सहेली साथ
कैसे तूँ अकेली दधि बेचन को जाति है।। २६७।।

A *nayak* speaks to a *nayika*, O my beloved! That place is so isolated that no one can hear you, the only sounds there are those of the cuckoo and the pigeon. There the creeper clings to the trees and there are so many bees that it is dark. You are all alone there without any friends. How do you go there to sell curd? [267]

दोहा

तोकौं देउँ बताय हौं तूँ कत होत उचाट।
ग्वालिन दधि बेचन गई बंसीबट की बाट।।२६८।।

A *gopi* speaks to a *nayak*, O *nayak*! That *nayika* has gone this way towards the grove to sell curd. Now that I have told you, do not be depressed. [268]

क्रियाचतुर लक्षण

करै क्रिया सौं चातुरी जो नायक रसलीन।
क्रियाचतुर ताकौं कहत कबि मतिराम प्रबीन।।२६९।।

Kriya chatur is one who cleverly finds time for love sports by his actions. [269]

उदाहरण (सवैया)

नँदलाल गयो तित ही चलिकै
जित खेलति बाल अलीगन मैं।
तहाँ आपु ही मूँदे सलोनी के लोचन
चोरमिहीचनि खेलन मैं।
दूरिबे को गई सिगरी सखियाँ
मतिराम कहै इतने छिन मैं।
मुसकायकै राधिका कंठ लगाय
छिप्यो कहूँ जाय निकुंजन मैं।।२७०।।

Krishna went to the place where Radhika and her *sakhis* were playing hide and seek. There he shut the eyes of his beloved. When the other *sakhis* went away to hide Krishna smiled and embraced Radhika and the two hid in a grove. [270]

साँझ समैं वा छैल की छलनि कही नहिं जाय।
बिन डर बन डरपाय कैं लई मोहिं उन लाय।।२७१।।

O *sakhi* ! What can I say of the pranks of this beloved? He frightened me in a forest and without any fear, embraced me. [271]

प्रोषित नायक लक्षण

नायक होय बिदेस मैं जो बियोग अकुलाय।
तासों प्रोषित कहत हैं जे प्रबीन कबिराय।।२७२।।

Proshit is a *nayak* who lives abroad and is distressed by his separation from his beloved. [272]

उदाहरण

प्यार पगे बचन-पियूष पान करि-करि,
उमँगि-उमँगि तिय आनँद बिसेखिहौं ;
कबि 'मतिराम' तन-तपनि बुझाय जैहै,
तब निज जनम सफल करि लेखिहौं।
हीतल को सीतल करन चारु चाँदनी-सी,
मंद मृदु मुसकानि अनमिख पेखिहौं ;
ह्वैहै तब निसा मेरे लोचन-चकोरनि को,
जब वाको आनन अमल इंदु देखिहौं।।२७३।।

A *nayak* dreams of returning home and being united with her beloved. "I long for that day when I will drink the nectar of her words with delight. The fire of my body will be assuaged by her presence and my life will be fulfilled. Her sweet smile is like the cooling moonlight. My *chakor*-like eyes will experience night only when I see her face. [273]

प्रफुलित सुमन-समाज मैं करबी आनँद केलि।
सो नीके दिन लागिहैं उर सोने की बेलि।।२७४।।

It will be a glorious day when I, like fully blossomed flowers, will sport with my delightful beloved who will be close to my heart. [274]

दर्शन भेद

दरसन आलंबनहिं मैं कबि मतिराम सुजान।
स्रवन स्वप्न अरु चित्र त्यौं पुनि प्रत्यच्छ बखान।।२७५।।

There are four types of *darshan bhed, shravan, svapna, chitra* and *pratyaksha*. [275]

श्रवण-दर्शन

उदाहरण

आनन-पूरनचंद लसै अरबिंद-बिलास-बिलोचन पेखे।
अंबर पीत लसै चपला छबि अंबुद मेचक अंग उरेखे।
कामहूँ तें अमिराम महा मतिराम हिये निहेचै करि लेखे।
तैं बरनैं निज बैनन सौं सखी
मैं निज नैनन सौं जनु देखे।।२७६।।

A *sakhi* speaks to a *nayika*.
The *nayak*'s face is as radiant as the moon. His eyes are as beautiful as that of a lotus. The *pitambar* on his body adds to his beauty. It seems as if lightning is shining in black clouds. Krishna seems to me more beautiful than Kama. Having heard this the *nayika* said, O *sakhi* ! You have described him so well to me with your words that I feel as if I have seen him with my own eyes. [276]

दोहा

जैसो बरन्यो तैं सखी रूप कान्ह को आय।
तैसोई मेरे चखन रह्यो आइ ठहराय।।२७७।।

O *sakhi* ! Your description of Krishna's beauty has come to reside in my eyes. [277]

स्वप्नदर्शन

उदाहरण (सवैया)

आवत मैं सपने हरि को
लखि नैसुक बाट सकोचन छोड़ी।
आगे ह्वै आड़े भए मतिराम
चली सु चीतैं चख लालच वोड़ी।
ओठन को रस लेन को मोहन
मेरो गहो कर काँपति ठोड़ी।
औरु भटू न भई कछु बात
गई इतने हीं मैं नींद निगोड़ी।।२७८।।

O *sakhi* ! In my dream, I saw Krishna coming in front of me and I stepped aside to let him go by. But he persisted to stay in front of me and wanting to see him, I kept on walking ahead. Then Krishna held me with trembling hands wanting to kiss me. Just then, I swore at him and I woke up from my sleep. [278]

दोहा

पियमिलाप को सुख सखी कह्यो न जात अनूप।
सौतुक सो सपनो भयो सपनो सौतुक रूप।।२७९।।

O *sakhi* ! The pleasure of seeing my beloved in my dream was beautiful and it is difficult to describe it in words. After the dream, everything around me looks false while the dream seems true. [279]

चित्रदर्शन

उदाहरण (सवैया)

अचल भए हैं गात परस न जान्यो जात
कही न सुनत बात जात बात न कही।
सूँघै न सुबास न सुमन की समुझि परै
टकटकी बड़े बड़े दृगन में उलही।
कबि मतिराम तोहि नैक परवाह नहीं
ऐसी भाँति भई वह तेरे नेह सों नही।
ऐरे चितचोर चलि चाहि चंदमुखि तोहि
चित्र ही में चाहि चाहि चित्र ही मै ह्वै रही।।२८०।।

O *nayak* (stealer of hearts)! The *nayika* has become infatuated with you after looking at your picture and her entire body has become restless. She has forgotten the sense of touch and smell and cannot recognise flowers and spends her time staring. She has fallen in love with you and you do not seem to care. O stealer of her heart! Why don't you come and see how she loves you? Since she cannot see you, she is tied to your picture and sees nothing beyond it. [280]

दोहा

चित्रहि में जाके लखे होत अनंत अनंद।
सपनेहुँ कबहूँ सखी सो मिलिहैं ब्रजचंद।।२८१।।

When I get so much happiness by looking at Krishna in a dream, how much more pleasure would I get if I actually saw him. [281]

साक्षात् दर्शन लक्षण

कवित्त

मोहनलला को मन मोहनी बिलोकि बाल
कस करि राखति है उमग उमाह को।
सखिन की दीठि को बचायकै निहारति है
आनँदप्रबाह बीच पावत न थाह को।
कबि मतिराम और सब ही के देखतहूँ
ऐसी भाँति देखति छिपावत उछाह को।
वेई नैन रूखे-से लगत और लोगन को
वेई नैन लागत सनेह भरे नाह को।।२८२।।

After seeing Krishna, the *nayika* controls her desires and excitement. She gazes at Krishna while avoiding the staring *sakhis*. The sight of Krishna fills her mind with a sea of delight but she is unable to get her attention. The poet says that she gazes at Krishna in the middle of many people in such a way that no one suspects her feelings. Her eyes seem devoid of love to others, but her beloved detects love in them. [282]

दोहा

नँदनंदन के रूप पर रीझ रही रिझवारि।
अधमूँदी अँखियन दई मूँदी प्रीति उघारि।।२८३।।

The *nayika* is infatuated with Krishna's looks. Her half-closed eyes apparently reveal her love. [283]

उद्दीपन लक्षण

चंद कमल चंदन अगर ऋतु बन बाग बिहार।
उद्दीपन शृंगार के जे उज्जल संभार।।२८४।।

The moon, lotus, sandalwood, incense, spring, forest, garden, these facilitate romance. They are called facilitating emotions. [284]

उदाहरण (सवैया)

पूरनचंद उदोत कियो घन
फूलि रही बनजाति सुहाई।
भौंरन की अवली कल कैरव
कुंजन-पुंजन में मृदु गाई।
बाँसुरीताननि काम के बाननि
लै मतिराम सबै अकुलाई।
गोपिन गोप कछू न गने
अपने अपने घर तें उठि धाई।।२८५।।

The full moon was in the sky. The trees and shrubs had blossomed in the forest. Bees were humming on creepers in the grove. Just then the mellifluous notes of Krishna's flute began to be heard and it was like arrows of Kama on the hearts of the *gopi*. The *gopi*s ignored their husbands and left their home and came to the grove. [285]

दोहा

प्रथम कामिजन मनन कौं रँगत सुरभि रितु राग।
मंडत है नवपल्लवनि पुनि पीछे बन बाग।।२८६।।

Fragrance, music, the spring season, forest, garden and new leaves on trees all gladden the hearts of those in love. [286]

उद्दीपन भेद

सखी दूतिका जानिये उद्दीपन के भेद।
नायक अरु नायका को हरै बिरह को खेद।।२८७।।

The *sakhis* and *dutis* are aware of the situations of the *nayak* and *nayika* and help them in lessening the pain of their separation. [287]

सखी लक्षण

जा तिय सौं नहिं नायका कछू छिपावे बात।
तासौं बरनत कह सखी, सब कबि मति अवदात।।२८८।।

A *sakhi* is a confidante of the *nayika*. [288]

सखी के काम

मंडन अरु सिच्छाकरन उपालंभ परिहास।
काज सखी के जानियो औरो बुद्धि-बिलास।।२८९।।

A *sakhi* has four duties towards the *nayika*, to adorn, to teach, to complain with sarcasm and to make humour. [289]

मंडन उदाहरण

जावक रंग रँगै पगपंकज,
नाह को चित्त रँगै रँगु जातैं;
अंजन दै करि नैनन मैं
सुखमा बढ़ि स्याम सरोज प्रभातैं।
सोने के भूषन अंग रचे,
'मतिराम' सबै बस कीबै की घातैं;
यों हीं चलै न सिँगार सुभावहि,
मैं सखि भूलि कही सब बातैं।। २९०।।

A *sakhi* is adorning the *nayika* and explains the importance of the various adornments. It is important to apply the red dye of the feet as this colours the mind of the *nayak* and makes it ready for love. Applying corrylium to the eyes is important as it adds to the beauty of the eye and the blue lotus wilts on seeing them at dawn. Wearing adornments increases the beauty of the limbs. All these will bring the *nayak* under your influence. Only ordinary adornments will not do. Please forgive me, for I have erred. This was just a joke. Actually your beauty does not need any adornments. [290]

दोहा

सखी प्रिया की देह मैं सजे सिँगार अनेक।
कजरारी अँखियान मैं भूली काजरु एक।।२९१।।

The *sakhi* adorned the *nayika* with a number of adornments. But she forgot to put corrylium in her eyes. But acutally, her eyes in their natural state look so dark as if corrylium is applied to it. [291]

शिक्षा उदाहरण

मलय पवन मंद-मंद कैं गमन लाग्यौ,
फूलन के वृंदनि तैं मकरंद ढारने;
कबि 'मतिराम' चितचोर चारौं ओर चाहि,
लाग्यौ चैत-चंद चारु आँदनी पसारने।
अलिन की आली, आली मैन कैसे मंत्र पढ़ि,
लागी सब माननी के मान मद झारने;
सुमन सिँगार साज सेज सुख साजि करो,
लाज करो आज ब्रजराज पर वारने।।२९२।।

The month of Chaitra is here, the soft Malay winds are blowing, dew drops are dropping from flowers, the intoxicating moon is spreading its light everywhere, rows of bees are buzzing and it seems that they are chanting a *mantra* and assuaging offended women. So please decorate the bed with flowers. Today you must shower Krishna with your love. [292]

कहत सजनी ह्वै अनमनी अँसुवा भरति संसक।
बड़े भाग नँदलाल सौं झूठहु लगत कलंक।।२९३।।

O *sakhi* ! Why are you sad? Why are there tears in your eyes? If on account of Nandlal you are called a liar then it is a matter of good fortune. [293]

उपालंभ उदाहरण

पान की कहानी कहा, पानी को न पान करै,
आहि कहि उठति अधिक उर आधि कैं;
कबि 'मतिराम' भई बिकल बिहाल बाल,
राधिके जिवावरे अनंग अवराधि कैं।

याही को कहायो ब्रजराज दिन वारि ही मैं,
करी है उजारि ब्रज ऐसी रीति नाधि कैं;
जैसे तुम मोहन ! बिलोक्यौ वाकी ओर तैसे,
बैरिहू सौं बैरी न बिलोकै बैर साधि कैं ।।२९४।।

O Krishna ! Ever since you lovingly looked at Radha she is not herself. Leave aside eating betel, she does not even drink water. When she is very sad all she can do is to sigh. She is very distressed. Our prayer to Kamadev is to keep Radha alive. For such cruel deeds, you proclaim yourself to be the king of Braj. Not even an enemy would look at Radha the way you have. Your piercing gaze has become a curse for Radha. Even an enemy does not behave the way you did. [294]

वाको मनु तीने लला, बोलो बोल रसाल ।
झुकत तनक ही बात मैं ललित बेलि बर बाल ।।२९५।।

O *nayak*! By speaking sweet words you have captured the heard of the *nayika*. She is as tender as a creeper that bends even in the slightest breeze. [295]

परिहास

उदाहरण (सवैया)

गौने के द्यौस सिंगारन को
मतिराम सहेलिन को गनु आयो।
कंचन के बिछुवा पहिरावत
प्यारी सखी परिहास बढ़ायो।
प्रीतम स्रौन समीप सदा
बजै यों कहिकै पहिले पहिरायो।
कामिनी कौल चलावनि कौं कर
ऊँचो कियो पै चल्यौ न चलायो।।२९६।।

On the day of the *gauna* a group of *sakhis* came to adorn the *nayika*. When they were putting a toe-ring one *sakhi* spoke in jest to the ring, "may you always ring in his ears". Feigning anger, she lifted a lotus as if to hit her but then thinking of her beloved, her hand became limp. [296]

दोहा

प्रभा तरौना लाल की परी कपोलन आनि।
कहा छपावत चतुर तिय कंत-दंतछत जानि।।२९७।।

The *nayika* is bashful about the reflection of the ear ornament on her cheek and is trying to hide it. The *sakhi* in jest asks her not to hide it and says that it is not because of your love sports but a mere reflection of the ear ornament. [297]

दोहा

भुज फुलेल लावत सखी कर चलाय मुसकाय।
गाढ़े गहे उरोज तिय बिहँसि भौंह चढ़ाय।।२९८।।

A *sakhi* speaks to a *nayika* :
A *sakhi* is applying fragrant adornments to the *nayika*. During this, her eyes fell on the love marks on the *nayika*'s breasts. She said, "it seems that your beloved has tightly held your breasts". She pretended to be angry, but remembering the romantic pleasure she broke into a smile. [298]

उत्तमादि त्रिविध दूती-भेद वर्णन

निपुन दूतता मैं सदा दूती ताहि बखान।
उत्तम मध्यम अधम यौं तीन भाँति सौं जान।।२९९।।

The *duti* is a messenger who arranges meetings between the beloved and conveys messages between the two. There are three types of messengers: *uttama, madhyama* and *adhama*. [299]

उत्तमा दूती लक्षण

मोहै जो मृदु बोलिकै मधुर बचन अभिराम।
ताहि कहत कबिराज हैं उत्तम दूती नाम।।३००।।

Uttama duti is one who pleases everyone by her sweet speech. [300]

उदाहरण (कवित्त)

जा दिन तैं देखे मतिराम तुम ता दिन तैं
बढ़ी रहै मुसकानि वाके जियराई पर।
भावत न भोजन बनावत न आभरन
हेतु न करत सुधानिधि सियराई पर।
चलो उठि देखौ बड़े भाग हैं तिहारे अब
राखो धरि राधिकै कन्हाई हियराई पर।
दूनी दुति छाई देह आई दुबराई पिय
राई लौनु वारिये तिया की पियराई पर।। ३०१।।

O Krishna ! Since the day Radhika has seen you, there is a smile on her face. But she has lost interest in food and does not adorn herself and does not have the heart to look at moonlight. So get up and go and see her state for yourself. You are a person of good fortune, so please give her your love. Due to her separation from you she has become lean, but her radiance has doubled. Her body has become pale. We should remove the evil spell from her with mustard seeds and salt. [301]

दोहा

तिय के हिय के हनन कौं भयो पंचसर बीर।
लाल तुम्हैं बस करन कौं रहे न तरकस तीर।।३०२।।

A messenger speaks to the *nayak*. O Krishna ! Why is your heart devoid of love? It seems that to pierce the heart of that tender damsel Kama used all his skill. All his arrows are now exhausted and he does not have any more arrows to capture you. [302]

मध्यमा दूती लक्षण

कछू बचन हित के कहै बोलै अहित कछूक।
मध्यम दूती कहत हैं तासौं सुकबि अचूक।।३०३।।

A messenger speaks to a *nayak* :
Kamadev has used all his arrows to fill her heart with love and there are none left. [303]

उदाहरण (कवित्त)

चरन धरैं न भूमि बिहरैं तहाँई जहाँ,
फूले-फूले फूलनि बिछायौ परजंक है;
भार के डरनि सुकुमारि चारु अंगनि मैं,
करति न अंगराग कुंकुम को पंक है।
कबि 'मतिराम' देखि बातायन बीच आयो,
आतप मलीन होत बदन मयंक है;
कैसें वह बाल लाल बाहिर बिजन आवै,
बिजन बयारि लागैं लचकत लंक है।।३०४।।

A messenger speaks to a *nayak*. O Krishna ! The *nayika* is very delicate. She does not put her feet on the ground but steps only where flowers have spread. She is so soft that even saffron applied to her skin feels hard. Even if a few rays of sun come through the window her moon-like face withers. How can such a delicate maiden come and meet you in a secluded place? Even a draft of wind from a fan is a burden on her slim waist. [304]

रीझि रही रिझवारि वह तुम ऊपर ब्रजनाथ !
लाज सिंधु की इंदिरा, क्यौंकर आवै हाथ ?।।३०५।।

A messenger speaks to a *nayak* :
O Krishna ! The *nayika* is in love with you. But she is very shy. She is like the Lakshmi of all bashful women. She will never surrender to your advances. [305]

अधमा दूती लक्षण

अधम दूतिका जानिए बचन कहत सतराय।
ग्रंथन को मति देखि कैं बरनत सब कबिराय।।३०६।।

She is a messenger who gets angry and always speaks harsh words. [306]

उदाहरण

जानत कछू न पै कहावत रसिकराय,
ल्याउ-ल्याउ अबहीं तिहारे यह टेक है;
कूरन की रीति है जु डेल ऐसो डारि देत,
'मतिराम' चतुराइ चतुर लिए कहै।
बोली ना नवेली कछू बोल सतराय वह,
मनसिज ओज को सुहानौं कछु सेक है;
बातन सुनत अँगरात अलसात गात,
सौहैं करि नैन बिहसोहैं भई नेक है।।३०७।।

A messenger speaks to Krishna:
You claim to be an accomplished lover but you do not know anything. All you do is to keep on wishing that your beloved be here. You do not know how to speak properly. Your words sound like the sound of a drum. Intelligent people should speak with dignity. The *nayika* is young and out of fear she does not say anything but there is a suggestion of love on her face. She lovingly twists her body and is ready for love. While her face may say no, her eyes are smiling, for there is a hint of love in them. [307]

जोबन मंडित आपनैं अजौ न जानत गात।
तो चित्त मैं अति चटपटी निपट अटपटी बात।। ३०८।।

That *ajnatayauvana mugdha* is still unaware that youth has touched her body. On the other hand, you are so impatient making strange proposals. [308]

अनुभाव वर्णन लक्षण

जिनते चित रतिभाव को
आछो अनुभव होय।
रस सिंगार अनुभाव तिहि
बरनत कबि सब कोय।।३०९।।

Anubhav is that state which helps in experiencing the erotic sentiment. [309]

लोचन बचन प्रसाद मृदु हास भाव धृति मोद।
इनते प्रगटत भाव रति बरनहि सुकबि बिनोद।।३१०।।

All poets are of the opinion that in expressing love you need a combination of: eyes, speech, easygoing temperament, sweet smile, gestures, courage and happiness. [310]

उदाहरण (सवैया)

गहि हाथ सौं हाथ सहेली के साथ
मैं आवत ही वृषभान लली।
मतिराम सुबास तैं आवत नीरे
निवारत भौंरन की अवली।
लिखिकै मनमोहन कौं सकुची कस्यो
चाहत आपनी ओट चली।
चित चोरि लियो दृग जोरि तिया
मुख मोरि कछू सकुचाय चली।।३११।।

Radhika was walking hand in hand with her *sakhis* and she kept on removing the cluster of bees that had surrounded her, having been attracted to her because of her fragrance. All of a sudden, she saw Krishna and she was confused and wanted to hide with her *sakhis*. She turned her face and smiled and her eyes met those of Krishna and her heart was stolen. [311]

दोहा

सहज बात बूझत कछू
बिहँसि नवाई ग्रीव।
तरुण हिये तरुणी दई
नए नेह की नीव।।३१२।।

The *nayika*, when asked a question, bent her head and smiled. The *nayak* was attracted by this gesture and it was as if the *nayika* had planted a new seed in her heart. [312]

सात्त्विक भाव

ते अनुभावै जानियो जे हैं सात्विक भाव।
रसग्रंथनि अवलोकिकै बरनत सब कबिराव।।३१३।।

Those situations that express a *sattvik* state of the mind are being expressed on the basis of canons of aesthetics. [313]

स्तंभ स्वेद रोमांच सुर भंग कंप बैबर्न।
आँसू औरो प्रलय कहि आठौं ग्रंथनि बर्न।।३१४।।

Canons describe eight types of situations: being frozen, being speechless, getting goosebumps, loss of voice, trembling, pallor, tearing and death. [314]

स्तंभ लक्षण

लज्जा हर्षादिकन तैं अचल होत जहँ अंग।
स्तंभ कहत हैं ताहि को जे प्रबीन रसरंग।।३१५।।

Stambha sattvik is the state when the body freezes on account of being shy and happy. [315]

उदाहरण (सवैया)

देखत ही मतिराम रसाल गही
मति प्यारी की प्रेमन गाढ़ी।
चाहिबे को चितचाह भई
हिय तैं कुलकानि न जाति है काढ़ी।
संग सखीन को जानि दुरावति
आनन आनँद की रुचि बाढ़ी।
पाइँ परे मग मैन मरुकै
भई मिस लाजन के फिर ठाढ़ी।।३१६।।

She became very emotional when the *nayika* saw the mango grove and could not think clearly. There was an intense desire to see her beloved. But she could not walk ahead because of fear of censure. Her face was radiant with love but she wanted to hide this from her friends, for she did not want to reveal her love. She started to walk but stopped on account of inhibition. [316]

दोहा

पाय इकंत निकुंज मैं भरी अंक ब्रजनाथ।
रोकन कौं तिय करति पै कह्यो करत नहिं हाथ।।३१७।।

In the pleasure grove, Krishna embraced the *nayika*. The *nayika* wanted to resist him, but her hands would not listen to her. [317]

स्वेद लक्षण

हरष लाज भय कोप श्रम इत्यादिक तैं होय।
पानी परगट देह मैं स्वेद कहावत सोय।।३१८।।

Sved is the state when pleasure, shyness, fear, anger and fatigue burn the body. [318]

उदाहरण (सवैया)

किंकिनि नेवर की झनकारनि
चारु पसार महारस जालहि।
काम कलोलनि मैं मतिराम
कलानि निहाल कियो नँदलालहि।
स्वेद के बूँद लसैं तन मैं रति
अंतर ही लपटाय गुपालहि।
मनो फली मुकता फल पुंजन
हेमलता लपटानी तमालहि।।३१९।।

The *nayika* was fully engaged in love sports, her waistband and anklet resounded with the sound of bells and she was able to please Krishna. After that the *nayika* embraced Krishna. It seemed as if a creeper had clung to a *tamal* tree. [319]

दोहा

कुच तैं श्रम जलधार चलि मिलि रोमावलि रंग।
मनो मेरु की तरहटी भयो सितासित संग।।३२०।।

During love sports streams of sweat were pouring from the *nayika*'s breasts and in it was mixed a bit of blue colour and it seemed as if at the foothills of Sumeru Ganga and Yamuna were flowing. [320]

रोमांच लक्षण

हरष भयादिक तैं प्रगट रोम उमँग जो अंग।
ताहि कहत रोमांच हैं कबिजन सुमति उतंग।।३२१।।

Romanch is a state where happiness causes goosebumps. [321]

उदाहरण (कवित्त)

चंद्रमुखी हाँसी मैं चमेली की लता सी होति
चंपकलता सी अंग जोति को धरति है।
कबि मतिराम तेरे अंग की सुबास लहै
कौन बेली ऐसी हिये जानि न परति है।
नैसुक निहारे ते नबेली नैन कोरन सौं
ऐसी अदभुत की कलानि आचरति है।
ललित ललाम स्याम रसिक रसाल को
कदंब मुकुलित के कुलनि सौं करति है।।३२२।।

When the *nayika* smiles she looks like a creeper of *chameli* and the radiance of her body is like the full-blossomed creeper of *champa*. Matiram says that the fragrance of the *nayika*'s body makes one wonder whether any creeper can compete with her. And when she looks at anyone even for a moment with cross eyes, it is as if a wondrous event has taken place. If Krishna casts a glance on that coy Radha, she reacts in such a playful gesture that Krishna appears as a *kadamba* tree full of blossom. [322]

दोहा

जौन अंग ढिग ह्वै कढ़ी छुई छैल की छाँह।
अजहूँ लौं अवलोकिये पुलक पटलता ताह।।३२३।।

A *sakhi* speaks to another *sakhi*:
The *nayika*, while leaving, touched her body to that of the *nayak* and goosebumps are still seen on his body. [323]

स्वरभंग-लक्षण

क्रोध हर्ष मद भीति तैं बचन और बिधि होय।
तहि कहत स्वरभंग हैं कबि कोबिद सब कोय।।३२४।।

Svarbhang is a state where anger, pleasure and fear prevents one from talking rationally. [324]

उदाहरण (सवैया)

ताहि लै आई अली रतिमंदिर
जाकी लगै रति हूँ परछाँहीं।
आय गयो मतिराम तहीं
जिन कोटिन काम कला अवगाहीं।
देखत ही सगरी डगरी
पकरी हँसिकै तिय को पिय बाँहीं।
लाजनि तैं मति मंद भई
सुकढ़ी मुखचंद, मरू करि नाहीं।।३२५।।

Sakhis brought the *nayika*, who was more beautiful than Rati, into the pleasure chamber. At that time, the *nayak* who was well versed in love sports also arrived there. On seeing the *nayak*, the *sakhis* ran away and the *nayak* smiled and held the *nayika's* arms.

She was afraid and in that confusion all she could say was "no". [325]

दोहा

कहा जनावति चातुरी कहा चढ़ावत भौंह।
अधनिकरे अखरान सों सौंह कीजे सौंह।।३२६।।

A *nayika* has returned after a romantic meeting with her beloved and when the *sakhis* tease her, she gets angry at them. A *sakhi* speaks to the *nayika*.

O *sakhi* ! Why are you being clever and raise your eyebrows in anger? You tell us on oath that you have not engaged in romantic sports, but it is a lie because your words are incoherent. [326]

कंपन लक्षण

क्रोध हर्ष भय आदि तें थरथराति जो देह।
तहि कंप यौं कहत हैं कबि कोबिद मतिगेह।।३२७।।

Kampan is a state where anger, pleasure and fear cause the body to tremble. [327]

उदाहरण (सवैया)

चंद्रमुखी अरबिंद की बालनि
गूँदत रूप अनूप सुधाख्यो।
कामसरूप तहाँ मतिराम
अनंद सों नंदकुमार पधाख्यो।
देखत कंप छुट्यो तिय के तन
यौं चतुराई को बोल उचाख्यो।
सीरे सरोज लगे सजनी कर
काँपतु जातु न हार सँवाख्यो।।३२८।।

The moon-faced *nayika* adorned her body with half open lotuses. Matiram says that at that time the *nayak*, more handsome than Kama, appeared there. On seeing him the *nayika*'s body began to tremble and she cleverly said, "My arms are shaking because of the cold lotuses and that is why I am not able to hold the garland." [328]

दोहा

लाल बदन लखि बाल के कुचन कंप रुचि होति।
चपल होत चकवा मनो चाहि चंद को जोति।।३२९।।

On seeing the *nayak*, the *nayika*'s breasts started trembling and it seemed as if two *chakva* birds had become restless in moonlight. [329]

वैवर्ण्य लक्षण

मोह कोह भय आदि तें बर्न और बिधि होय।
ताहि कहत बैबर्न हैं सकल सयाने लोय।।३३०।।

Vaivarnya is a state where infatuation, anger, fear cause the colour of the face to change. [330]

उदाहरण (कवित्त)

छल सों छबीली कों सहेलिन लिवाय करि
ऊपर अटारी जाय रूप रच्यो ख्याल को।
कबि मतिराम भूषनन की झनक सुनि
चाय भो चपल चित रसिक रसाल को।
अली चली सकल अलीक मिस करि-करि
आवत निहारि करि मदनगोपाल को।
लालन को इंदु सों बदन अवलोकि करि
अरबिंद सों बदन कुम्हिलाय गयो बाल को।।३३१।।

Once, *sakhis* of the beautiful *nayika* tricked her to go to the terrace and they began to play. Matiram says that on account of the sounds of the movements of the ornaments Krishna had a desire to play with them and he went there. On seeing him, the *sakhis* went away from there with one pretext or the other. When the *nayika* saw the moon-faced *nayak*, her face wilted like the lotus. [331]

दोहा

बाल रही इकटक निरखि लाल बदन अरबिंदु।
सियराई नैनन परी पियराई मुख इंदु।।३३२।।

A *sakhi* speaks to a *sakhi* :
The *nayika* is staring at the *nayak*'s lotus-like face. Her eyes are peaceful but her face has turned pale. [332]

अश्रु लक्षण

हरष दुःख भय आदि तें जल आवे अँखियान।
ताहि बखानत आँसु कहि ग्रंथन को मत जान।।३३३।।

Ashru is a state where pleasure, sorrow, fear cause tears. [333]

उदाहरण (कवित्त)

बैठे हुते लाल मनमोहन छबीली बाल
छिनक सकोच राख्यो गुरुजन भीर को।
कबि मतिराम दीठि और की बचाय देखै
देखत ही औरै भय राखै अब धीर को।
तन को न मोह धरै मन की खबरि भूली।
आँखिन में छायो पूर आनँद के नीर को।
उमँगि हिये तें आयो प्रेम को प्रवाह तातें
लाज गिरि गई जैसे तरुवर तीर को।।३३४।।

All the family members were sitting in the home and Krishna and Radha were there too. Out of respect to them, their heads were turned down. When Radha looked at Krishna even for an instant love surged within her and she overcame her shyness. She was unable to contain herself or control her body or mind and tears of joy filled her eyes. Shyness within her disappeared just as a tree falls in the river. [334]

दोहा

बिन देखे दुख के चलैं देखैं सुख के जाहिं।
कहौ लाल इन दृगन तें अँसुवा क्यौं ठहराहिं।।३३५।।

Tell me my beloved, when I am away from you then tears flow from my eyes because of pain. When you are in front of me I am happy and even then tears of joy flow from my eyes. Please tell me how can my eyes be without tears? [335]

प्रलय लक्षण

जीवित तनु में होत है ईहा सकल निरोध।
हर्ष दुःख भय आदि तें प्रलय कहत मतिसोध।३३६।।

Pralaya is a state where even though one is alive the bodily functions come to a standstill. [336]

उदाहरण (सवैया)

जा दिन तें छबि सौं मुसक्यात
कहूँ निरखे नँदलाल बिलासी।
ता दिन तें म नही मन में
मतिराम पियै मुसक्यानि सुधा सी।
नेकु निमेष न लागत नैन
चकी चितवै तिय देवतिया सी।
चंद्रमुखी न हलै न चलै
निरबात निवास में दीपसिखा सी।।३३७।।

The day the *nayika* saw the smile of Krishna she is constantly drinking the nectar of his lips. That face constantly remains in front of her eyes she is frozen and keeps on looking at them and like a fish does not even blink. In this state, she does not move and it seems as if a row of lamps is burning in a room where there is no wind. [337]

दोहा

तो में अनमिषनैनता मोहन मूरति मैन।
अनमिष नैन सुनैन ये निरखत अनमिष नैन।।३३८।।

Radha and Krishna were gazing at each other and at that time Radha's *sakhi* told her, O Radha! You are looking at Krishna's image as it were that of Kama and he in turn is staring at you. [338]

जृंभा लक्षण

जृंभा कौं कबि कहत हैं नव यौं सात्विक भाव।
उपजै आलस आदि तें बरनत सब कबिराव।।३३९।।

Within all the *sattvik bhava* there is one called *jrimbha* and it arises from laziness. [339]

उदाहरण (कवित्त)

केलिकै सकल राति प्रात उठि अँगिराति
नींद भरे लोचन जुगल बिलसत है।
लाजनि तें अंगनि दुरावति है बार बार
खैंचि करि बसन बिहारी बिहँसत है।
कबि मतिराम आई आलस जँभाई मुख
ऐसी मनभावती की छबि सरसत है।
अरुन उदोत मनौ सोभा के सरोवर में
सोभा मानि सोभा को सरोज बिकसत है।।३४०।।

After an entire night of love-making the *nayika* got up in the morning and stretched herself. Her lazy eyes were looking beautiful. Out of shyness she is covering herself but Krishna pulls at them and laughs. When she yawned she looked even more beautiful. Her body was a sea of beauty, her red mouth was the rising sun and the open mouth the red lotus. [340]

दोहा

आयो पीव बिदेस तैं बहुतैं द्योस बिताय।
सखी उठाई पास तैं साँझहि तैं जमुहाय।।३४१।।

The *nayika* was sitting with her friends. Just then, she was told that her husband was about to return from abroad. She dispersed all her friends and started yawning, pretending to be sleepy. [341]

शृंगार वर्णन

जो बरनत तिय पुरुष को कबि कोबिद रतिभाव।
तासौं रीझत हैं सुकबि सो सिँगार रसराव।।३४२।।

Those poets who compose poetry about erotic love between a man and a woman are most appreciated. [342]

कहि सिँगार रसभाव द्वै प्रथम कहत संयोग।
ग्रंथन को मत देखिकै दूजो कहत बियोग।।३४३।।

There are two types of romantic emotion, love in union and love in separation. [343]

संयोग शृंगार लक्षण

प्रमुदित नायक-नायका जिहिं मिलाप मैं होत।
सो संयोग-सिँगार कहि बरनत सुमति उदोत।।३४४।।

Samyog shringara is a state of the pleasures of love-making. [344]

सवैया

प्रानप्रिया प्रिय आनँद सौं
बिपरीति रची रति रंग रह्यो भ्वै।
कामकलोलनि मैं मतिराम रही
धुनि त्यौं कटिकिंकिनी की ह्वै।
आनन की उजियारी परी
श्रमबूँद समेत उरोज लखै द्वै।
चंद की चाँदनी के परसैं
मनौ चंदपखान पहार चले च्वै।।३४५।।

Once the *nayak* and the *nayika* were in a state of bliss and decided to make love in the reverse position. During that, the bells on her waistband rang loudly. On account of fatigue, sweat appeared on her breasts and the radiance of her face fell on them. It seemed as if under the light of the moon the moonstone began to dissolve. [345]

दोहा

छुवत परसपर हेरिकैं राधा नंदकिसोर।
सबमैं द्वै ही होत हैं चोर मिहीचनि चोर।।३४६।।

Radha and Krishna play blind man's bluff and close each other's eyes from time to time. [346]

हाव लक्षण

दँपति के संयोग मैं होत प्रगट जे भाव।
ते संयोग सिँगार मैं बरनत सब कबि हाव।।३४७।।

When both the *nayak* and the *nayika* are full of love it is called *hava*. [347]

लीला प्रथम बिलास पुनि
त्यौं बिच्छित्ति बखान।
बिभ्रम किलकिंचित बहुरि
मोट्टाइत मन आन।।३४८।।
बहुरि कुट्टमित कहत हैं
पुनि बिब्बोक बखान।
ललित बरनि अरु बिहित कहि
सकल हाव दस जान।।३४९।।

There are ten types of *hava*: *lila, vilas, vicchiti, vibhrama, kilkinchita, mottayit, kutttmita, bibbok, lalit* and *vihit*. [348, 349]

लीला हाव लक्षण

पिय भूषन बचनादि की लीला करै जो बाल।
तासौं लीलाहाव कहि बरनत सुकबि रसाल।।३५०।।

Lila hava is a state where the *nayak* and the *nayika* exchange their clothes and ornaments. [350]

उदाहरण (सवैया)

प्यारपगी पगरी पिय की घर भीतर आपने सीस सँवारी।
एते मैं आँगन तैं उठिकै तहाँ आय गयो मतिराम बिहारी।
देखि उतारन लागी पिया पिय सौंहनि सौं बहुर्यो न उतारी।
नैन नवाय लजाय रही उर लाय लई मुसकाय पियारी।।३५१।।

The *nayak* was in the courtyard and the *nayika* was in the room. When she saw his turban, love surged within her and she felt that his turban was a token of her love so she decided to wear it. Matiram says that in the meantime, the *nayak* came inside and on seeing him she decided to remove the turban. But the *nayak* wanted to see her a bit longer with his turban, so he asked her not to remove it. She kept on wearing the turban and bashfully stood there with downcast eyes. The *nayak* smiled and embraced her. [351]

दोहा

मेरे सिर कैसी लगै यौं कहि बाँधी पाग।
सुंदरि रति विपरित नैं प्रगट कियो अनुराग।।३५२।।

The *nayika* placed the *nayak*'s turban on her head and asked the *nayak* how she looked. Thus she suggested reverse coitus. [352]

विलास हाव लक्षण

गवन नयन बचनादि में
होत जु कछुक विसेष।
बरनत ताहि बिलास कहि
रसमय सुकबि असेष।।३५३।।

When the *nayika* is full of love then her gait, gaze and speech are very special. This is called *vilas hava*. [353]

उदाहरण (कवित्त)

किंकिनी कलित कल नूपुर ललित रव
गौन तेरो देखिकै सकतु करि गौन को।
मृदु मुसकानि मुखचंद चारु चाँदनी सों
राख्यो कैं उज्यारो अभिराम द्वार भौन को।
सहज सुभावनि सों भौंहनि के भावनि सों
हरति है मन मतिराम मनरौन को।
रूपमद छकी आजु छबि सों छबीली देति
तिरछी चितौनि मैन बरछी सी कौन को।।३५४।।

A *sakhi* speaks to the *nayika* : O *sakhi* ! When you walk the bells on your waist as well as your ankle bells make a sweet sound. Anyone who sees your attractive gait will stop to watch. Your smile is like moonlight and your face is verily the moon. The radiance of our face fills the whole house. Your eyebrows attract the *nayak*. Your oblique glance looks like the bow of Kamadev and all in all you look so beautiful today. I wonder who will be wounded by your beauty today. [354]

दोहा

तेरी चलनि चितौनि मृदु
मधुर मंद मुसकानि।
छाय रही लखि लाल की
सखियन मिस अँखियानि।।३५५।।

The *nayak* looks at your gait, your gestures, you delicacy, sweetness and soft smile. It seems as if while gazing at you, the *nayak*'s eyes have become your friend. [355]

विच्छित्ति हाव लक्षण

थोरे ही भूषन बसन जहँ सोभा सरसाय।
ताहि कहत बिच्छित्ति हैं जे प्रबीन कबिराय।।३५६।।

Vichhita hava is a state where clothes and ornaments add to the beauty of the persons wearing them. [356]

उदाहरण (कवित्त)

बारने सकल एक रोरी ही की आड़ पर
हा हा न पहिरि आभरन और अंग में।
कबि मतिराम जैसे तीछन कटाछ तेरे
ऐसे कहाँ सर हैं अनंग के निखंग में।
सहज सुरूप सुघराई रीझो मन मेरो
डोलत है तेरी अद्भुत की तरंग में।
सेत सारी ही सों सब सौतें रँगी स्याम रंग
सेत सारी ही सों रंगे स्याम लाल रंग में।।३५७।।

A *nayak* talks to a *nayika* : Just one *tilak* on your forehead has made you so beautiful that anyone would bestow everything on you. I implore you not to adorn your body any more. Matiram says that your gaze is even more powerful than the arrows of Kama. I am infatuated by your simple unpretentious beauty and am drowning in it. Her white *sari* has made the faces of the co-wives turn dark and the dark Krishna, on the other hand, has become red with passion. [357]

दोहा

नथुनी गज मुकतान की लसत चारु सिंगार।
जिन पहिरे सुकुमारि तनु और आभरन भार।।३५८।।

A *sakhi* speaks to a *nayika* :
The elephantine nose ring suits you and completes your adornment but do not add

any more weighty adornments on your delicate body. [358]

विभ्रम हाव लक्षण

उलटे भूषन बसन की होतु जु है पहिराव ।
तासौं विभ्रमहाव कहि बरनत सब कबिराव ।।३५९।।

Vibhrama hava is a state when the *nayika* in a state of confusion does not wear her ornaments and clothes properly. [359]

उदाहरण

साँझहि तैं चलि आवत जात,
जहाँ-तहाँ लोगनि हूँ न डरौंगी;
प्रीतम सौं रति ही यह रूप धौं,
ह्वैहै कहाँ जब अंक भरौंगी ?
जानति हौं 'मतिराम' तऊ,
चतुराई की बात नहीं उरचौंगी ?
किंकिनि को उरु हारु किए,
कहि कौन सौं जाय बिहार करौंगी ?३६०।।

The *nayika* in a hurry to meet her beloved wore her waist ornament around her neck. The *sakhi* talks to her : O *sakhi* ! As evening came, you have left your home to meet your beloved. Are you not afraid of who will cross your path and see you? You can attract your beloved just with your good looks. But what will happen when you embrace him? I know, but still I ask. You are about to engage in romantic activity with a waist ornament around your neck. [360]

अली चली कहि कौन पै? बड़े कौन के भाग ।
उलटी कंचुकि कुचन पै कहै देत अनुराग ।।३६१।।

O *sakhi* ! Who is the fortunate one you are hurrying to meet? It is obvious from the way you have worn your *choli* backwards that you are deeply in love with someone. You are in so much of a hurry that you have ignored the way you dress. [361]

किलकिंचित हाव लक्षण

हरष, गरब, अभिलाष, स्रम, हास, रोष अरु भीति ।
होत एक ही संग हैं, किलकिंचित यह रीति ।। ३६२।।

Kilkinchita is a state where happiness, pride, expectation, fatigue, joy, anger and fear are all expressed at the same time. [362]

उदाहरण

लालन बाल के द्वै ही दिना तैं
परी मन आनि सनेह की फाँसी;
काम कलोलनि मैं 'मतिराम'
लगैं मनौ बाँटन मोद की आँसी ।
पीतम के उर बीच चुभ्यो
दुलही के बिलास मनोज की गाँसी;
स्वेद बढ्यौ तन कंप उरोजनि,
आँखिन आँसू कपोलनि हाँसी ।। ३६३।।

A *sakhi* speaks to another *sakhi* :
Within a few days of meeting, the *nayak* and the *nayika* are deeply in love and giving each other pleasure through romantic sports. Kama's arrows have pierced the *nayika* as if she was a bride. The glances of that newly wed *nayika* pierce the heart of *nayak* like that of cupid's arrow. On her body we can see sweat, trembling breasts, tears of happiness in her eyes, and a smile spreads on her pinkish face. [363]

सकुचि न रहिए साँवरे!
सुनि गरबीले बोल ।
चढ़त भौंह, बिकसत नयन,
बिहँसत गोल कपोल ।। ३६४।।

A *sakhi* speaks to a *nayak* :
O Krishna ! Do not be bothered by her sharp words and raised eyebrows. She is truly in love with you. In addition to her arrogance and anger, the radiance of her eyes give away her happiness and her rounded cheeks speak of her smile. [364]

मोट्टाइत हाव लक्षण

बातन को बिघटन भए, पुनि मिलाप की चाह ।
सो मोट्टाइत जानियो, बरनत सब कबिनाह ।।३६५।।

Mottayit hava is the desire to meet even though one does not want to talk or listen. [365]

उदाहरण

फूलि रहे द्रुम बेलनि सौं मिलि
पूरि रहीं अँखियाँ रतनारी;
मोहिं अकेली बिलोकि यहाँ कछू
और ही-सी भई दीठि तिहारी ।
जैसी हुती हमसौं तुमसौं
अब होयगी ऐसिये प्रीति निहारी;

चाहत जो चित मैं हित तौ
जिन बोलिए कुंजन बीच बिहारी ।। ३६६।।

Mottayit hava is when even though there has been no conversation between the two but yet the lovers have a desire to meet.

O Krishna ! In this grove, creepers have wound around trees and there are flowers everywhere. I see that your eyes are rested and seeing me, there is different gaze in them. We can restore our love but if you truly love me then do not invite me in this secluded grove. [366]

दोहा

झूठे ही ब्रज में लग्यौ मोहि कलंक गुपाल।
सपने हू कबहूँ हिए लगे न तुम नँदलाल ।।३६७।।

A *nayika* speaks to the *nayak* :

O Krishna ! The slander in Braj that I am in love with you is not correct. You have, not even in your dreams, kept me close to your heart. [367]

कुट्टमित हाव लक्षण

ईहा दुख अरु सुक्ख की प्रकट करे जहँ बाम।
परम ललित यह हाव है होत कुट्टमित नाम।।३६८।।

Kuttamita hava is a state where the *nayika's* frolics express both sorow and happiness. [368]

उदाहरण (कवित्त)

सोने की सी बेलि अति सुंदर नबेली बाल
ठाढ़ी ही अकेली अलबेली द्वारा महियाँ।
मतिराम आँखिन सुधा की बरखा सी भई
गई जब दीठि वाके मुखचंद पहियाँ।
नेकु नीरे जाय करि बातनि लगाय करि
कछु मन पाय हरि वाकी गही बहियाँ।
चैनन चरजी लई सैनन थकित भई
नैनन मैं चाह करै बैनन में नहियाँ।।३६९।।

The golden-complexioned beautiful *nayika* stood alone at the door. When Krishna's gaze fell on the moon-faced one nectar rained on his eyes and he held her in his arms. With Krishna's touch, her restless eyes became still and this gave away her pleasure. While she was resisting Krishna with words her eyes were conveying the opposite message. [369]

दोहा

प्रीतम को मनभावती मिलति बाँह दै कंठ ।
बाहीं छूटै न कंठ तैं, नाहीं छूटै न कंठ ।।३७०।।

The *nayika* put her arms around the *nayak*'s neck. When the *nayak* advanced towards her, she said no despite her firm embrace. [370]

बिब्बोक हाव लक्षण

जो पिय को, अभिमान तैं, करै अनादर बाम ।
ताहि कहत बिब्बोक हैं, जे प्रबीन गुण धाम ।।३७१।।

Bibboka hava is a state where the *nayika* insults the *nayak*. [371]

उदाहरण

मानहु आयो है राज कछू
चढ़ि बैठे हो ऐसै पलास के खोढ़े;
गूँज गरे सिर-मोर पखा
'मतिराम' हों गाय चरावत चोढ़े।
मोतिन को मेरो तोरयौ हरा,
गहि हाथन सों रहे चूनरी पोढ़े;
ऐसें ही डोलत छैल भए
तुम्हें लाज न आवत कामरी ओढ़े ।।३७२।।

A *nayika* speaks to a *nayak* : The way you have secured a place on the tree it seems as if you are like a king. With a necklace of *gunja* seeds and a peacock feather crown on your head, you tend cattles with great pleasure. Do you not feel bashful the way you cover yourself with black garment and dance? You broke my pearl necklace and tore my *odhni*. [372]

दोहा

प्रान पियारो पग परयौ, तू न तकत यहि ओर ।
ऐसो उर जु कठोर तौ न्यायहि उरज कठोर ।।३७३।।

A *sakhi* speaks to a *nayika* :

O *sakhi* ! Your beloved prostrates before you yet you have not recognised him. Your heart is so hard that it is but natural that your breasts are hard too. [373]

ललित हाव लक्षण

बनै बानिकन सौं सरस सकल आभरन अंग।
ललितहाव तासौं कहैं जे कबि बुद्धि उतंग।।३७४।।

Lalit hava is a state when the *nayika* adorns herself profusely with clothes and ornaments. [374]

उदाहरण (सवैया)

मंद गयंद की चाल चलै कटि किंकिन नेवर की धुनि बाजै।
मोती के हारनि सौं हियरो हरिजू के बिलास हुलासनि साजै।
सारी सुही मतिराम लसै मुख संग किनारी की यौं छबि छाजै।
पूरन चंद पियूष मयूष मनौ परबेष की रेख बिराजै।।३७५।।

When the *nayika* walks, the bells on her anklets and waistband jingle and it looks as if an intoxicated elephant is walking. The pearl necklace on her chest causes Krishna to love her even more. She has worn a blue *sari* and the border covers her face and it seems as if nectar has outlined the moon. [375]

दोहा

बिरी अधर अंजन नयन मिहँदी पग अरु पानि।
तनु कंचन के आभरन नीठि परत पहिचानि।।३७६।।

The *nayika*'s mouth is full of betel, her yes are full of corrylium, henna on her hands and feet, and golden ornaments on her body. With all these adornments, it is hard to believe that she is a village girl. [376]

विहित हाव लक्षण

जो परिपूरन होत नहिँ पिय समीप अभिलाख।
ताकौं बिहित बखानहीं जिनकी कबिता दाख।।३७७।।

Vihit hava is a state when the *nayika* fails to be united physically with the *nayak* despite being near him. [377]

उदाहरण (कवित्त)

सकल सहेलिन के पीछे पीछे डोलति है
मंद मंद गौनु आजु हिय को हरत है।
संमुख होत मतिराम सुख होत जबै
पौन लागे घूँघट को पट उघरत है।
कालिंदी के तट बंसीबट के निकट
नंदलाल कौं सकोचन तैं चाह्यो न परत है।
तनु तो तिया को बर भाँवरे भरत मनु
सामरे बदन पर भाँवरै भरत है।।३७८।।

The *nayika* was walking behind her *sakhis* and her intoxicated gait was captivating. When the wind blows her *odhni* away her face looks even more beautiful. When she reaches the bank of the Yamuna she wanted to see Krishna, but modesty prevented her from doing this. In this state, she was going round and round but her mind was circumambulating Krishna. [378]

दोहा

रूप साँवरो साँचु है सुधासिंधु मैं खेल।
लखि न सकैं अँखियाँ सखी परी लाज की जेल।।३७९।।

Krishna's dusky appearance is like a sea of nectar. The *nayika* is unable to see him fully as she is imprisoned by her shyness. [379]

वियोग शृंगार

प्यारी पीव मिलाप बिनु होत नहीँ आनंद।
सो बियोगशृंगार कहि बरनत सब कबिबृंद।।३८०।।

When there is sadness on account of the separation of the *nayak* and the *nayika*, it is called *viyog shringara*. Love in separation is when the lover and the beloved unhappy because they are not together. [380]

वियोग शृंगार भेद

कहि पूरब अनुराग अरु मान प्रबास बिचारि।
रस सिँगार बियोग के तीन भेद निरधारि।।३८१।।

There are three divisions of *viyoga sringara*, i.e. *purvanurag, mana* and *pravasa*. [381]

पूर्वानुराग लक्षण

जो प्रथमहिँ देखे सुने बढ़ै प्रेम की लाग।
बिन मिलाप जो बिकलता सो पूरब अनुराग।।३८२।।

Purvanurag is the state of love at first sight. [382]

उदाहरण

न्योते गए कहुँ नेह बढ्यौ 'मतिराम' दुहूँ के लगे दृग गाढ़े।
ऊँचे अटा पर काँधे सहेली के ठोढ़ी दिए चितेवैं दुख बाढ़े।
लाल चने सुनि कैं गृह कौ, तिय-अंग अनंग की आगि सौं डाढ़े।
मोहनजू मन गाढ़ो करैं,
पग द्वैक चलैं फिर होत हैं ठाढ़े।।३८३।।

The *nayak* and the *nayika* were invited to someone's home. At that place, their eyes met and they fell in love at first sight. The *nayika* then stepped on a high platform and started to look at the *nayak* who was in the garden and was preparing to leave.

The *nayika*, had tears in her eyes and she was saddened and her body developed a fever. The *nayak* was stepping forward but stood there hoping to catch a glimpse of the *nayika*. [383]

दोहा

निरखो नेह दुहून की दई नई यह बात।
सूखति देँह दुहूँन की त्यों पानिप सरसात।।३८४।।

The love of these two is a bit different. Their bodies seem to be wasting away but the glow of their bodies increases. [384]

मान वर्णन

मान कहत हैं तीनि बिधि लघु मध्यम गुरु नाम।
तिनके भेद बनायकै बरने कबि मतिराम।।३८५।।

There are three types of sulking: little, middling and large. These are being explained here. [385]

लघुमान लक्षण

और बाल कौं लखत जहँ, लखै कंत कौं बाल ।
बरनत हैं लघुमान सो छूटत तनकहि ख्याल ।।३८६।।

When a *nayika* who catches the *nayak* looking at another woman and is offended it is called *laghu mana*. [386]

उदाहरण (सवैया)

देखत और तियाहि छबीले कौं मान छबीली के नैनन छायो।
प्रीतम यों चतुराई करी मतिराम कछू परिहास बढ़ायो।
रीति रची बिपरीति जु प्रीति सौं ताको कवित्त बनाय सुनायो।
भूलि गई रिस लाजन तैं
मुसकाय पिया मुख नीचे कौं नायो ।।३८७।।

When the *nayika* saw the *nayak* looking at another woman, her eyes were filled with anger and the *nayak* said something in jest. He recited a line from poetry describing reverse love-making. Hearing this, the *nayika* forgot her anger and hung her head in shame. [387]

दोहा

मानु जनावति सबनि कौं मन न मान को ठाट।
बाल मनावन कौं लखे लाल तिहारि बाट।।३८८।।

A *sakhi* speaks to a *nayak*. O *nayak* ! The *nayika* is not angry. She is just waiting to be won over by you. [388]

मध्यम मान लक्षण

पिय मुख औरहि नारि को सुनै नाँव जब नारि।
होत मान मध्यम तहाँ बरनत सुकबि बिचारि।।३८९।।

Madhyama mana is a state where the *nayika* hears the name of another woman and gets angry. [389]

उदाहरण (सवैया)

दोऊ अनंद सौं आँगन माँझ
बिराजैं असाढ़ की साँझ सुहाई।
प्यारी को बूझत और तिया को
अचानक नाउँ लियो रसिकाई।
आयौ उनै मुँह मैं हँसी
कोपि प्रिया सुरचाप सी भौंह चढ़ाई।
आँखिन तैं गिरे आँसू के बूँद
सुहासु गयो उड़ि हंस की नाई।।३९०।।

It was the month of Ashadha and the *nayak* and the *nayika* were sitting in the courtyard enjoying each other's company. During the conversation the *nayak* spoke the name of another woman. When he realised his mistake the *nayak* smiled and said that he was speaking in jest, but the *nayika* got angry and then like the taut bow-string, her face became cross. She was also saddened and tears rolled down her eyes and the smile on her face flew away like a swan. [390]

दोहा

भई देवता भाव बस वह तुमकौं बलि जाउँ।
वाही को मन ध्यान है वाही को मुख नाउँ।।३९१।।

The *nayika* is offended and the *nayak* is worried that he might lose her. Looking at this, the *sakhi* speaks to the *nayak*. O Krishna ! I surrender myself to you. I do understand that a *gopika* has made a god-like image in your heart. That is why you always remember her and recite her name. [391]

गुरुमान लक्षण

बोलत और तियान सौं पिय कौं देखै बाम।
होत तहाँ गुरुमान, सो बरनत कबि 'मतिराम'।।३९२।।

When a *nayika* who finds the *nayak* talking to another woman and is offended. [392]

उदाहरण

तेरे प्रान्प्यारे कहूँ सहज सुभाय प्यारी !
कहा भौ कहीं जो कछू बात काहू बाल सौं;
ताको ऐतो रिस है अयानिन की रीति तू तौ,
दीप की-सी जोति जगे जोबन रसाल सौं।
कबि 'मतिराम' मेरो कह्यौ उर आनि आली !
ठान जिन मान ऐसे मदनगुपाल सौं;
भौंहैं करि सूधी बिहसौंहैं कै कपोल नैंक,
सौंहैं करि लौचन रसौहैं नंदलाल सौं ।।३९३।।

O *sakhi* ! You have been offended just because your beloved spoke to another woman. This is the way ignorant people behave. You are youthful and full of love and the lamp of your affection burns brightly. (Your beloved will not be attracted to anyone else). Listen to me and do not be offended with Madangopal. [393]

बहु नायक सौं बात मैं मानु भलो न सयानु ।
दुख-सागर मैं बूड़िहै, बाँधि गरे गुरु मानु ।।३९४।।

A *sakhi* speaks to a *nayika* :
O *sakhi* ! You should not stay offended with your beloved and if you continue to be indifferent to him, you will enter a sea of sorrow. If you keep getting offended with trivial matters then your beloved might get offended too. [394]

प्रवास लक्षण

पीतमबसेबिदेसमैं बिरहजहाँ सरसाय।
बरनततहाँ प्रवासकहि जेप्रबीनकबिराय।।३९५।।

Pravasa is the state when the state of longing increases when the *nayak* is away. [395]

सवैया

धुरवानि की धावनि मानो अनंग की
तुंग धुजा फहरान लगी।
नभमंडल ह्वै छितिमंडल छवै
छनदा की छटा छहरान लगी।
मतिराम समीर लगै लतिका
बिरही बनिता थहरान लगी।
परदेस मैं पीव सँदेस न पायो
प्योद्घटा घहरान लगी।।३९६।।

Low-lying clouds were moving around and it appeared as if Kama was flying his banner. Lightning shone, joining the sky with the earth. Matiram says with the wind both the lonely *nayika* and the creeper begin to shake. The beloved is abroad and there is no news from him and the clouds are thundering. [396]

दोहा

चलत लाल के मैं कियो सजनी हियो पखान।
कहा करौं दरकत नहीं इतैं बियोग कृसान।।३९७।।

A *nayika* speaks to her *sakhi*. When my beloved left on a journey, I made my heart as hard as stone that is why it did not wilt in the fire of separation. [397]

नव दशा वर्णन

होत वियोग सिँगार मैं प्रगट दसा नव जानि।
प्रथम कहै अभिलाष पुनि चिंता समृति बखानि।।३९८।।
गुनबर्नन उदबेग पुनि कहि प्रलाप उन्माद।
ब्याधि बहुरि जड़ता कहत कबि कोबिद अबिबाद।।३९९।।

Separation leads to nine mental states, desire (*abhilasha*), anxiety (*chinta*), remembrance (*smriti*), praise (*gunavarnana*), anguish (*udvega*), gossip (*pralapa*) intoxication (*unmada*), fever (*vyadhi*) and stupor (*jadata*). [398, 399]

अभिलाष लक्षण

ताहि कहत अभिलाष हैं जो मिलाप की चाह।
प्रेम कथन तैं जानिये बरनत सब कबिनाह।।४००।।

Abhilash is a state when there is a desire of meeting but they are separated. [400]

उदाहरण (सवैया)

मोरपखा मतिराम किरीट
मनोहर मूरति सौं मनु लैगो।
कुंडल डोलनि गोल कपोलनि
बोल सनेह के बीज से बैगो।
लोल बिलोचनि कौलनि सौं
मुसकाइ इतैं अरुझाइ चितैगो।
एक घरी घन से तन सौं
अँखियान घनौं घनसार सौं दैगो।।४०१।।

With a crown of peacock feathers Krishna showed his charming face and stole my mind. With the movements of his earrings, his chubby cheeks and his speech he has planted a seed in my mind. Looking at me with his lotus eyes and smile, he has left my mind rattled. I saw him only for an instant but it is as if he threw camphor in my eyes. [401]

दोहा

मो मन सुक लौं उड़ि गयो, अब क्यों हूँ न पत्याय।
बसि मोहन बनमाल मैं रह्यो बनाउ बनाय।।४०२।।

O *sakhi*! My mind is not under my control. Like the parrot, it has flown away from my body as it wants to make its home in Krishna's garland. [402]

चिंता लक्षण

दरसन सुख की भावना करे चित्त की चाह।
चिंता तासौं कहत हैं जे प्रबीन रस-नाह।।४०३।।

Chinta is a state when a *nayika* worries about meeting her beloved. [403]

उदाहरण

जैयै अकेली महाबन बीच
तहाँ 'मतिराम' अकेलोई आवै;
आपने आनन चंद की चाँदनी
सो पहिलै तन-ताप बुझावै।
कूल कंलिदी के कुंजन मंजुल
मीठे अमोल वै बोल सुनावै;
ज्यौं हँसि हेरि लियो हियरो हरि,
त्यौं हँसिकै हियरे हरि लावै।। ४०४।।

I wish to go alone to the forest and Krishna will come there too. First, he will cool the heat of my body with the cool moonshine of his face and then we will sit on the bank of the Yamuna and will exchange sweet words. And then he will embrace me close to his heart. [404]

दोहा

काजु कहा कुलकानि सौं लोक लाज किन जाय।
कुंजबिहारी कुंज मैं कहूँ मिलै मुसकाय।।४०५।।

O *sakhi*! What do I care about the honour of my family? I do not care if people censure me. All I want is to meet Krishna with a smile on his face at the bower. [405]

स्मृति लक्षण

लखी-सुनी पिय बात को, जो सुमरन मन होय।
स्मृति तासौं कबि कहत हैं, सब रसग्रंथ बिलोय।।४०६।।

Smriti is a state when one remembers the words or the face of the beloved. [406]

उदाहरण

आलस बलित कोरे काजर कलित,
'मतिराम' वे ललित बहु पानिप धरत हैं;
सारस सरस सोहैं सलज सहास सगरब,
सबिलास ह्वै मृगनि निदरत हैं।
वरुनी सघन बंक तीच्छन तरल बड़े,
लोचन कटाच्छ उर पीर ही करत हैं;
गाढ़े ह्वै गड़े हैं न निसारे निसरत मैन-
बान-से बिसारे, न बिसारे बिसरत हैं।।४०७।।

A *virahini* Radha describes to her *sakhi* the qualities of Krishna's eyes. "O dear Sakhi! His [Krishna's] kohl-smeared and languid eyes are most attractive. These lotus-like pinkish and bashful eyes are so beautiful that even antelopes feel ashamed on seeing them. The glances of these sharp, elongated, limpid and large eyes cause great pain in one's heart. Once these eyes get embedded in the very core of one's heart, they remain there forever. Like the arrows of Kamadeva, the pain caused by these eyes cannot be forgotten." [407]

दोहा

सोभा सो रति सुंदरी, नव सनेह सौं बाम।
तन बूड़त रँग पीत मैं, मन बूड़त रँग स्याम।।४०८।।

That *nayika* who is more beautiful than Rati has just experienced love. She has now been entangled with Krishna. Physically she is attached to her husband, but emotionally she is devoted to Krishna. [408]

गुणवर्णन लक्षण

बिरह बीच जो पीव की सुंदरतादि सराह।
गुनबर्नन तासौं कहैं जो प्रबीन कबिनाह।।४०९।।

Guna varnan is the state where you praise the *nayika* to assuage the pain of separation from him. [409]

उदाहरण (सवैया)

मोरपखा मतिराम किरीट मैं
कंठ बनी बनमाल सुहाई।
मोहन की मुसकानि मनोहर
कुंडल डोलनि मैं छबि छाई।
लोचन लोल बिसाल बिलोकनि
को न बिलोकि भयो बस माई।
वा मुख की मधुराई कहा
कहौं मीठी लगै अँखियान लुनाई।।४१०।।

Krishna's feather crown and his garland of forest flowers are very beautiful. His captivating smile and the movement of his earrings add to his beauty. When he looks here and there with his large eyes who would not fall a victim? And what to talk of his sweet speech? All I say is that his salty eyes look sweet. [410]

दोहा

सरद चंद की चाँदनी
जारि डारि किनि मोहि।
वा मुख की मुसकानि सम
क्यौंहूँ कहौं न तोहि।।४११।।

A *virahini nayika* looks at the moon of Kartik and says to the moon, "even if the moonlight burns me I will never tell you about the beauty of Krishna. You are nothing compared to his smile." [411]

उद्वेग लक्षण

बिरहबिथा की बिकलता जहाँ कछू न सुहाय।
ताहि कहत उदबेग हैं जे प्रबीन कबिराय।।४१२।।

Udveg is the state where nothing pleases one in the despair of separation. [412]

उदाहरण (सवैया)

चाहि तुम्हैं मतिराम रसाल
परी तिय के तनमैं पियराई।
काम के तीछन तीरन सौं
भरि भीर तुनीर भयो हियराई।
तेरे बिलोकिबे कौं उतकंठित
कंठ लौं आय रह्यौ जियराई।
नैक परे न मनोज के औजनि
सेज सरोजनि मैं सियराई।।४१३।।

O *nayak*, after falling in love with you the *nayika*'s body has turned pale. Her heart has been wounded by the arrows of Kama. Now, in her desire to see you her heart has come into her throat. Her body burns with the fire of separation and even a bed of lotuses will not cool it. [413]

दोहा

जे अंगनि पियसंग मैं बरसत हुते पियूख।
ते बीछू के डंक से भए मयंक-मयूख।।४१४।।

When my beloved was with me, a moonlight on my body felt like nectar. Now that he is away that same moonlight is like the bite of a scorpion. [414]

प्रलाप लक्षण

उतकंठा ते कहत हैं जहाँ मोहमय बैन।
बरनत तहाँ प्रलाप हैं जे प्रबीन रस ऐन।।४१५।।

Words spoken in separation from the beloved is called *pralap*. [415]

कवित्त

कहियो सँदेसो प्रानप्यारी को गमन कीनो
बिक्रम बिलास जे वे आपने परस के।
चंदकर बरछीन छेदि छेदि हार्‌यौ तीर
तीछन मनोज के कछुक करि न सके।
कबि मतिराम ये कुलिस कैसे घाय क्यौंहू
गनत न कोकिल की कूकन के कसके।
कैसे दरकतु मेरो उर सदा सहि रह्यौ
तेरे कुच निपट कठोरनि के मसके ।।४१६।।

The separated and lovelorn *nayak* sends a message through a messenger to his beloved that the tender marks she had made on his person have vanished. Eventually the moon with its spear-like sharp beams failed to pierce his heart. The same was the fate of Cupid's arrows. Even the heart rending cry of the cuckoo could not harm me. How could my heart not be effected by all these, as it was accustomed by embracing your hard and firm breasts? [416]

दोहा

बिकल लाल कौं बाल तू क्यौं न बिलोकति आनि।
बोलि कोकिलनि सौं कहै बोल तिहारे जानि।।४१७।।

A *sakhi* speaks to the *nayika* : O *sakhi* ! Krishna is very distressed because of being separated from you. When a cuckoo sings he begins to talk to it. It is such a strange state of that love-lorn *nayak*. [417]

उन्माद लक्षण

उतकंठा तैं मोहमय वृथा करत कछु काज।
ताहि कहत उन्माद हैं कबि कोबिद सिरताज।।४१८।।

Unmad is a state when on account of her longing for her beloved, she performs unrelated activities. [418]

उदाहरण (सवैया)

जा छिन तैं मतिराम कहै
मुसकात कहूँ निरख्यौ नँदलालहि।
ता छिन तैं छिन ही छिन छीन
बिथा बहु बाढ़ी बियोग की बालहि।
पोछति है कर सौं किसलै गहि
बूझति स्याम सरीर गुपालहि।
भोरी भई है मयंकमुखी भुज
भेटति है भरि अंक तमालहि।।४१९।।

Since the day the *nayika* saw Krishna smiling she is wasting away and she is in a state of longing. She picks tender leaves and taking them as the body of Krishna, wipes the dust from them. She is so distraught that she embraces even the *tamal* tree considering it as Krishna. [419]

दोहा

रोय उठै छिन हँसि उठै छिन उठि चलै रिसाय।
बौरी करी बनायकै रूप ठगौरी लाय।।४२०।।

A *sakhi* speaks to Krishna : O Krishna ! My friend cries then smiles and then sulks and walks away. You have used your beautiful form to cast a spell on her and made her insane. [420]

व्याधि लक्षण

काम पीर तैं पियरई, ताप दूबरी होय ।
तासौं ब्याधि बखानहीं कबि-कोबिद सब कोय ।।४२१।।

A *sakhi* speaks to Krishna: O Krishna ! The *nayika* has wasted away on account of being separated from you and when she lies on the bed, one cannot see her. It is only on account of her burning body that one knows that she is there. [421]

उदाहरण

वरषा-सी लागी निसि बासर बिलोचननि,
बाढ़ो परबाह भयो नावनि उतरिबौ;
सहौ जान कौन पै सुकबि 'मतिराम' अति,
बिरह अनल ज्वाल जालन ते जरिबौ ।
जैयतु समीप तो उडैयत उसासनि सौं,
हमकौं तौ होतु उत हेरत हहरिबौ;
कियौ कहा चाहत सु करो न कुँवर कान्ह,
रह्यौ अब वाको उपचारनि को करिबौ ।।४२२।।

A *sakhi* describes the longing of the *nayika* : O Krishna ! There is a stream of tears in her eyes all day and night. The rain of tears is so much that the only way to go to her is to take a boat. Who can suffer the heat of her longing? When we go close to her we hear her sighing breaths and it seems as if we would be blown away by it. We do not know what to do and only you can cure her. [422]

दोहा

देखि परै नहिं दूबरी सुनियो स्याम सुजान।
जान परै परजंक मैं अंग आँच अनुमान।।४२३।।

A *sakhi* speaks to a *nayak* :
O Krishna ! You are a reasonable person. You should listen to the *nayika*'s sad story and try and understand her situation. That *nayika* has become so feeble on account of being separated from you that even though she is lying on the bed, one cannot see her. The only indication that she is alive comes from the heat of her body on account of longing. [423]

जड़ता लक्षण

उतकंठादिक तैं जु हवै अचल चित्त अरु अंग।
तासौं जड़ता कहत हैं कबि कोबिद रसरंग।।४२४।।

Jadata is the state of being frozen because of longing. [424]

उदाहरण कवित्त

सूँघै न सुबास रहै राग रंग तैं उदास
भूलि गई सुरति सकल खान पान की।
कबि मतिराम इकटक अनमिष नैन
बूझै न कहति बात समुझै न आन की।

थोरी सी हँसनि में ठगोरी तैने डारी स्याम
बौरी कीनी गोरी तैं किसोरी बृषभान की।
तब तैं बिहारी वह भई है पखान की सी
जब मैं निहारी रुचि मोर के पखान की।।४२५।।

O Krishna ! with just a smile, what magic have you done on Radha? She is beside herself. She cares neither for fragrance nor taste. She looks blank without moving her eyelids, does not respond to questions, nor does she listen to anyone. Ever since she has seen your peacock crown she has become frozen like a stone. [425]

दोहा

अनमिष लोचन बाल के यातैं नंदकुमार।
मीच गई जरि बीच ही बिरहानल की झार।।४२६।।

O Krishna ! the eyes of the *nayika* are frozen and a stream of tears flows. If she is living, it is due to the tears that extinguish the fire of separation. [426]

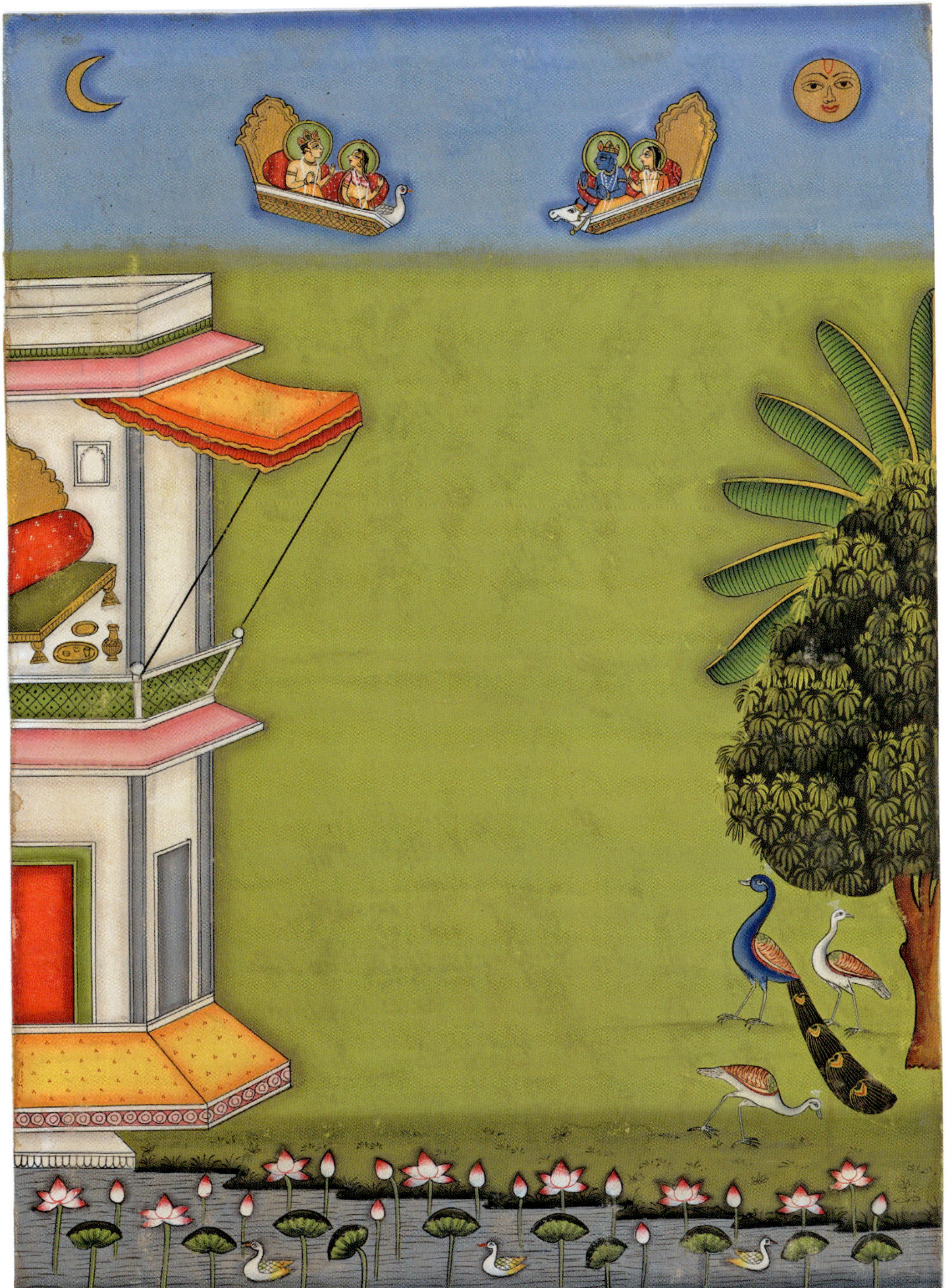

Painting by Trilok Soni

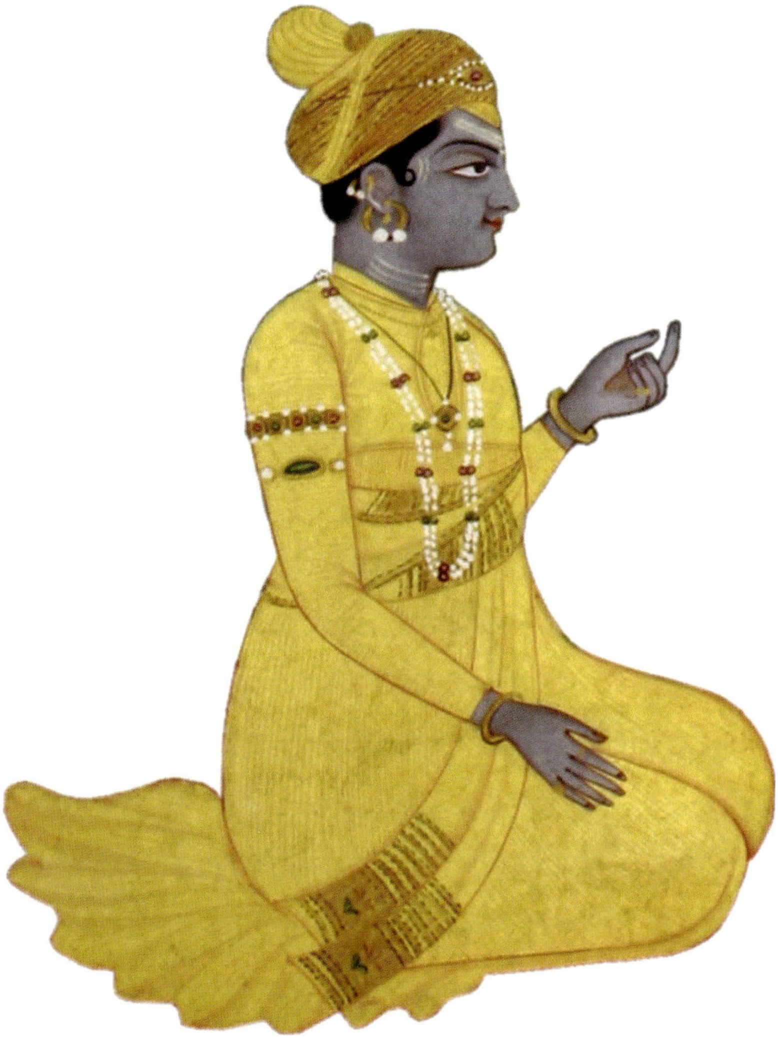

The Poetics of Ritikavya

Four periods in the history of Indian poetry are generally recognised: *adikal* (ancient period), *bhaktikal* (devotional period), *ritikal* (mannered period) and *adhunikkal* (modern period). These are like four streams of poetry, deriving their inspiration and strength from the same source, but meandering through different terrains, intersecting at times, running parallel at others and taking off in its own independent direction at others, but never losing its moorings in the roots of Indian civilisation and especially its literary traditions and culture. Of these four genres *bhaktikal* and *ritikal* are closely associated, as they must, as *shringara* for the Indian mind encompasses both romance and devotion. It has been rightly said that socio-historical conditions have a direct bearing on the arts, and this is true of romantic literature, as it is of other arts and probably even Indian thought. The *bhakti* movement of medieval India was directly related to the climate of psychological insecurity and lack of certainty for the Hindus, vulnerable as they were to the tension and aggression of the waves of multiple Muslim invasions. The Vaishnava *bhakti* cult, and that of Krishna in particular, was a direct result of this, as Krishna *bhaktas* sought refuge both in personal and private worship as well as communal veneration of Krishna in secure spaces and away from menacing eyes.

The origin and the evolution of *ritikal*, its language and poetry and its transformation into miniature painting, is closely tied to the culture of Braj and in particular to the history, sociology and politics and above all to its aesthetics of Brajbhasha. Braj has a very ancient history and on its soil many religious traditions have thrived. The Puranas identify Braj as the site of Krishna's earthly incarnation. But it was during the early decades of the sixteenth century, which was a time of devotional Vaishnavism of the *bhakti* movement, that it became home to Krishna *bhakti,* and the cult of Krishna got intimately tied with Braj. Vallabha (1479-1531) and Chaitanya (1486-1533), two contemporary Vaishnava theologians, located Krishna's *lila* in Braj's geography and thus it is that the Braj country sees an admixture of both Pushtimarg and Gaudiya Vaishnavism. With the advent of Mughal rule, and especially during the reign of Akbar, Jahangir and Shah Jahan, Muslim invasions and harassment had come to an end, there was political stability in north India and the Hindu mind was greatly assuaged and ready for the evocation and celebration of their *ishtadevatas,* and the Krishna culture of Braj thrived in the stable and tolerant political environment of that time. It has been correctly commented that the combination of a Muslim-dominated political structure with a largely Hindu populace fostered a cultural symbiosis which was richly productive in the interconnected realms of music, art and literature. One of Akbar's courtiers was Abdurrahim Khankhana, also known as Rahim. He was a Krishna *bhakta* and a noted *ritikal* poet. Another Muslim who was a Pathan and who converted to the Vallabha *sampradaya* was Raskhan, who also wrote beautiful *ritikal* poetry.

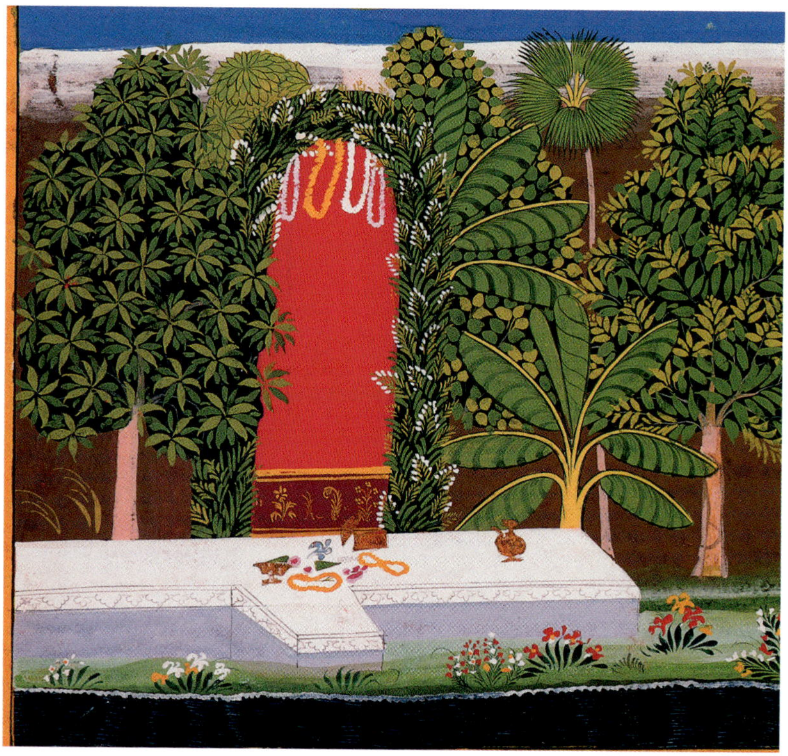

Brajbhasha, or the language of the Braj country, is probably a descendant of the Middle Indo-Aryan Apabhramsha and drew from Sanskrit, Prakrit, Persian and Arabic sources. In particular, it borrowed from the vocabulary of *barahmasa* folk songs in local dialects which featured the lament of the woman in love who was separated from her beloved. It was also influenced by the *bija mantras* of the Ragamala literature. While Awadhi was to produce epic poetry like the *Ramcharitmanas* and the *Padmavat*, Brajbhasha remained confined to *muktak kavya* (fragmentary poetry), and took mainly three forms: *bhakti* (devotional), *niti* (moral and ethical) and *shringara* (romantic). The most common format of poetry in Brajbhasha was the *pada,* a metrically simple song composed in rhyming couplets. These were transmitted orally, and by the time they were written by and it is not inconceivable that miniature artists were privy to these and created a painting based on a *pada* they had heard and not seen in its written form. Brajbhasha *padas* took many forms and among them are: the *nakh-shikh varnan* (the description of the romantic heroine from tresses to the toes), *solah shringara* (the adornment of the *nayika* with the sixteen traditional adornments), *shad ritu varnan* and *barahmasa* in which *viraha* lamentations are set against the changing seasons and then perhaps the most important genre of *ritikal kavya*, namely *nayika bhed*, which portrayed the many different hues and textures and the many situations of the woman in love.

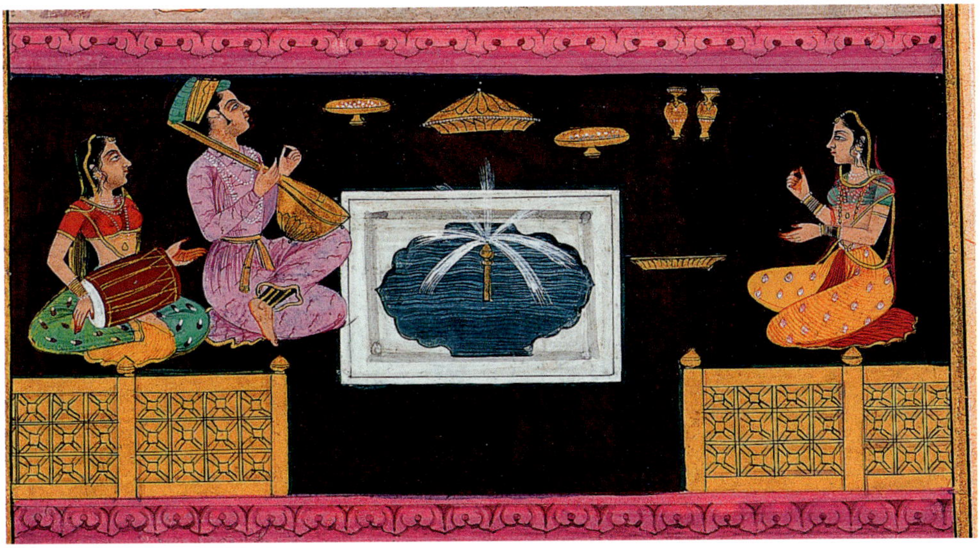

scribes there was an element of corruption in the written *pada*, and when these were used by visual artists there was room for further mistakes. This could account for some disparities between the inscriptions and the paintings of *ritikavya*. While some paintings have inscriptions written on the front or the back, other paintings must have been created through the inspiration these *padas* provided to the artists and may not have written inscriptions on them. The *padas* were sung by people in homes and *havelis*, fairs and bazaars, Brajbhasha has a musical texture, its consonants are soft and its words have many vowels, and this is why its best form is a song and not a written text and further this made it the perfect language for romantic poetry. It has been rightly been said that Brajbhasha poets wove a garland of flowers with its words and kept it fragrant with the silken threads of metre and texture. The romance that Braj poetry portrays is courtly and not pastoral, its concerns are the many nuances and situations of romantic love at the human level, a love that is earthy and not celestial, it is concerned with matters of the heart and not of the state, it is driven by heart-throbbing emotion and not religious dictates or moralising ethics. It is worth stressing Prof. Ramananda's words that *ritikavya* is concerned with *lokranjan* (human pleasure) and not *lokmangal* (human emancipation). However, at the same time, even though the *nayak* and *nayika* are courtly and secular figures, the images of Krishna and Radha are always in the background and *ritikavya* operates at least two levels simultaneously. The beauty and the strength of *ritikavya* is that it moves effortlessly and fluidly between the secular and the sacred, from courtly to devotional, from sensuous to spiritual and all this because and through the persona of Krishna, who is now a human and now a god.

While devotional poetry in Braj touched Gujarat, Maharashtra and Bengal, *shringara* poetry in Brajbhasha reached even non-Hindi speaking areas like Punjab and Rajasthan and this is a contribution and strength of *ritikavya.* It is worth noting that towns like Nabha, Patiala, Lahore and Suketmandi were home to poets like Gwal, Chandrashekhar Vajpeyi and Navin. *Padas* in Brajbhasha blended with music and were incorporated as *bandishes* in *chhota khayal* and *thumris* and this further strengthened its aural presence, and songs in Brajbhasha became a living and performing art, and ensured that *shringara rasa* resonated with the *raja* and the *praja* and in homes and *havelis* alike. Brajbhasha became the preferred language, not just for the performing arts like music and dance, but inspired artists to create visual poetry through their paintings.

Ancient India had produced *shringara rasa kavya,* initially in Prakrit and Tamil and then in Sanskrit. Hala's *Saptashati*, Bhartrhari's *Shrigara-Trayi*, Amaru's *Shringara-Shataka* and the *Aham* poetry in Tamil had shown that ancient Indian poets were well accomplished in the literary arts of romantic poetry. In medieval India, romantic poetry as an offshoot of *bhakti* poetry, was to emerge once again in Rajput courts and *havelis* and this was to occur through Brajbhasha and it was because of this that Brajbhasha acquired the status of a major literary language and became the vehicle of Krishna's *shringara rasa.* Brajbhasha could bridge both *riti* and *bhakti,* and although this was in large measure due to the personae of Krishna, but it was also helped by the nature of the language, its sounds and rhythms, a language that not only had the rhetoric of *bhakti* but the sensuality of *riti* at the same time. Thus, it was the perfect vehicle for *shringara rasa.* Both the language and the sociology of Braj were to come together in the celebration of the romantic and courtly Krishna from the seventeenth to the nineteenth centuries in *ritikavya* in Brajbhasha. Music and dance that flourished in these courts was also to add to the ambience of the representation and enjoyment of *shringara rasa,* and in this Brajbhasha was also to play an important part, as *khayal bandishes* were also composed in Brajbhasha. It is well known that romantic arts thrive in a settled environment, in an ambience of peace and prosperity, when life is secure and religious beliefs are not threatened, and there is leisure and opportunity to entertain matters of the heart rather than attend to conflicts of the state. This was the heyday of *ritikavya* and *khayal bandishes* in Brajbhasha, where under the umbrella of Krishna *bhakti, riti*, *shringara* could flourish at the same time in poetry, dance and music, and all this was to translate into miniature painting in the ateliers of Rajput courts. It was Brajbhasha that was to seamlessly bring these arts together and weave them into a tapestry of love.

Ancient Sanskrit, Prakrit and Tamil poetry had provided the models for expressing the romantic sentiment in small and fragmentary verses and Brajbhasha was to inherit its motifs and metaphors but then go on to inaugurate a new genre of romantic poetry by creating new situations and metaphors of *shringara rasa.* In using many of the well-worn motifs and metaphors of love, but moving away from the strict dictates of classical Sanskrit poetry, *ritikal* poets by using Brajbhasha were attaching themselves to the ancient Indian *parampara* of *shringara rasa kavya*, and signalling that *shringara rasa* was indeed ancient and that it had a distinctly Indian texture, but furthermore the celebration of *shringara rasa* through its depiction of moments of romantic love in the *bhashas* had a place in the lived lives of people. Brajbhasha could touch people at all levels as it was the language of the people and not of courtly and philosophic discourse.

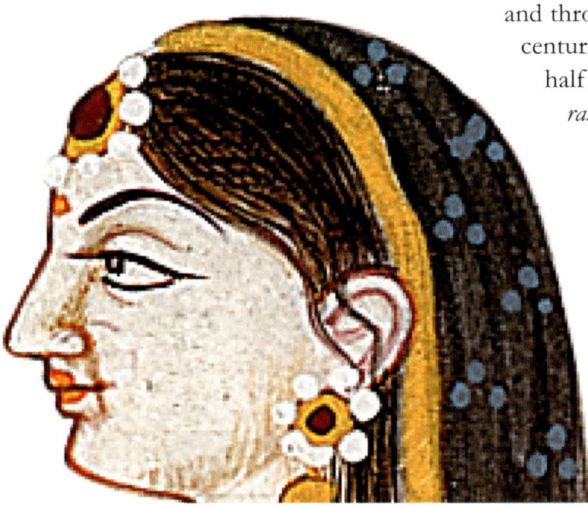

It was in the *dashama skandha* of the *Bhagavata Purana* that the *shringara rasa* of Krishna and the *gopis* was given a textual presence. The *gopis*, who are the romantic heroines of the *Bhagavata* and who engage in deeply moving romantic relationships with Krishna in the idyllic Vrindavana, were transformed in a couple of hundred years into Radha by Jayadeva in the *Gita-Govinda*. And at the same time, the pastoral Krishna with his *lilas* and *kridas* underwent a transformation from divinity to humanity as Jayadeva humanised Krishna. This was the first major shift in *shringara rasa kavya* in the post-*Bhagavata* period in ancient India. From the generic and universal *gopis* of the *Bhagavata* we now had a specific heroine (*nayika*) namely Radha in a romantic relationship with Krishna. This was to bring in a major shift in the texture of *shringara rasa kavya* and its representations in painting. Once Radha became the central *nayika* in the *shringara rasa* of Krishna, *harishringara* (the love of Krishna) for the *gopis* could be transformed into *ratishringara rasa* (romantic love) between a *nayak* and a *nayika*. This was the backdrop upon which *ritikavya* developed as the pastoral Krishna became a courtly Krishna.

Towards the end of the sixteenth century and throughout the seventeenth/ eighteenth centuries, roughly the period of two and a half centuries from 1591 to 1830, *shringara rasa kavyas* were to take a different turn, particularly in the genre of *kavyas* in the *bhashas*. I have chosen 1591 as the landmark date for *ritikavya*, for that is the date of Keshavdas' *Rasikapriya* which is undoubtedly the foundational text of *ritikavya*. Kriparam (1541), Nanda Das (1559) and Rahim (1583) were precursors of Keshvadas and some would include them as forerunners of *ritikavya* but Keshavdas should be given pride of place as the father of the *ritikavya*. While the *Bhagavata*, the *Gita-Govinda* and the rich treasure of poetic creations by the *ashtachhap kavis* like Surdas of the Nathadvara *pushtimarg* tradition, remained the bedrock of the celebration of the *harishringara* or the evocation of the romantic Krishna of Vrindavana, and in this the *shringara bhakti* of Krishna was the primary driving emotion of this poetry, we saw the emergence of *ritikavya* and courtly poetry of *shringara rasa* in the eighteenth/nineteenth centuries, and with it came the genre of *nayak-nayika bhed* (the myriad taxonomies of the romantic hero and heroine), their many moods and manipulations, their persona and psyche, and this was to dominate the ateliers of the Rajput courts in Rajasthan, central India and the Punjab Hills, and colour the way we enjoyed and celebrated the love of Krishna, not only through poetry, but equally through painting. Krishna during this period indeed remains the romantic hero or the central *nayak,* but he is portrayed as a courtly figure, while Radha as the urbane and sophisticated *nayika* takes on many different colours and forms, as she continues her romantic relationship with Krishna in a courtly setting. The courtly Krishna in *ritikavya* is seen as more human than divine, more regal than pastoral, his behaviour and graces are those of a prince was nurtured through martial conflicts, but when he was not at war, the Rajput wanted to celebrate his own Vaishnava identity, and this he did by upholding the romantic Krishna of Vallabhacharya's *pushtimarg sampradaya.* This assertion was not only through religious rituals but equally by aesthetic rejuvenation through song, dance and painting. In the earlier centuries the Sultans of Delhi, as they were called, and later the Mughals, had dominated north India both militarily and culturally. The *bhakti* movement which originated in the south was sweeping the country in medieval India, and in parts of India that were dominated by the Muslims it led to the celebration of the divine in personal and courtly spaces rather than in temples or through ostentatious public

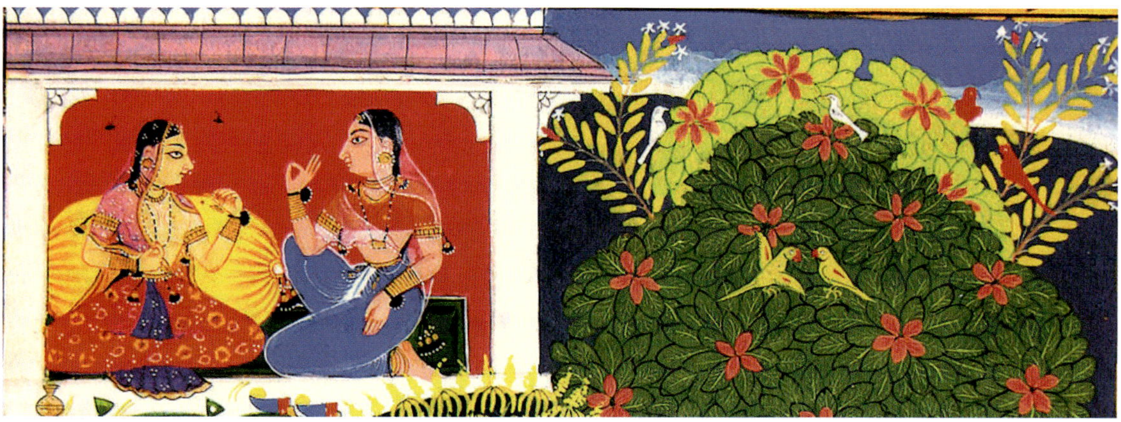

and not a peasant, and the ambience of his romantic dalliance is more ceremonial than spontaneous, more mannered and not pastoral. *Ritikavya* humanised Krishna and brought him into closer association with the daily routine of life and love, the turmoil and toil, the longing and the belonging of the ordinary man and woman, and the pleasures and pain of not only the common man but equally of the Rajput royalty and courtier.

The rise of the Rajput courts of the seventeenth and eighteenth centuries represents the resurgence of the Hindu ethos in the north despite the domination by Muslims, and the Mughals in particular. The Rajput psyche

display or by temple arts. Dance, music and painting, which could develop in courtly ateliers, were the preferred art forms and not sculpture. As the Rajputs reasserted their dominance both politically and culturally, the time for both the grand Sanskrit narrative *mahakavya* (epic poetry) and the Puranas was over, no new monumental temples were built although their influence was very much a part of the culture. Krishna had already been established and valourised as the prototypical romantic hero in the *Bhagavata*, the *Gita-Govinda* and by the *ashtachhap kavis*, and the time was ripe not for the enjoyment of grand romantic narratives but of romantic moments through the *bhashas,* in all its rich and varied sensuality and manifold situations, but which was never far removed from an underlying spirituality of the classical *shringara rasa*. *Harishringara* and *ritishringrara* could never be totally separated. The ethos of the time was one of courtly ceremony and not of temple rituals, of sophisticated courtiers and not of rustic cowherds, of urban pleasures and not of pastoral enjoyment, of urbane settings and not idyllic pastures and of a princely Krishna that was valourised through poetry in the *bhashas* and not the Krishna of the idyllic and bucolic Vrindavana, it was a bardic and not a Puranic Krishna. It has been rightly said that art in Rajput courts became sweet and tender in the celebration of romantic love, but yet elusive, at once both heart-piercing and tranquil in its revelation as mystical experience through its in-built metaphors and all this through *ritikavya* in Brajbhasha and its paintings in the miniature genre. But the pastoral Krishna always remained in the background like the faded writing on a palimpsest and underpinned the courtly *nayika*.

Ritikavya is mainly court poetry and the milieu of the court is central to the creation and enjoyment of this genre of poetry. Protypically the poet was under the patronage of a king or nobleman and in addition to writing romantic poetry, would very often write invocatory panegyric verses in honour of the king. An essential part of the court was the court dancer who would not only be skilled in music and dance but would also quite often be a poetess herself. Many examples come to mind, starting with Padmavati, who inspired Jayadeva to write the *Gita-Govinda* but then later in the *ritikal* period, two names come to mind and those are of Sujan and Parvinrai. Parvinrai was not only an accomplished dancer but a poetess as well and received instruction from none other than Keshavdas in the court of Indrajit of Orchha. Sujan was the dancer at the court of Mohammad Shah Rangila and it is said that Ghanananda, who was the court-poet was in love with her. The story goes that one day the king wanted to hear poetry and asked Ghanananda to recite some verses. Ghanananda was in no mood and refused the king's request. The king's minister whispered in his ear that Ghanananda would surely accede if Sujan asked him, and he did, but with his back to the king. The king was pleased to hear the romantic couplet but banished Ghanananda from his court for insulting him. Ghanananda became a recluse and settled in Mathura. It is said that when Nadir Shah laid siege to Delhi his men went to Mathura and asked Ghanananda to show them where the gold and the jewels were. Ghanananda threw dust at them implying that the dust of Braj was richer than gold, for it had the footprints of Krishna in it. The marauders felt insulted at this gesture and cut his hands off and with dripping blood he wrote a couplet in the dust. It is entirely possible that this is an apocryphal story but that does not undermine the importance of the court dancer and the liaison between her and the court-poet. It also reminds us that *ritikavya* was essentially a performing art where music and dance were essential components to the enjoyment of poet and the celebration of *shringara rasa*.

The aesthetic space of the romantic Krishna was already created in the *Bhagavata* and *Gita-Govinda*, and in the post-Bhagavata period around the fifteenth and the sixteenth centuries there was a shift in the romantic literature from Sanskrit to the *bhashas*. One of the early creations in Brajbhasha were those of Surdas and the *ashtachhap kavis* of the Nathadvara *sampradaya,* and then in about a hundred years after this, *ritikavya* was born. *Ritikavya* celebrates that same romantic love of Krishna of the *Bhagavata* but it now moves fluidly between religious devotion and urbane romanticism, moving seamlessly between *riti* and *bhakti* and between the court and the *haveli*. The *ritikal* poets richly embraced the romantic love of the courtly Radha and Krishna and north India resonated with their beautiful compositions, and the love of Radha and Krishna took on yet another dimension, another nuance, and the Rajput ateliers hummed with *ritikavya* as well as the *Bhagavata*, and a new phase of *shringara* poetry and painting was ushered in, a genre which would see Krishna and Radha, as *nayaks* and *nayikas* in a courtly setting.

There were significant changes in the tone and texture, style and rhythm, of *ritikavya* in Brajbhasha as compared to both the romantic poetry of *adikal* and *bhakti* poetry of medieval India that preceded it. We hasten to add that *bhakti* and *riti* are branches of the same tree, and while they are distinct in some ways and have their own characteristics, they are rooted in Vaishnava sensibility. *Ritikavya*

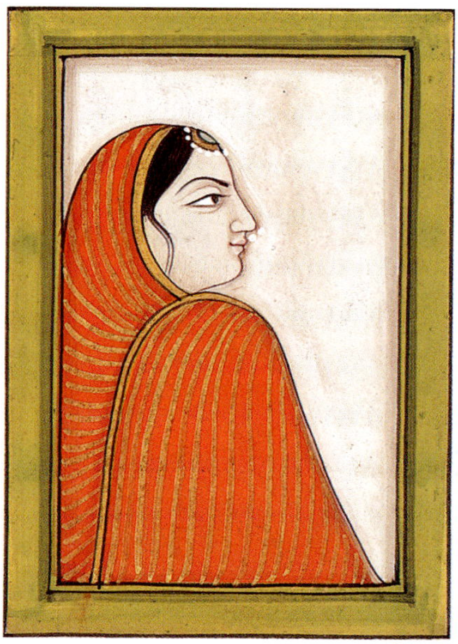

was mannered and stylised, short and fragmentary, and it was richly nuanced and not direct, and was not overtly devotional. Krishna and Radha in *ritikavya* were not always referred to directly, neither were romantic sentiments and situations presented literally, and it did not have the devotional veneration and surrender of *bhakti* poetry. In *ritikavya* Krishna and Radha were ever present in the background, so that every *nayak* and *nayika* were reflections of Krishna and Radha, and amorous exchanges and engagements were to be imagined and not presented as such. So strong was the paradigm of the Krishna and Radha as a romantic couple and as protagonists of *shringara rasa*, that every *nayak* and *nayika* in *ritikavya* were in the likeness of Krishna and Radha. *Ritikal* poets were Krishna *bhaktas* but were able to achieve the nuances and shades of *shringara rasa* with well-sculpted and minimal words, through the use of words in Brajbhasha that was both metaphoric and musical and equally pithy and measured. However, in spite of this courtly ambience of *ritikavya*, the piety surrounding the persona of Krishna nor the underlying divinity of Krishna, and equally the *paramatman jivatman* metaphor of the individual *atman* and the cosmic *atman*, was never lost sight of.

The *nayika* in the hands of *ritikal* poets was not a rustic *gopi* of the *Bhagavata* or Radha of *Gita-Govinda* anymore, but the perfect *nayika* or romantic heroine of courtly love, she was both *kamini* and *ramani* a sensuous and desirable woman, and she was projected in all her amorous manifestations and myriad romantic moods in a courtly setting. She was assertive and self-effacing, artful and coy, versed in the many arts of love and innocently desirous of amorous pleasures, all at the same time. By being so many different *nayikas*, the *nayika* in *ritikavya* becomes both depersonalised and universalised, a symbol rather than an individual. She is no woman in particular but stands for every woman in love. *Ritikavya* not only expressed the sensuality of romance but equally provided an extensive taxonomy of and prescribed models of romantic love in a courtly setting. The *ashtanayikas*, the eight heroines of Bharata now increased manifold. The innocence and charm of the pastoral love of the Bhagavata set in Vrindavana had changed and was replaced by courtly elegance and even intrigue. *Ritikavya* is built on the well-worn idioms and rhetoric of Sanskrit romantic poetry that preceded it, as in the *Amarushataka*, *Bhagavata* and the *Gita-Govinda*, but it went on to create a distinct and striking style of poetry and hence the term *riti* (style or mannered). In enunciating a strongly secular tone and in staying clear of overt devotion, *ritikavya* in Brajbhasha occupies a unique place in romantic poetry in the Indian tradition and became the fountainhead of paintings in the Rajput courts in Rajasthan and the Himalayan kingdoms. *Ritikavya* was essentially court poetry and flourished under the patronage and in the courtly ambience of the many Rajput kingdoms of north and central India. Its words were sonorous, its lyrics mellifluous and in the courtly ambience *ritikavya* was not just literature but became a performance, and in turn provided inspiration for other performing and visual arts such as song, dance and painting. The romance it portrayed, whether it was of longing or togetherness, was courtly not pedestrian, the ethos it created was one of graceful dignity and refined finesse within the ambience of a court or a *haveli* and not the idyllic environs of Vrindavana, the mood it painted was singularly devoid of banality, the romantic personae it brought to life were idealised and not stereotyped, and despite this, love in their artistic depictions was not just sensual but equally spiritual, as *riti* and *bhakti* were never far apart. This was because of Krishna who was always in the background of *ritikal* poetry and could span the sensual and the spiritual, the pastoral and the courtly, and ensure that the simple pleasures of love were understood for their larger purpose and not become hedonistic.

Three types of poets mark *ritikal*: poets whose compositions were mainly in praise of their patron, poets who wrote romantic poetry and those who wrote heroic and moral poetry. Our concern is mainly with romantic poetry. The *ritikal* poets presented numerous and a variety of beautiful romantic moments that defined courtly love and they did not set out to write a love story or an epic poem in the classical mould. Critics of *ritikavya* have said that *ritikavya* lacks depth and grandeur. Pandit Jaggannath, was one of the last poets who wrote in classic Sanskrit and he was a contemporary of the *riti* poet Sunder and scholars have compared the two. Classicists maintain that *ritikavya* was not able to match the majesty and grace of classical Sanskrit poetry. If this is true, it is perhaps because both the patron and the audience for which *ritikavya* was created were mainly pleasure-seeking connoisseurs and not intellectuals or scholars. Added to this was the absence of dedicated patronage for *riti* poets, for the historic period of *ritikal* was devoid of prosperous and powerful dynasties or empires and poets like Matiram had to move from one patron to another. However, what *ritikavya* lacked in classic refinement, finesse and depth it more than made up in its emotional richness.

Ritikavya spans the entire gamut and texture of romantic emotions but its principal preoccupation is with *nayika bhed* or the taxonomy of the many and varied romantic heroines. One reason for this is that in the ultimate analysis, the *nayika* is the paradigm of *prakriti* in search of *purusha* and as such, *prakriti* is multicoloured and multilayered, fickle and changing, while *purusha* is singularly steadfast. It has also sometimes been argued that *riti* poets over-ornamented their poetry, and while this could be true in some cases, the basis of *ritikavya* is *shringara* and ornamentation is only an accessory to it and enhances the romantic mood. Another criticism of *ritikavya* is that unlike classical Sanskrit poetry, *ritikavya* pays scant attention to the world of birds and blossoms, plants and planets. This criticism is unfair because *ritikavya* is all about romantic love that unfolds within the cloistered and elegant spaces of courts and *haveli*s, where the language of the eyes or subtle gestures of the body, play a more important part than the rustling of leaves and the whisper of blossoms. It is the *nayika*, the courtly woman in love, who is the centre of the poet's attention, her sensuality from the tresses to the toes, her heart-throbbing romance, her ecstasy and poignancy in moments of belonging or longing, her thrill of a loving glance and her expectation of a tender touch, all this and more are the concern of the poet, and this the poet executes with well-sculpted words and sonorous sounds within the space of a few lines, which pulsate and tremble with every nuance and texture of romantic love.

The changing social conditions of *ritikal* are evident in many different ways but especially through the depiction of the love messenger in the poetry of this period. The *sakhis* in *ritikavya* were not *gopis*, as they were in earlier poetry of the *Bhagavata* and the *Gita-Govinda*, where they were playmaids of Radha, but in *ritikavya* they were women of the town, of a lower social order such as the wife of the gardener or the barber, and who were able to move freely from *nayak* to *nayika*, as they fulfilled their role as ideal functionaries of the elite, and in many situations become the point of entry for the audience whether it was in poetry or painting. The change in the social structure of the *sakhi* however, did not rule out the possibility that she would also become the object of male gaze during the transactions of romance, but at all times she remains the poet's voice for us and it is she who makes accessible to us the world of courtly love. She is the *sutradhar*, as it were, who unfolds the drama of romance for us. She makes sure that we are not mere voyeurs but participants in the beautiful romantic moments that unfold before us. At one level, the romance is secret and clandestine but at another, it is the *sakhi* that makes it public for us. This is particularly true in *ritikavya* and the paintings it inspired.

So great was the appeal of *ritikal* poetry that it did not remain confined to courts and *havelis* but eventually reached the common people of the Hindi heartland as well, and also non-Hindi-speaking areas and entered the songs and conversations of the peasant and the potter; it was heard at fairs and festivals and sung by the mother and the bride alike. In this sense, it even surpassed the appeal of Jayadeva and Vidyapati. The lore of Radha and Krishna and their beautiful romantic love through *ritikavya* became the heart-throb of north India and it was as if the poets had recreated the celestial Vrindavana in the Braj country and the bowers of Vrindavana gave way to the sophisticated *pranay mandapas*, the love pavilions of courts and *havelis*, and all this in turn was to inspire artists to create movingly magnificent paintings of Krishna in the Rajput courts. And all of this through the aegis of Brajbhasha.

Fleeting but intense passion, whether of union or longing, the thrill of an amorous moment and the excitement of a charged sensuality are the hallmarks of romantic love and this kind of love is best expressed in the brevity of *ritikavya*, fragmentary poetry, and also in the beautiful and sensual space of a miniature painting. It does not take an epic poem or a grand mural to depict the thrill of the exchange of glances, the hushed joy of a clandestine meeting, the expectation and anticipation of a tryst or the pathos of longing, for this can be done even with a few well-sculpted words of a skilful poet or deft strokes of a miniature painter. Romantic love, as presented in *ritikavya*, is all about that beautiful, charged, amorous, intense, albeit transient moment, it is not meant to be an elaborate love story with moral overtones and social underpinnings. By its very nature romantic moments are evanescent, spontaneous, unexpected and unrehearsed and exist outside the strict dictates of *dharma* and it is only the skilled *ritikal* poet like Matiram, or the consummate Rajput miniaturist, who is able to capture that heart-throbbing moment and convert it to a moment of beauty in an artistic creation. These evanescent romantic moments are complete in themselves, for what they lack in their grand narrative content they more than make up in their emotional surcharge, for in that momentary and intense romantic happening there is not only the outpouring of the heart, but in that poetic moment is the fulfilment of one's very being. The beauty of that moment can only be captured poetically, whether it be through lyrics of the *ritikal* poet or the brush of the artist of the Rajput court. To convert that poetic moment into a painting needed the poetic imagination and skill of an artist like Sahibdin of Mewar and Purkhu of the Pahari region of the nineteenth century. That poetic moment, both in poetry and painting, is alive and throbbing, moving and sensuous, in that brief moment depicted in painting there is a whole universe of feelings, it is a still moment within orbits of amorous movements and activities. It is a moment of sheer romantic beauty, be it of longing or rejoicing, of belonging or expectant waiting, of bubbling joy or heart-rending remorse, of anger or jealousy, of the many seasons and faces of romance, all of that and more, fully alive and present in that brief but beautiful poetic and pictorial moment. It is that brief but beautiful poetic moment which epitomises the *shringara rasa nayika* of *ritikavya*.

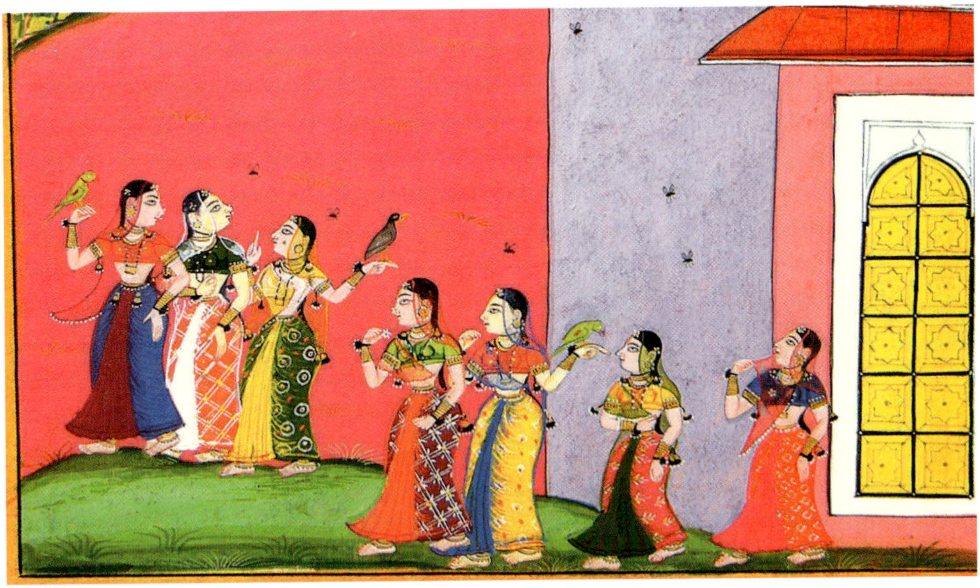

Our tradition of *smriti*, *purana*, *mahakavya* and *natya*, grand epics, mythic lore, epic poetry and drama, are rich with the treasure of love stories where romantic moments are a small part of a larger narrative. Romantic moments in these art forms are subservient to the unfolding of cosmic and human drama, of the expression of religious and metaphysical truths; in other words, of *dharma* under the aegis of the dynamics of storytelling and all this was not a feature of *ritikavya*.

Keshavdas is considered the father of *ritikavya* and his monumental *Rasikapriya* and *Kavipriya* are a *lakshana grantha,* the foundational text of *ritikavya*. Keshavdas set the tone of the courtly *nayak-nayika bhed* and created numerous aesthetically charged and romantically sensuous situations for the amorous *nayak* and the emotionally sensitive *nayika* to arrange countless meetings in an elaborate taxonomy of love. It is difficult to match Keshavdas' mastery of language, rich with motifs and metaphors and his vividness of imagination as he covers every possible interaction between two people in love, their many moods and meetings, the pleasures of belonging and the pain of longing, in varied locations and changing circumstances along with the people who surround them. In creating the *Rasikapriya* Keshavdas was breaking new ground and ensuring that the genre of *nayak-nayika bhed* no longer remained the prerogative of the poet but could be transformed into visual poetry through the skill of the *kalam* of the artist in the ateliers of Rajput courts. Were it not for *ritikavya*, paintings of *shringara rasa* would have been limited to the poetry of the *Bhagavata Purana* and the *Gita-Govinda*. Keshavdas opened the floodgates of romantic situations for the painter and painters such as Sahibdin of Mewar and Purkhu of Kangra who in turn made full use of that to create timeless

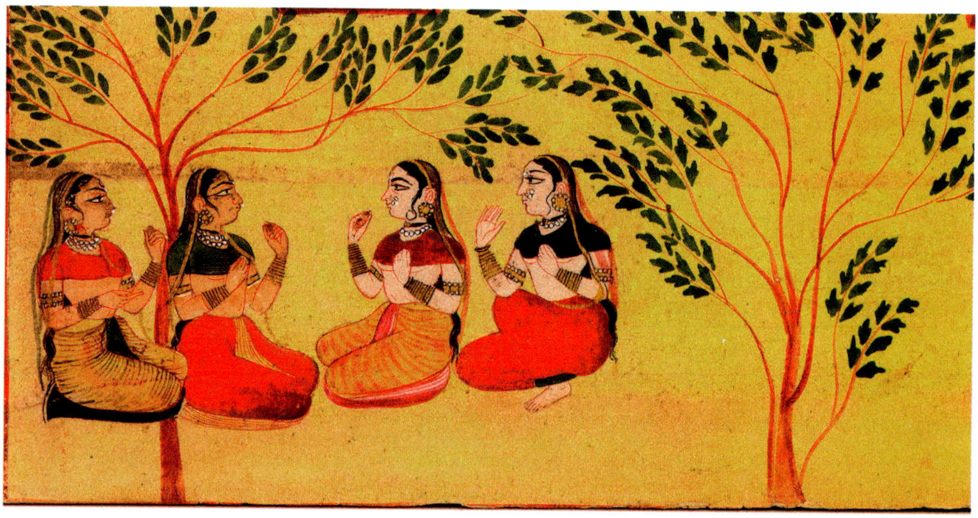

paintings of exquisite beauty that rank as one of the finest depictions of *shringara rasa* in the history of Indian painting. Keshavdas wrote beautiful poetry but equally ensured that there would be a rich transformation of this poetry into painting or visual poetry and he remains both a poet's poet and an artist's poet.

Readers in English are aware of only a few *ritikal* poets and chief of them are Keshavdas and Bihari. The entry of English readers into *ritikavya* was mainly through painting and which was brought to their attention by pioneers like Coomaraswamy, Havel and Archer, and the two *ritikal* poets who featured commonly in paintings were Keshavdas and Bihari. However, countless other poets remain unknown to the English readers. Literature in the *bhashas* however, is replete with these other poets and their works. And foremost among the second tier of *ritikal* poets is Matiram. Other noteworthy *ritikal* poets are:

Chintamani Tripathi (*Kavikulakalpataru*),
Kulapati Mishra (*Rasarahasya*),
Somnath (*Rasapiyushnidhi*),
Bikharidas (*Kavyanirnaya*),
Gwal (*Sahityananda*),
Sunder Kaviray (*Sunder Shringara*),
Beniparvin (*Navarasatarang*),
Dev (*Rasavilas*),
Padmakar (*Jagadvinod*),
Kalidas Trivedi (*Vadhuvinod*),
Udaynath Kavindra (*Rasachandrodaya*),
Chandrashekhar Vajpeyi (*Rasikvinod*),
Rasiksumati (*Alamkarachandrodaya*),
Raghunath (*Rasikmohan*),
Govind (*Karnabharan*),
Dulah (*Kavikulakanthabharan*),
Ramsinh (*Alamkara Darpana*),
Sukhdev Mishra (*Vrittavichar*)
Muralidhar Bhushan (*Chandohridayaprakash*),

Lal (*Chatraprakash*),
Sujan (*Sujancharit*),
Shridhar (*Jangnama*).
Other notable poets of *ritikavya* are
Raskhan, Alam, Ghanananda, Thakur.

Ritikavya had beautifully transformed the rustic *gopi* into a courtly *nayika* and Vrindavana was now changed into the charmed aesthetic space within the Rajput courts where *bhakti* and *riti* were not bipolar, but a continuum emotion of the exalted human state. While poetry gave words to *shringara rasa*, and lyrics gave colours to the *kalam* of the artist in the Rajput court, it was piety stemming from the *pushtimarg* Vaishnavism that was to drive and sustain the celebration of Krishna in the courts even through the oral and visual

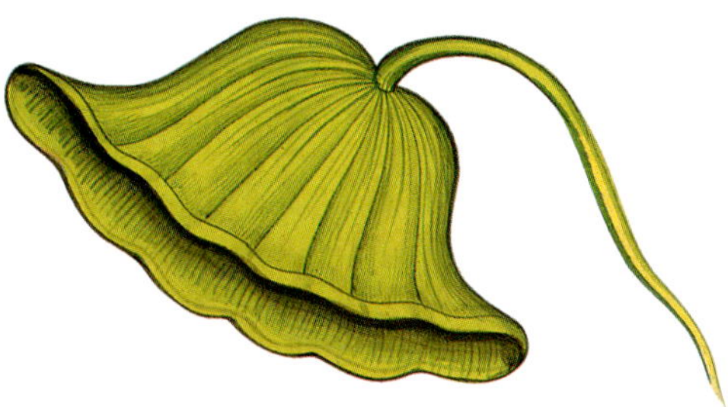

ritikavya. The Rajput kings were not only ardent *bhaktas* of Krishna of the Nathadvara tradition but some even identified themselves completely with Krishna in real life. A case in point is Savant Singh of Kishangarh, who wrote:

God created the moon-faced Radha
like a flame of light for this earth
As ill-luck would have it this
flame is dying
O Krishna ! Refresh this flame with
your oil (love)
So that the three worlds are not
immersed in darkness.

Nihal Chand, the court painter of Kishangarh, transformed the image of Savant Singh and Bani Thani into that of Krishna and Radha. It is said that another Rajput king Pratap Singh would see Krishna in his dreams and his court painter depicted him in this dream vision, showing once again the many different ways in which the Rajput kings identified themselves with Krishna, emphasising that Krishna in *ritikavya* was a courtly person and not a distant god. This was a feature of the *ritikal* and not of the *bhaktikal,* for in *bhaktikal* the relation is between a devotee and deity.

Rajasthani paintings that were an evocative visualisation of *ritikavya* concentrated towards the representation of the depth, beauty and serenity of man's life, rooted in the awakening, maturation and climax of love. That love in Rajput courts of the seventeenth and eighteenth centuries was underpinned by the *harishringara* of the *Bhagavata* but was expressed mainly through the *shringara rasa* of *ritikavya* and the courtly paintings that it inspired. The centre of romantic activity in *ritikal* paintings is the *pranaya mandapa*, also called the *keli bhawan* or the *rati kaksh*. The various pleasures of love unfold in this small but richly ornamented chamber.

Seventeenth and eighteenth-century Rajput romantic paintings based on *ritikal* poetry are set in a courtly ethos. Instead of the verdant groves or *kunj* that one sees in early western Indian paintings of the *Bhagavata Purana* and the *Gita-Govinda*, the locale in these Rajput paintings shifts to pavilions of love or *pranaya mandapa*. These pavilions take their inspiration from the local architecture and especially that of Mandu. It was Baz Bahadur, who was responsible for the evocative palaces that were built in Mandu, especially for his consort Rupamati, and this was to serve as inspiration for Mughal architecture that was to follow and more importantly, for the artists in the Rajput ateliers.

In its simplest form, a pavilion had four pillars and a canopy and were located either on the terrace or in the main building, with the space open to the outside, overlooking either the palace gardens or into the courtyard. In their time, these *mandapas* were decorated with curtains and carpets and furnished with *divans* and settees. Large bolsters with either embroidered or printed fabrics added a touch of graceful luxury and cushions invited those who entered for a moment of unhurried pleasure. The pavilions had carafes or bottles of wine, decanters of perfume, boxes of condiments, fruit stands and the *huqqa*. The walls of these pavilions had niches or alcoves where there were either lamps or carafes. Water fountains or reflecting pools often adorned the outside of these pavilions which featured lotuses and ducks. Musicians and dancers would be seated outside the pavilions ready to strike the right note.

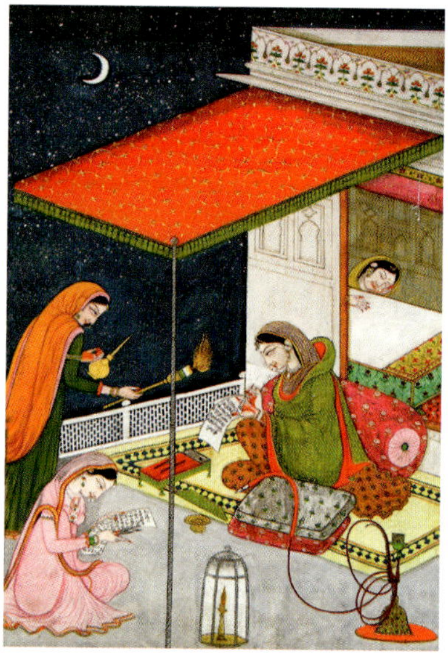

While the floor and the walls of these *mandapas* were important, what was most significant was the ceiling, for it recreated the sky and provided a protective canopy above our heads. The concept of a canopy runs deep in the Indian tradition. The ceiling of the *rangamandapa* is ornately decorated with musicians and dancers, *surasundaris* and *madanikas*. The shrine of a mother goddess, especially in Gujarat, is adorned with the *chandarvo*. The king's throne is never without a parasol and even when he travelled on a horse or an elephant there was an umbrella over him. The Buddha sat under the *pipal* tree which became a protective canopy while he meditated. While providing protection from the wind and the rain, sun and dust are some of the obvious reasons for a canopy, a canopy in the ultimate analysis is the human recreation of the sky, a representation in finite terms of what is infinite, it brings what is celestial and distant close and reachable to us. In order to feel complete we need to create an *axis mundi* which connects the earth to the sky, our earthbound and limited life to the vastness and freedom of the sky. A canopy is that recreation of the sky, which would otherwise remain abstract and distant.

These *pranaya mandapas* provided the right ethos for the pleasures of love and the sweet delights of romance. It was here that the *nayika* would prepare and wait with anticipation and excitement for her beloved. Often accompanied by her *sakhi*, the *nayika* would check her adornments in a mirror or be comforted by her *sakhi*. The *sakhi* would assuage her feelings when the waiting became painful and bring news of his coming. It was here that sandalwood paste would cool the burning body. And when the *nayak* arrived, the pavilion would come to life and poignant longing would give way to the pleasures of belonging. Wine and conversation would flow, music was heard and dancers would bring romantic lyrics of *thumris* to life.

Pranay mandapas are beautiful spaces.

There may be auspicious mythical creatures, such as a *makara* lurking at the summit or base of the columns. The walls of the pavilion are sometimes painted with brightly coloured flowers but more often, they are covered with niches filled with delicate bottles and jars and the floor is covered with a richly patterned carpet. In the foreground, there may be a stream or a pool festooned with lovely lotuses and saucy little ducks. Crowding in at the edges or retreating into the distance, there are ranks of full, lush trees. Perhaps there is a peacock close by or a clutch of musicians and there may be other small luxuries such as a *huqqa*, sweetmeats, wine or fruit to complete the picture of serene celebration.

This is the pavilion of love, which provides the setting for the ritual enactment of age-old stories of love and longing. It is here that the courtly Rajput *nayak* and *nayika* anxiously wait for the other, come joyously together or take their sorrowful leave. Very few of the details of the scene are new but in the hands of the Rajput painters of the day, they are combined to permit a deeper level of meaning. The lovers have taken on mythical proportions and they have invested their surroundings with equally heroic dimensions.

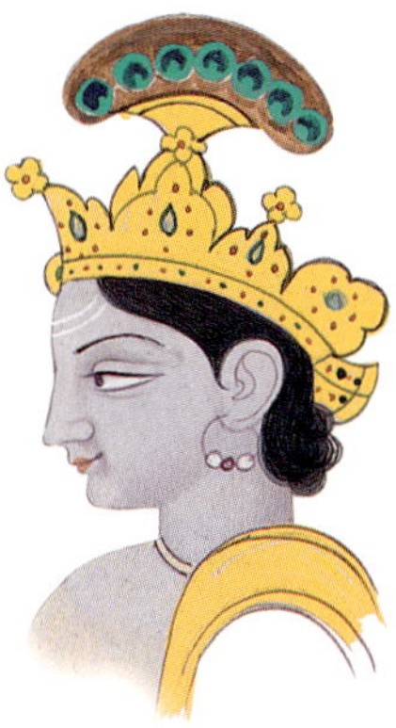

Nothing in this anointed space is accidental or incidental. The *makara*, a fearsome mythological creature is nevertheless an auspicious symbol. As the vehicle of the divine Ganga, it is a water symbol providing protection and calling to mind the primal life source. The lotuses swaying gently in a river or pond, or adorning one or other of the lovers, are part of the most ancient and universal repertory of symbols in India. Rising from the cosmic waters, they bestow grace, beauty and peace and remind us that we are witness to a transcendent love. The peacock also has an ancient pedigree. In its earliest manifestation, it promised immortality, a fitting heritage for its role as harbinger of the life-giving monsoon. Fruits such as the luscious mango or the succulent grape and even the jars and carafes filled with heady perfumes or sweet liquors, recalling the *purna kalasha*, are potent symbols of fertility and the power of sexual union.

All the details of the pavilion setting contribute to the mood of luxurious sensuality in the paintings. As with the time of day, the season or the weather in which the scene is located, they are carefully chosen for their dramatic and symbolic value. But they are not merely props or atmospheric flourishes. Like the pavilion they adorn, they have taken on ritual significance in a complex illustration of the purpose and power of love.

The *pranaya mandapas* of Rajput courts were a repository of aesthetic delights and romantic pleasures and were the prototype of these pavilions in miniature paintings. It is important to note that there is a difference between the *pranaya mandapas* of Rajasthani paintings such as those of Sahibdin of Mewar and those created in the Pahari ateliers such as those presided by Purkhu. While the Mewari *mandapas* emphasise architecture both inside and outside the pavilion, the Pahari pavilion of love centres itself around the *nayika* and is therefore more lyrical; blossoms and birds are as important as walls and doors. Purkhu and his school excel in creating romantic and beautiful pavilions, sensually charged spaces that resonate with the equally sensuous love that unfolds within it. In this respect, he surpasses the excellence of the Seu family whose strength was in creating luxuriant landscapes. *Ritikavya* is the art of love that unfolds in a *mandapa* and not in bucolic and pastoral spaces.

And so if the dashama skandha of the

Bhagavata gives Krishna a romantic presence and inaugurates the grand Vaishnava theme of *harishringara*, and in its hallowed pages we see and celebrate his various *kridas* and *lilas* as a pastoral cowherd, then in the *Gita-Govinda* we see Radha occupy centrestage as she teases and woos, dallies and dances with Krishna and brings him down to earth. It is in *ritikavya* such as the *Rasraj* of Matiram and the paintings in the ateliers of Rajput courts, like those of Purkhu under the patronage of Sansar Chand of Kangra, that they inspired, that Krishna becomes totally human. The *riti* poets do not engage in presenting a romantic epic, rather they are interested in depicting fleeting moments of love, where there is a whole universe of feelings in a passing moment. In the *ritikavya* of Matiram, *harishringara* is transformed into *shringara rasa*, where Krishna is a prince who enlivens the courts of the Rajputs, and ensures that more important than military exploits and political intrigue is to live so as to love, and to love so as to be fully human, where matters of the state are put aside and affairs of the heart are heeded, where the many situations of longing and belonging must be negotiated with a certain romantic finesse, where under canopies of love and in pleasure gardens in stately mansions, unhurried romance takes precedence over worldly concerns, where flasks of wine, bowls of fruits, containers of sandalpaste and flower garlands are always present as accessories for the celebration of fleeting romantic moments, where *sakhis* and *sakhas* ensure that beautiful and intimate moments of love are safeguarded, where mirrors of adornment are a statement not of one's status but of the importance of making that amorous situation perfect and beautiful, for in that beautifully romantic courtly moment is the eternity of love.

This is the message of *ritikavya* of Matiram and the courtly paintings of the seventeenth, eighteenth and nineteenth centuries that it inspired.

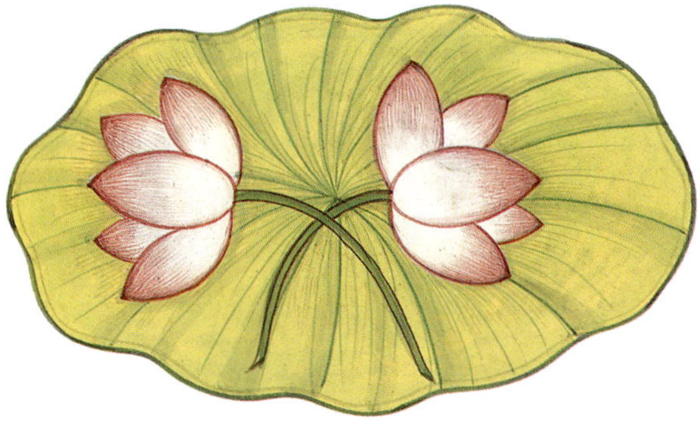

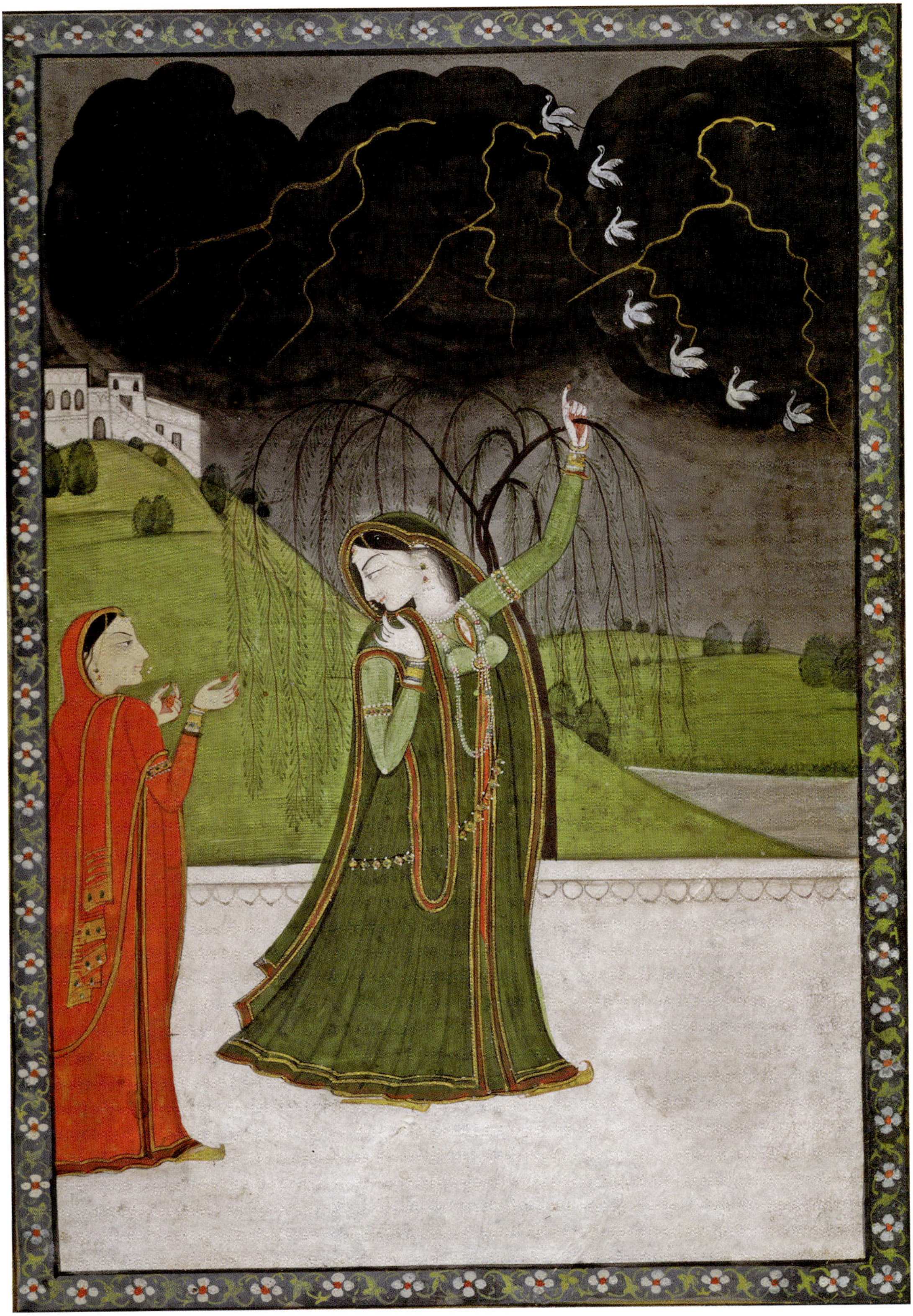

Virahini Nayika, Kangra, CE 1830-50, Dehejia collection

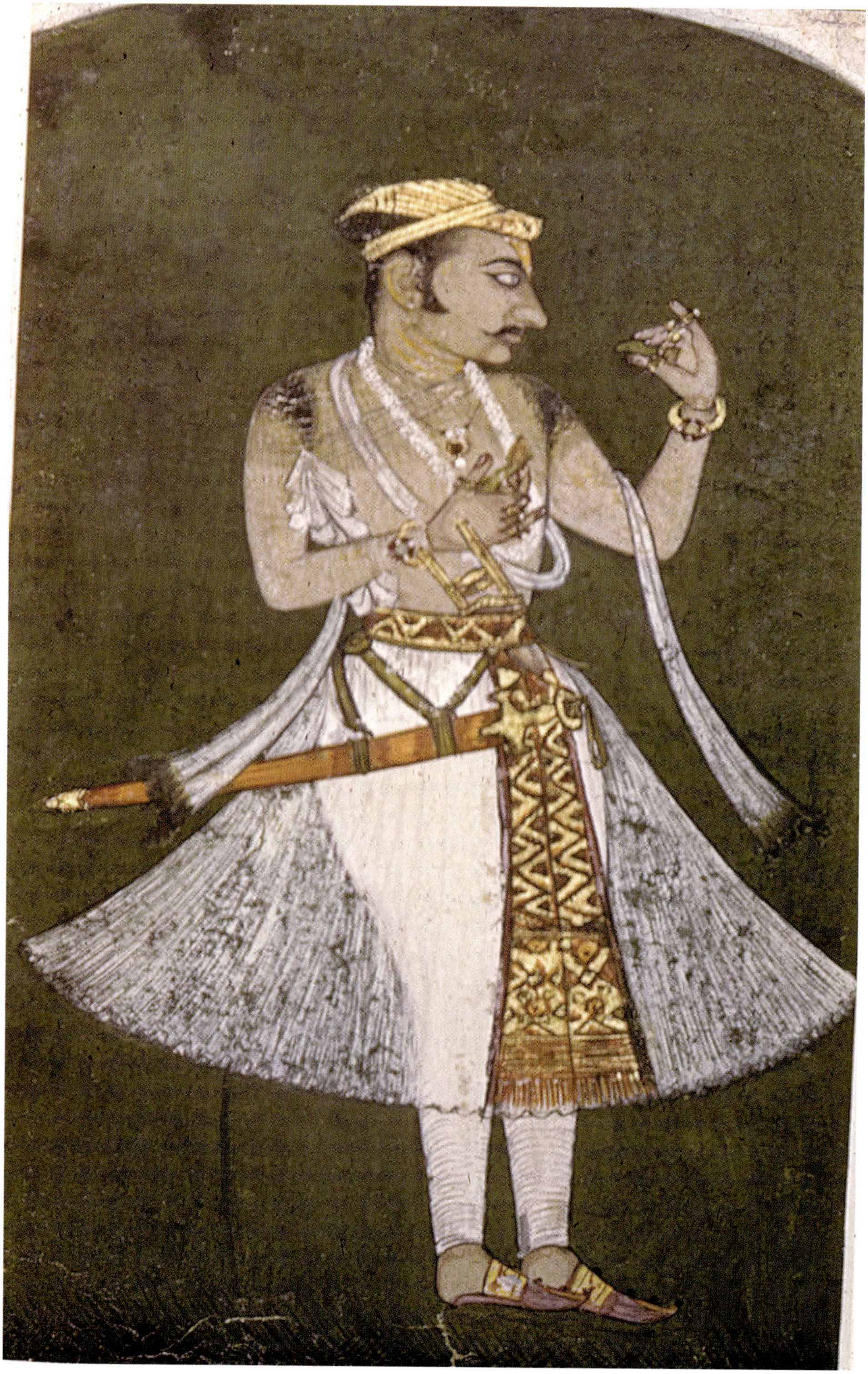

Raja Chattar Sal of Bundi, *c.* CE 1650, private collection.

Courtesy: Milo Beach

Matiram: The Poet and His Poetry

Ritikal, or the period of ornamented poetry which covered the period from the sixteenth to the nineteenth centuries has a special place in the genre of *shringara rasa*, and it would not be wrong to call this period *shringarakal* (the period of romantic poetry). *Ritikavya* is mannered poetry and is bound by certain structural literary conventions. Such is the beauty and the strength of its words that even within a few words it is able to convey vistas of sensuous meanings and layers of romantic feelings and thus it is that it could give us even in two lines, a rich and evocative taste of romantic love.

While Keshavdas and Bihari are considered foundational poets of *ritikavya*, Matiram also stands as a beacon and commands equal respect and attention. Matiram was born in 1603 and lived a long life and passed away in 1693. He was a gifted child and his first poetic composition was written at the age of 18. He came from a Kanyakubja brahmin family that was known for its literary accomplishments. His father Ratnakar Tripathi and his brothers Chintamani and Bhushan were accomplished poets themselves and they lived in a village by the name of Tikampur on the Yamuna, not far from Kanpur. During his life Matiram was patronised by several kings and among them are Raja Chhatrasal (also called Shatrushal 1631-58) and Raja Bhao Singh (1658-82) both of Bundi, the Mughal emperor Jehangir, Raja Gyan Chand and Fateh Singh Bundela of Shrinagar. His first composition was *Phoolmanjari*, which he wrote when he was only 18 years old and its 60 verses are evocations of different flowers. His other compositions are *Rasraj*, *Lalit Lalam*, *Satsai*, *Sahityasar* and *Lakshana Shringara*. *Rasraj* which was written between 1633-43, and which was not commissioned by any patron but composed for his own pleasure, is considered his flagship work. Even during his lifetime, Rasraj attracted the attention of other poets and within a few years commentaries were written on the *Rasraj*. *Lalit Lalam* was written during 1661-64 under the patronage of Raja Bhao Singh of Bundi. His *Satsai* was written between 1678 and 1681.

Like other *ritikal* poets Matiram was influenced not only by literary conventions and traditions that preceded him, but also by the courtly ethos of the times in which he lived and worked. This was a time of the Rajput courts in north-west India where romantic poetry was enjoyed in the company of connoisseurs and accompanied by music and dance. It was also the heyday of Brajbhasha, which was ideally suited to express the many and varied romantic emotions.

However, all of this did not restrict his creativity and Matiram emerged as a significant *ritikal* poet in his own right and his poetic creations shine like a jewel in the store of *ritikal* poetry.

Romantic poetry has an ancient and hoary past in the Indian literary tradition. Bharatmuni in his *Natyashastra* was perhaps the first to enumerate the different *nayikas* and this was followed by centuries of romantic poetry in Sanskrit, Prakrit and Tamil. Names such as Vatsyayana, Hala, Amaru, Mammata, Kalidas, Jayadeva, the *ashtachhap kavis* of the Vallabha *sampradaya*, Vidyapati and Chandidas, shine radiantly in the corridors of Indian romantic poetry. It was Bhanudatta's Sanskrit composition *Rasmanjari* that was to leave a lasting stamp on erotic poetry in Sanskrit and also influenced *riti* poets in Hindi.

Matiram, while remaining within the confines of the traditions of *shringara kavya* set before him and influenced by it, was able to assert his own individual style to emerge as a significant *acharya* of *ritikal*. He was also aware of the courtly ethos of royalty and the nobility but even this did not restrict him from his innate understanding of *shringara rasa*. Matiram's strength in *ritikavya* lies in creating varied and touching situations to portray the different *nayikas*, situations that he drew from the quotidian life of the ordinary rural householder, rather than from the lives of the royalty and nobility or the urban elite. The following *doha* will serve as an example:

bhitar maun ke dvar khari
sukumar tiya tan kamp bisekhai |
gunghat ko pat aut diye
pat aut kiye piyko mukh dekhai | |

The young wife, eager to see her beloved
who has returned from a journey
stands behind the door covering her face
with her *odhni*.

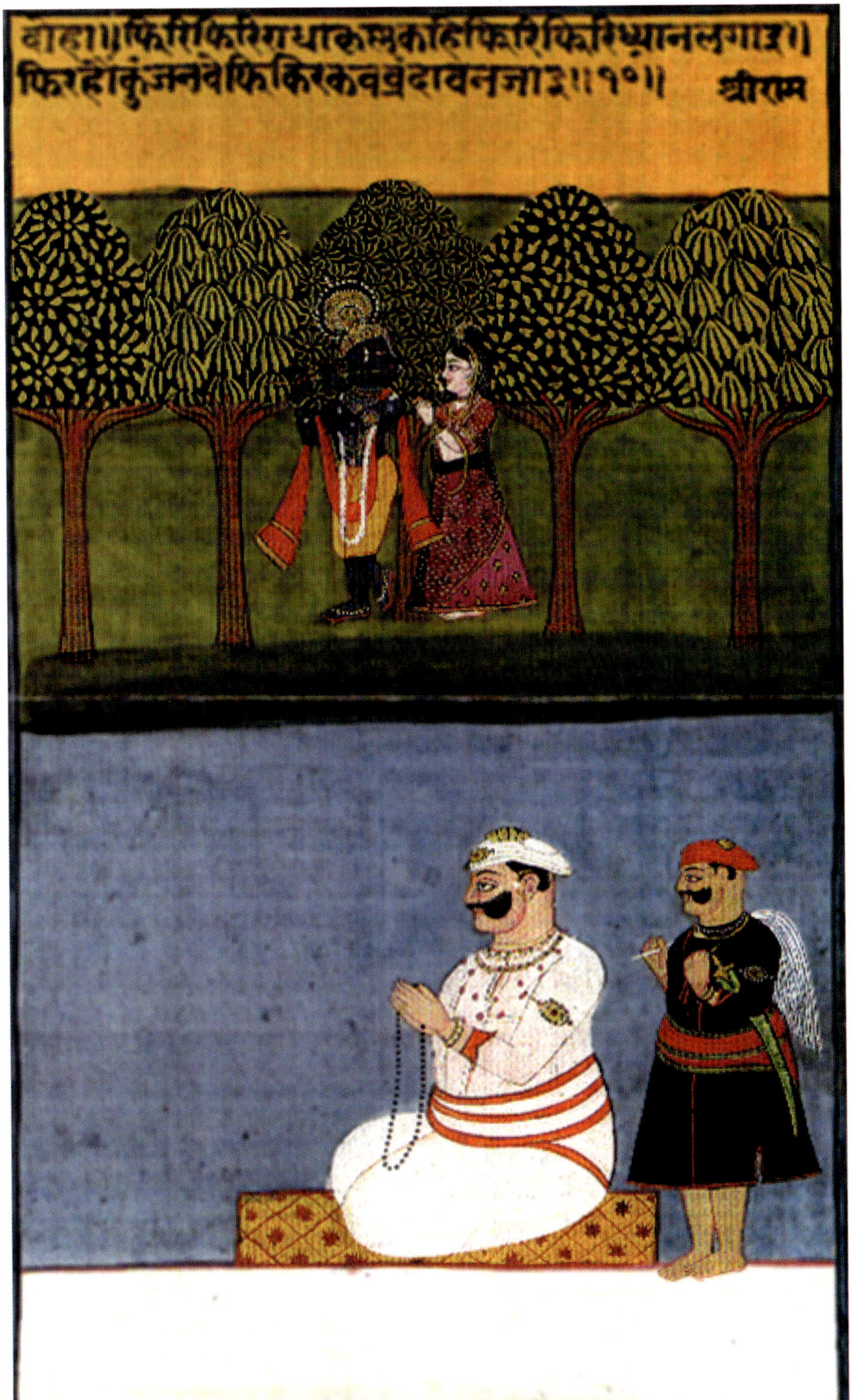

Vikram Singh venerating Krishna, Datia, eighteenth century, Dehejia collection

Many *ritikal* poets would choose to portray *parakiya nayikas* or romantic women in adulterous relationships, for that would create exciting romantic situations. Matiram broke away from them and excelled in portraying the young, shy and coy *svakiya nayika*, a maiden who is even ignorant of her bodily signs of adolescence and who is married into a traditional joint family. When it came to an *ajnyat mugdha nayika*, or a *nayika* who is unaware of her approaching adolescence, Matiram, in keeping with his conservative tenor, stresses emotional rather than physical changes in the maiden, thereby avoiding depicting erotic sensuality. Matiram's time was one of child marriages and his compositions take us from the entire gamut from the *mugdha* to the *praudha nayikas* and every shade in between and all within the orbit of the *svakiya*. And even though his *nayikas* were conservative and traditional they did not lack sensual charm, elegant beauty and emotional sophistication. In one of his celebrated *dohas*, he writes that "even the colour of gold fades before that of the *nayika*, her smile was such that with its charm she could sell anything, she is so beautiful that the closer one gets to her, it seems that every limb and part of her body overflows with beauty".

If Matiram's *nayika* is shy in the company of the elders of the family, she could become self-possessed and self-assured when she was alone with her beloved and turn herself into a *svadhinapatika*. In moments of belonging and the pangs of longing, Matiram's *nayikas* emerge as sensitive and sensuous women. And yet she is ever so innocent when she tells her beloved not to come in contact with camphor before he touches her, for she does not realise that her tears are caused by her romantic excitement and not by camphor. She is also skilled in the arts of love as when she evades the prying eyes of her friends and steals a glance of her beloved. When she gradually becomes a *praudha* she cannot totally be free of her inherent bashful nature. Even while respecting the elders in her home she decorates the bed chamber for the pleasures of love and stealing away from the family, comes and lies on the bed awaiting her beloved and thus she becomes a *vasaakasajja*. But when days have passed and her beloved has not yet come, she becomes anxious and then jealous and wonders if he is with another woman. Just then, a yellowish moon rises and she turns pale like the moon. And then when she is distressed beyond measure, she discards her ornaments and thus becomes a *vipralabdha*. When however her beloved does come and paints her feet, arranges her tresses and gives her a flower garland, she is now a *svadhinapatika*. As she grows more assured and secure in her love, the *nayika* becomes an important member of the household and takes on the responsibility of running the home. Her beloved equally becomes more assertive and once when he wished to spend romantic pleasures with her in the middle of the day, he called for her saying he was thirsty. The elder sister-in-law understood his intentions and asked the young *nayika* to take some water for him. Even though he was winking at her she took a glass of water and left it at the threshold as she did not want to transgress the honour of the elders. This is the *vishrabdha navodha* of Matiram. Even under these conditions, Matiram does not exceed the propriety and limitations of a traditional home. When the elders in the family wanted a grandchild she protected the honour of her husband and declared herself sterile rather than let them point a finger at him. Sincere and simple, coy and caressing is her love, so that even if she is dressed in a plain white *sari* she looks so beautiful that the co-wives become pale and her beloved turns red on looking at her.

In every type and shade of *nayika*, whether it is the pleasures of belonging or the pathos of longing Matiram's *nayikas* are demure never defiant, coy never crass, sensuous but not flirtatious, respectful of the traditions and honour of a joint family and yet in spite of this always throbbing with romantic love, ever seeking amorous excitement with her beloved.

Matiram, while remaining true to the conventions of *ritikavya*, departs from the rather austere and arid style of Keshavdas to create sensually evocative and romantically throbbing images of the *nayika*.

In this, he exceeds even Keshavdas. Matiram's poetic compositions are more sensuous, his images for lyrical, the landscape in his poetry more melodious. It is as if his *kalam* is honeyed and it was left to Purkhu to take this honey from his *kalam* and transform his *tulika,* so that Matiram's sonorous words become Purkhu's sensual images.

Even remaining under the spell of the prevailing traditions of *ritikavya*, Matiram's well-sculpted words and chiselled images remain unique and secure for him an honoured place in the hallowed chambers of *ritikal* poets of the seventeenth and eighteenth centuries.

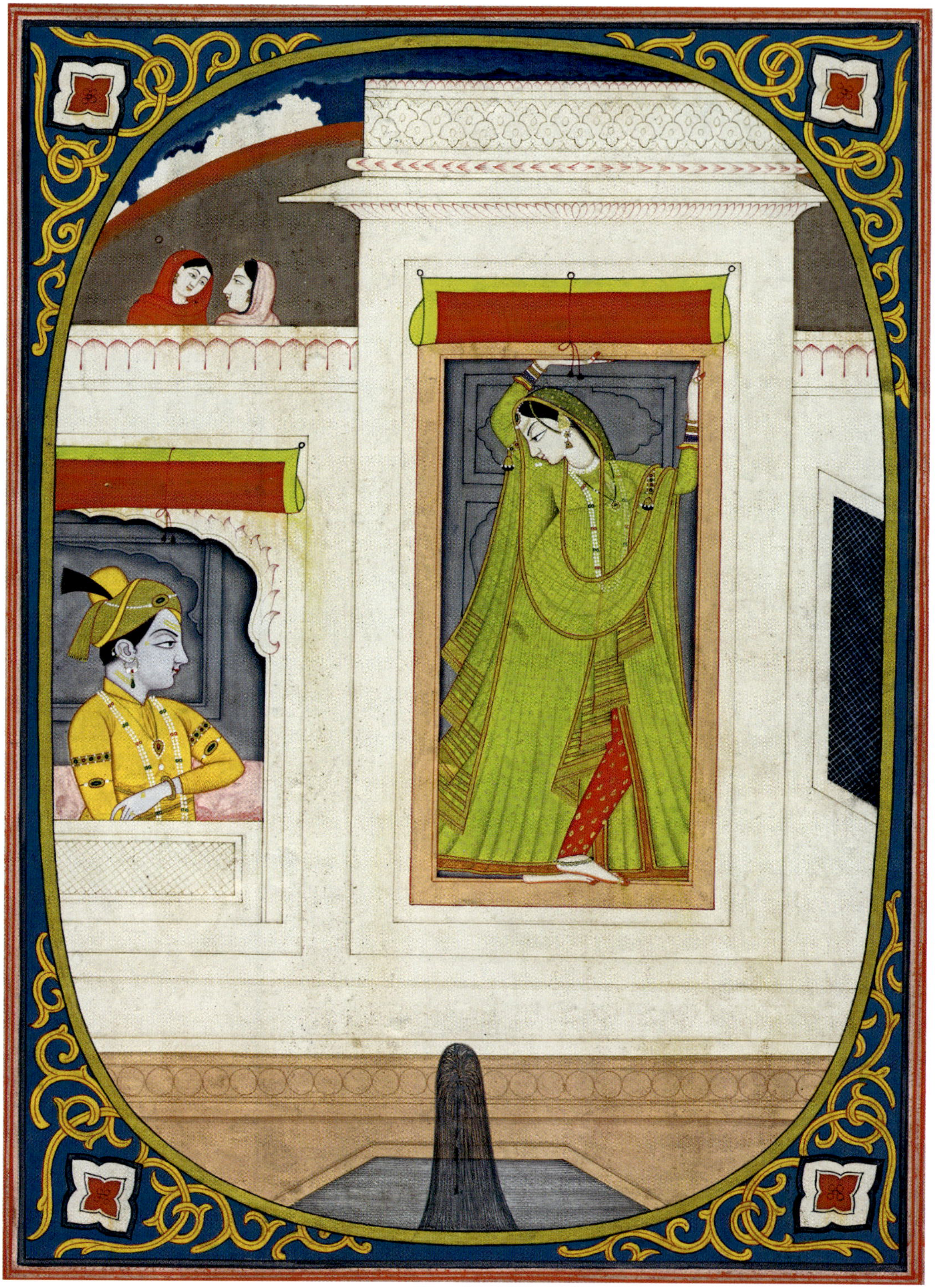

Madhya Nayika, school of Purkhu, Kangra, CE 1785-90, Dehejia collection.

A Bouquet of Pahari Paintings

मध्या

केलिभवन की देहरी खरी बाल छबि नौल।
कामकलित हिय को लहै लाजकलित दृगकौल ।।

Madhya Nayika

Standing at the threshold of a pavilion the newly blossomed damsel captures the heart of a nayak *by casting glances with her bashful lotus-like eyes.*

The poet Matiram has placed these words in the mouth of a *sakhi*, who whispers to another *sakhi* who is seen in the background of the picture. Matiram's taxonomy has three types of *nayikas*, *mugdha, madhya* and *praudha*. A *madhya nayika* is one who is neither a novice nor proficient in the arts of love. In the resplendent love pavilion which the poet describes as *keli-bhawan*, a young maiden stands at the threshold of the chamber. The adolescent *nayika* is sumptuously dressed in a pale green dress and stares intensely at the *nayak*. Her face is soft. Though she advances towards her beloved, her bashful nature seems to restrain her. Yet the sensuous contours of her body can be seen through it. Leaning against the wooden door frame, the fair complexioned *nayika* seems to be lost in her thoughts, while the Krishna-like *nayak* constantly gazes towards her. The *nayak* wears a yellow *jama* and a turban topped by a plume, a sign of royalty.

The figure of the *nayika* is the focal point in the picture. Her static posture with upraised arms suggests that she is in a romantic mood. The background is monochromatic without any detail, save the streaks and floating clouds in the turbulent sky. The marble building is less embellished. A cistern in the foreground and a latticed window to the right of the picture help in balancing the pictorial composition. The patterns at the four corners of the oval frame with rosette designs are typical of the Kangra painting at the court of the Katoch chief, Sansar Chand of Kangra.

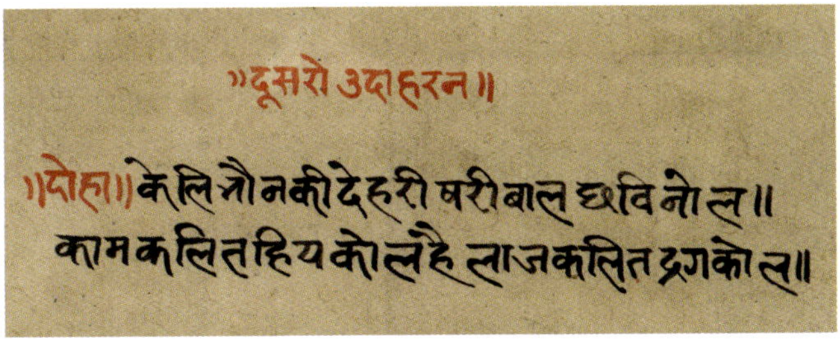

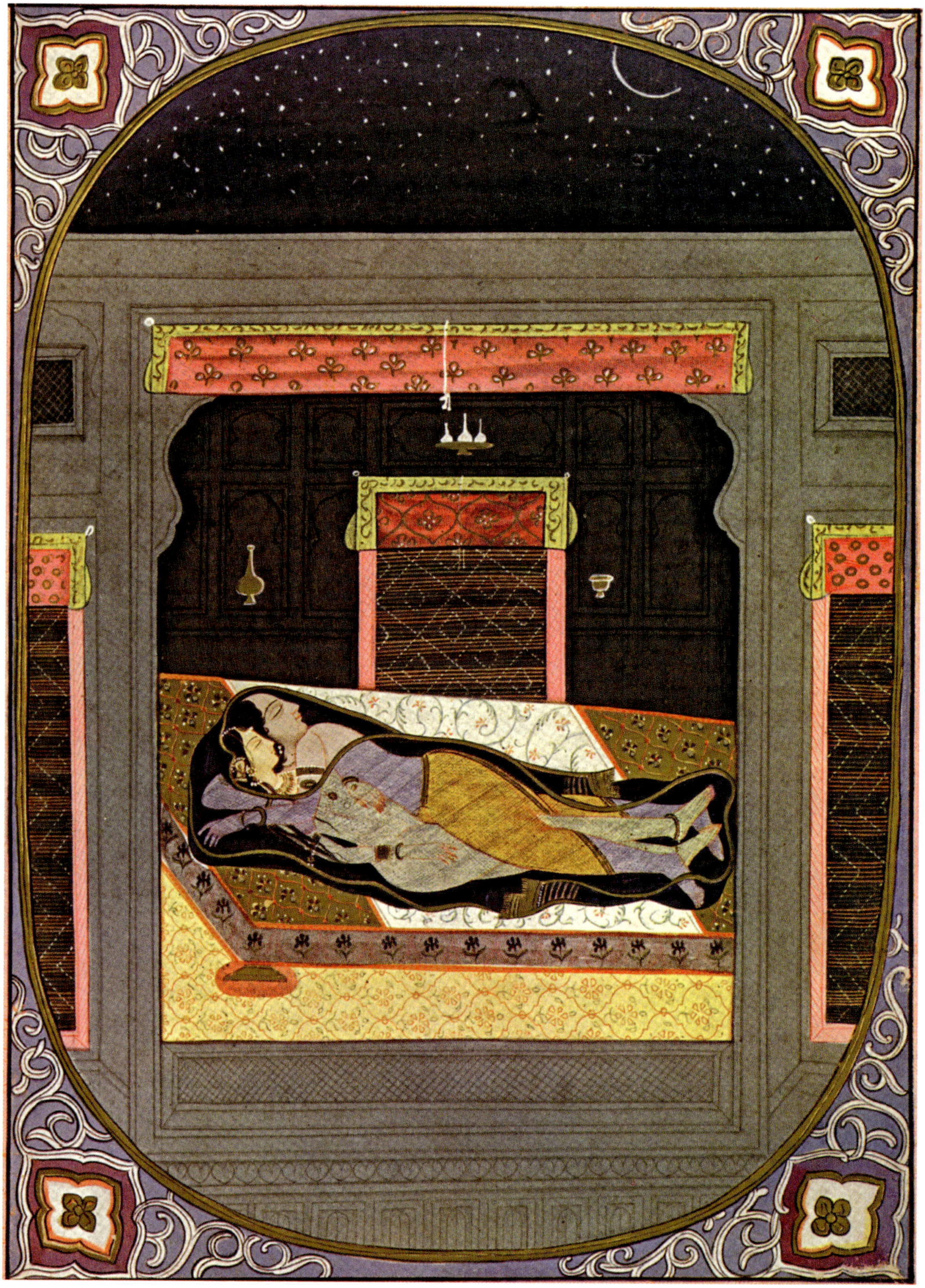

Praudha Nayika, school of Purkhu, Kangra, CE 1785-90, National Museum, Delhi.

प्रौढ़ा

लपटानी अति प्रेम सो दै उर उरज उतंग।
घरी एक लौं छुटेहु पर रही लगी-सी अंग।।

Praudha Nayika

Embracing her lover the praudha nayika *sleeps on the bed in her chamber. Though she has fallen in deep sleep yet she does not let loose the grip of his embrace even for a moment.*

It is a romantic night with a crescent moon and a starry sky. The vestiges of the deep night sky suggest that it is the dead of night. In the innermost chamber of the *haveli* there is a palpable serenity and the air is still and quiet, and lover and beloved are in a deep and romantic embrace on a raised white bedstead. Their eyes are shut and bliss is written all over their faces even as their bodies express the sensuality and warmth of love. In his two arms, he holds his beloved in a sweet sleep of love. The bodies of the two lovers are entwined in a blue diaphanous veil, yet the contours of their bodies are clearly visible.Though the paraphernalia of love are absent from the chamber, some wine bottles and cups placed in the niches of the bedroom suggest a romantic aura. There is a subdued ambience of love all over. The rolled up pink curtains and dark grey walls add to the quiet elegance of this moment of love. The inky blue sky strewn with a galaxy of stars and the diaphanous veil wrapping the lovers indicate the season of summer. The artist succeeds in presenting a quiet, serene, and intimate moment of love. He composes the painting in a symmetrical manner. The painting is enclosed in an oval-shaped border with a decorated design, typical of the Sansar Chand period.

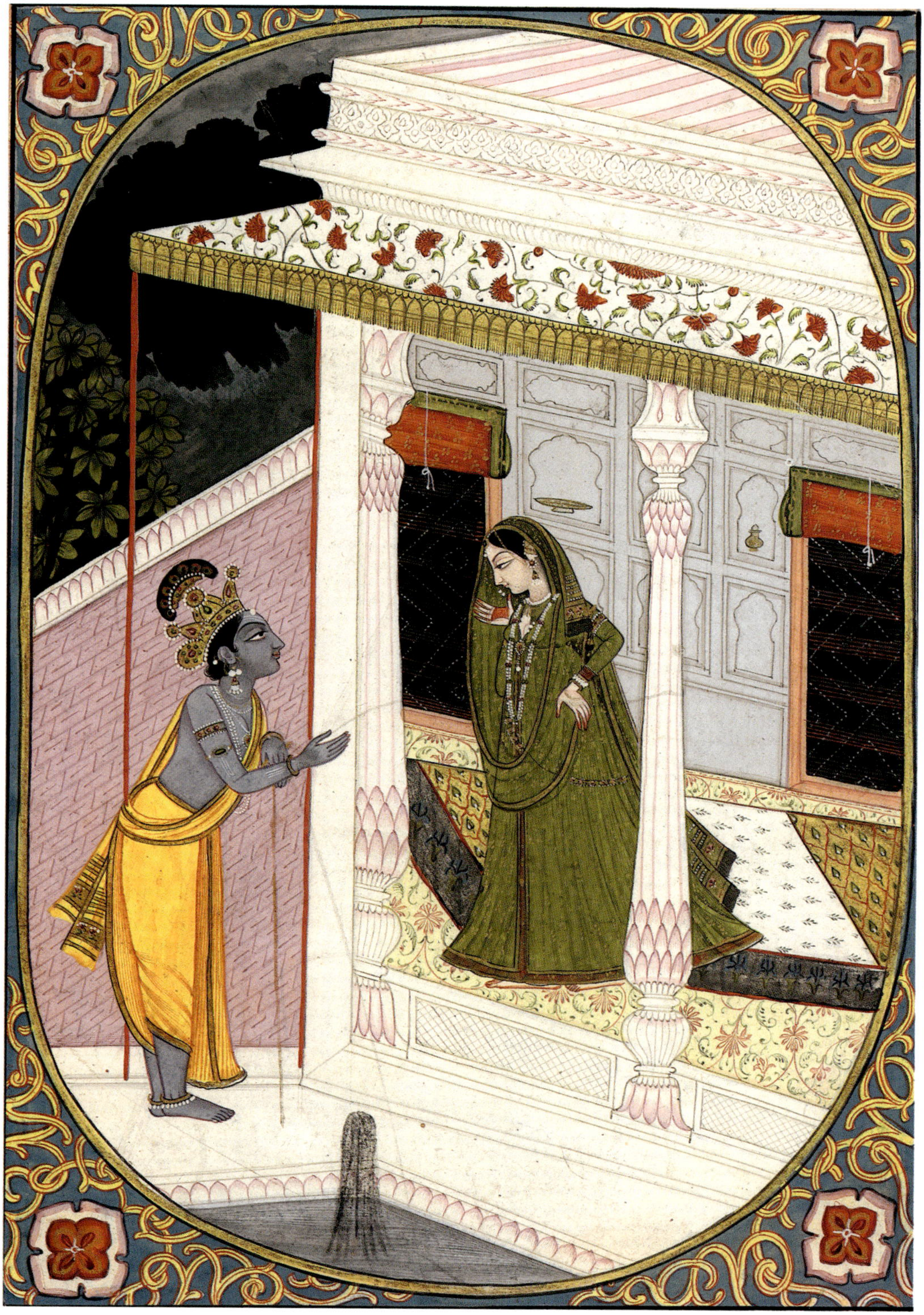

Madhya Dhira-Adhira Nayika, school of Purkhu, Kangra, CE 1785-90, Dehejia collection.

मध्या धीराधीरा

तुमसौं कीजै मान क्यौं बहु नायक मनरंज ।
बात कहत यौं बाल के भरि आए दृगकंज ।।

Madhya Dhira-Adhira Nayika

A nayika *speaks to her* nayak, *who has just returned after spending time with another woman: You are so smart and liked by several women. O dear! Why should I feign anger and be displeased with you? Saying these words, tears rolled down from the eyes of that young* nayika.

Clad in a green *peshwaz*, the *madhya dhira adhira* heroine stands between the two fluted lotus pillars of her apartment. Sumptuously dressed in anticipation of union with her beloved, she waits for a long time. The *nayak* arrives late at night after enjoying the company of another woman. The offended *nayika* expresses her anger with mild words and reflects on her own state of mind.

Night is suggested by a pitch dark sky laden with rainy clouds. Leaning against a staff, the *nayak* who is none other than Krishna, wearing a crown topped with a peacock feather and sporting a *pitambar*. The *nayak* is shown standing outside the pavilion beneath a fringed canopy. In order to assuage his sulking beloved, he raises his right hand to explain the reason for his late arrival. Dark clouds in the sky suggest that it is late in the night. The coy *nayika* occupies the focal place in the pictorial composition and casts glances towards her husband from the veil. Her *henna* smeared feet and palms and tapering red fingers apparently suggest that she had fully prepared for a romantic union with her lover.

The painter exhibits his skill in capturing the melancholic emotions that are discernible on the *nayika's* otherwise bashful face. He renders minute detailing in the designs seen in the fringed umbrella sported with poles, floral carpet and a bedstead. Even the intricate details in the architectural edifices, especially in the fluted columns are well depicted. The entire atmosphere brings an air of placid ambience that enhances the mood of romantic suggestions. The decorative design in four corners of the oval frame is the hallmark of the painter of this extensive series.

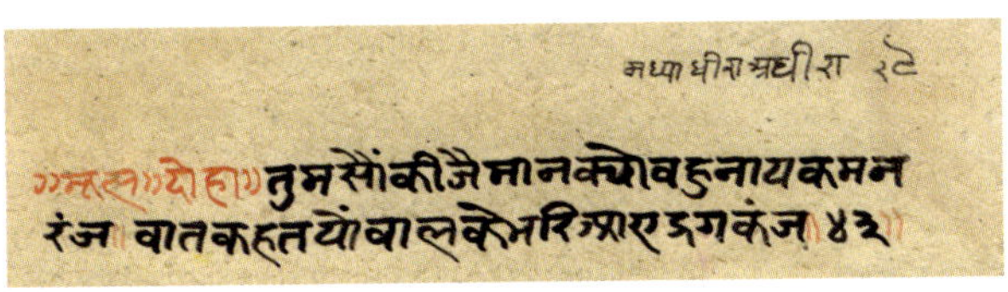

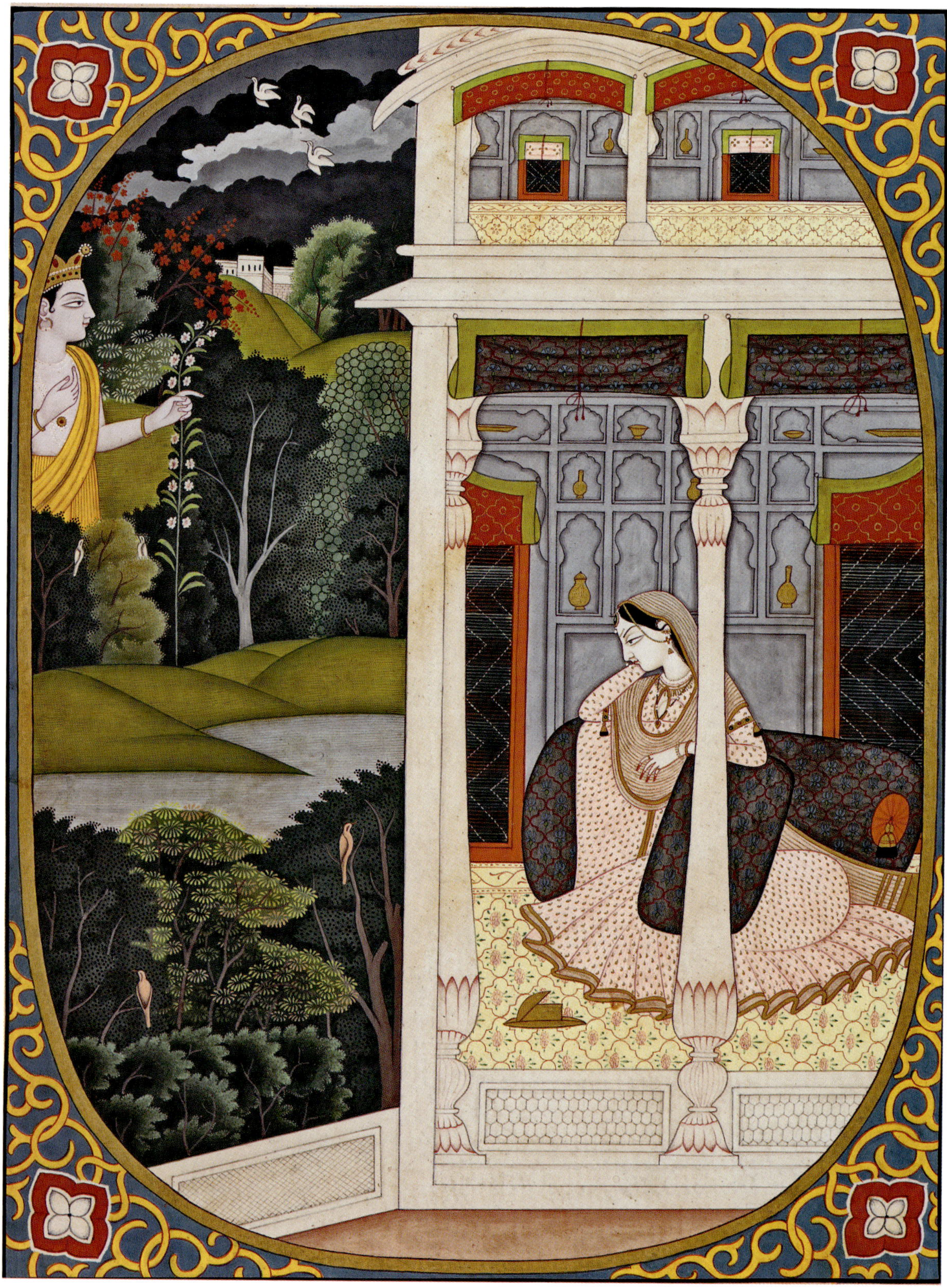

Anusayana Nayika, school of Purkhu, Kangra, CE 1785-90, Dehejia collection

अनुसयना

अनुसयना छरी सपल्लव लाल कर लखि तमाल की हाल ।
कुम्हिलानी उरसाल धरि फूलमाल ज्यौं बाल ।।

Tritiya Anusayana Nayika

When Radha saw Krishna holding a branch with leaf and blossoms freshly plucked from a tamala *tree, her heart was filled with remorse at not having kept the appointed tryst. She turned pale and withered like a flower.*

The Devanagari text at the verso mentions the *nayika* as *anusayana*, or one who is overcome with sorrow. The *anusayana* suffers remorse because of her helplessness to go to the appointed rendezvous, where her beloved has already reached. In the depiction of Anusayana Radha in this picture which has been composed in an oval format, she is seen seated on a carpet leaning against large bolsters. Clad in a richly embroidered pink outfit with detailing of golden dots, she is richly adorned with jewellery. Her costume is delicately rendered. The artist skilfully depicts the emotion of sorrow on her face. On the farther hill just opposite Radha's resplendent palace, the crowned Krishna carrying a leafy branch freshly plucked from a *tamala* tree, wears a yellow garment and a crown topped by lotus buds. He intentionally holds the branch of the *tamala* tree just to make Radha aware that she had not kept her rendezvous.

The turbulent sky, laden with dark grey rainy clouds, the flight of cranes and clusters of leafy green trees suggest the monsoon season. Some houses peeping behind the receding hillock suggest a village locality. Two birds that the painter cleverly depicts on the trees near Radha's chamber are shown symbolically in opposite directions. Perhaps these birds suggest the mental anguish of both the lovers. The painter skilfully paints the niches of the chamber and prefers to use a silvery colour for the curtains and bolsters which have now been oxidised with the course of time.

On the basis of compositional conventions and craftsmanship, this painting can be attributed to the painter Purkhu at the atelier of Sansar Chand of Kangra.

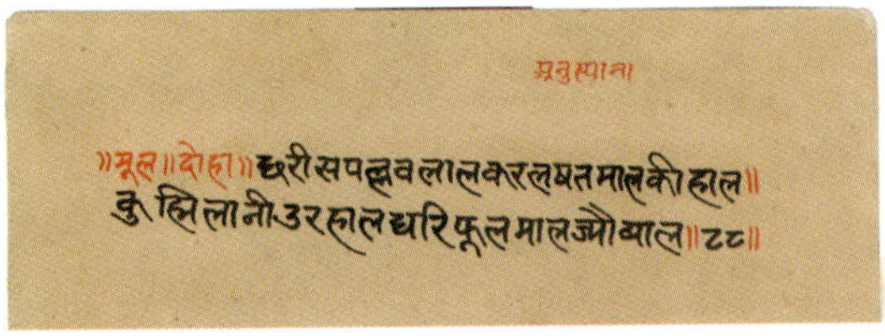

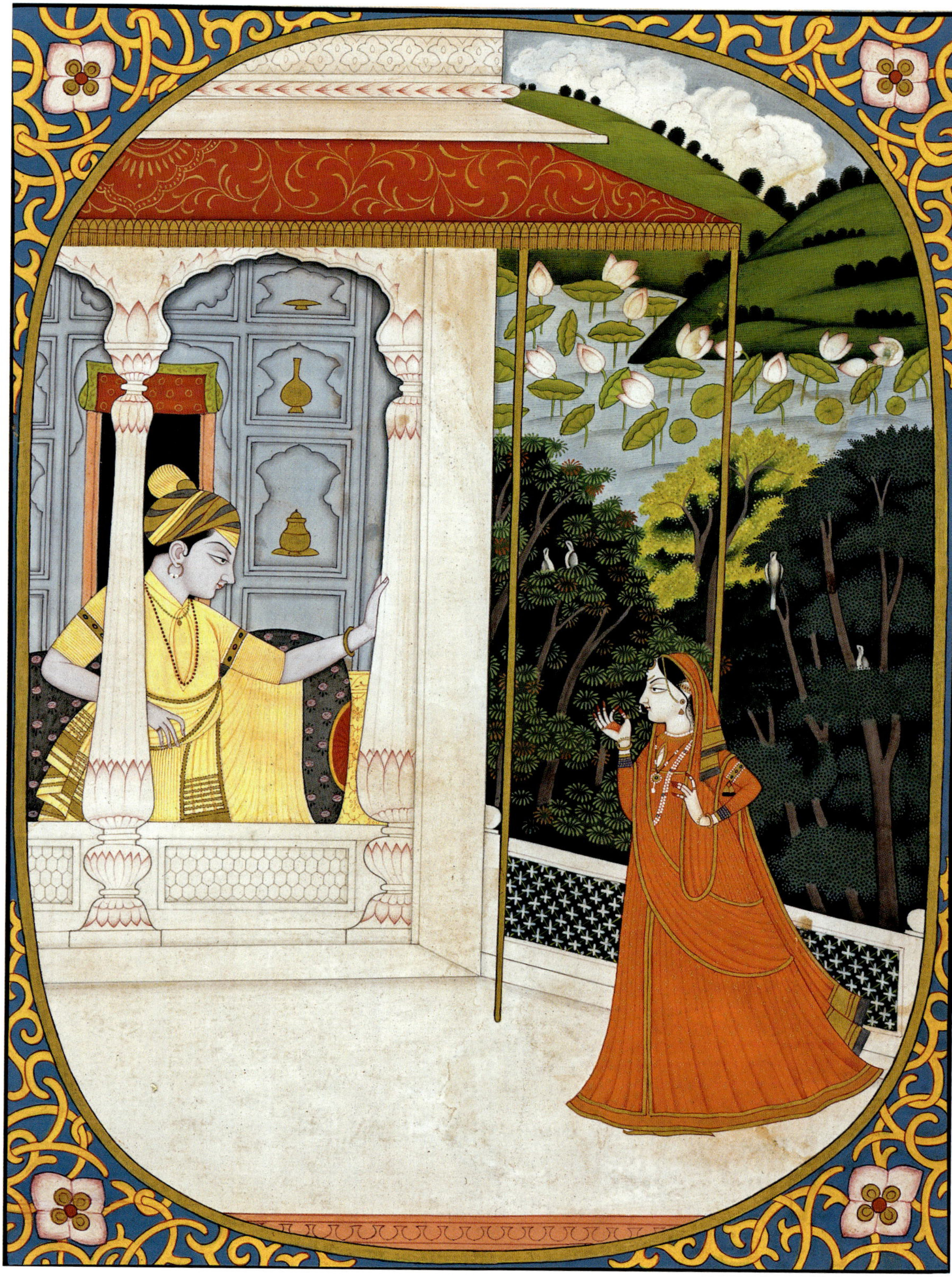

Ganika Nayika, school of Purkhu, Kangra, CE 1785-90, Dehejia collection.

गणिका

लाल कर चरन रदन छद नख लाल, मोतिन की रदन रही है छबि छाइकै ।
कबि मतिराम मुख सुबरन रूप रहि, रूपखानि मुसकानि सोभा सरसाइकै।
आनन कौं इंदु जान आँखैं अरबिंद मानि, इंदिरा रजनि दिन रहति सिहाइकै ।
नायक नवल क्यों न देय धन-मन ऐसे, सुतनु कौं सुतनु अतनु-धन पाइकै ।।

Ganika Nayika

The ganika nayika *decorates her body by applying henna to her tapering fingers and alta to her feet. Her scarlet lips are attractive and teeth glitter like pearls. Matiram says that the* nayika's *radiant face glows like gold as if she is a mine of beauty. She looks exceedingly charming when she smiles. Her fair complexioned face appears like the moon and her elongated eyes are like two lotus buds. She is beautiful and wealthy to the extent that even Goddess Lakshmi feels envious. The young* nayak *gladly offers favours to that* ganika nayika. *Though the* ganika *surrenders only her body to the cupid-like* nayak, *yet in return she captures not only his wealth but heart too.*

A *ganika* (courtesan) is *rupa jiva* or one earns money on account of her beauty and whose sole concern is to extract money from her lovers. It is a charmed moment and everywhere there is delight and joy. The lotuses that sway in the wind seem to be singing a love song. Birds perched on trees seem to be whispering words of love to each other. One tree has burst into yellow blossoms as if to fill the air with the colours of spring. The ambience is charged with love and there is an air of sweetness. Just then a *ganika nayika*, sumptuously dressed in a red *peshwaz* and tastefully bejewelled, her right hand raised in a *mudra* of love looks at the *nayak* seated in the window and who peeps through the window and her eyes lock with his. It is in the coming together of their gaze that the romantic moment is complete. Nothing is said but a lot is understood between the two and the world around concurs. The Kangra artist has created a beautiful composition where human love resonates with love all around and we who partake of this cannot but be touched by it. The painter has used the art of perspective by showing receding hills and a placid lake strewn with lotuses. Designs at the four corners of the oval format further enhances the beauty of this Kangra painting.

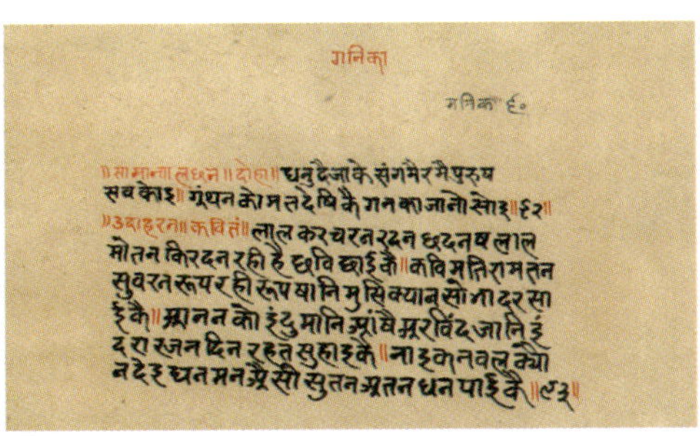
गनिका

गनिका ६०

॥सामान्या लछन॥दोहा॥ धनु देजाके संगमेर मैपुरुष
सबकोइ॥ गुंधन कोमत देषि कै गनका जानो सोइ॥६२॥
॥उदाहरन॥कवित्त॥ लाल कर चरन रदन छदन ष लाल
मोतन किरदन रही है छवि छाई कै॥ कवि मतिराम तेन
सुवरन रूप रही रूप षानि मुसिक्यान सोभा दरसा
ईकै॥ आनन को इंदु मानि आंषै अरविंद जानि इं
दरा रजन दिन रहत सुहाइकै॥ नाइक नवल क्यों
न देइ धन मन ऐसी सुतन अतन धन पाईकै॥६३॥

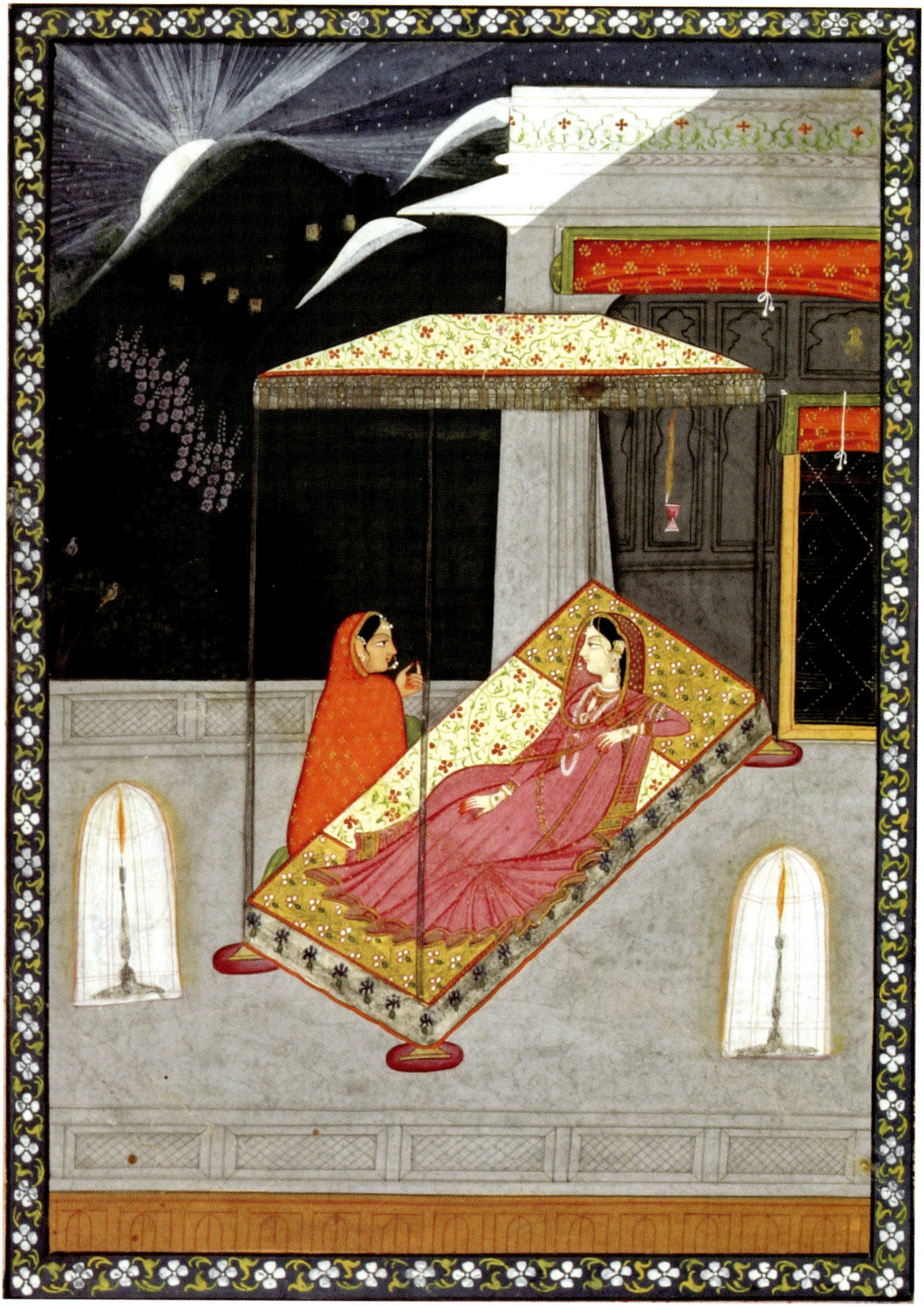

Mugdha Utkanthita Nayika, school of Purkhu, Kangra, CE 1785-90, Harish Patel, New York.

मुग्धा-उत्कंठिता

बीत गई जुग जाम निसा मतिराम मिटी तम की सरसाई ।
जानति हौं कहुँ और तिया से रहे रस में रमिकै रसराई ।
सोचति सेज परीयों नबेली सहेली सौं जाति न बात सुनाई ।
चंद चढ़ो उदयाचल पै मुखचंद पै आनि चढ़ी पियराई ।।

Mugdha Utkanthita Nayika

When half the night had passed and the nayak *(Krishna) did not come to the rendezvous, the bashful heroine's heart filled with anxiety. She assumed that the* nayak *must have engaged in romantic pleasures with another woman. The love-lorn* nayika *is unable to describe her condition even to her intimate companions. When she was thinking thus the moon began to rise at the horizon. Looking at the silvery moonbeams, that heartbroken* nayika's *face too turned pale with anguish.*

The pitch black background and two lanterns placed in the foreground suggest night time. On a palace terrace, an elegant and bashful *nayika* reclines on a canopied bed placed diagonally. She is fashionably dressed and richly adorned with jewellery. The *utkanthita nayika*, as described by the poet, is clad in a multi-pleated full length pink robe (*peshwaz*) revealing the sensuous curves of her shapely body. The porcelain-like beauty of the charming *nayika* is characterised by slim waist, pointed bosom and *henna*-coloured tapering fingers.

For a long time the *nayika* has waited for her lover, who failed to keep his promise to meet her. Though she looks keenly towards her companion sitting before her, she hesitates to reveal her mind. However, a subtle hint of discreet frustration is discernible on her lips. The dazzling moonbeams coming out from the horizon further increase the *nayika's* anguish.

The facial type of *nayika* represents the Kangra style that was prevalent at the atelier of Sansar Chand of Kangra during the last decade of eighteenth century, i.e. 1790-1800. The workmanship of this picture is characterised by precise brush work and a palette of soft, muted colours. He places the decorated bedstead diagonally in the middle of the picture to highlight the figure of the demure *nayika*. Two illuminating lanterns placed in the foreground on either side of the bed balances the composition of the painting.

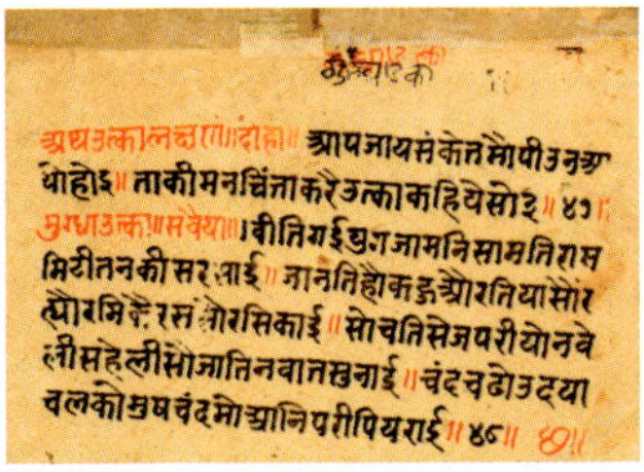

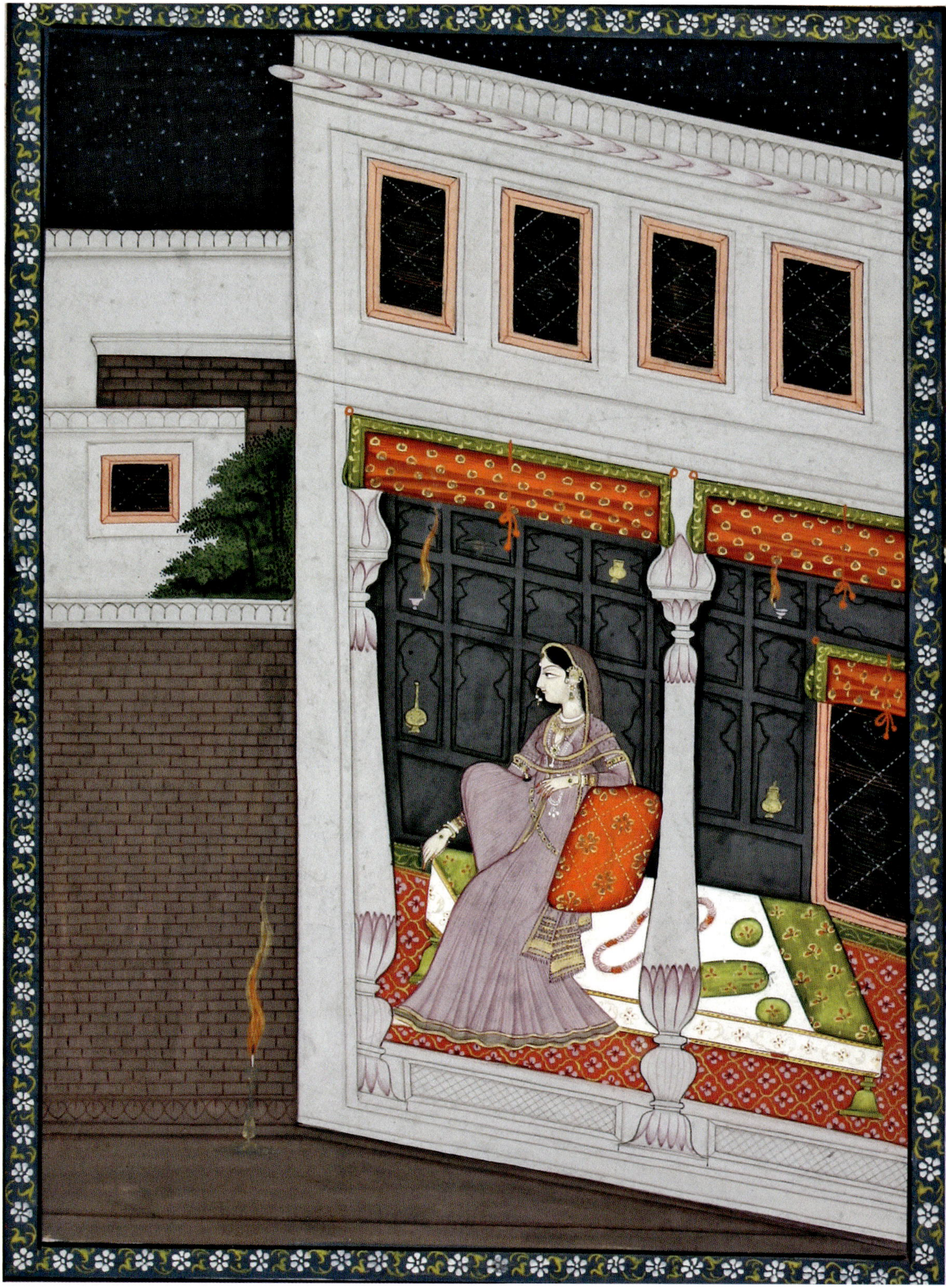

Praudha Vasakasajja Nayika, school of Purkhu, Kangra, CE 1785-90, Art of the Past, New York.

प्रौढ़ा-वासकसज्जा

बारनि धूपि अँगारनि धूप कै धूम अँध्यारी पसारी महा है ।
आननचंद समान उगो मृदु मंद हँसी जनो जोन्हछटा है ।
फैलि रही मतिराम जहाँ तहाँ दीपति दीपनि की परभा है ।
लाल तिहारे मिलाप को बाल ने आजु करी दिन में ही निसा है ।।

Praudha Vasakasajja Nayika

> *The freshly bathed* nayika *dries her hair in the sun. Then she scents them with aromatic herbs burnt on charcoal. There is smoke all around and that fair complexioned* nayika's *radiant face shines like the full moon and her sweet smile spreads like moonlight. She has adorned herself profusely with dazzling jewels and the sparkling adornment on her garment twinkles like tiny lamps.* O nayak! *The passionate* vasakasajja nayika *has created a nocturnal ambience during the day for amorous sports.*

To adorn oneself is to beautify and to ornament oneself is to extend an invitation. Such is the emotional state of the *vasakasajja* who is mature in the arts of love. As she sits expectantly and in readiness dressed in a mauve *peshwaz* there is an air of confidence about her. The bed reflects her desires with bolsters and a flower garland waiting to be used during love sports that will follow. Two lamps containing camphor and oil light and perfume the room and richly decorated curtains are ready to be drawn. She will convert day into night and hesitation into sport, such is her charm. The *praudha vasakasajja* contemplates the amorous pleasures that await her. As night passes, she is impatient for the promised meeting. A flare outside the pleasure pavilion awaits the arrival of the beloved.

The painter divides the bedroom by placing fluted columns, which draws our attention to the *nayika*. The *nayika* has decorated her chamber with various objects. She has placed on the bed a floral garland to greet her lover. The red carpet and rolled cloth curtain further add elegance to the painting.

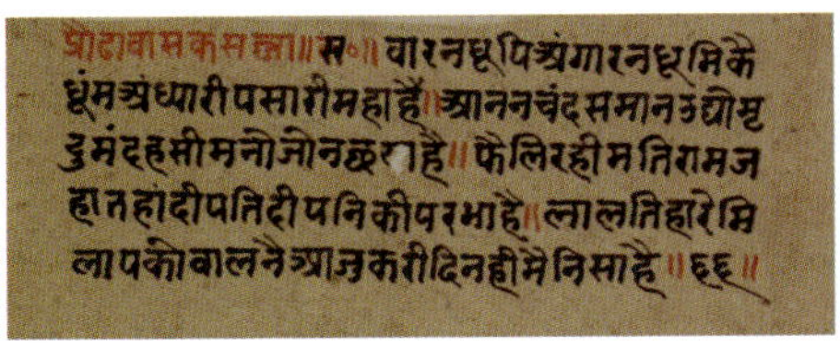
प्रौढावासकसज्जा ॥ स० ॥ वारनधूपिअंगारनधूमिके
धूंमअंध्यारीपसारीमहाहैं ॥ आननचंदसमानउगोमृ
दुमंदहसीमनोजोन्हछटा है ॥ फैलिरहीमतिरामज
हांतहांदीपतिदीपनिकीपरभाहै ॥ लालतिहारेमि
लापकोबालनेआजुकरीदिनहीमेनिसाहै ॥ ६६ ॥

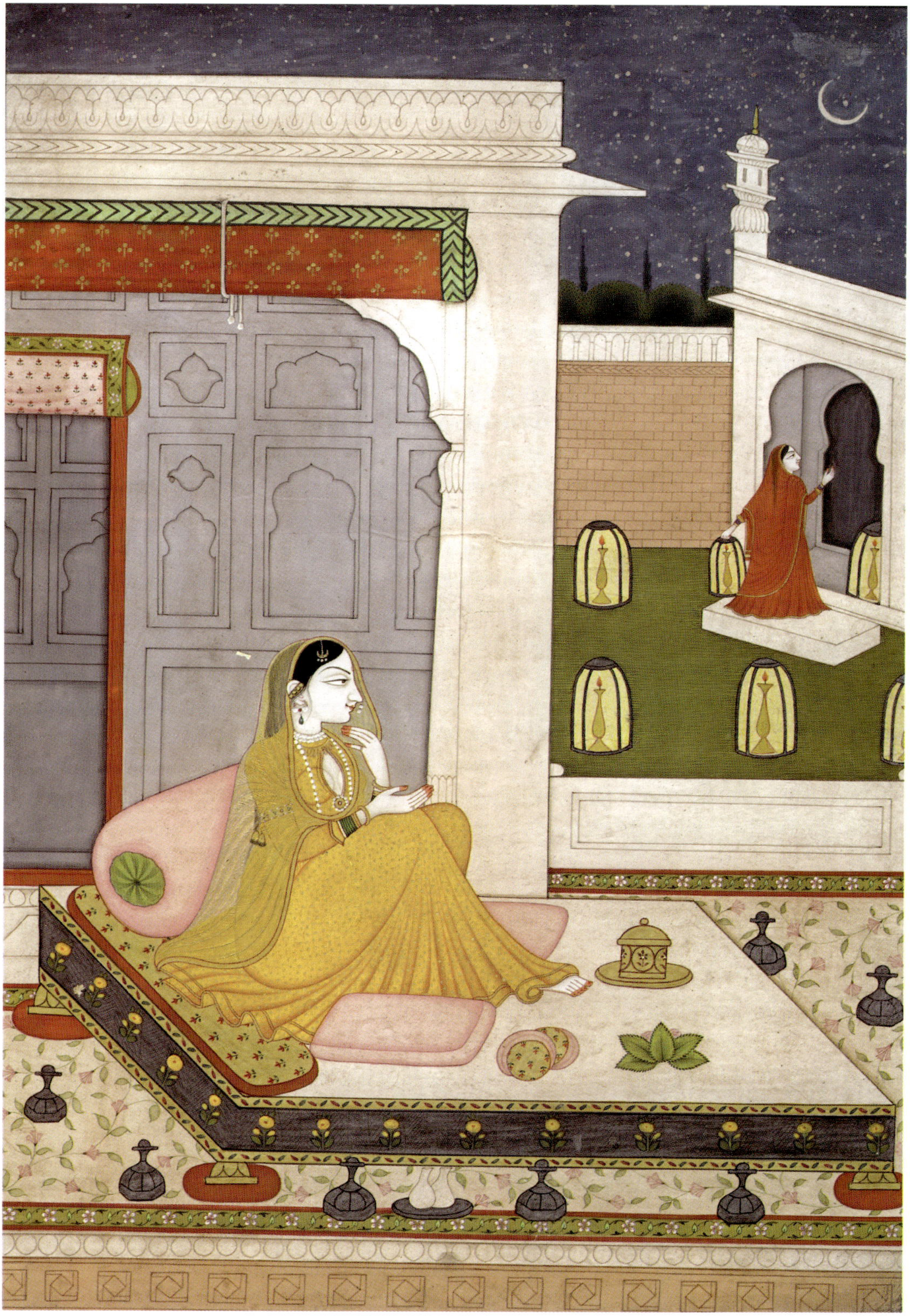

Vasaksajja Nayika, school of Purkhu, Kangra, CE 1785-90, Dehejia collection.

वासकसज्जादूसरा
सब सिँगार सुंदरि सजै बैठी सेज बिछाय।
भयो द्रौपदी को बसनु बासर नाहिं बिहाय।।

Vasaksajja Nayika

> *After adorning herself profusely, that coy* nayika *sits on a bedstead anticipating the arrival of her lover. Thus time appears to her as long as Draupadi's stretched garment.*

It is a starry night with a crescent moon in the sky. A *sakhi* waits at the door expectantly placing even as lanterns illuminate the garden. It is a moment of anticipation of the arrival of the *nayak*. After taking in this landscape, one's eyes settle on the *vasakasajja nayika* who anxiously awaits her beloved. Elegantly clad in a golden *ghaghra* and resting against a pink bolster, her eyes look into the distance through her *odhni*. Her hands speak of longing and expectation. The *chauk* on which she sits is empty, as is her heart, save for the betel box and freshly plucked flowers, which is a reminder of romantic moments that will follow once the beloved returns. A carafe of wine is placed in the foreground to serve the *nayak*. But that wait is unending like the *vastra* (garment) of Draupadi. The Kangra artist has rendered a fine painting where every detail eloquently describes the mood of expectation and longing, the pain of *viraha* and the emptiness of life without the beloved. The niches of the wall in the chamber are devoid of any object or decoration. The row of bulbous trees in the background and a turret above the cornice of the entrance suggest the period of this Kangra work in the last quarter of the eighteenth century.

The painting is probably not from the workshop of Purkhu, yet a remarkable influence of the Seu-Nainsukh family style is clearly discernible in this work. The silver colour used in the bedstead and the utensils filled with scented water placed around the bed seems to have been tarnished with the course of time.

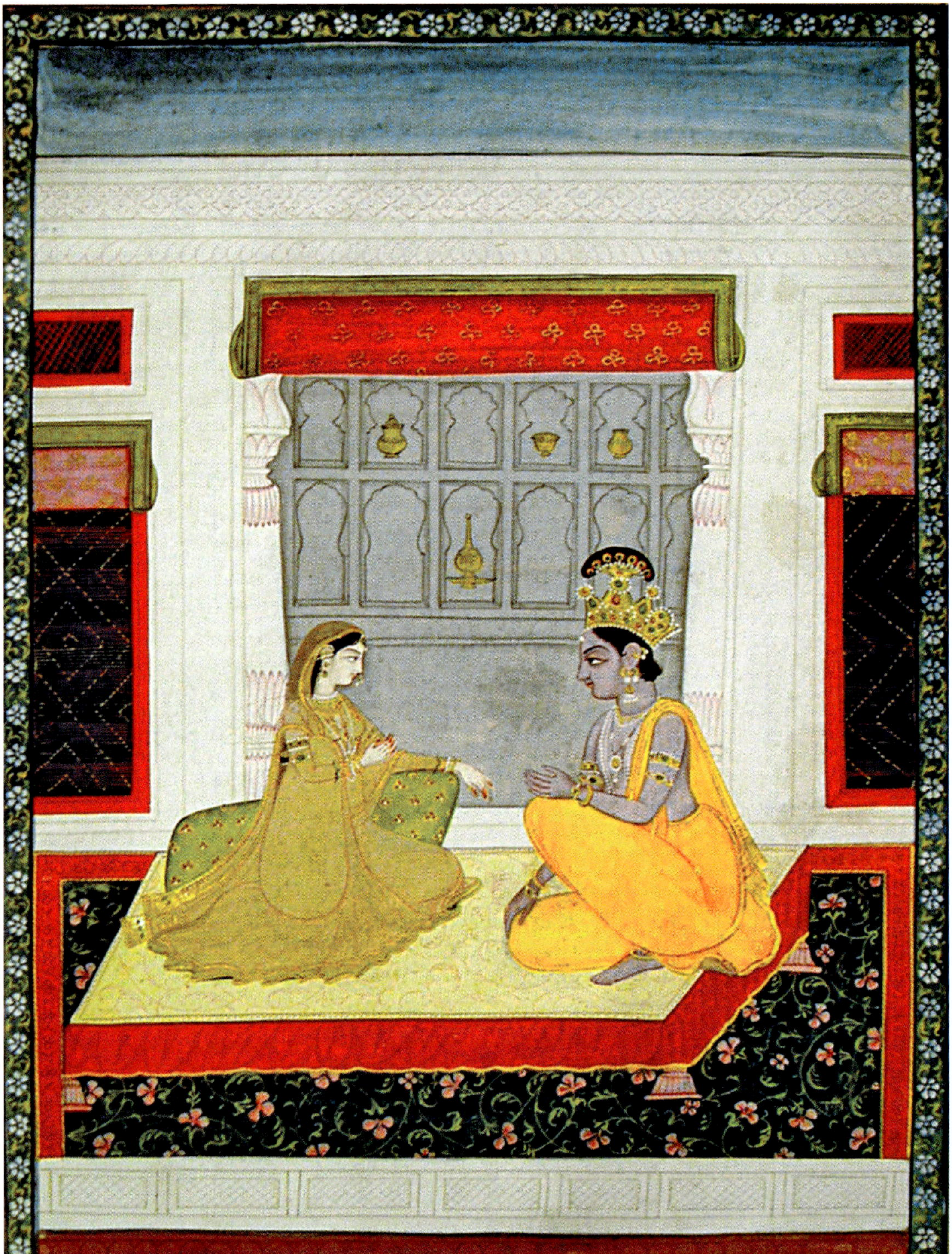

Mugdha Svadhinapatika, school of Purkhu, Kangra, CE 1785-90, private collection

मुग्धा-स्वाधीनपतिका

आपने हाथ सौं देत महावर आप ही बार सँवारत नीके ।
आपनु ही पहिरावत आनिकै हार सँवारिकै मौरसिरी के ।
हौं सखि लाजनि जात मुरी मतिराम सुभाव कहा कहौं पी के ।
लोक मिलैं घर घैरु करैं अबही ते ये चेरे भए दुलही के ।।

Mugdha Svadhinapatika

Rapt in seeing the sublime beauty of that bashful mugdha svadhinapatika nayika*, it appears to the* nayak *as if his eyes have taken a dip in the occean of nectar.*

In a resplendent mansion the *mugdha swadhinapatika nayika* sits on a raised couch resting against bolsters. Clad in a light green-coloured dress, the fair complexioned *nayika* is richly decorated with ornaments. An emotion of shyness can be seen on her benign face. She faces towards the *nayak* (Krishna) who intently casts glances on the *nayika*'s charming limbs. The coy *nayika* is of *svadhinpatika* type, whose *nayak* is subject to her wish and is never far from her.

Here, the purple-coloured *nayak* is shown wearing a yellow *dhoti* and an *uttariya.* He sports a bejewelled crown topped by a peacock feather (*mora-mukuta*) like that of Krishna. The *rasika nayak* sits in *virasana* posture, as if in readiness to fulfil *nayika*'s every wish. His transfixed gaze at *nayika*'s radiant face reveals that his eyes are engaged in enjoying the *rasa* of her sublime beauty.

The dark blue sky with white streaks suggests the night time. The scene is composed in a symmetrical setting. The palace architecture is simple and devoid of any decorative motifs. Fluted lotus columns, which are invariably seen in paintings of Rasraj are shown. However, the painter balances the composition by adding detailing like latticed ventilators and entrance gates covered with curtains. Further, he renders intricate brushwork in the depiction of the floral pattern on the carpet. A wine bottle and cup suggests romantic pleasures. Like other paintings from the same series, the artist encloses the painting by a decorative border with tendril pattern. Here the painter prefers to render the *nayak* wearing a crown topped with peacock feathers as Krishna, rather than a courtly *nayak* in a *jama* and *kuledar* turban.

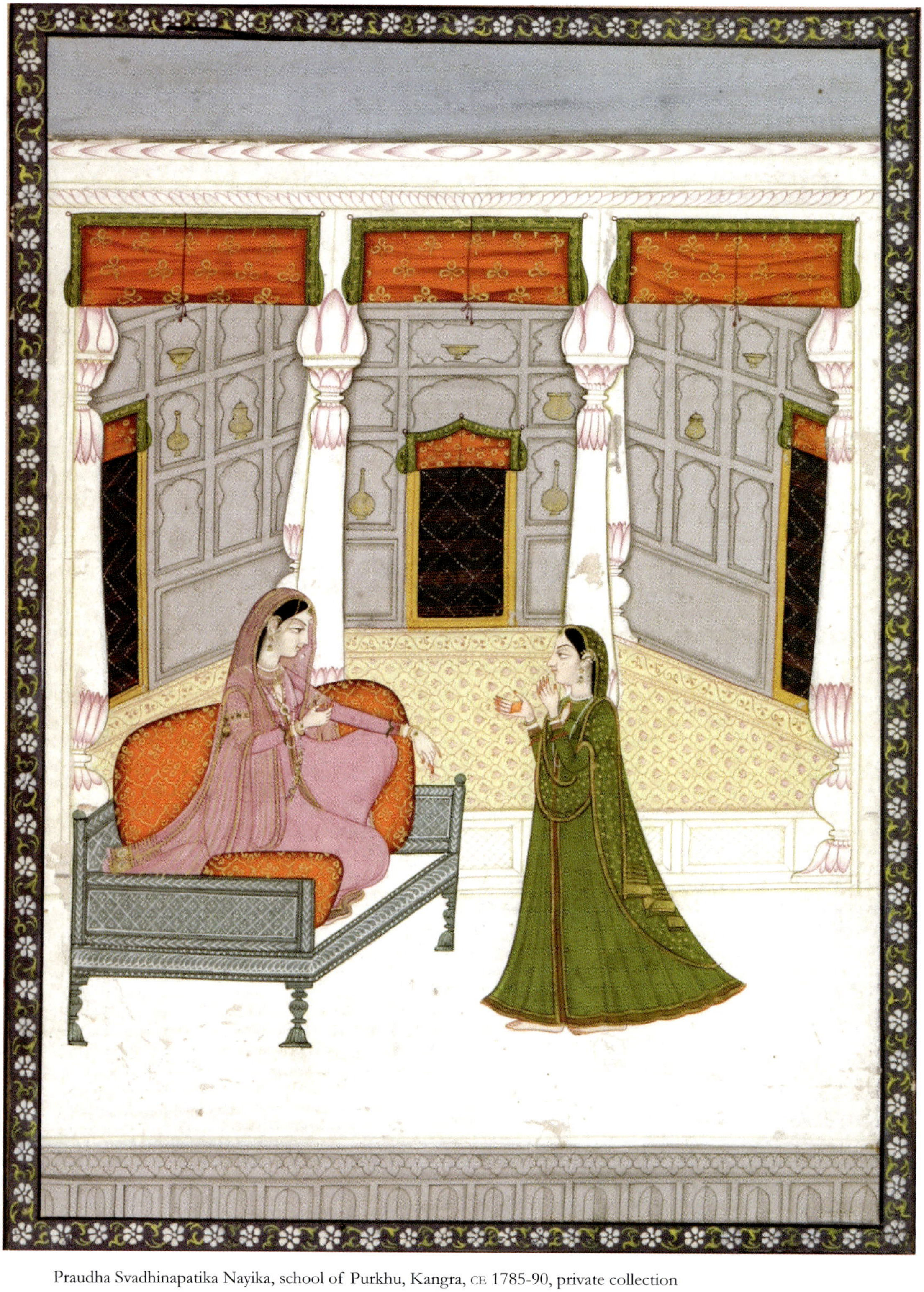

Praudha Svadhinapatika Nayika, school of Purkhu, Kangra, CE 1785-90, private collection

प्रौढ़ा स्वाधीनपतिका

सुधा-मधुर तेरे अधर सुंदर सुमन सुगंध।
पीय जीव को बंध यह बंधुजीव को बंध।।

Praudha Svadhinapatika Nayika

Your lips are sweeter than nectar and more fragrant than flowers. Your redness is enough to capture your beloved. It looks as if it is related to dupahriya *flowers.*

Matiram places these words in the mouth of a *sakhi* who is shown standing before the *praudha svadhinapatika nayika*. Fluted columns adorned with lotuses support rolled up curtains in the inner apartment with understated elegance save a floral carpet. A *nayika* dressed in a pink *peshwaz*, seated on a raised couch, has her left hand elegantly resting on her knee while the right hand seems to be questioning the certitude of her love. Across from her is her animated *sakhi* who gestures words of reassurance to her. It seems as if the *nayika* is unsure of herself and her *sakhi* assuages her and confirms that her charm has captivated her beloved and that he is under her control. In this work, which has a symmetrical composition, it is the hands that are most evocative and draw our attention. The painter has used intricate detailing on the walls to create a beautiful painting in the typical Kangra style. The diagonal walls and the fluted columns seen in the background create a feeling of perspective. The pale-coloured carpet and the resplendent white marble floor in the foreground help enhance the contrast of the main figures.

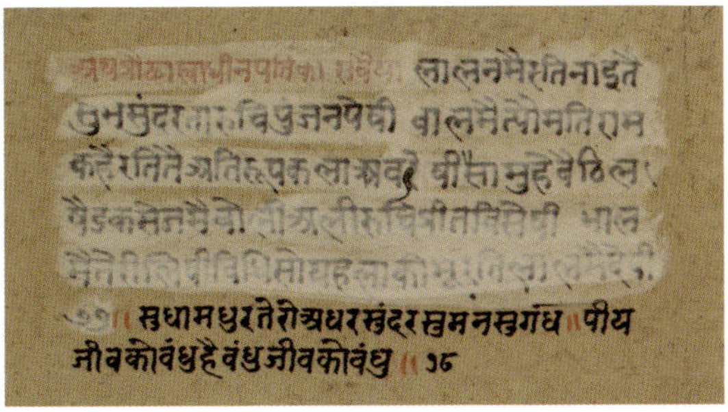

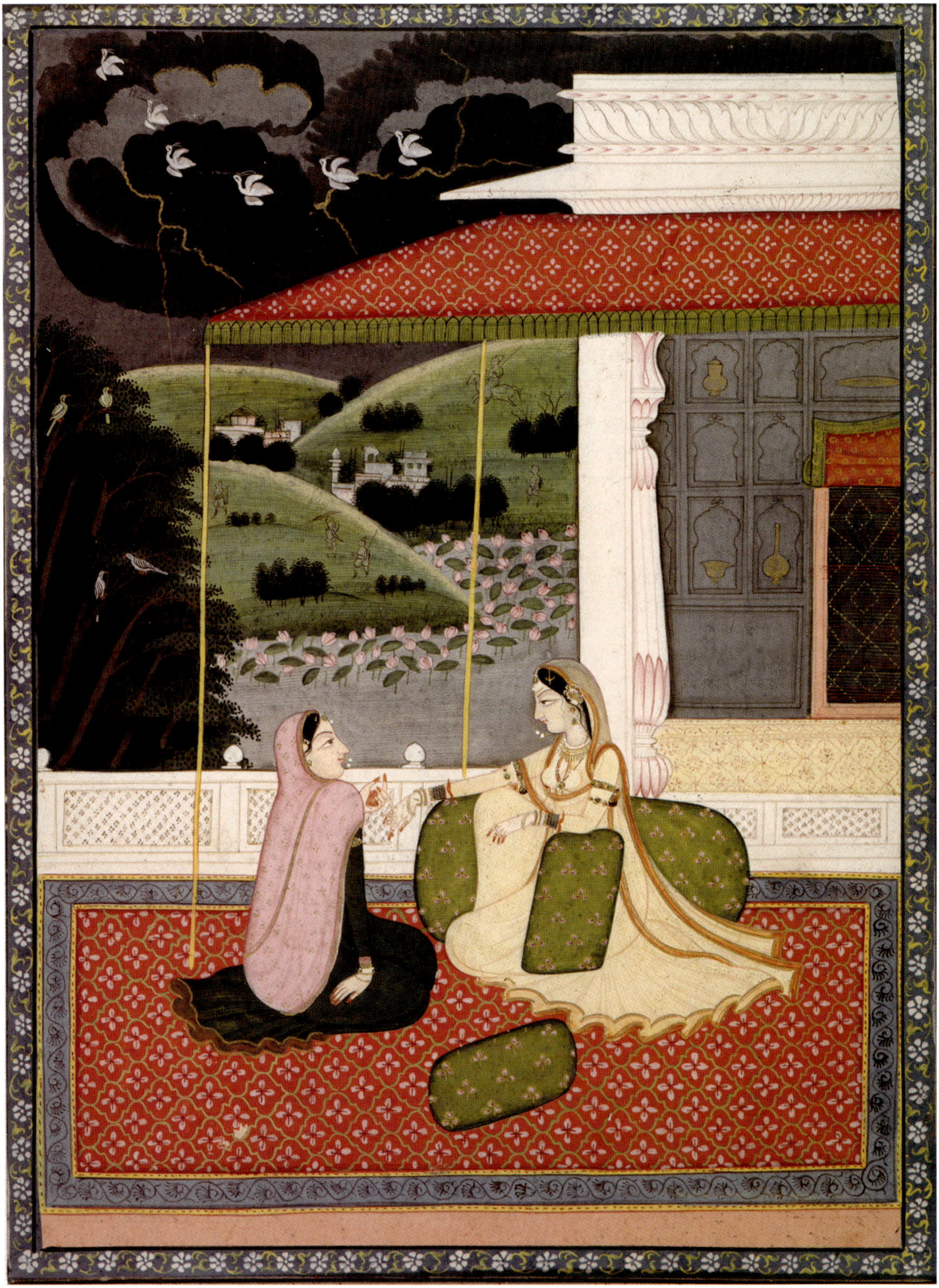

Ganika Svadhinapatika Nayika, school of Purkhu, Kangra, CE 1785-90, Dehejia collection.

गणिका स्वाधीनपतिका
आपुहि पान खवात आई सहेलिन आवन पावत नेरे ।
भूषन अंबर लयावत आपु रहै पहिरावत को मुख हेरे ।
पूरि रहे मनभावन के गुन मान कौ ठौर नही मन मेरे ।
ता पिय सौ रिस कैसे करो मतिराम कहे सिख ऐ सखि तेरे॥

Ganika Svadhinapatika Nayika

O friend! Always staying near me, he (nayak) *offers me betel leaf and presents sumptuous gifts like garments and ornaments and decorates me while looking at my face. I am so much grateful to him that there is hardly any room for anger. So dear! I cannot heed your advice to offend such a magnanimous lover!*

A *svadinapatika* is a *nayika* whose husband is subject to her wish and remains always devoted to her. Thus, this *nayika* is full of joy and expresses her feelings to her friends. Leaning against a bolster, a richly clad coy *nayika* sits confidently on a floral carpet underneath a fringed canopy. Overwhelmed by her husband's fidelity and passion she converses with her *sakhi*. The scene is set in an open terrace of the palace. It is the monsoon season as is seen by dark clouds and a flight of cranes. The placid lake is strewn with lotus flowers. The receding green hills with pale rims remind one of the hilly landscape of the Kangra Valley. A certain sense of perspective can be seen as the painter depicts tiny human figures in the farther hills. Two pairs of birds perched near the balustrade are symbolic of romantic suggestions. The artist adds minute detailing in the rendering of architectural edifice, carpet and canopy as well.

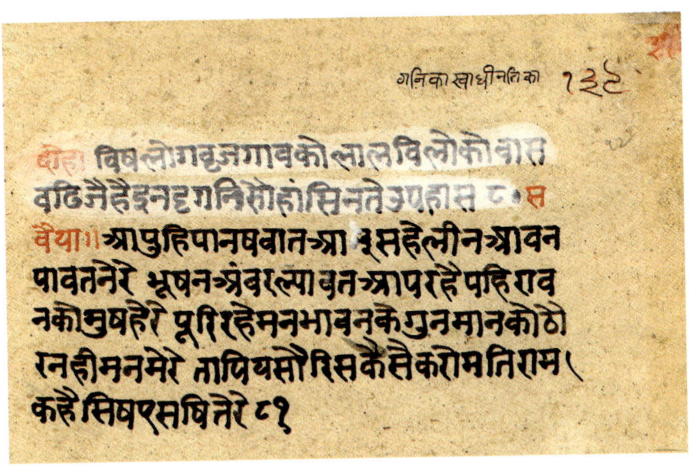
सवैया॥ आपुहिपानषवातआई सहेलीनआवन
पावतनेरे भूषनअंबरल्यावतआपरहेपहिराव
नकोमुषहेरे पूरिरहेमनभावनकेगुनमानकोठो
रनहीमनमेरे तापियसौरिसकैसेकरोमतिराम
कहेसिषएसषितेरे ८१

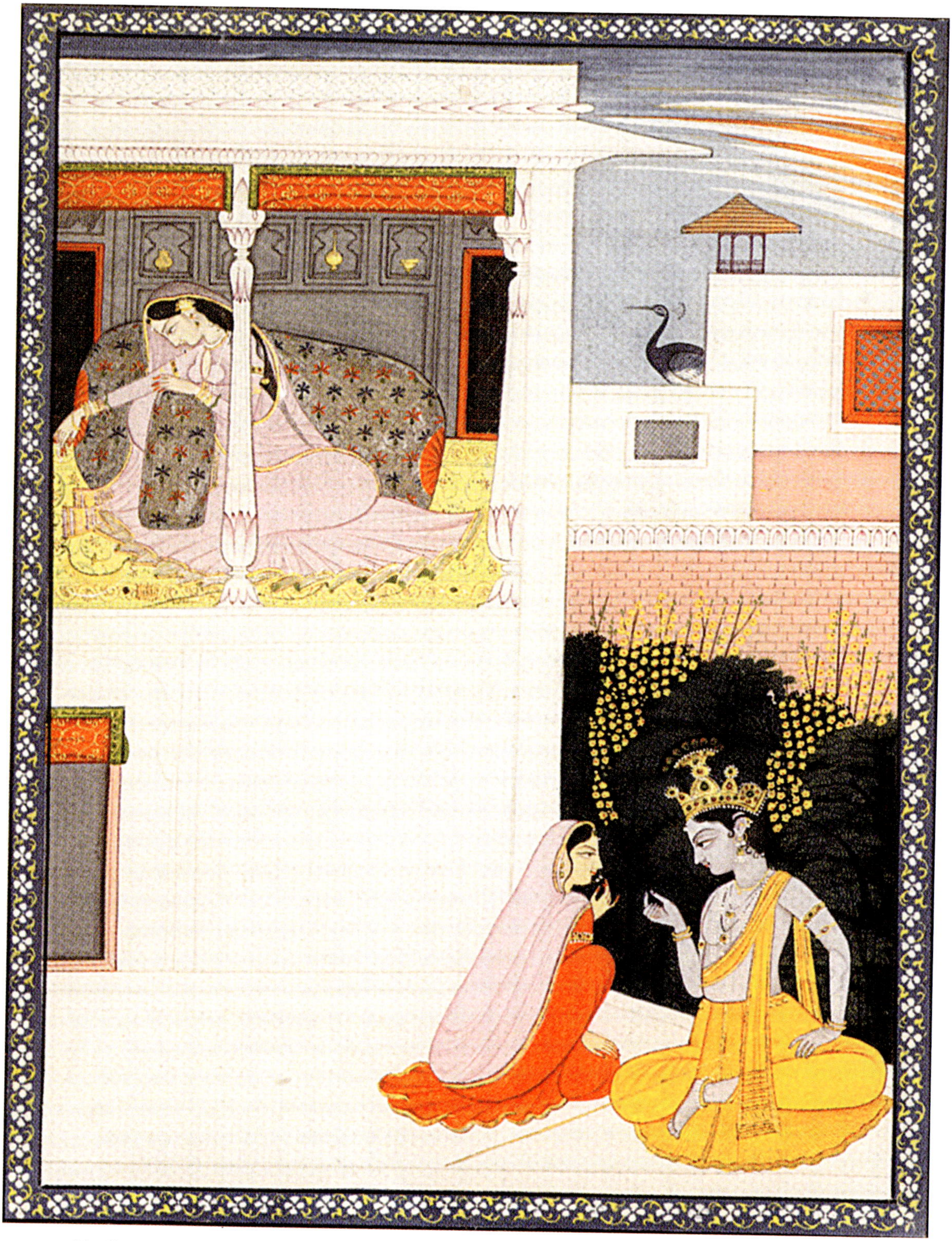

Mugdha Pravatsyatpreyasi Nayika, school of Purkhu, Kangra, CE 1785-90, private collection.

मुग्धा-प्रवत्स्यत्प्रेयसी

जा दिन तें चलिबे की चरचा चलाई तुम, ता दिन तें वाके पियराई तन छाई है ।
कहै मतिराम छोड़े भूषन बसन पान, सखिन सों खेलनि हँसनि बिसराई है ।
आई ऋतु सुरभि सुहाई प्रीति वाके चित्त, ऐसे में चलो तो लाल रावरी बड़ाई है ।
सेवत न रैन दिन रोवत रहति बाल, बूझे तें कहति मायके की सुधि आई है ।।

Mugdha Pravatsyatpreyasi Nayika

A sakhi *addresses the* nayika's *husband*:
That coy nayika'*s body has turned pale from the very day you announced that you will be leaving for a distant land. She has given up wearing ornaments and nice clothes. She put away the betel and stays aloof from her companions. Since the spring season has enhanced her romantic passion, it would be nice of you to turn your attention towards her. Now that young woman does not sleep in the night and sheds tears all the day long. If someone asks, she pretends that it is due to the remembrance of her parents.*

This is visual reportage at its best in the Kangra style. The narrative takes place in two parts. In the upper chamber we see a *nayika* in despair. Her body speaks of her pain, head downturned and her right arm drooping and eyes downcast. The room lacks cheer. On the terrace below a *sakhi* conveys the *nayika*'s pain to the *nayak*. The hand gestures convey a sense of the conversation. She implores and he listens, she urges and he considers. While the three human figures dominate the composition one cannot ignore the blossoming trees outside the *haveli* which adds to the poignancy of the impending separation.

The painter depicts vermilion and white streaks in the sky suggesting morning. He purposely paints yellow blossoms in the plants protruding out of the dark green trees to suggest the season of spring. A lonely peacock on the terrace further enhances the emotion of despair of the *nayika*.

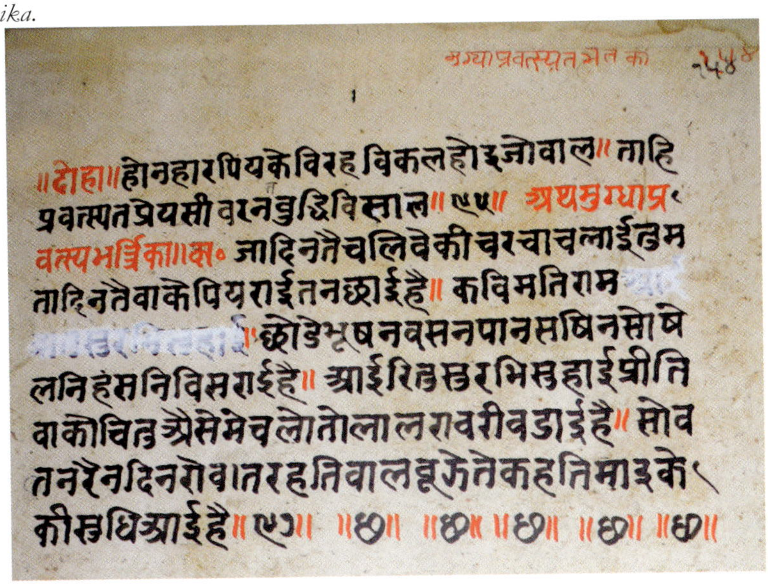
मुग्धाप्रवत्स्यतप्रेत का ॰५५४

॥दोहा॥होनहारपियकेविरहविकलहोइजोवाल॥ ताहि
प्रवत्स्यतप्रेयसीवरनवुद्धिविसाल॥ ९५॥ अथमुग्धाप्र॰
वत्स्यभर्त्रिका॥क॰ जादिनतेंचलिवेकीचरचाचलाईतुम
तादिनतेंवाकेपियराईतनछाईहै॥ कविमतिराम
॥छोडेभूषनवसनपानसषिनसोषे
लनिहंसनिविसराईहै॥ आईरितुसुरभिसुहाईप्रीति
वाकोचित्तऐसेमेचलोतोलालरावरीवडाईहै॥ सोव
तनरैनदिनरोवातरहतिवालवूझेतेकहतिमाइके
कीसुधिआईहै॥ ९३॥ ॥छ॥ ॥छ॥ ॥छ॥ ॥छ॥ ॥छ॥

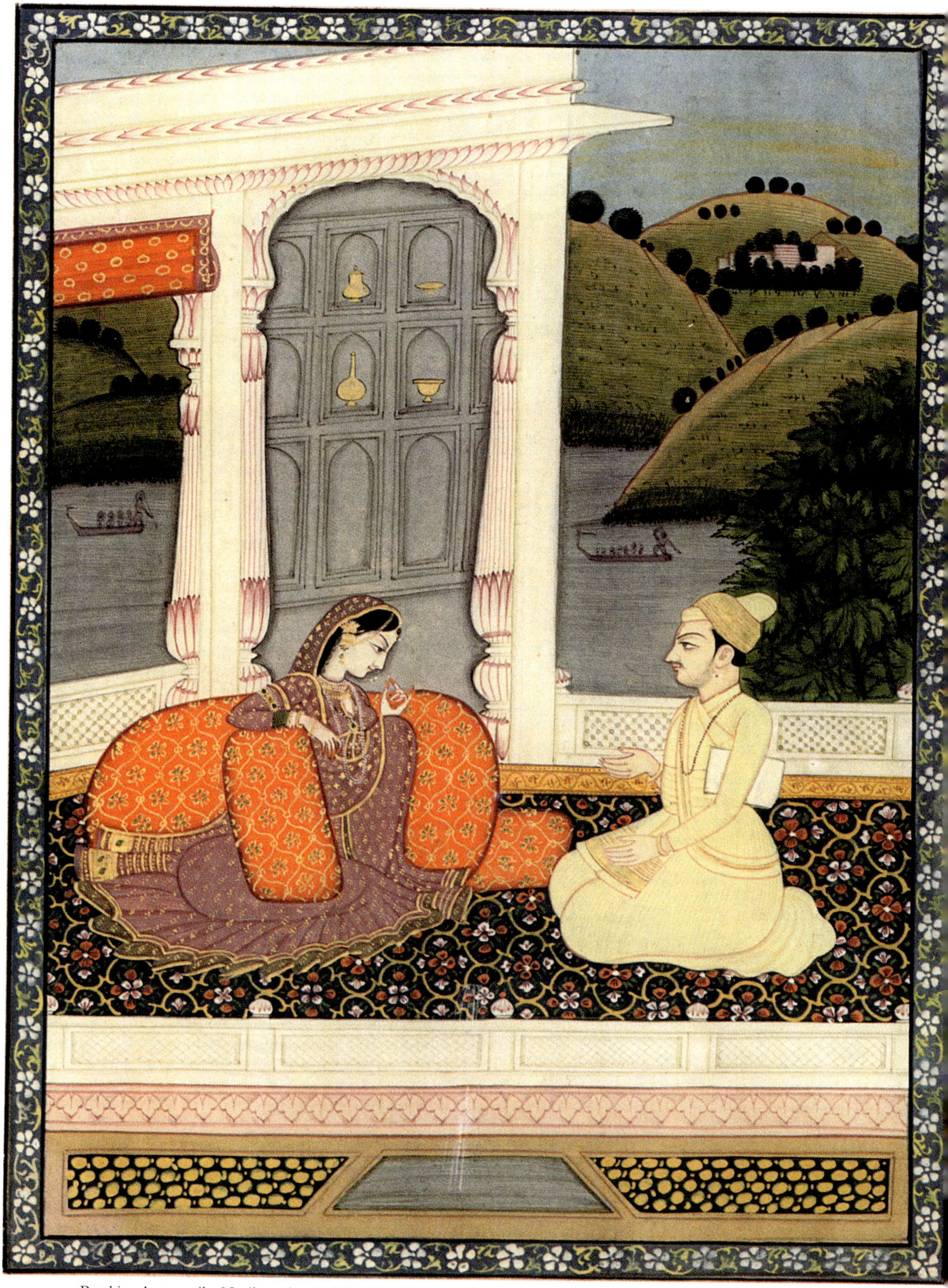

Parakiya Agatapatika Nayika, school of Purkhu, Kangra, CE 1785-90, private collection.

परकीया-आगतपतिका

आयो बिलंब बिदेस तें बालम बाल बियोग बिथा बिसराई ।
आई तहाँ तिनके संग हवै सब गाँव की जे जुवती मिलि आई ।
देखत ही मतिराम कहै अँखियान में आनँद की छबि छाई ।
लाजन क्योंकर बैन कहै। सु कह्यो दुख देहँहि की दुबराई ।।

Parakiya Agatapatika Nayika

On seeing her paramour returning home after a long sojourn, the parakiya agatapatika nayika *forgets her pangs of separation. Together with some neighbouring women, she rushes eagerly towards the* nayak's *home. As soon as she sees her lover, her eyes are filled with immense joy. The* nayak *too understands the poignant condition of her love-lorn beloved. Though helpless in expressing her agony, her trembling body reveals her suffering.*

The scene is the balcony of a *haveli*. Behind the *haveli* is a placid river where two pleasure boats ply. The landscape shows rolling hills and the ambience is one of silent pleasure. Seated against a red bolster and dressed in a mauve *ghaghra* is the *parakiya agatapatika nayika*. She has waited long for his arrival and when the moment of the meeting has come she coyly turns her head down in hesitation. The *nayak*, who squats in front of her, extends his hand in a gesture of invitation and asking about her welfare and under his left arm holds a packet, which is probably a gift for her. The *nayika*'s mind throbs with excitement as she thinks of romantic moments to follow and even though she controls her emotions, her body gives them away.

Behind the *haveli* is a placid river where two ferry boats ply. The landscape shows receding hills with pale rims. At the farther hill some houses peep from the cluster of trees suggesting a village. The artist renders the scene with finesse and attention to intricate details. The floral pattern on the clothes and the carpet, the flower garden and the cistern in the foreground, the wall with flasks and containers are all signs of romantic moments that await the couple after a long wait. The fluted lotus columns and the decoration of the arch with caramine colours appear in Kangra paintings of the late eighteenth century. The detailing of the carpet and bolsters is noteworthy.

One comes away from the painting sharing the muted excitement of a romantic rendezvous.

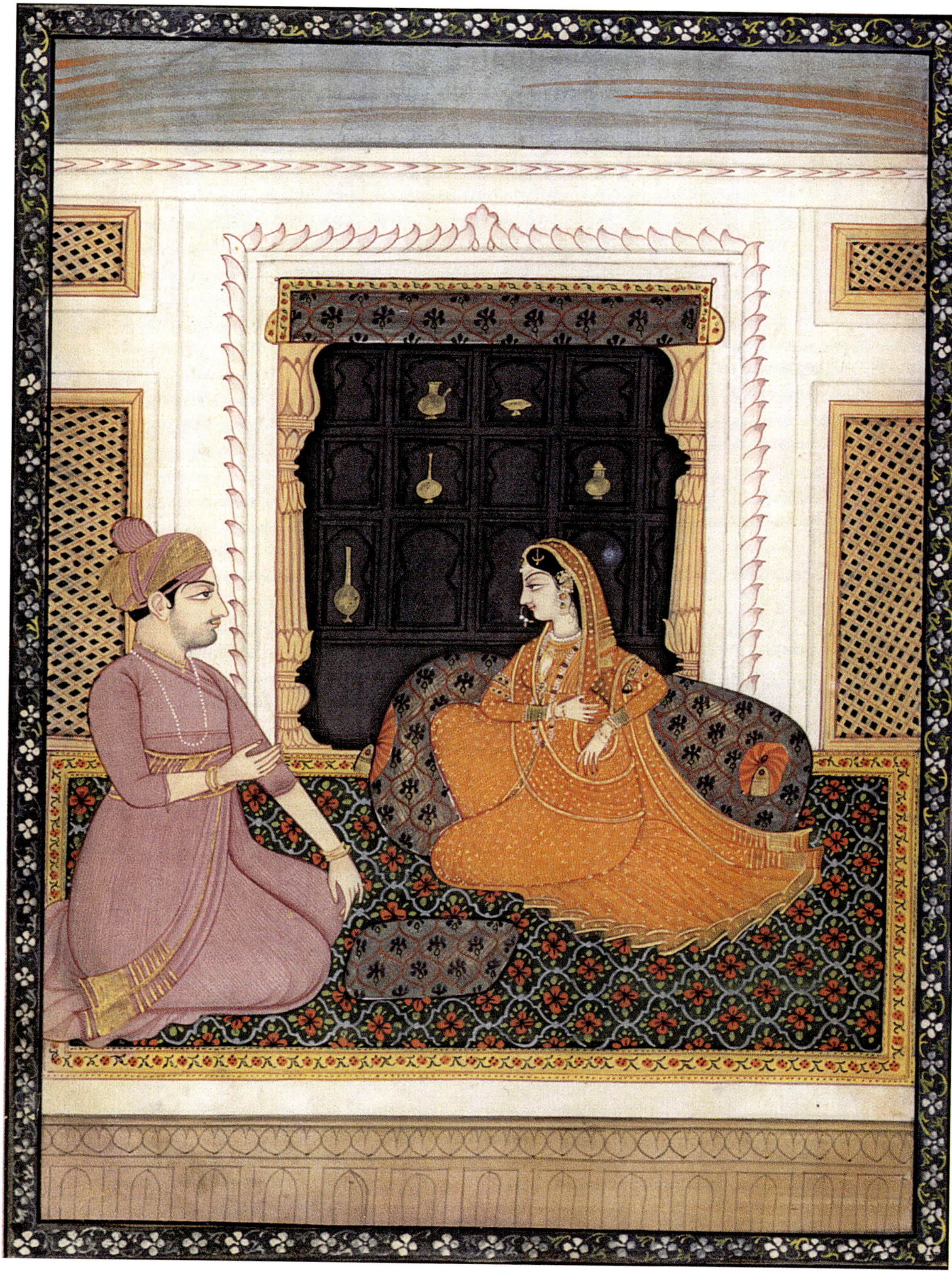

Ganika Agatapatika Nayika, school of Purkhu, Kangra, CE 1785-90, private collection.

गणिका-आगतपतिका

नागर बिदेस मैं बिताय बहु द्यौस आयो, नागरि के हिय मैं हुलासन की खान की ।
कबि मतिराम अंक भरत मयंकमुखी, नेह सरसाय मोही मति सखुदान की ।
सबुरनबोलिकैबतावतिहैसबुरन, हीरनजनावतिहैछबिमुसकान की।
आँखिन तैं आनँद के आँसू उमगाय प्यारी, प्यारे को दिखावति सुरति मुकतान की ।।

Ganika Agatapatika Nayika

Staying for a long time in the distant land, the nayak *has returned home. Thus, the* ganika agatapatika nayika *has become a mine of happiness. Matiram says that the moon-faced* nayika *clings to her lover and expresses her joy by embracing him tight in her arms. The delighted nayak too inclined towards that ravishing* nayika, *whose sweet speech appears to him like that of gold. When she smiles, her sparkling teeth look like jewels. And the tear drops rolling down from her eyes due to extreme joy appear to the* nayak *like pearls.*

The *ganika agatapatika*, though lonesome in his absence, is more self-assertive and locks her gaze with his. Seated gracefully, she exudes confidence and at the same time conveys an invitation to the *nayak* to participate in the pleasures of love. The vermilion *ghaghra* speaks of her passion while her sumptuous jewellery of her adorned mood. The understated elegance of the resplendent *haveli* represents the excitement of romantic moments that await them. The *nayak* is in a light mauve *jama* tied at the waist with a long fluttering *kamarband* (sash) and expresses his pleasure with his extended right hand as if to say that while the separation was difficult for him as well he returns with renewed love and a commitment towards the celebration of their romance.

He sports a *kuledar* turban decorated with brocade. Such turbans can be seen in several portraits of Sansar Chand. The dark grey wall in the centre of the composition and the oxidised silver pigment of the bolster and the dark green floor silhouettes the figure of the *nayika*. The niches on the wall that contain the paraphernalia of romance, is a perfect backdrop as our eyes stay focused on the romantic couple.

The Kangra artist does justice to the romantic moment with another fine composition surcharged with the colours and the textures of romance. Vermilion streaks over the sky suggest that it is early evening.

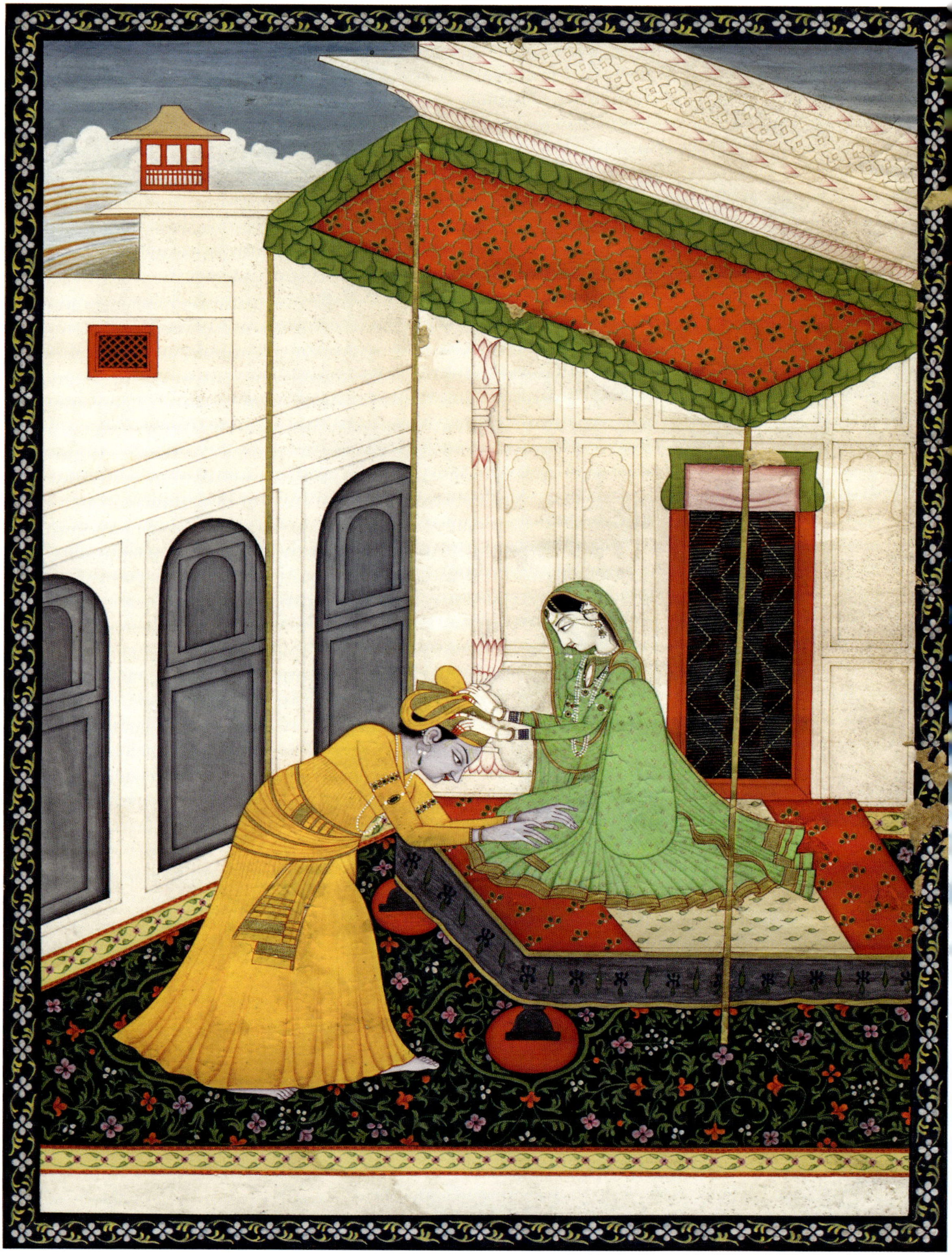

Madhyama Nayika, school of Purkhu, Kangra, CE 1785-90, Dehejia collection.

मध्यमा-नायिका

पियसौंहितनैंहितकरैअनहितकीनेमान। ताहिमध्यमाकहतहैंकबिमतिरामसुजान।।
कवित्त आयो प्रानपति राति अनतैं बिताय बैठी, भौंहन चढ़ाय रँगी सुंदरि सुहाग की।
बतन बनाय पर्यो प्यारी के चरन आय, छल सौं छिपाई छैल छबि रतिदाग की।
छूटि गयो मान लगी आपु ही सवँ रन कौं, खिरकी सकु बि मतिराम पिय पाग की।
रिस ही के आँसू रस-आँसू भए आँखिन मैं, रोस की ललाई सो ललाई अनुराग की।।

Madhyama Nayika

After spending the night elsewhere with another woman, the husband returns in the morning to his offended wife who is angry on account of his fickleness. In order to appease his sulking wife, he prostrates at her feet, thus cleverly hiding signs of love-play on his body. The nayika's *pride dwindles and she rearranges the loose turban of her lord. The teardrops of wrath turn into the tears of joy and love and the red anger in her eyes is transformed into the red of passion.*

Matiram classifies *nayikas* according to their conduct with erring lovers. They are *uttama* (best), *madhyama* (middling) and *adhama* (lower). Here is a example of a *madhayama nayika* who shows her anger at the fickleness of her beloved.

The morning time is suggested cleverly by the painter by showing red streaks at the horizon and the rising sun peeping from the upper left of the palace architecture. The blue-complexioned, erring *nayak* is shown bending at the feet of the offended *nayika* for assuaging her anger and to ask her for pardon. His loose turban suggests that he has been in an amorous play with another woman. The scene is set inside a chamber of the palace. Clad in light green garments the *nayika* is shown seated on a decorated bedstead underneath a canopy supported by golden poles. Her raised arms is a gesture of forgiveness. A white spacious building with diagonal architectural elements, the carpet, bed and a fringed canopy with richly decorated floral patterns all suggest the date of this painting. It seems to be from the family workshop of Purkhu who was the court painter in the late nineteenth century of the noted Katoch chief Sansar Chand (1775-1823) of Kangra. This painter's style is seen from the typical facial types, rich colouring and intricate details. The *bel buti* (tendril) design on the blue black border and three rules in vermilion besides the border are seen at times on other folios of this series and is a hallmark of this painter.

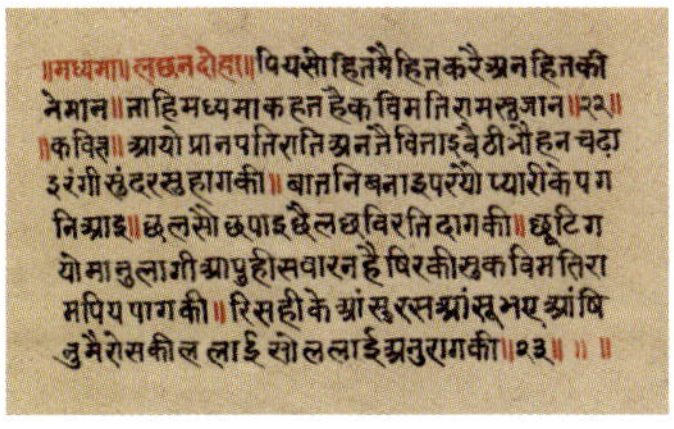
॥मध्यमा॥ लछनदोहा॥ पियसौ हितनै हितकरै अनहितकी
नेमान॥ ताहि मध्यमा कहत हैं कवि मतिराम सुजान॥२२॥
॥कवित्त॥ आयो प्रानपति राति अनतै विताइ बैठी भौंहन चढ़ा
इ रंगी सुंदर सुहागकी॥ बातनि बनाइ पर्यो प्यारीके पग
नि आइ॥ छलसो छपाइ छैल छवि रति दागकी॥ छूटि ग
यो मानु लागी आपुही सवारन है षिरकी सुक वि मतिरा
म पिय पागकी॥ रिस ही के आंसु रस आंसु भए आंषि
नु मै रोसकी ललाई सो ललाई अनुरागकी॥२३॥ ॥ ॥

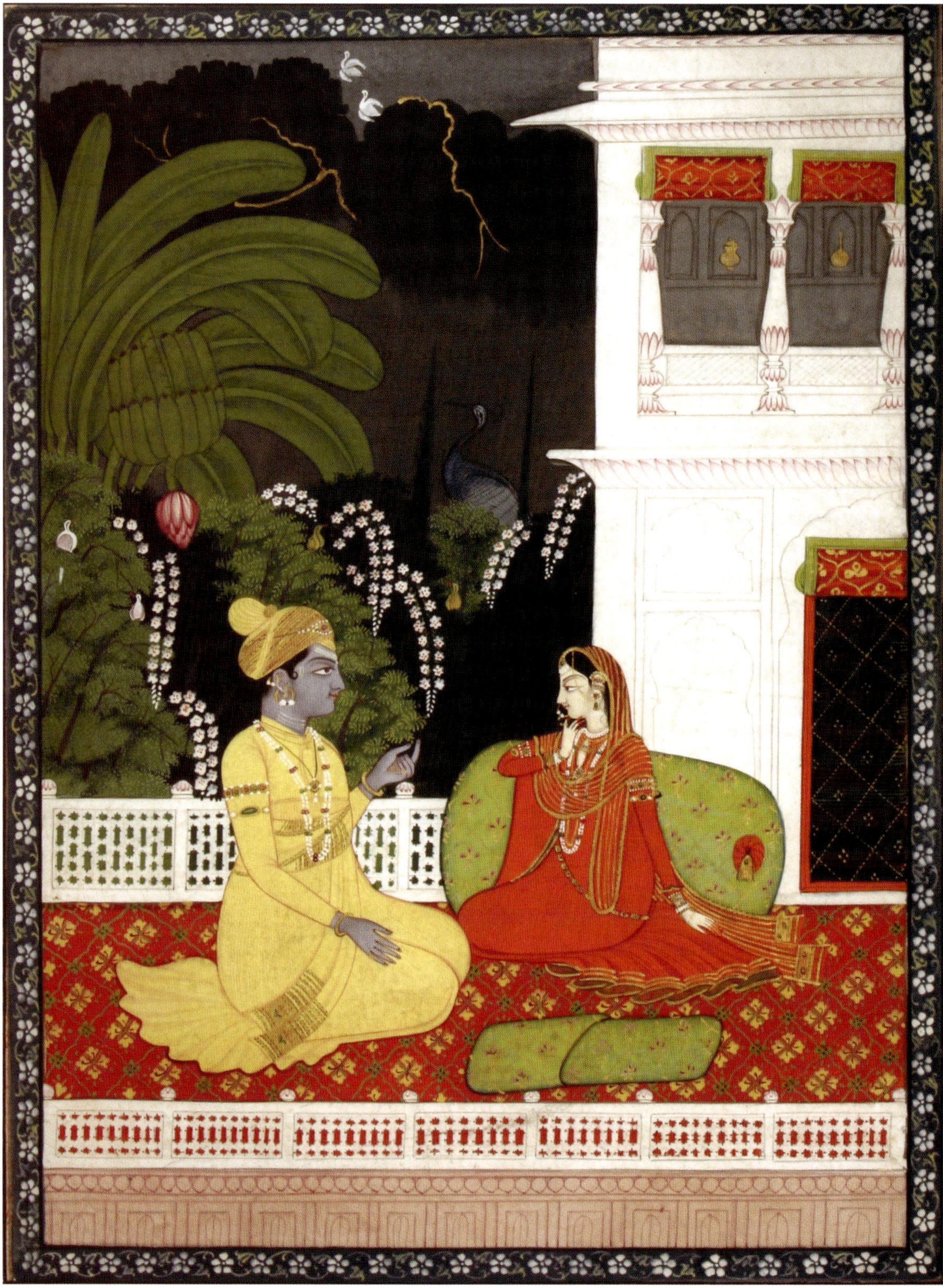

Shatha Nayak, school of Purkhu, Kangra, CE 1785-90, Harish Patel, New York.

शठ नायक

पियत रहैं अधरान को रस अति मधुर अमोल ।
तातें मीठे कढ़त हैं बालबदन तें बोल ।।

Shatha Nayak

The shrewd nayak *tyring to win over the* nayika *says, My dear! The words that come out of your mouth drink sweet nectar from your lips. That is why whatever words you speak are sweeter.*

The word *shatha* means cunning, who despite being scolded by the *nayika* is still trying to assuage her by speaking sweet words.

It is a moment to savour and the artist creates a visual feast. It is a stormy night and lightning illuminates a dark sky as we see two cranes fly away. Luxuriant trees with hanging bananas and delicate blossoms create the perfect backdrop for sweet romantic conversations. Between white latticed balustrades and covered by a red floral carpet the *nayak* and the *nayika* are engaged in matters of the heart; he dressed in a yellow *jama* and she in a red *peshwaz*, both beautifully bejewelled. The cunning and shrewd *nayak* tries to assuage the *nayika* who patiently hears the sweet words spoken by her beloved. Resting against a green bolster, she is a picture of self-assured composure. He, squatting on his knees, exudes regal confidence. The empty *haveli* with colourful drapes provides an elegant backdrop to this finely rendered composition. The artist, in this charming painting, creates a visual delight leaving only the sweet words exchanged between the two to our imagination. The blue-complexioned *nayak* appears to be Krishna, but his yellow *kuledar* turban is devoid of peacock feathers. The white latticed balustrades in the back and front of the picture suggest perspective.

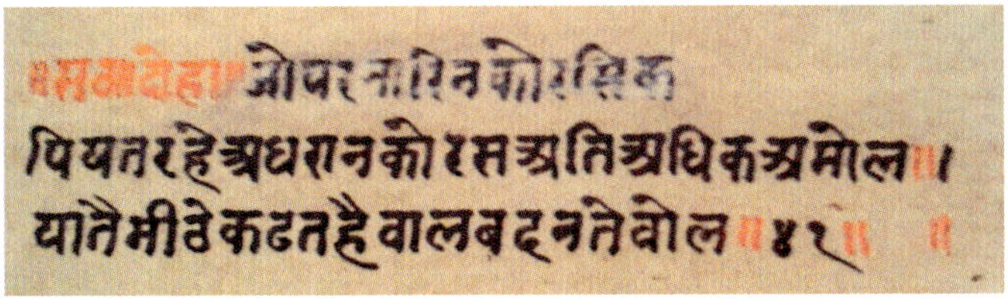
॥सखी दोहा॥ ओपर नारिन कोरसिक
पियतरहेअधरानकोरसअतिअधिकअमोल॥
यातेमीठेकढतहैवालबदनतेवोल॥४२॥ ॥

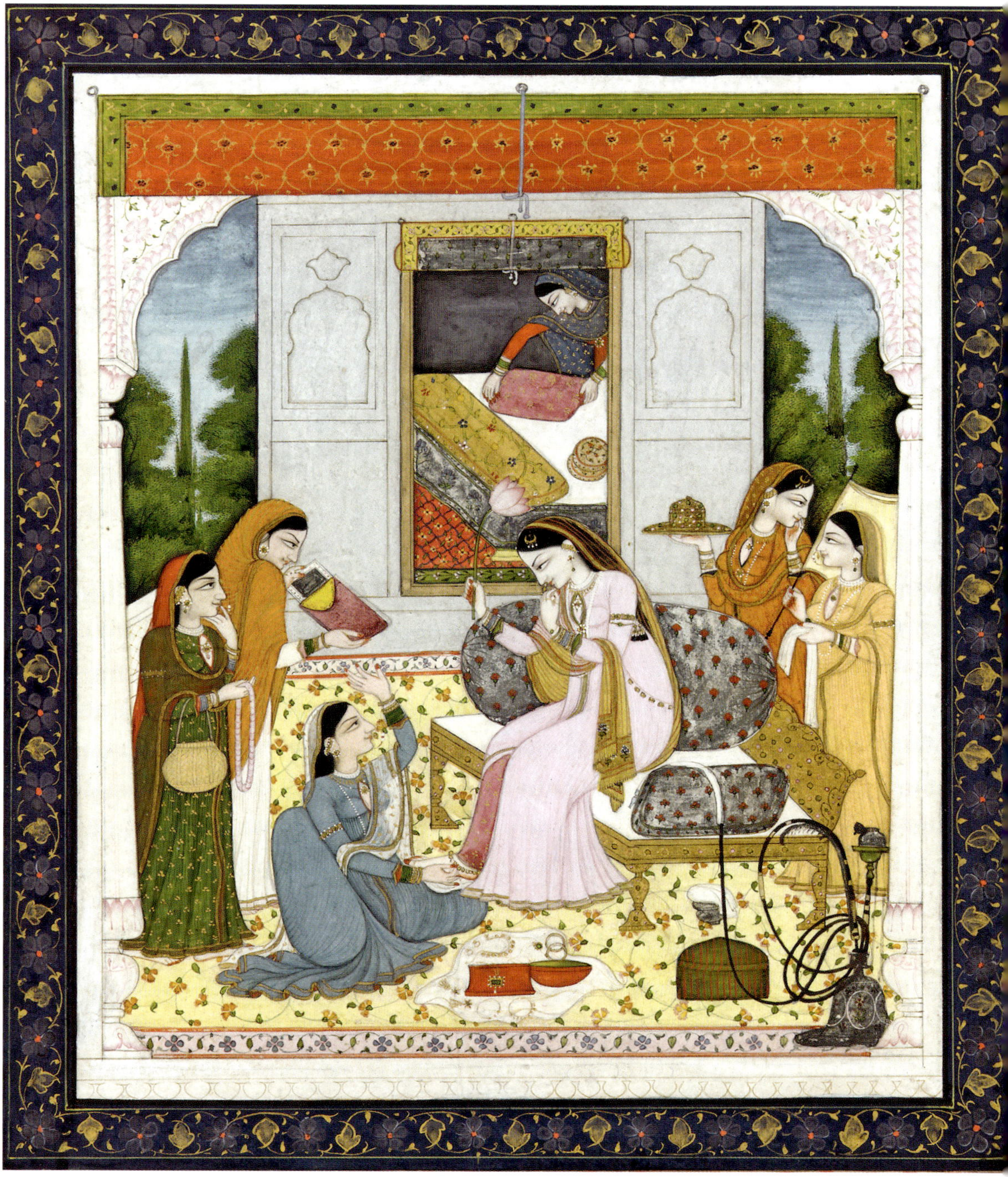

Sakhi Parihasa Nayika, Kangra, CE 1800, National Museum, Delhi

परिहास

गौने के द्यौस सिँगारन को मतिराम सहेलिन को गनु आयो।
कंचन के बिछुवा पहिरावत प्यारी सखी परिहास बढ़ायो।
प्रीतम स्रौन समीप सदा बजै यों कहिकै पहिले पहिरायो।
कामिनी कौल चलावनि कौं कर ऊँचो कियो पै चल्यौ न चलायो।।

Sakhi Parihasa Nayika

A nayika *is getting ready to go to her in-laws' home and the poet describes the jovial mood of her* sakhis *as they prepare her to leave. Before her first meeting with her husband, the newly-wed heroine's* (nayika) *companions* (sakhis) *came to adorn her. While putting a ring studded with tiny, jingling bells on the heroine's big toe, one of the companions remarked in jest: "May these bells forever jingle in the ears of your beloved husband." Understanding the pun, the bashful heroine playfully held a lotus* (lila-kamala) *as if to hit her companion but did not do it.*

Matiram elucidates in his *Rasraj* various duties of the *sakhi* or the love messenger. One of them is *parihasa* or a *sakhi* that creates humour with the *nayika*.

Several paintings of various Pahari schools depict toilette scenes, in which the *nayika* is usually shown being adorned with ornaments by her friends. The paintings depicting such situations are generally referred to as the adornment of a heroine. A finely executed painting from a Kangra workshop depicts a coy young *nayika* seated on a raised couch and being adorned by her friends.

It is a special day and the *nayika* is supposed to go to her husband's house for the first time after her wedding. Dressed in a decorative bridal garment, the young damsel is surrounded by some of her intimate companions. One of the *sakhis* who sits near her leg puts *bichhua*, an ornament studded with jingling tiny bells, to her toe. At the same time she passes a naughty remark to the *nayika*. Understanding the pun the shy *nayika* tries to strike her friend with a lotus flower (*lila-kamal*) held in her raised hand. Since this picture does not carry any poetic verse, it is not easy to understand its precise meaning as to why the *nayika* attempts to strike her companion with a stemmed lotus. The painting in all likelihood seems to be based on a poetic verse of Matiram, who very eloquently describes the situation.

The composition of this painting, arranged in an architectural setting, does provide an air of romantic ambience. It is early evening and a maidservant is preparing the bed in the chamber in the background. Wrapped in a brocade veil the *nayika* can be seen smiling at the naughty remark. One of the friends standing in front of the *nayika* holds a mirror, while others are engaged in various activities. The words of the verse are placed in the mouth of a *sakhi* who sits just in front of the *nayika*. The charming and bright female faces, the rendering of the architectural edifices and fine brushwork suggest the typical Kangra style, though not from the workshop of Purkhu.

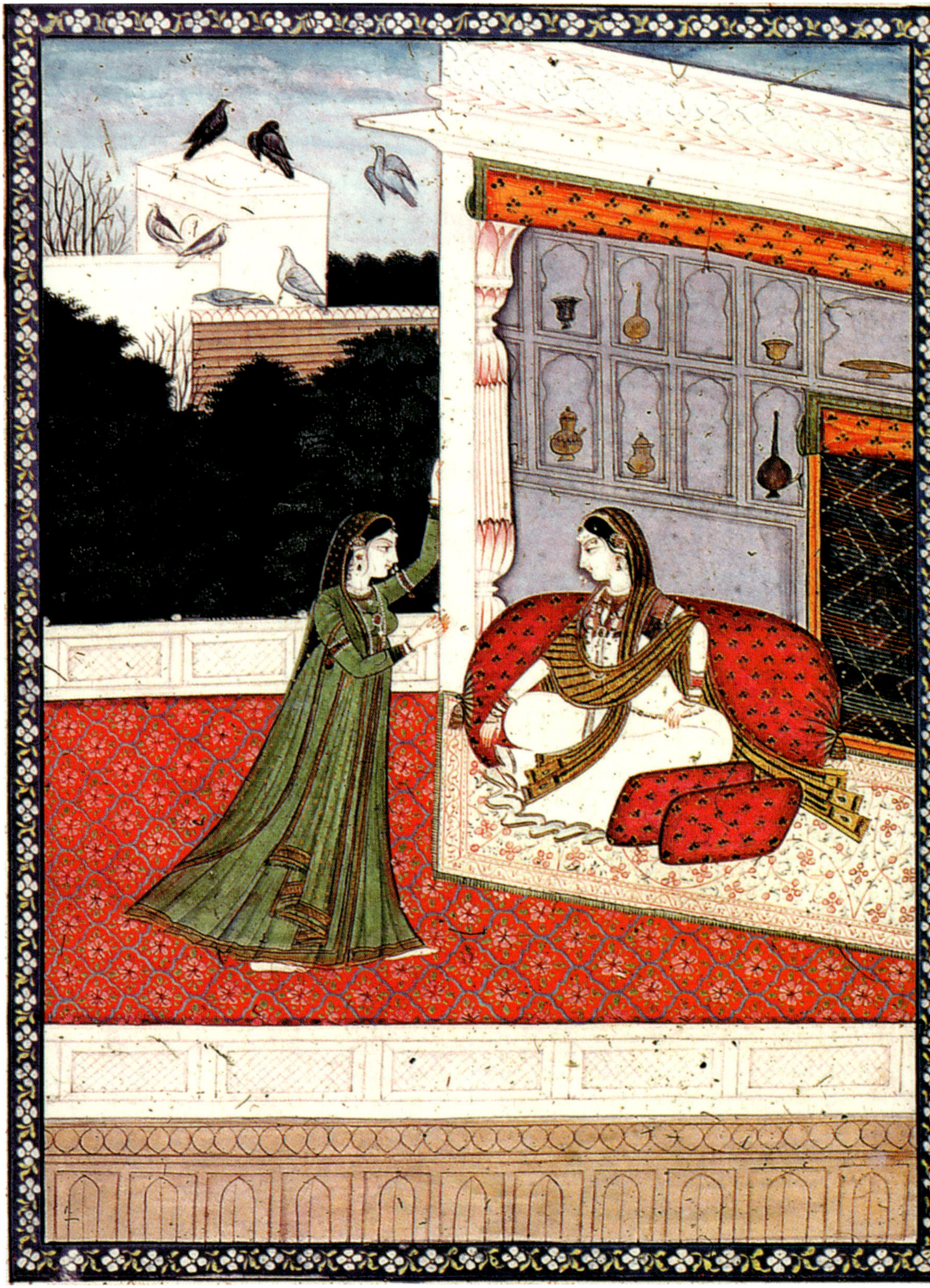

Mugdha Agatapatika Nayika, school of Purkhu, Kangra, CE 1785-90, Brooklyn Museum of Art, New York.

मुग्धा-आगतपतिका
आए बिदेस तैं प्रानप्रिया मतिराम अनंद बढ़ाय अलेखै।
लोगन सौं मिलि आँगन बैठि घरी ही घरी सिगरो घर पेखै।
भीतर भौन के द्वार खरी सुकुमारि तिया तनकंप बिसेखै।
घूँघट को पट ओट दिये पट ओट किये पिय को मुख देखै।।

Mugdha Agatapatika Nayika

The nayika's *husband has returned home from abroad and the* nayika's *heart fills with immense joy. Sitting in the courtyard of her home, the* nayak *is being greeted by people, yet his eyes seek the presence of his beloved. Meanwhile, standing at the door of her chamber, the* nayika's *body is thrilled with overwhelming joy. Being bashful by nature, that damsel does not step out of her room, but to look at her lover, she stealthily peeps through her veil.*

The Kangra artist portrays the *mugdha nayika* as she sits in anticipation of the arrival of her beloved. Crows on the roof suggest that a visitor is expected soon, which gladdens her heart. The *sakhi* is seen in an animated conversation with the *nayika*. Perhaps she is imparting some useful suggestions to the *nayika* for the anticipated blissful union. Dressed in a yellow *peshwaz* and seated on a foliated carpet against a vermilion bolster, she expresses the joy of an impending rendezvous. The wine bottles and carafes are ready for greeting the lover and also for the joyous reunion. There is an air of romantic expectation in this beautifully rendered painting. The artist has intentionally depicted pairs of pigeons at the backdrop of the painting, which suggests the *nayika*'s union with her beloved. The *nayak* is conspicuous by his absence.

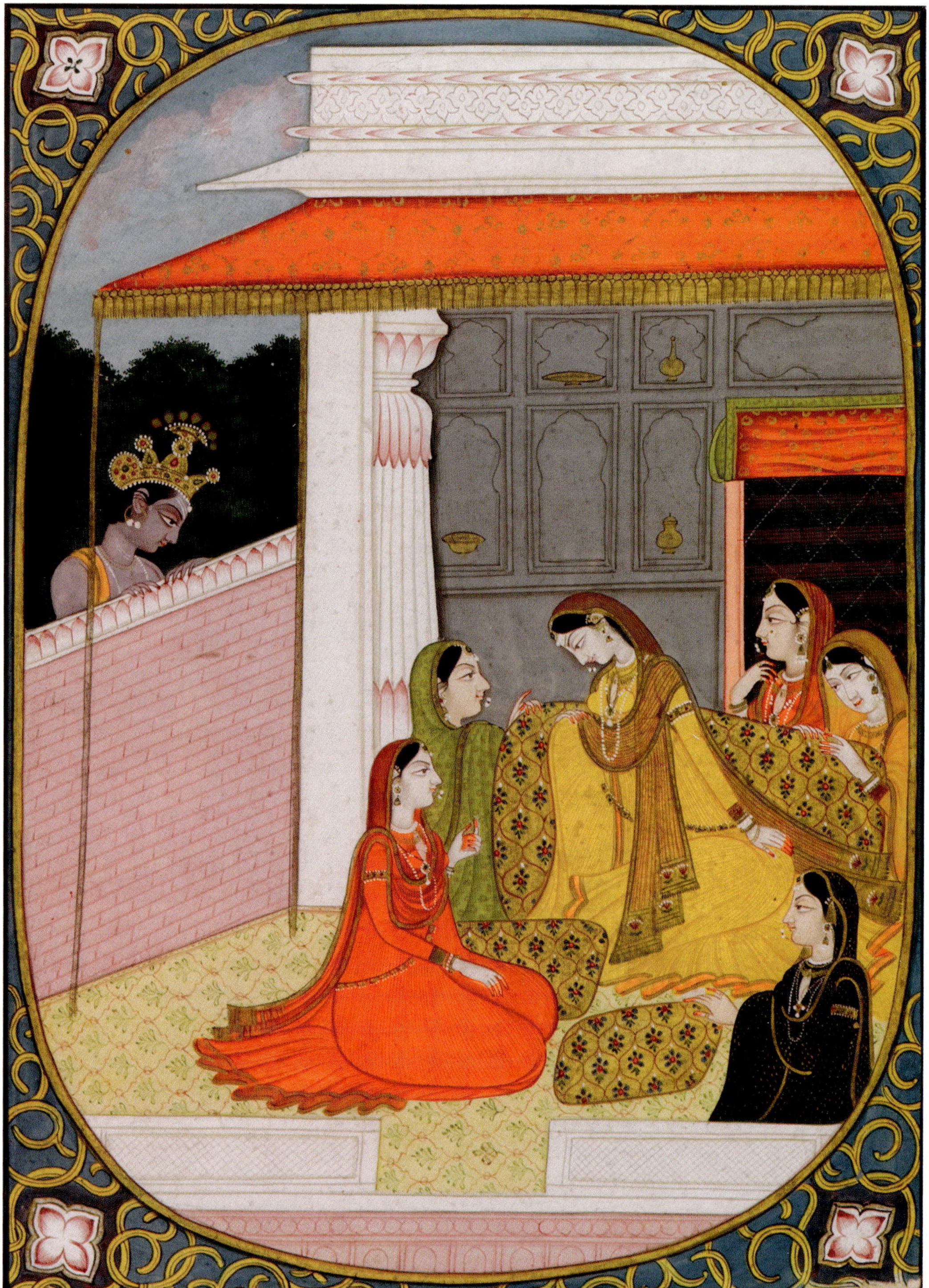

Kriya-vidagdha Nayika, school of Purkhu, Kangra, CE 1785-90, Brooklyn Museum of Art, New York.

क्रियाविदग्धा

बैठी तिया गुरु लोगन में रति ते अति सुंदर रूप बिसेखी।
आयो तहाँ मतिराम सुजान मनोभव सों बढ़ि कांति उरेखी।
लोचन रूप पियो ही चहैं अरु लाजनि जात नहीं छबि पेखी।
नैन नमाय रही हियमाल में लाल की पूरति लाल में देखी।।

Kriya-vidagdha Nayika

The nayika, *who surpasses Rati in beauty, was sitting amid her* sakhis. *Incidentally, at that time, the* nayak, *who was more beautiful than Kamadeva, came there. The coy* nayika *desired a glimpse of her beloved's beauty, but could not. So she held her head downwards to see the reflection of his graceful image in the ruby studded in her garland.*

It is a charged moment within the *haveli*. Sitting underneath an extended fringed canopy, a lonesome *nayika* is surrounded by her *sakhis*. Dressed in an elegant bright yellow-coloured *peshwaz* her head is lowered to catch a glimpse of her beloved in her necklace ornament. Across the wall Krishna is seen peeping inside. The group of *sakhis* wait in loving attendance upon the *nayika* and the artist renders each one of them individually and with attention to every detail, to their clothes and physiognomy. The typical oval format with floral corners completes a painting that is both elegant and pleasing and captures the mood of the moment in well-executed lines and evocative colours.

Though the coy *nayika* is *kriya-vidagdha* (clever in deeds) in nature, she is still bashful despite her desire to see her beloved passing by. She does not cast sidelong glances, rather she discreetly sees the vision of her beloved in her ruby-studded ornament. The painter has used a palette of soft, muted pigments in this painting. The focal point of the painting is the figure of the *nayika*, which the painter places in the middle of the composition.

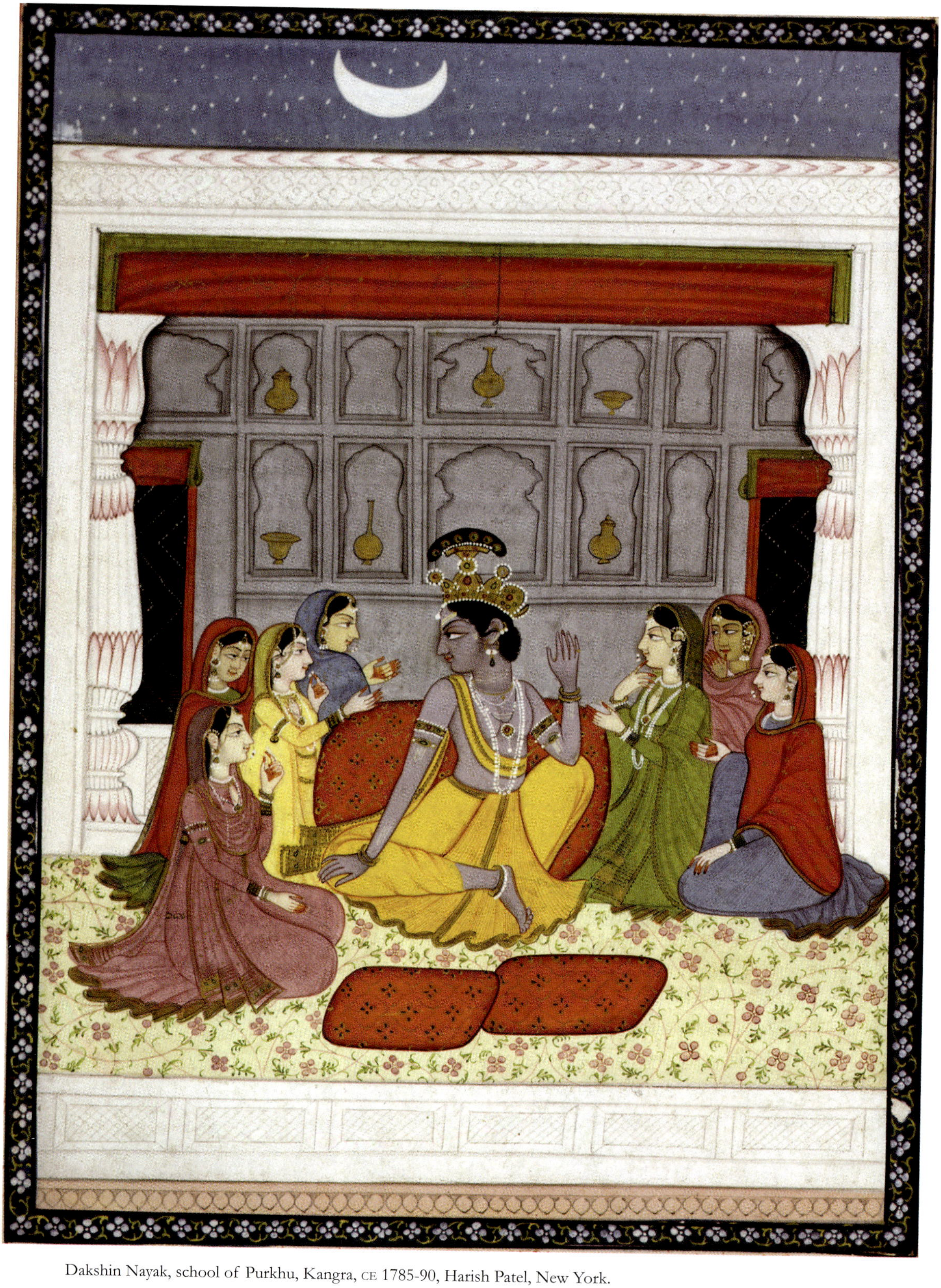

Dakshin Nayak, school of Purkhu, Kangra, CE 1785-90, Harish Patel, New York.

दच्छिन नायक

दच्छिन नायक एक तुम मनमोहन बृज चंद।
फुलए बृज-बनितान के दृग-इंदीवर बृंद।।

Dakshin Nayak

O Manmohan [Krishna]! Being a dakshin *kind of* nayak, *you are the moon of Braj. The lotus-like eyes of the damsels of Braj bloom on seeing your auspicious vision.*

Krishna is the cynosure of attention in this group of animated *nayikas*. Turning his head to the right he raises his left hand while the *nayikas* watch him in rapt attention. Even though each *nayika* is elegantly dressed and appears self-assured there is an organic wholeness to the group, for each is tied to Krishna and he in turn, lovingly belongs to everyone. A crescent moon in a star-studded sky gives the painting a nocturnal grace. Fluted columns and niches with carafes and bottles add to the romantic ambience of this finely executed Kangra painting.

The painter renders the figure of the *nayak* in the very centre of the picture. He is none other than Krishna as he is identifiable by his yellow garment and the crown topped by peacock feathers. Every maiden's eyes are turned towards him to have his vision. Krishna too sits in such a posture that he assures them all of his equal attention to every maiden. A juxtaposition of colours can be seen in the depiction of architectural edifices as well as in the figures.

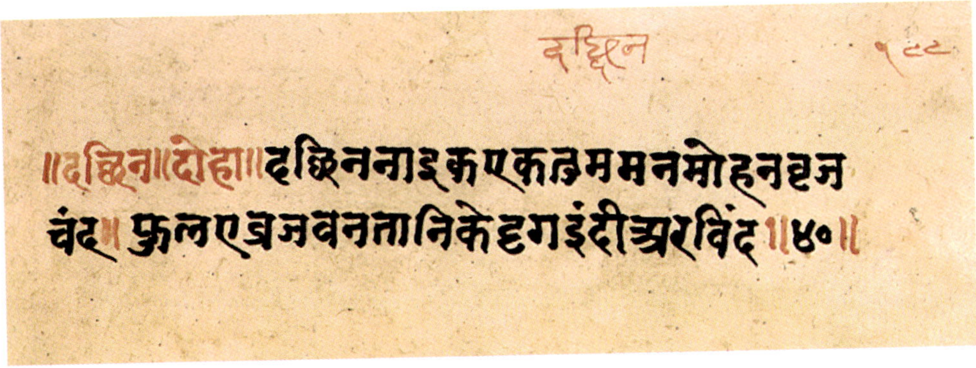
दछिन १८८
॥दछिन॥दोहा॥दछिननाइकएकतुममनमोहनव्रज
चंद॥फुलएव्रजवनतानिकेद्दगइंदीअरविंद॥४०॥

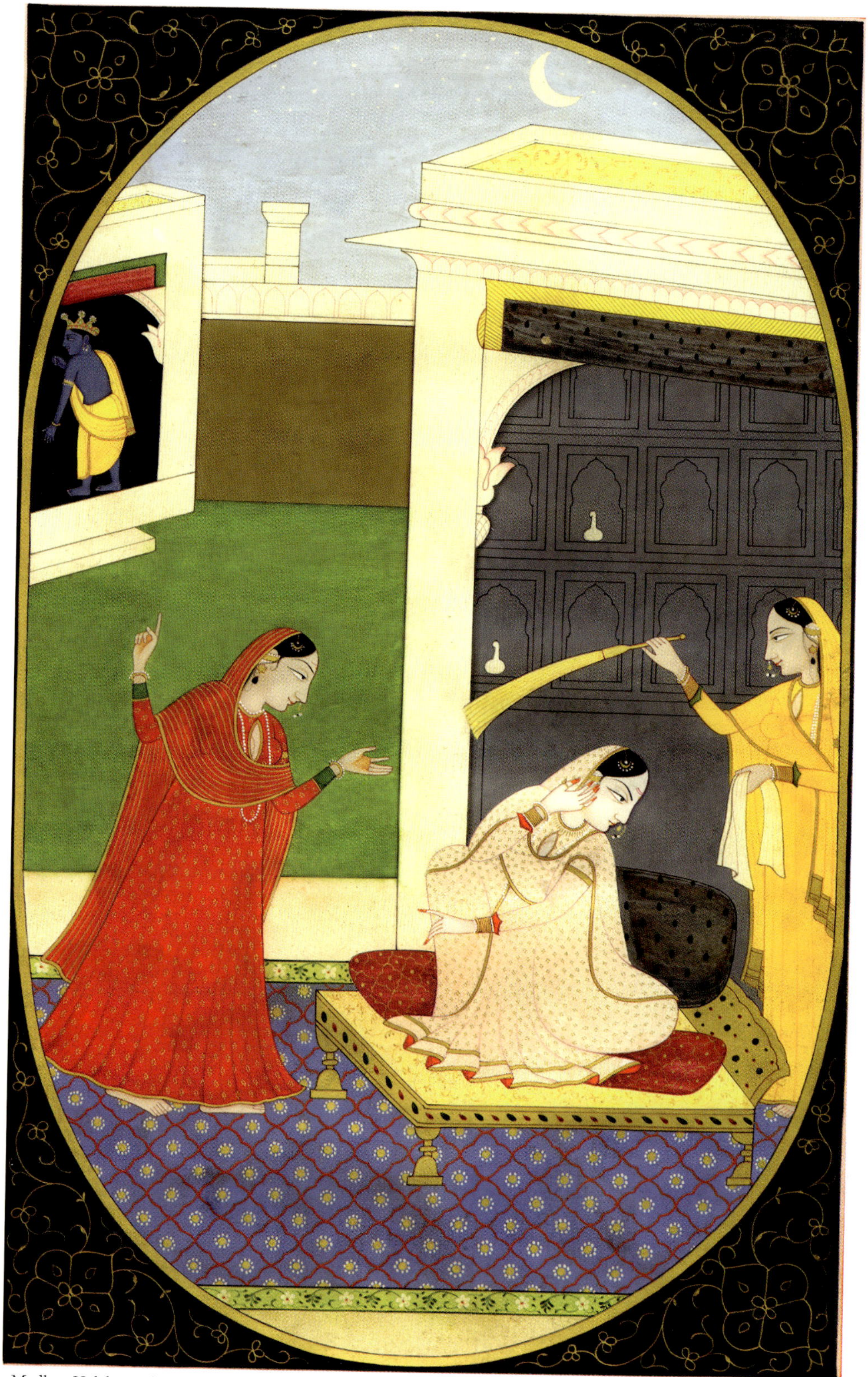

Madhya Kalahantarita Nayika, Late Kangra, CE 1890-1900, Dehejia collection.

मध्या-कलहांतरिता

पाँयन आनि परे तो परे रहे केती करी मनुहारि न झेली।
मान्यो मनायो न मैं मतिराम गुमान मैं ऐसी भई अलबेली।
प्यारो गयो दुख मान कहूँ अब कैसे रहूँ यहि राति अकेली।
आप ते ल्याउ मनाय कन्हाई को मेरो न लीजियो नाम सहेली।।

Madhya Kalahantarita Nayika

I will go and assuage the nayika *if you want me to. But I will make it clear that it is you who have sent me.*

A *nayika* tells her *sakhi*. He fell at my feet and stayed there for a long time and even though he tried to appease me I did not relent. I was so arrogant that I did not listen to him one bit. Now that my beloved has gone to whom shall I express my remorse and how shall I spend the night all alone? My dear *sakhi* please go and win over Krishna but do no let him know that I have sent you.

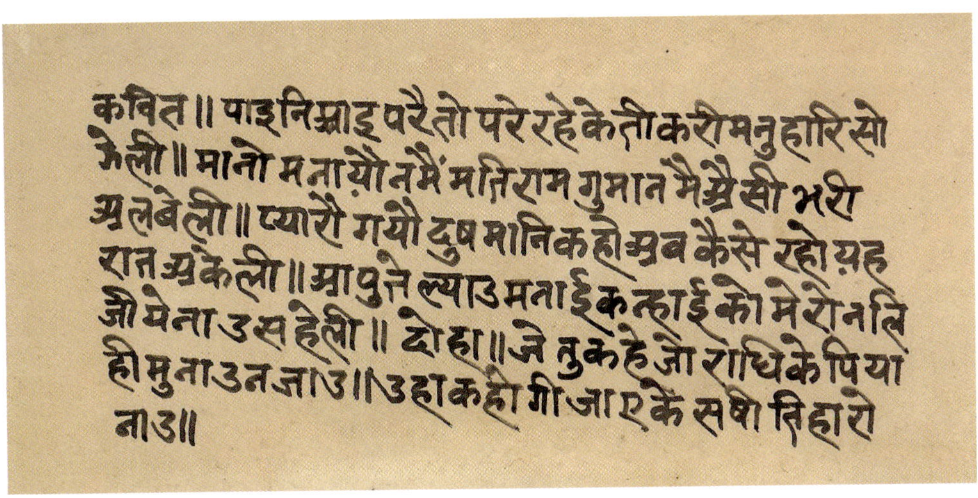
कवित ।। पाइनिआइ परै तो परे रहे केती करी मनुहारि सो
झेली ।। मानो मनायो न मैं मतिराम गुमान मैं ऐसी भरी
अलबेली ।। प्यारो गयो दुष मानि कहो अब कैसे रहो यह
रात अकेली ।। आपु ते ल्याउ मनाइ कन्हाई को मेरो न लि
जो येना उ सहेली ।। दोहा ।। जे तु कहे जा राधिके पिया
हो मुनाउन जाउ ।। उहा कहोगी जाए के सषी तिहारो
नाउ ।।

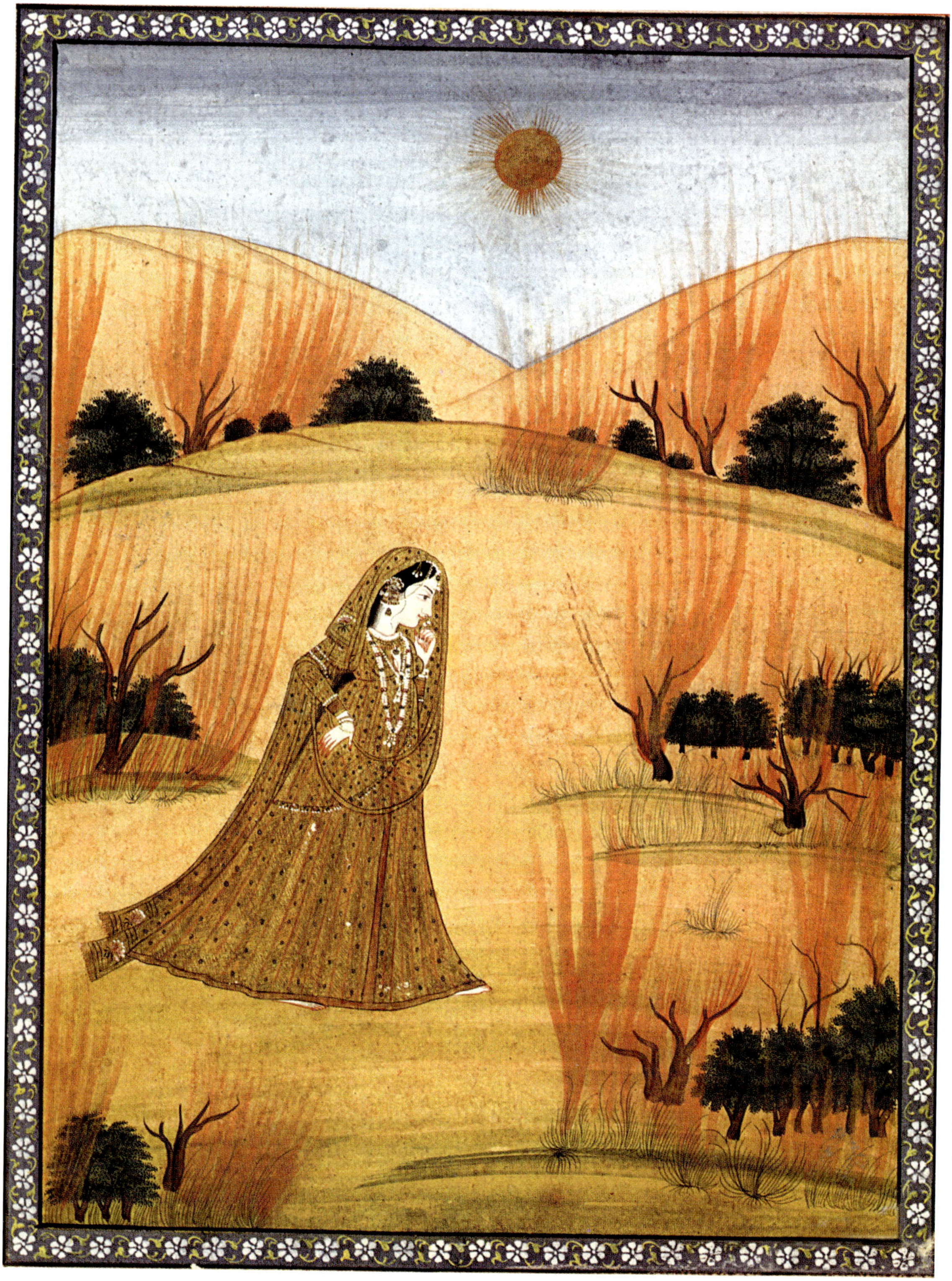

originally in the Paul Walter collection

Paheli Anusayana Nayika, Kangra, CE 1790-1800, private collection

पहलीअनुसयना
ग्रीषम ऋतु में देखिकै बन में लगी दवारि।
एक अपूरब बात यह जरत हिये बर नारि।।

Paheli Anusayana Nayika

It is summer and there is a fire in the forest and at the same time there is a fire in her heart as she would be meeting her beloved in that forest. Now their meeting place was destroyed.

At first sight, this seems like an unusual Pahari painting. The landscape is barren, there are no blossoms or bubbling brooks, neither chirping birds nor dancing peacocks, no meadows or picturesque *havelis*. Instead, there are leaping flames of fire and a scorching sun and burnt grass. A typical bejewelled Pahari *nayika*, dressed in a mustard *peshwaz*, her left hand held to her chin, huddles towards her romantic rendezvous. She is a *anusayana* kind of *nayika* who is in a state of despair upon seeing the destruction of the meeting place. The grove in the forest has completely burnt down on account of the fire and her heart also burns like the forest fire. It becomes apparent that this is not a typical Pahari landscape because the artist wanted to depict her mind. The composition radiates with warm colours like brown, orange and red and conveys the anticipation and anxiety of the *nayika*, which resonates with the fire in the landscape.

The painter has composed the picture with a very simple background. The figure of the *nayika* in despair is the sole centre of attention. She is profusely bejewelled, but in vain, for the meeting place has been completely destroyed by the fire.

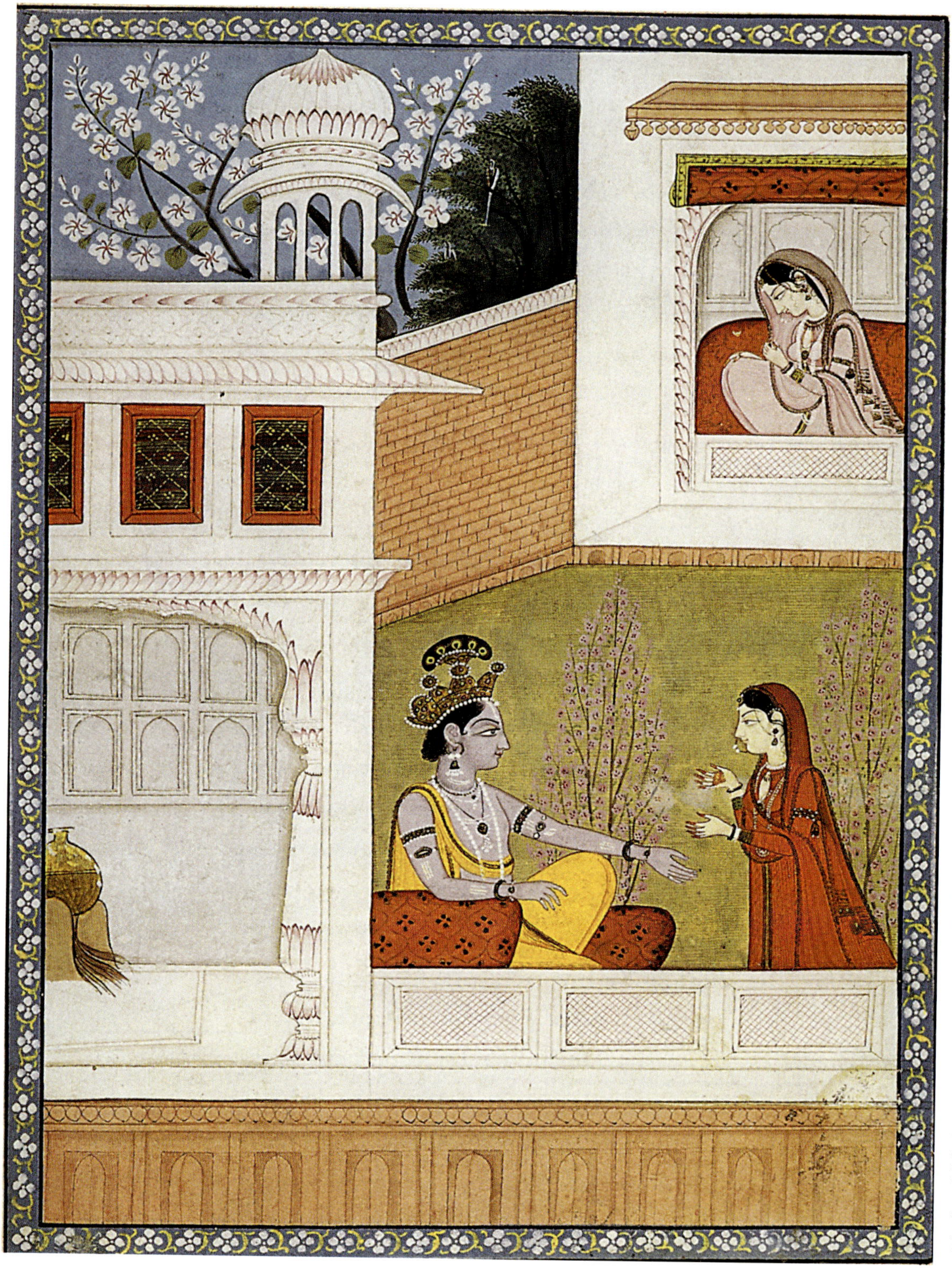

originally published in The Pleasure Gardens of The Mind

Upapati, Kangra, CE 1780, school of Purkhu, private collection

उपपति

नैन जोरि मुख मोरि हँसि नैसुक नेह जनाय।
आगि लेन आई हियै मेरे गई लगाय ।।

Upapati

Locking her gaze with mine and turning her face, smiling and showing some affection she had come to take embers but lit a fire in my heart.

In this picture, Radha and Krishna are shown in their respective apartments. The earthen hearth is shown in Krishna's kitchen just behind him from where Radha has just borrowed some embers. In India, it was common practice in times ancient to borrow embers for one's kitchen. Radha, in borrowing the embers, casts a magical spell on Krishna. Though Radha has reached her home, Krishna is now restless and expresses his passion to Radha's companion. It is important to note that Krishna is portrayed here as a paramour (*upa-pati*).

It is a beautiful Pahari setting with two *havelis* and an elegant cupola set amidst blossoming trees. In the courtyard, Krishna sits comfortably in conversation with a *sakhi*. With his extended left hand, he makes a point while the *sakhis*' gesture suggests surprise. In the yonder *jharokha* we see a lonesome Radha dressed in a pink *peshwaz*. The subject of the conversation becomes clear when we see a pot on a stove. Radha had come to borrow some embers but, as the *doha* says, she left Krishna with a fire in his heart. The Kangra artist executes a fine painting. Even though the colours are subdued, the passions are on fire. Fluted columns, trellised windows and blossoms in the courtyard complete the composition probably from the school of Purkhu.

The painter has skilfully composed the composition by depicting glistened *havelis* in the background and in front. He also places Krishna's figure prominently in the middle of the painting.

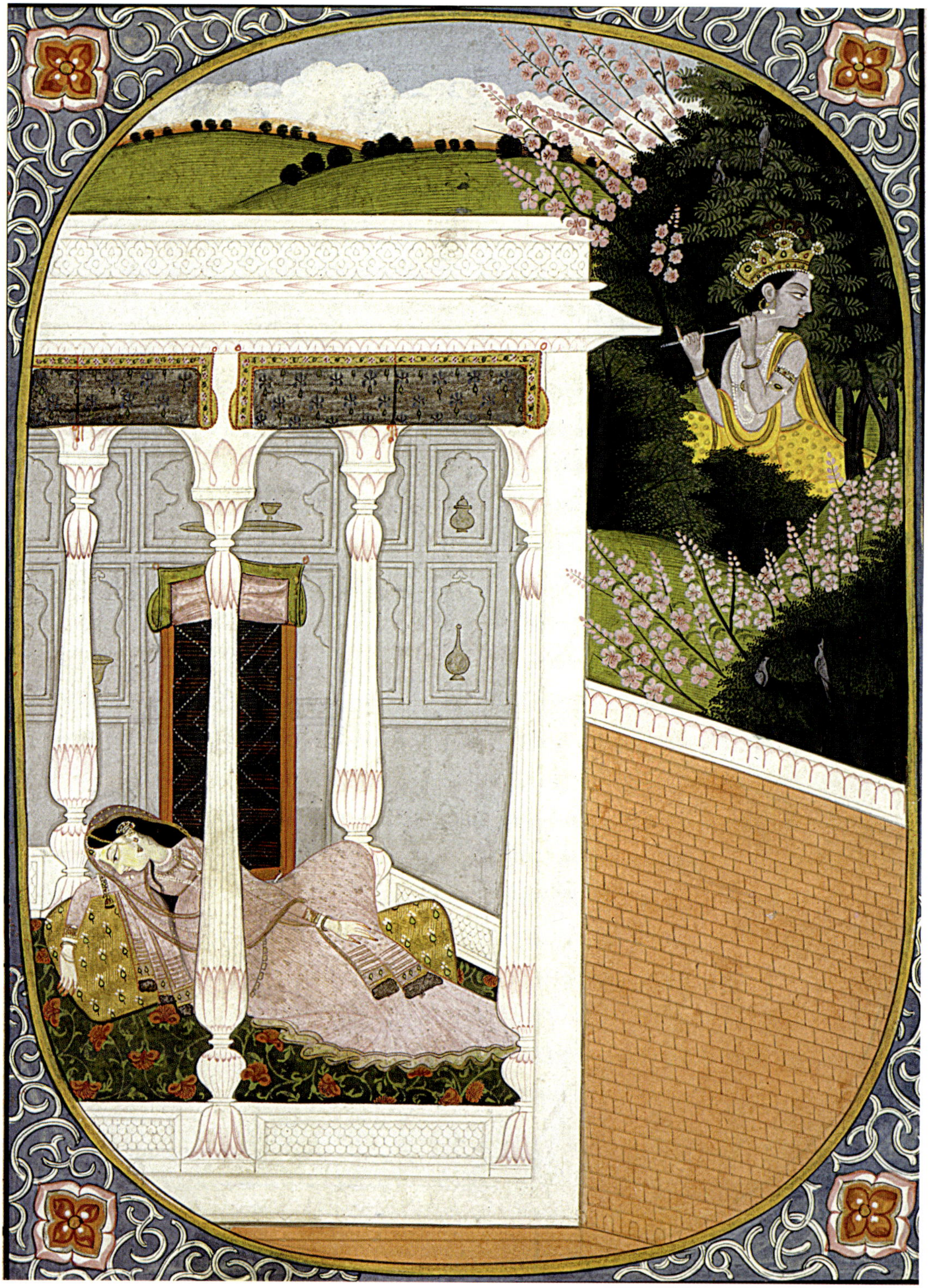

Svapna Darshan, Kangra, CE 1785-90, Harish Patel, New York

स्वप्न

पियमिलाप को सुख सखी कह्यो न जात अनूप।
सौतुक सो सपनो भयो सपनो सौतुक रूप

Svapna Darshan

A nayika speaks with her sakhi.
O sakhi ! The pleasure of seeing my beloved in my dream was beautiful and it is difficult to describe it in words. After the dream everything around me looks false while the dream seems true and it constantly comes before my eyes.

In this quintessentially Kangra charming painting we are led into the chamber of a *nayika* who has just awoken from a dream. Lying alone without her *sakhis*, with her head resting on her right hand, sleep written all over her body, her eyes however have not lost the vision in her dream. That vision was of Krishna and his mellifluous flute which we see in the upper right hand corner, enveloped in foliage. The fluted columns, the fine drapery, the floral bed and the marble jalis that enclose this private chamber are skilfully depicted. The foliate oval frame captures the dreamer and the dream in a beautiful composition.

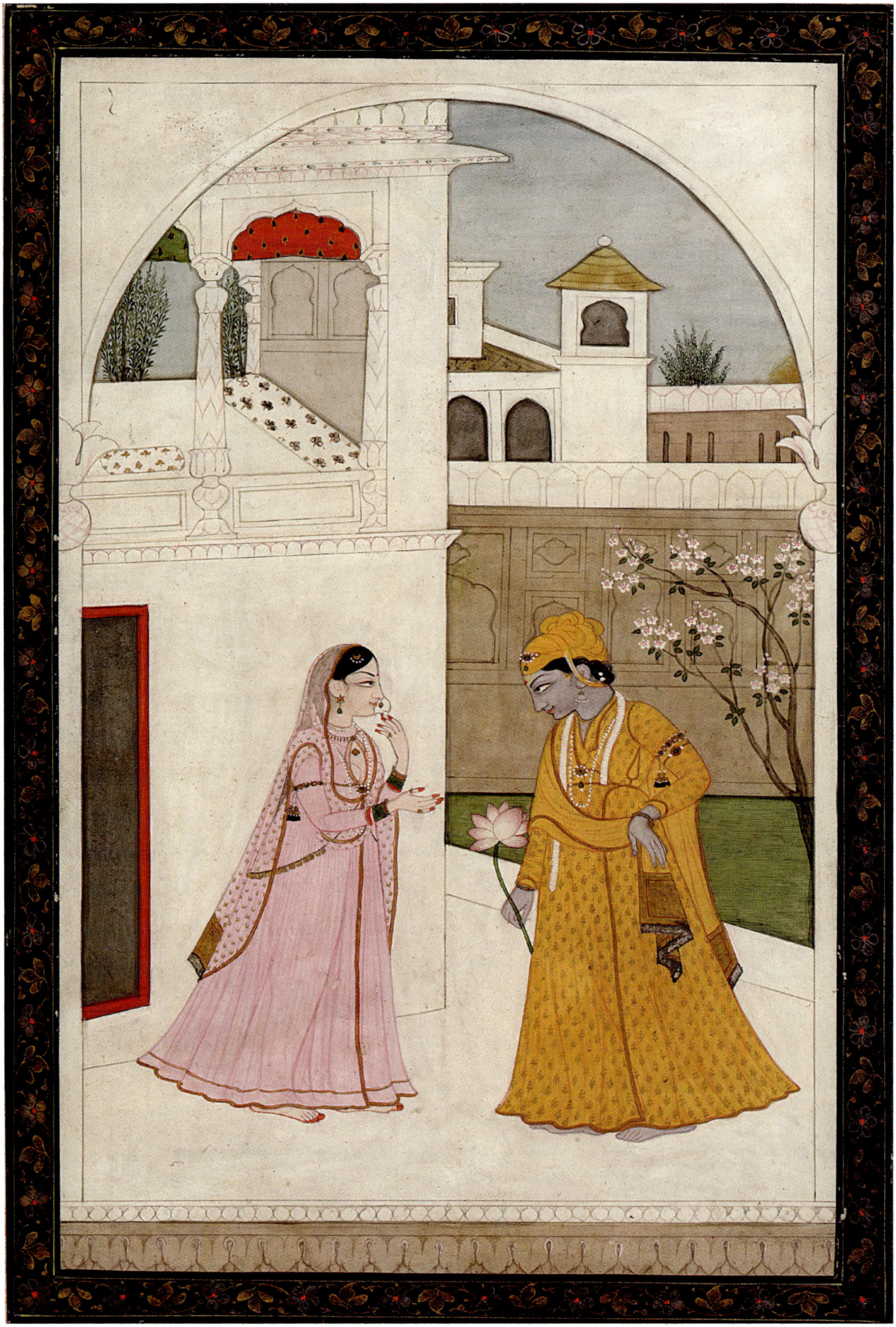

Madhya Khandita Nayika, Kangra, CE 1800-20, Kapoor Gallery, New York

मध्या-खंडिता
जावक लिलार ओठ अंजन की लीक सोहै
खैये न अलीक लोकलीक न बिसारिये।
कबि मतिराम छाती नखछत जगमगै
डगमगै पग सूधै मग मैं न धारिये।
कसकै उघारत हौ पलक पलक यातें
पलका पै पौढ़ि श्रम राति को निवारिये।
अटपटे बैन मुख बात न कहत बनै
लटपटे पेँच सिरपाग के सुधारिये।।

Madhya Khandita Nayika

A nayika *tells her* nayak, *"There are red marks on your forehead as you have prostrated yourself at another woman. There are marks of corrylium on your lips as you have kissed the eyes of another woman. So do not speak words of deceit. Matiram says that nail marks are clearly visible on your chest and you can barely walk straight and your eyes are drooping. So please lie down on the bed and recover from the fatigue of the night. Your speech is indistinct and your turban is dishevelled."*

It is a tense moment as a repentant *nayak* is accosted by an offended *nayika* outside the door of her *haveli*. With his head turned down he avoids eye contact with her and holds a fully bloomed lotus which indicates that it is dawn. He has returned after a romantic night away from her. His turban is dishevelled and his forehead is marked by a red spot clearly indicating his romantic involvement through the night. The bejewelled *nayika* is in a pink *peshwaz*, her left hand showing surprise while her right hand questions the *nayak*. The empty bed chamber at the top speaks of her long and anguished wait through the night, which she hides in her expression. The blossoming tree has also waited for amorous pleasures of this romantic pair, had the *nayak* arrived on time. The Kangra artist has rendered a fine composition and through subtle suggestions, has told the story of the *khandita nayika*.

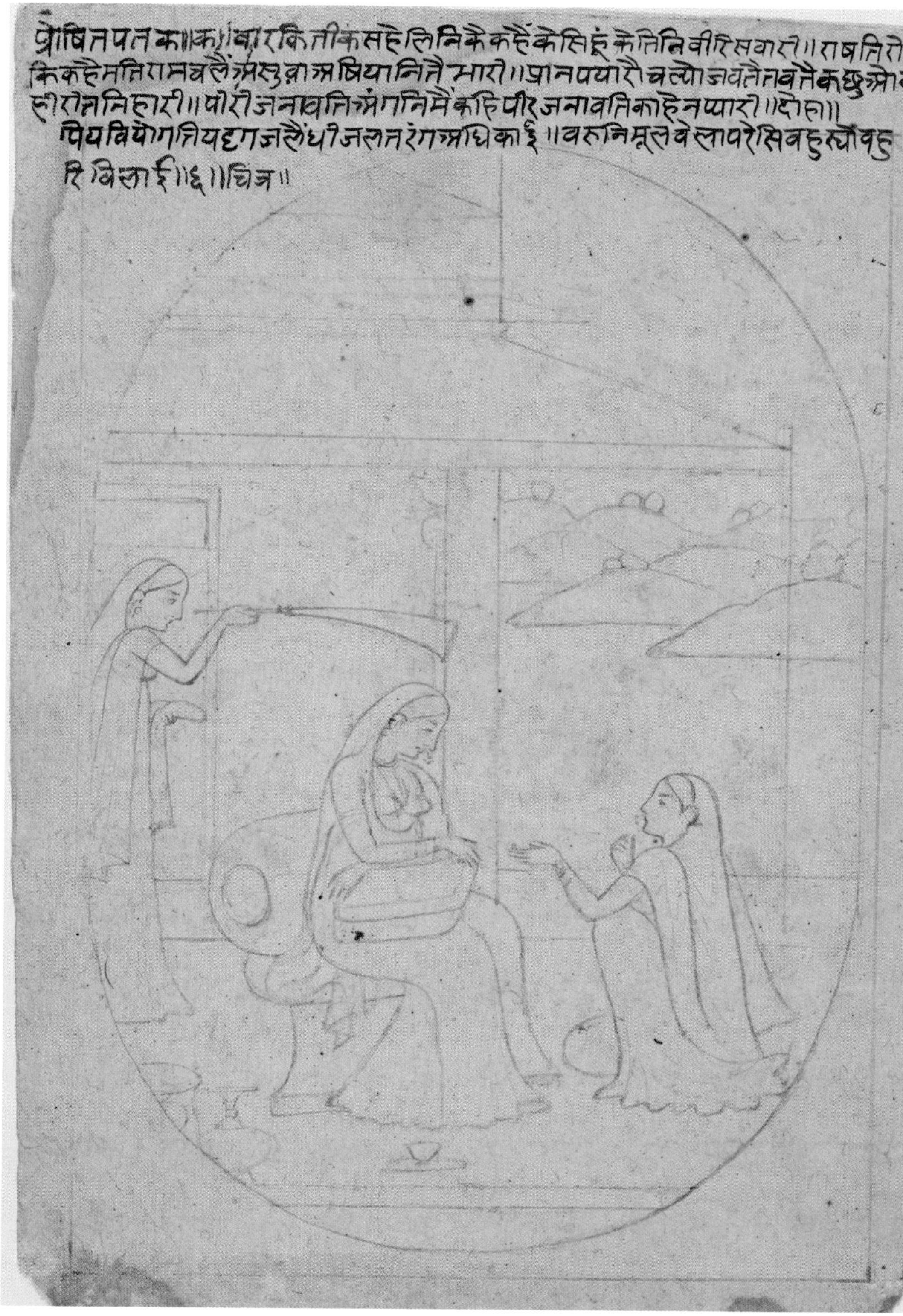

Mugdha Proshitapatika Nayika, drawing in Guler style, CE 1800, Museum of Fine Arts, Boston.

मुग्धा-प्रोषितपतिका

लक्षण बार कितेक सहेलिन के कहैं कैसेहूँ लेत न बीरी सँवारी ।
राखति रोकि कहै मतिराम चलैं अँसुवा अँखियानि तें मारी ।
प्रानपियारो चल्यो जबतें तबतें कछु और ही रीति निहारी ।
पीरी जनावति अंगन में कहि पीर जनावति काहे न प्यारी ।।

Mugdha Proshitapatika Nayika

The mugdha proshitapatika nayika *refuses to take a betel offered by her companions. Torrential stream of tears flows down from her eyes which she cannot control. Ever since her beloved has proceeded on a long tour to a distant land, her life has been affected. Her body has turned pale due to the pangs of separation. Her friend advises to share her anguish with other friends, so that she could be relieved from her suffering.*

In the same oval format on the reverse of the drawing is another sanguine drawing, probably by the same artist. Our eyes focus on the unhappy *nayika* in the middle of the composition. With folded hands and downcast eyes she refuses to engage with her *sakhi*, who pleads with her even as another *sakhi* attends to her with a fly whisk. The *proshitapatika*'s mind is written all over this drawing, a mind that is withdrawn and loveless, which finds the world around her meaningless and who is not interested in the pleasures of the home devoid of her beloved. Neither the landscape nor the concerns of her *sakhis* touch her, for there is no peace in heart at the prospect of being forlorn when her beloved embarks on a long journey.

The scene is composed on a palace terrace beside a river. The *nayika* rests on a raised couch leaning against a bolster. The poet describes that the *sakhi* offers betel to the *nayak*; however, the betel box is missing in the painting.

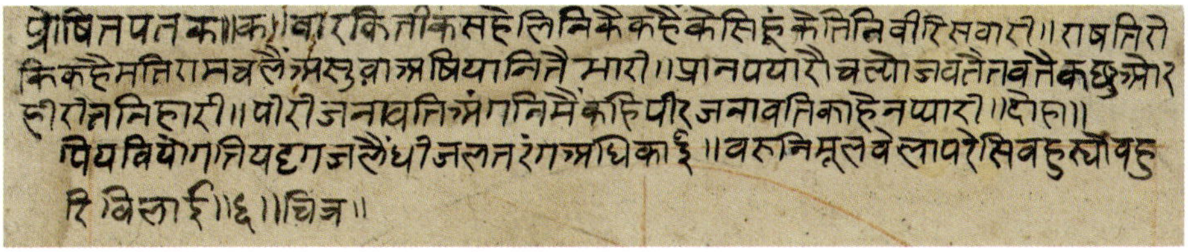
प्रोषितपतका ॥ कं ॥ बारकितीकसहेलिनिकेकहैंकेसिहूंकेतिनिवीरिसवारी ॥ राषतिरो
किकहेमतिरामचलैंअंसुवाअंषियानितैं मारी ॥ प्रानपयारैचल्योजवतैंतवतैंकछुओर
हीरीतनिहारी ॥ पीरीजनावतिअंगनिमैंकहिपीरजनावतिकाहेनप्यारी ॥ दोहा ॥
पियवियोगतियदृगजलैंधीजलजरंगअधिकाई ॥ वरुनिमूलवेलापरेसिवहुस्योंवहु
रि विलाई ॥ ६ ॥ चित्र ॥

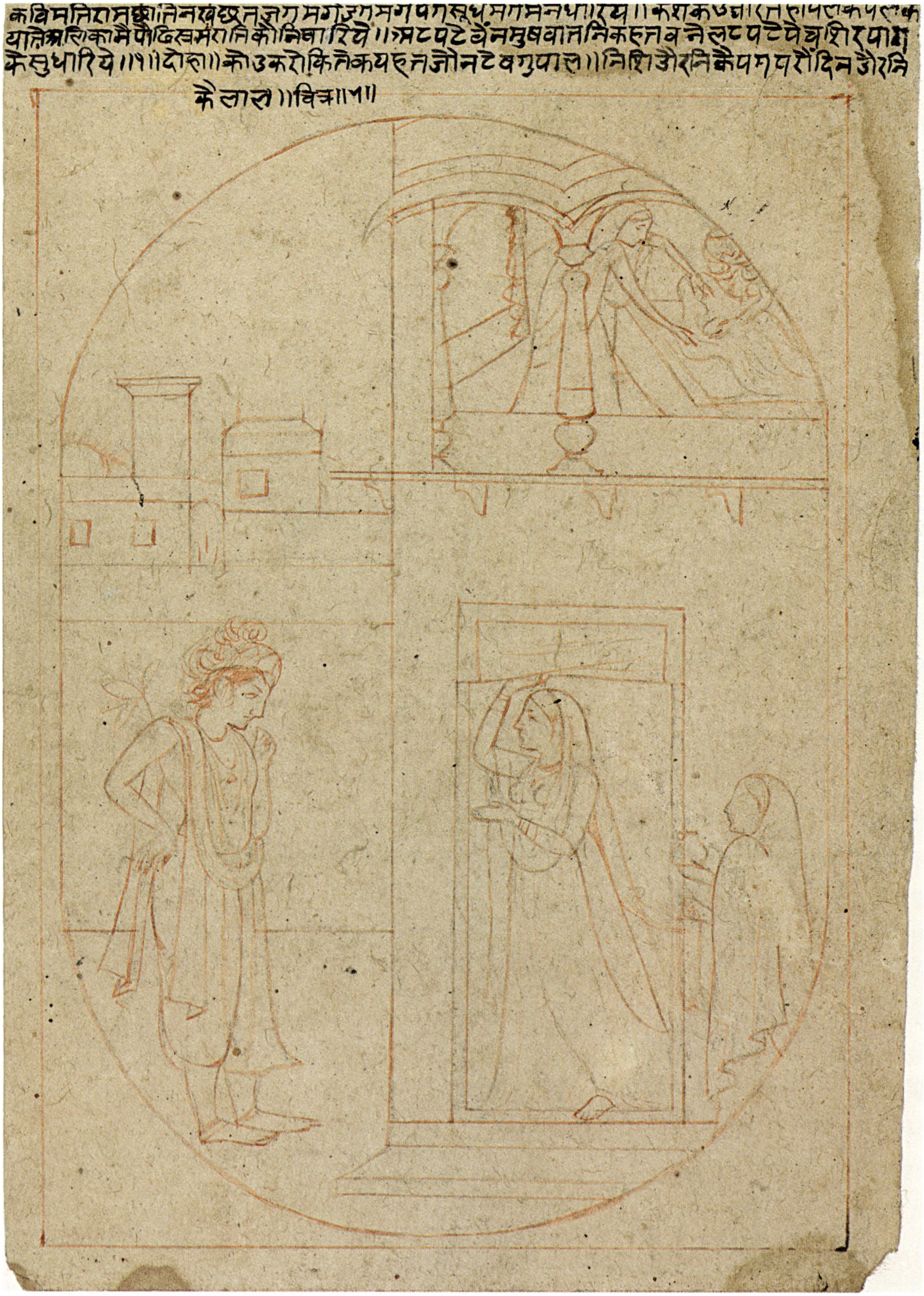

Madhya Khandita Nayika, drawing in Guler style, CE 1800, Museum of Fine Arts, Boston.

मध्या-खंडिता

जावक लिलार ओठ अंजन की लीक सोहै, खैये न अलीक लोकलीक न बिसारियै।
कबि मतिराम छाती नखछत जगमगै, डगमगै पग सूधै मग मैं न धारियै ।
कसकै उघारत हौ पलक पलक यातैं, पलका पै पौढ़ि श्रम राति को निवारियै।
अटपटे बैन मुख बात न कहत बनै, लटपटे पैंच सिरपाग के सुधारियै ।।

Madhya Khandita Nayika

A nayika *tells her* nayak, *"There are red marks on your forehead as you have prostrated yourself at another woman. There are marks of corrylium on your lips as you have kissed the eyes of another woman. So do not speak words of deceit. Matiram says that nail marks are clearly visible on your chest and you can barely walk straight and your eyes are drooping. So please lie down on the bed and recover from the fatigue of the night. Your speech is indistinct and your turban is dishevelled."*

Composed in an oval format, this sanguine drawing illustrates a verse of *Rasraj* of Matiram. The *madhya khandita nayika* is one who is angry with her husband and remonstrates for his fickleness. Standing at the threshold of her room, she encounters her erring husband, who has arrived at dawn after spending the night elsewhere with another woman. The *nayak* is depicted bare chested as the poet Matiram describes nail marks made on his breast during love-making. The tangled folds of his turban reveal his active involvement in his amorous activities. The speechless *nayak* with his head tilted downwards listens quietly to the oblique remarks made by his sulky wife.

The entire scene is set in the inner apartment of the palace. Though the painter has not shown the rising sun in the morning, yet he intentionally draws two maids cleaning the bed chamber of *nayika*, where she waited for her husband all the night in vain.

The sanguine drawing done in the typical Kangra style, datable to *c.* 1800, appears to have a fragment of another group of pictures than that of usual extensive series from Purkhu's workshop rendered for Sansar Chand, the Katoch chief of Kangra. Five lines of verse in Devanagari script corresponds to the *Rasraj* of the celebrated *riti* poet Matiram. Stylistically, this seems to be a creation of a painter other than Purkhu.

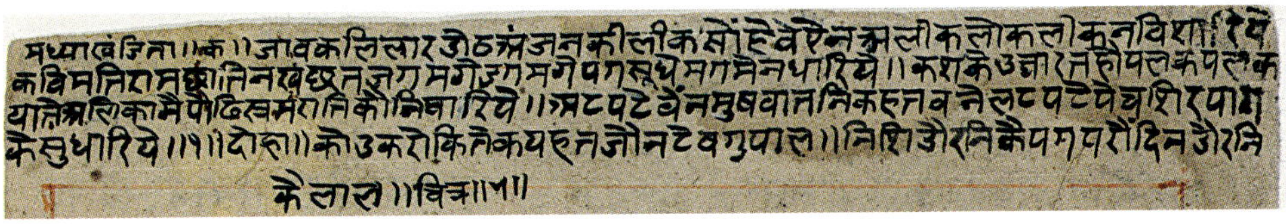

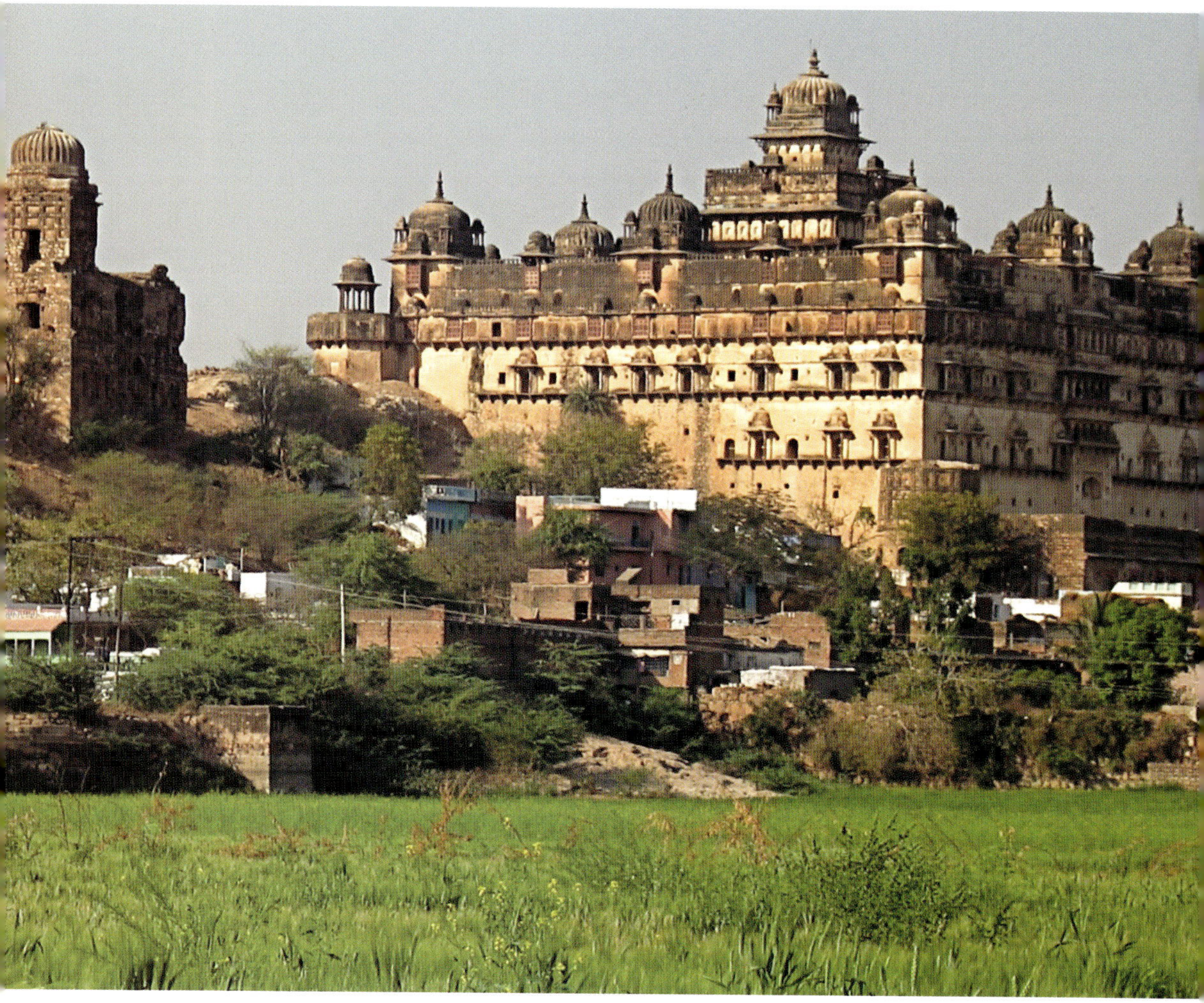

Govind Mahal, Datia, CE 1620-26.

The Atelier of Datia

Bundelkhand in present-day Madhya Pradesh was home to the many artistic expressions of the romantic emotion. It had seen *shringara rasa* immortalised in stone in the temples of Khajuraho in the tenth century where love resonates even today from every stone and wall of the magnificent temples built by the Chandellas. The Sultans of Malwa ruling from the city of Mandu were powerful rulers and the romance of Baz Bahadur and Rupamati still echoes in the palaces of Mandu. Mandu had a flourishing atelier and many landmark paintings were produced there. Even in spite of the Muslim influence, the Malwa *kalam* was stridently indigenous as is seen in the *Ramayana*, *Rasikapriya* and *Amarushataka* paintings that emerged from its atelier. The paintings from the Malwa school remain foundational in the history of Indian miniature painting.

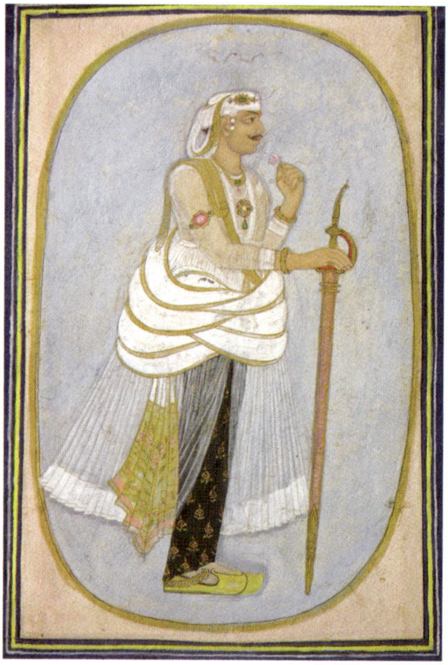

Raja Shatrujit, Datia, eighteenth century, National Museum, Delhi

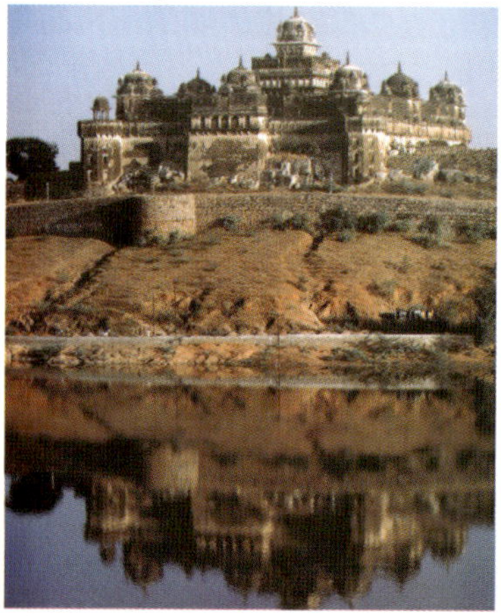

Jehangir Mahal, Orchha.

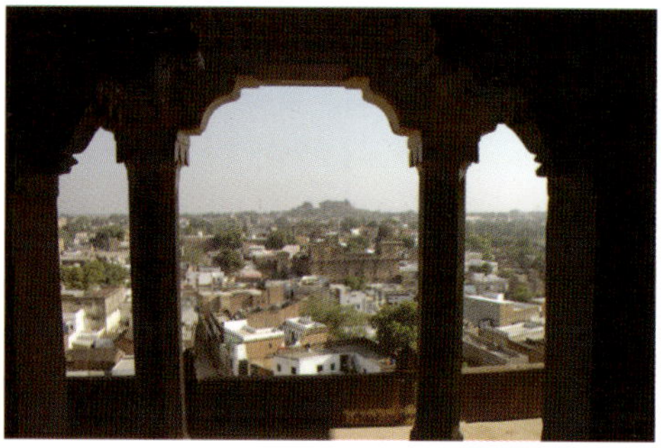

View of Datia.

The Tomars ruled from Gwalior and Raja Man Singh (1486-1516) was one of its most illustrious rulers. The Man Mandir palace is not only a fine piece of architecture but has figures carved in the Chaurapanchasika_style, which strongly suggests that this style of painting must have originated here. Gwalior was also the home of Tansen and music, especially *dhrupad*, flourished here.

It was Raja Rudra Pratap who founded the kingdom of Orchha on the river Betwa in 1531, and later under his son Madhukar Shah the kingdom prospered. Madhukar Shah was followed by Indrajit who patronised Keshavdas, the author of the encyclopaedic and foundational text of *ritikavya*, the *Rasikpriya*. It was under Bir Singh Deo in the early seventeenth century that Bundela art came into its own and despite the strong Mughal presence, retained its own style and ethos. Jehangir Mahal, built in 1614, could boast not only of beautiful architecture but its walls whispered the love of Radha and Krishna from its evocative murals. The murals of Orchha have robust figures, bright colours and sensitive compositions, which suggest that the artistic expression of romantic love had reached a high watermark in that state. Not much is known about miniature painting in Orchha but notwithstanding, it cannot be forgotten that it was the home of *ritikavya* and the patronage of Indrajit, of the poetic genius of Keshavdas and the dances of the courtesan Parvin Rai and all of this must have ensured that *shringara rasa* resonated in word and sound in its courts.

Bir Singh divided his kingdom of Orchha in 1626 and created the kingdom of Datia for his son Bhagvandas and Datia also became an important centre of Krishna painting in the seventeenth and eighteenth centuries. Datia had a thriving atelier and developed its own unique style of painting. Inspired by the Malwa *kalam* and perhaps influenced by Jehangiri Mughal painting, Datia remained resolutely Hindu not only in the ethos of its

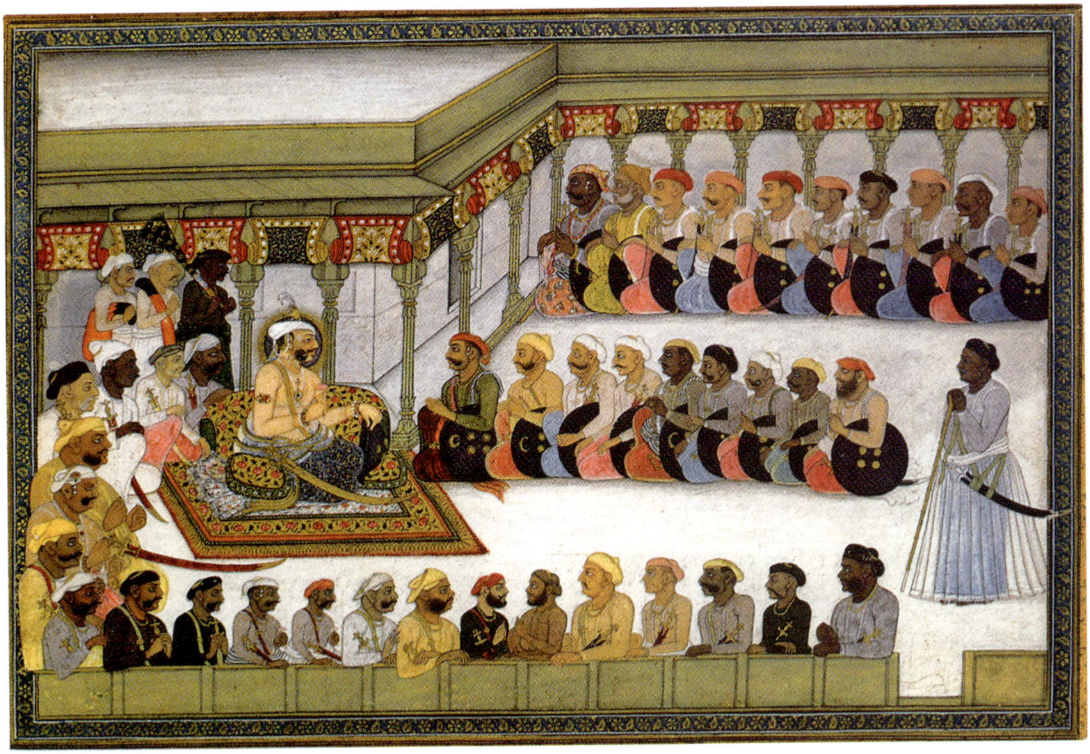

Shatrujit Singh holding court, *c.* CE 1780, Datia, private collection

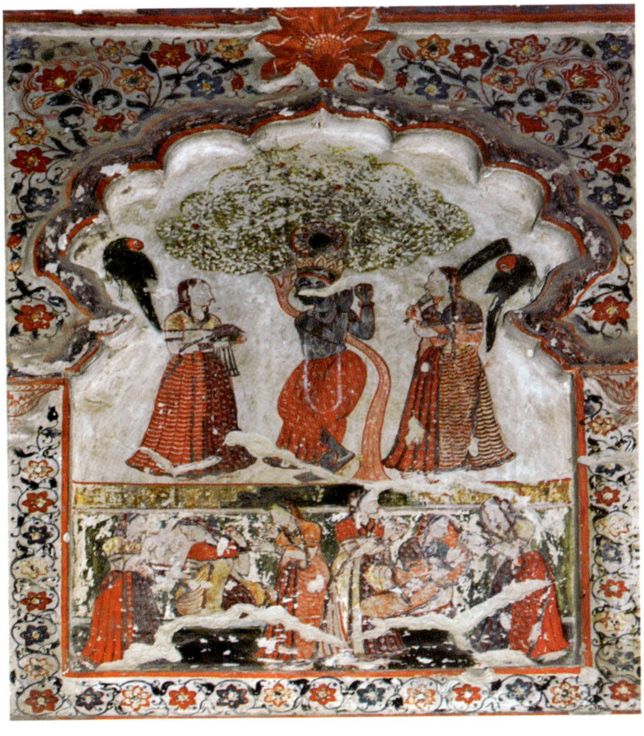

Mural, Jehangiri Mahal, Orchha

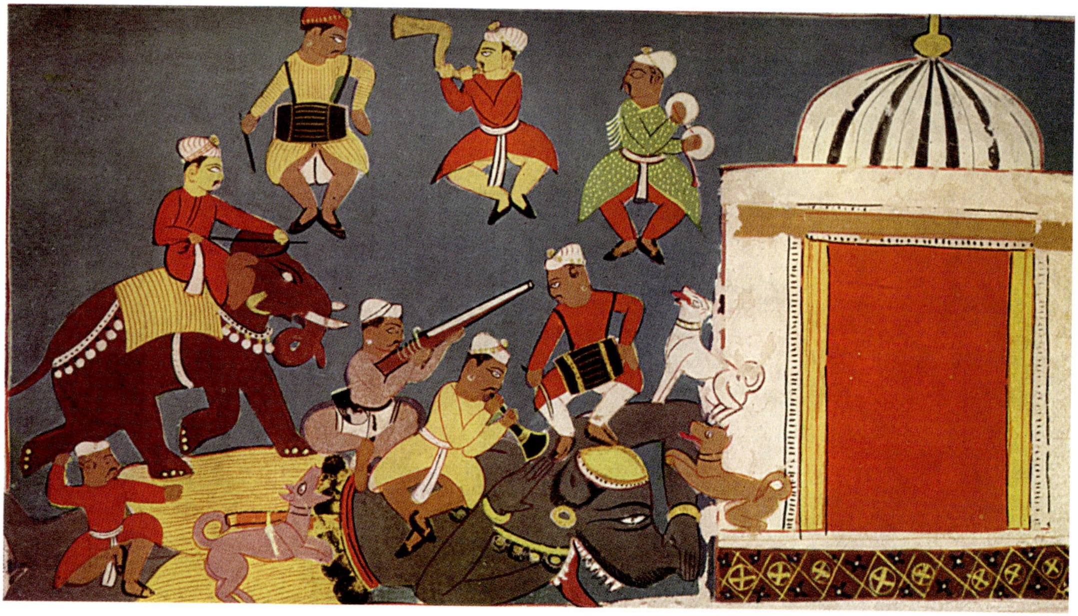

Ramayana, Malwa, eighteenth century, private collection.

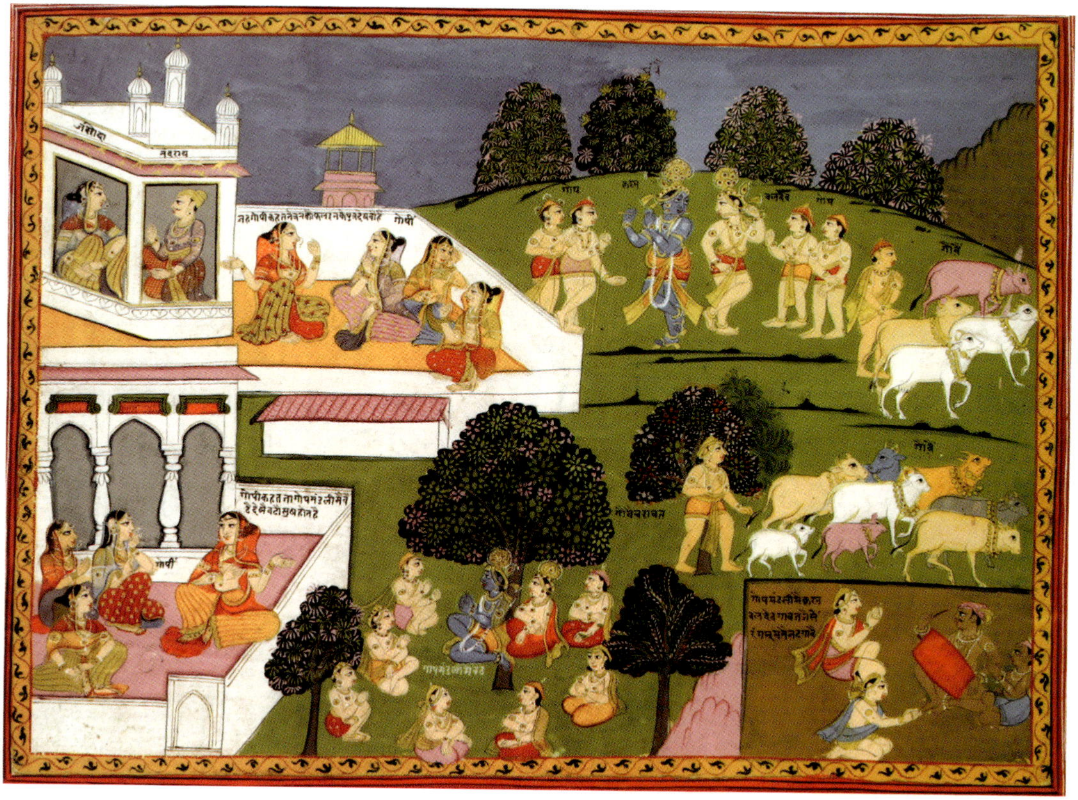

Bhagavata Purana, Datia, eighteenth century, Dehejia collection.

rulers and the culture of the courts but also in the tone and texture of its paintings.

Painting flourished especially under the patronage of Raja Shatrujit (1761-1803). Shatrujit was able to develop an atelier where poets and painters interacted to produce charming pictures, both narrative and portraits. Their *Ramayana* and *Bhagavata Purana* sets are truly remarkable and occupy a pride of place in the treasure of Indian paintings. Shatrujit is especially to be commended for the artistic activity at his court, as Bundelkhand in the eighteenth century was privy to repeated military conflicts, mainly sponsored by the Mughals. The conquest of Mandu by Azam Khan on behalf of Akbar, which led to the downfall of Baz Bahadur is only too well known and this sent shock waves throughout central India. Despite this, Shatrujit was able to keep an active atelier where evocative paintings were produced, driven not just by artistic excellence and sensitive patronage but equally by Shatrujit's commitment to Vaishnavism. This speaks not only of his love of art but even more of his Vaishnava faith. The Bundela kings of Orchha and Datia resolutely retained their Hindu ethos even in the face of a strong Islamic presence in their part of the country. The account of Madhukar Shah, his Orchha predecessor, who went to the court of Akbar with a large *tilak* on his forehead to express his Vaishnava heritage, defying the emperor's orders, is written in the dust of Bundelkhand and leaves no doubt about the strength and resilience of Hindu faith in that kingdom. There was a strong ethos of Vaishnavism in that state, even ahead of the *bhakti* cult that was to follow a couple of hundred years later. Shatrujit could not but be touched by such acts of religious zeal and it was this that drove him to have his artists produce paintings in the Vaishnava theme. Both the *Ramayana* and the *Bhagavata Purana* of the Datia atelier show a strong Hindu artistic touch. Multiple figures in the *Ramayana*, performing various activities, dancing or armed for a conflict,

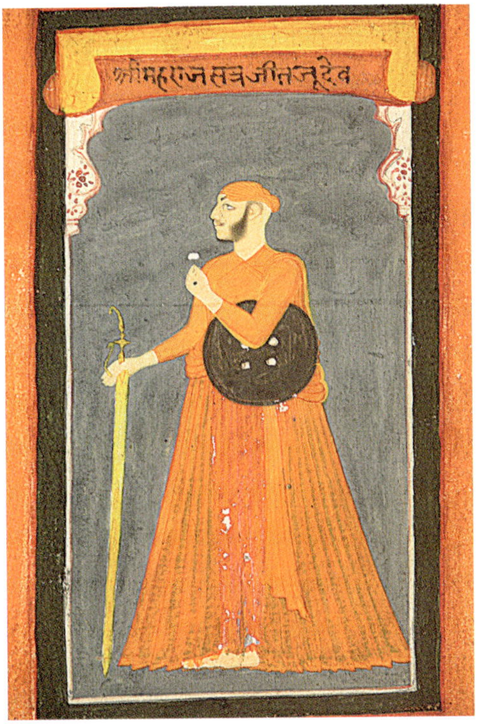

Raja Shatrujit, Datia, eighteenth century, National Museum, Delhi

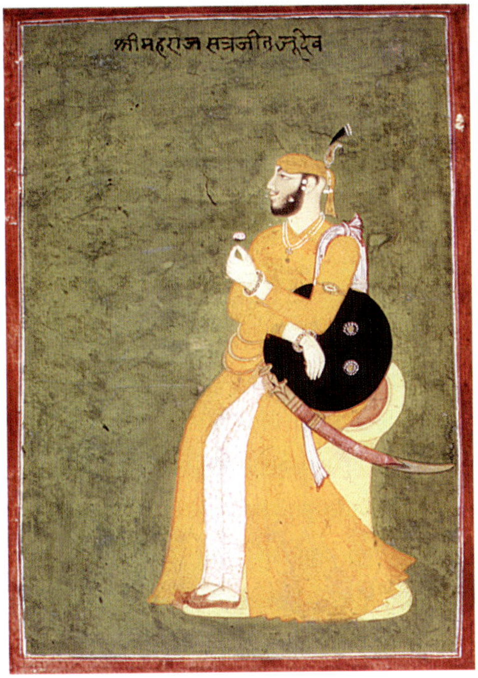

Raja Shatrujit, Datia, eighteenth century, National Museum, Delhi

resonate with a Hindu texture and show very little influence of the Mughal style. The *Bhagavata Purana*, on the other hand, captures both a courtly and pastoral ambience. Whether it is the ladies who sit in the *haveli* or *gopas* tending their cows in Vrindavana, there is no doubt that they drive their energy from the fluting Krishna standing under the *kadamba* tree. The Datia penchant for writing inscriptions in white is also clearly seen in this remarkable painting.

Another strength of Datia artists were portraits of royalty and nobility which are no less inferior in their artistic veracity than those that emerged from the atelier of Akbar or Jehangir. In their portraiture, the Datia artists looked up to their Mughal masters.

In Bundelkhand where the Narmada sings, and the dust whispers of the romance of Baz Bahadur, where the palaces in Orchha still resound with the ankle bells of the dance of Parvin Rai and the poetry of *Rasikapriya* is still heard and the footsteps of Keshavdas are still seen, the atelier of Datia is remembered fondly not only by connoisseurs of art but also by aficionados of *ritikavya*, and the paintings that emerged from its atelier occupy an honoured place in the corridors of Indian art.

Datia paintings show robust though stiff figures, set in a simple *haveli* devoid of architectural embellishments or the luxuriance of landscape. In strong monochromatic colours and bold outlines, the narrative emerges with a dynamism all its own. A characteristic of Datia paintings is inscriptions written in white either at the top or right in the painting itself.

The two paintings based on Matiram's *Rasraj* bear the unmistakable Datia stamp and so does the painting from Bihari's *Satsai.*

It can be emphatically said that Datia occupies an honoured place in the history of miniature paintings and especially in the paintings of *ritikavya.*

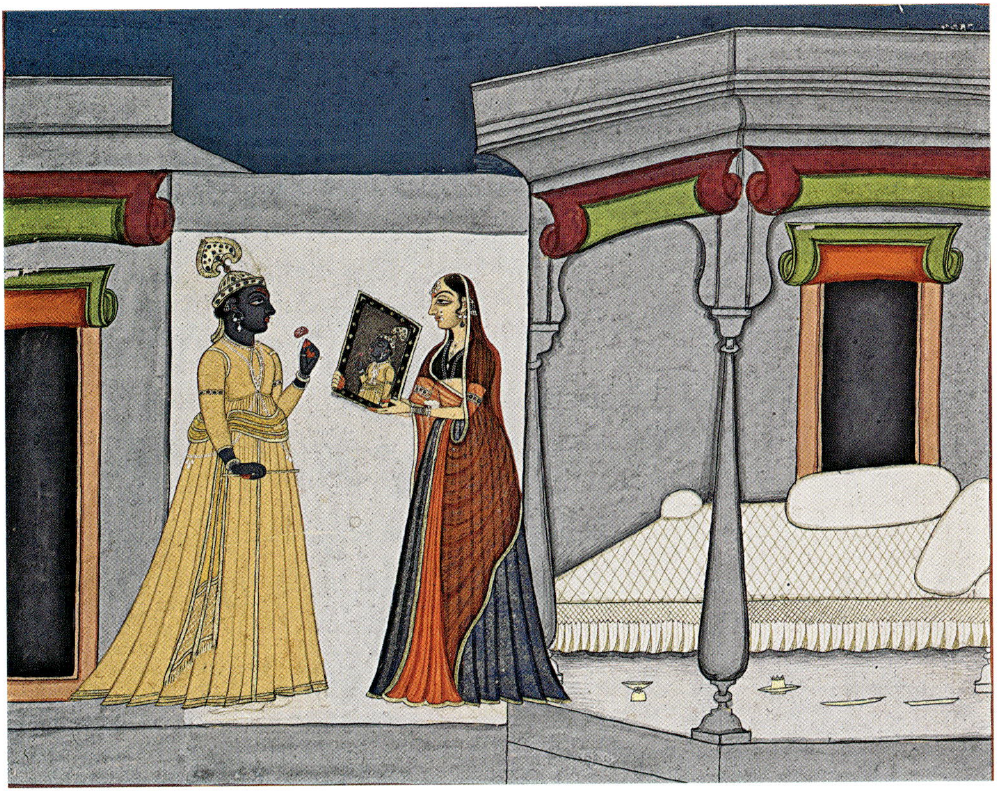

Sat Sai, Datia, eighteenth century, Museum of Fine Arts, Boston.

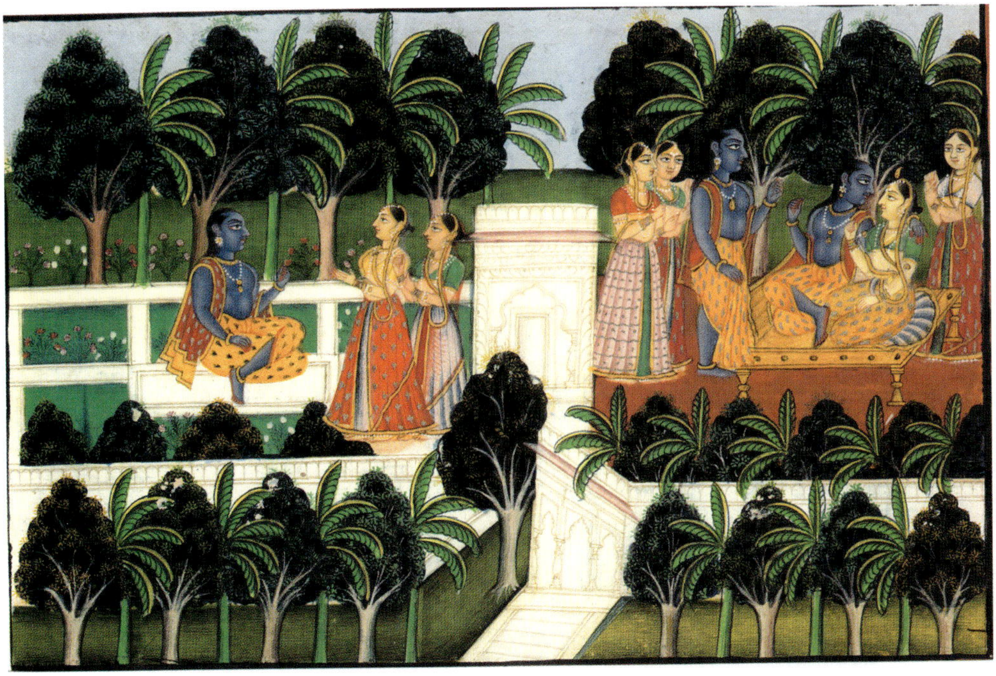

Datia, eighteenth century, Dehejia collection.

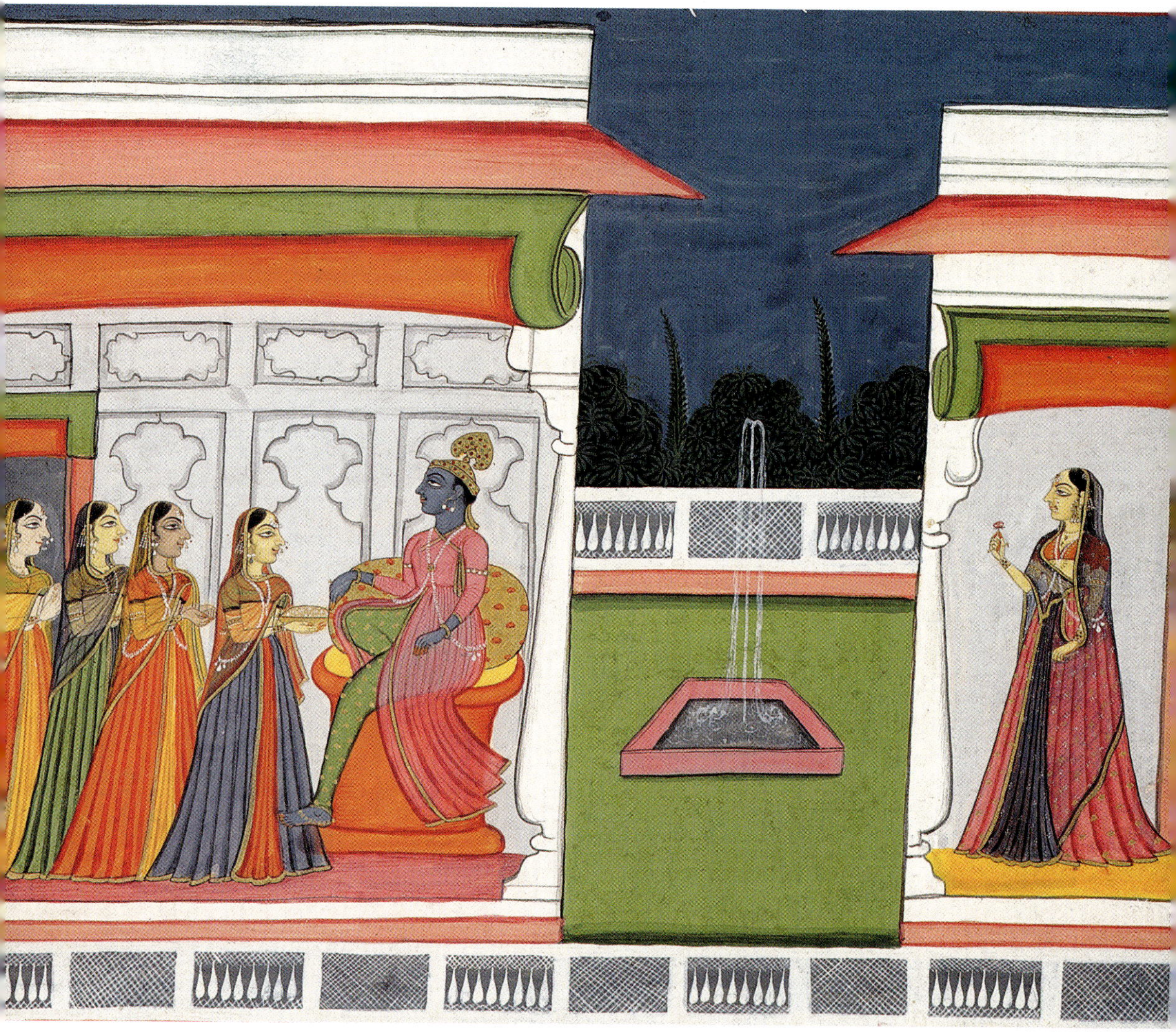

Ajnatayauvanamugdha Nayika, Datia, eighteenth century, Dehejia collection.

अज्ञातयौवना

निरषि नवोढा नारि तन छूटत तरकई लेस।
भौ प्यारो पीतम तियनि मानहु चलत विदेस।।

Agyatayauvanamugdha Nayika

One sakhi *talks to another. The* nayika *is gradually losing her childhood but she has not yet lost her innocence and it shows in some of her behaviour. When the beloved is getting ready to go away the* nayika *keeps on embracing him repeatedly.*

The composition is set in the typical Datia squarish format. A central fountain along with a distant landscape divides the composition in two *haveli*s. In the *haveli* on the left, a *nayika* stands gracefully dressed in a red *ghaghra* and a black diaphanous *odhni* with a flower in hand. Her deportment is regal. In the *haveli* on the other side is the courtly *nayak*, dressed in a green *jama* and a flowing red *uttariya* seated on a pedestal. Four *sakhis* are in attendance. Perhaps the attendants are offering a fond farewell as he is about to embark on a journey. The *nayika* on the other hand, is apprehensive and it seems that she is not ready to let him go. The Datia artist renders this painting in bold strokes and evocative colours which more than makes up for the simple landscape and minimal architecture.

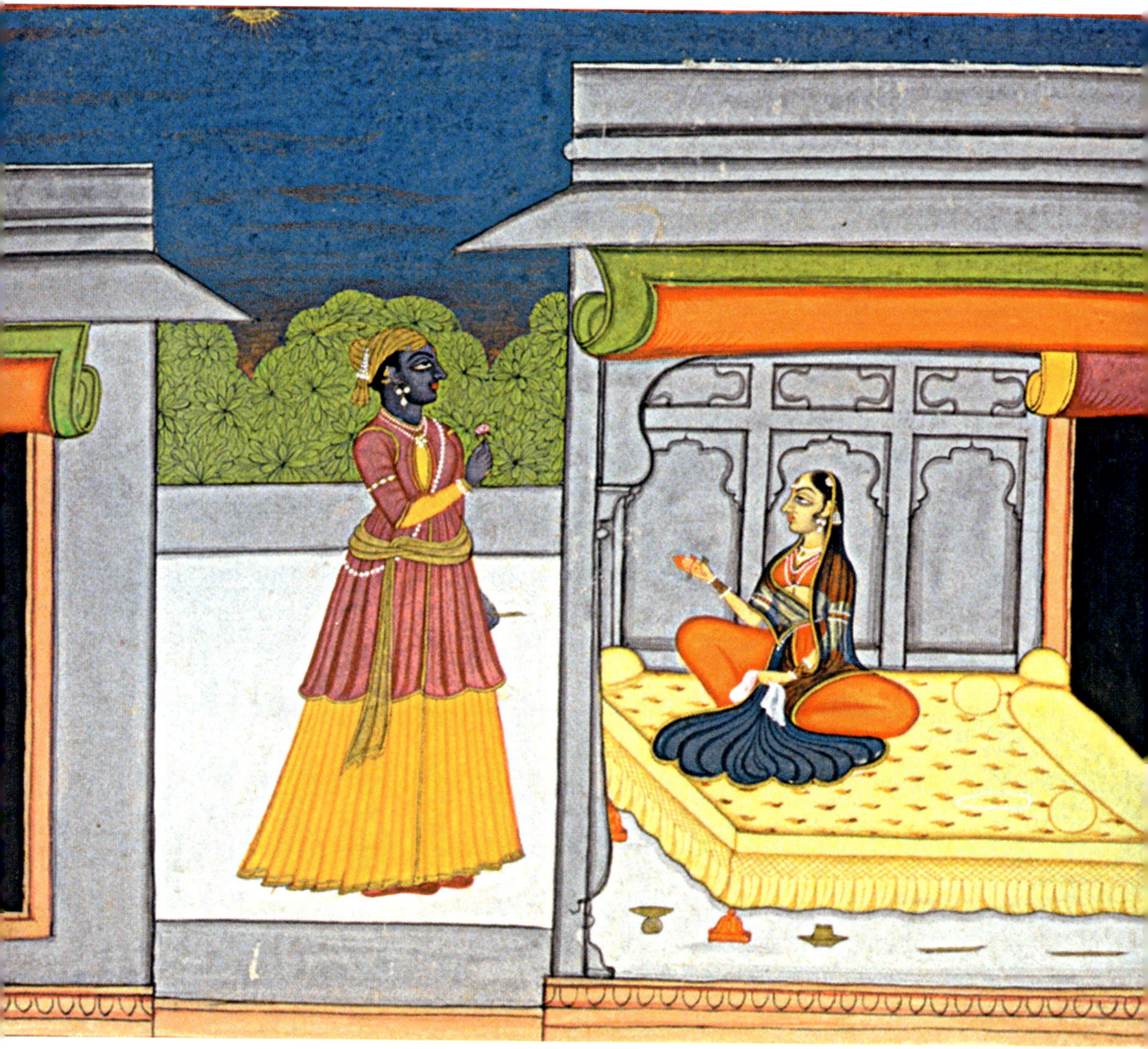

Khandita Nayika, Datia, CE 1780-90, R.K. Tandan collection

खंडिता

रह्यो चकित चहुँ बाचित चित मेरी मति भूलि।
सूर उदआय द्रगान रही सांझ सी धूलि।।

Khandita Nayika

A nayika *addresses her beloved who has spent a night with another woman. I am puzzled and my mind is confused. It is dawn but your eyes have the colour of dusk.*

It is a typical Datia composition, rectangular with monochrome backgrounds. Behind the trees the first rays of the morning sun are seen. The *nayika*, seated on a yellow bedstead, raises her arm to interrogate the repentant *nayak* who has arrived through the door on the right. Holding a flower in his hand and dressed in a yellow and red outfit, he is hoping to be forgiven for his trespasses. The Datia artist is economical and a minimalist when it comes to depicting the architecture or the landscape, but instead he makes beautiful iconic figures which almost speak. The painting has the standard while inscription at the top, which is again typical of Datia paintings.

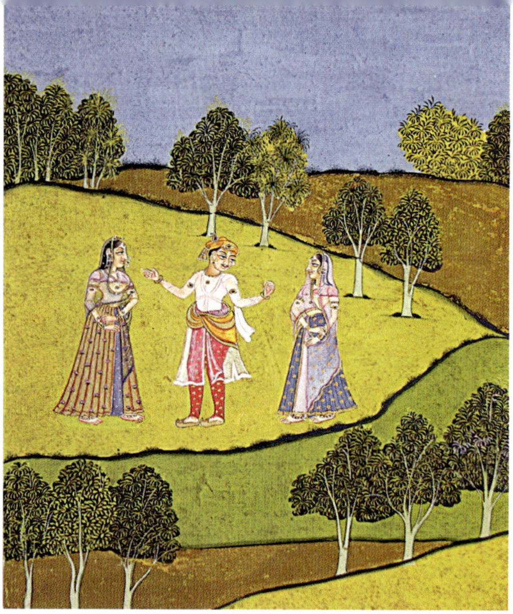

पियत रहैं अधरान को रस अति मधुर अमोल।
तातें मीठे कढ़त हैं लालबदन तें बोल।।२५२।।

The *nayak* is cleverly trying to win over the *nayika* and says, "My dear, your lips drink sweet nectar from my lips. That is why whatever words you speak are sweet because your lips have also become sweet". [252]

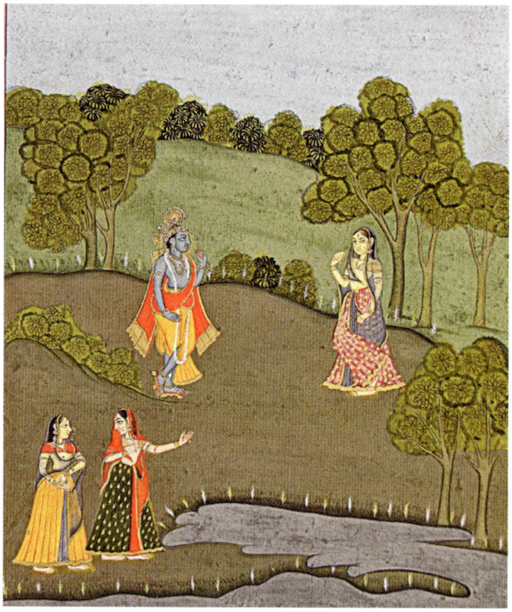

नँदनंदन के रूप पर रीझ रही रिझवारि।
अधमूँदी अँखियन दई मूँदी प्रीति उघारि।।२८३।।

The *nayika* is infatuated with Krishna's looks. Her half-closed eyes reveal her love. [283]

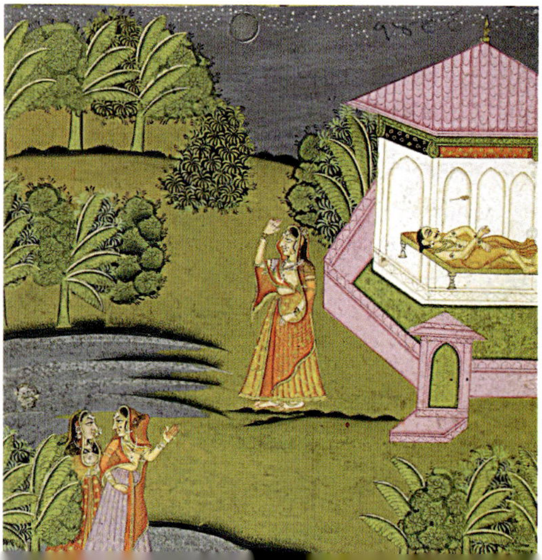

चली मतिराम प्रानप्यारे को मिलन घात
नैसुक निहारिकै बिसारि काज घर को।
पियरो बदन दुख हियरे समाय रह्यो
कुंजन में भयो न मिलापु गिरिधर को।
बिसरे बिलासु वे बिलाय गयो हासु छायो
सुंदरि के तन में प्रताप पंचसर को।
तीछन जुन्हाई भई ग्रीषम को घाम भयो
भीसम पियूषभानु भानु दुपहर को।।१५१।।

The *nayika* saw that the time was right and leaving behind her house-work set out to meet her beloved. When she did not see Krishna in the grove her face turned pale and her heart was filled with sorrow. She forgot all the love sports and the smile on her face vanished. Kama's five arrows created a state of longing in her heart so that the moonlight seemed to her like summer and the moon appeared to her like the afternoon sun. [151]

सखी के काम

मंडन अरु सिच्छा-करन, उपालंभ, परिहास।
काज सखी के जानियो, औरौबुद्धि-बिलास।।२९०।।

After applying red dye to her feet the *sakhi* tells *nayika* that her feet look so attractive that its hue will colour her beloved. Your eyes covered with corrylium look so beautiful that just as the blue lotus folds at dawn they will shut. Ornaments of gold that adorn your body will capture the entire world. These words of mine are false, for it is the beauty of your body that speaks and love is just an excuse. You are so beautiful that the ornaments do not make you beautiful but instead you make the ornaments beautiful. [290]

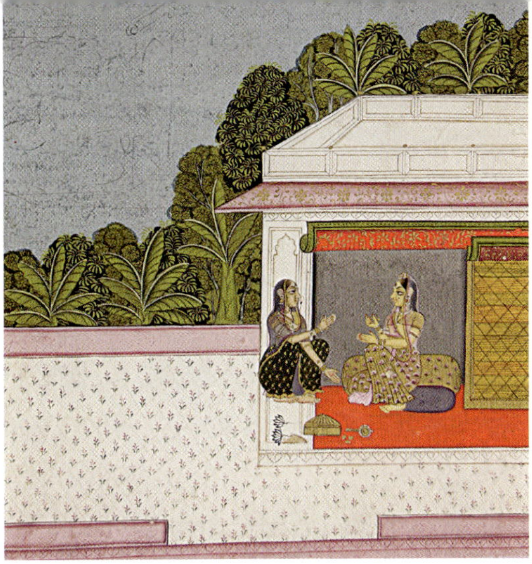

कैयो घरी निसि बीति गई अरु मेह चहूँ दिसि आयो उनैहै।
अंग सिँगार कै बैठी है साँवरे रावरी बाट बिलोकति ह्वैहै।
बैठे कहा मतिराम रसाल हो राति मनावत ही पुनि जैहै।
जाहु न बेगि तिहारी पियारी सु
दोसु बिहारी हमैं पुनि दैहै।।१६१।।

A *sakhi* talks to a *nayak*. "O *nayak* ! The night is advancing and there are dark clouds everywhere. Your beloved must be adorning herself and must await your arrival but yet you are still here. What if she is offended and the whole night would be spent in winning her over. Hasten and go to her, otherwise she might think that we were at fault in not sending you there." [161]

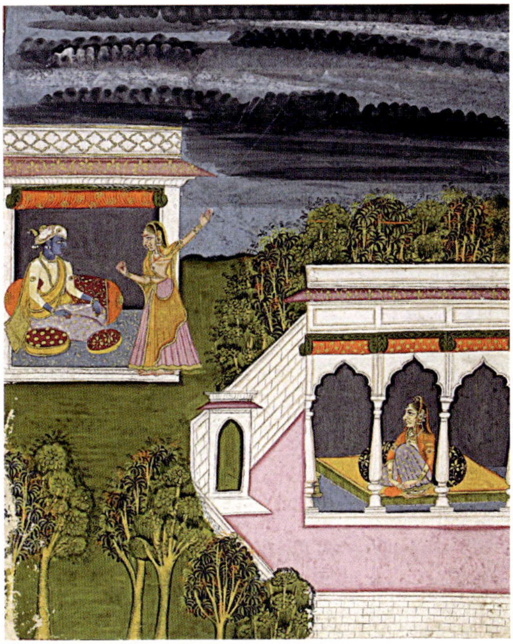

परकीया वासकसज्जा

मनमोहन के मिलन को कौर मनोरथ नारि।
धौर पौन के सामुहैं दियो भौन को बारि।।१७५।।

A *nayika* was very keen on meeting Krishna, so she hatched a plot. When night came, she lit the lamp but kept it in such a place that it would be exposed to the wind so that it would be extinguished soon and thus Krishna could easily enter her home. [175]

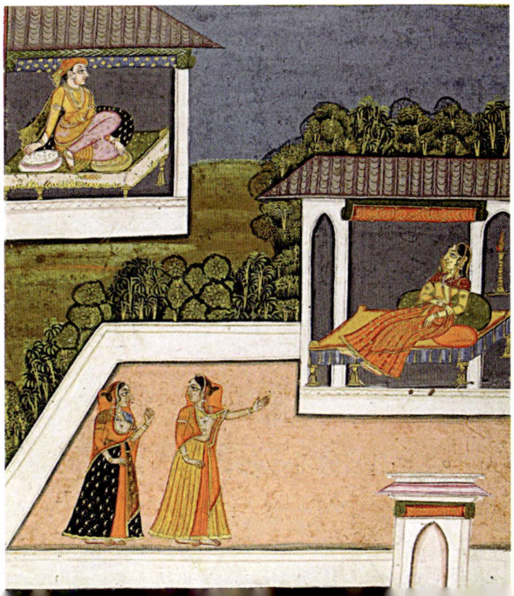

These six paintings are from the atelier of Datia in the late eighteenth century during the period of Raja Shatrujit.

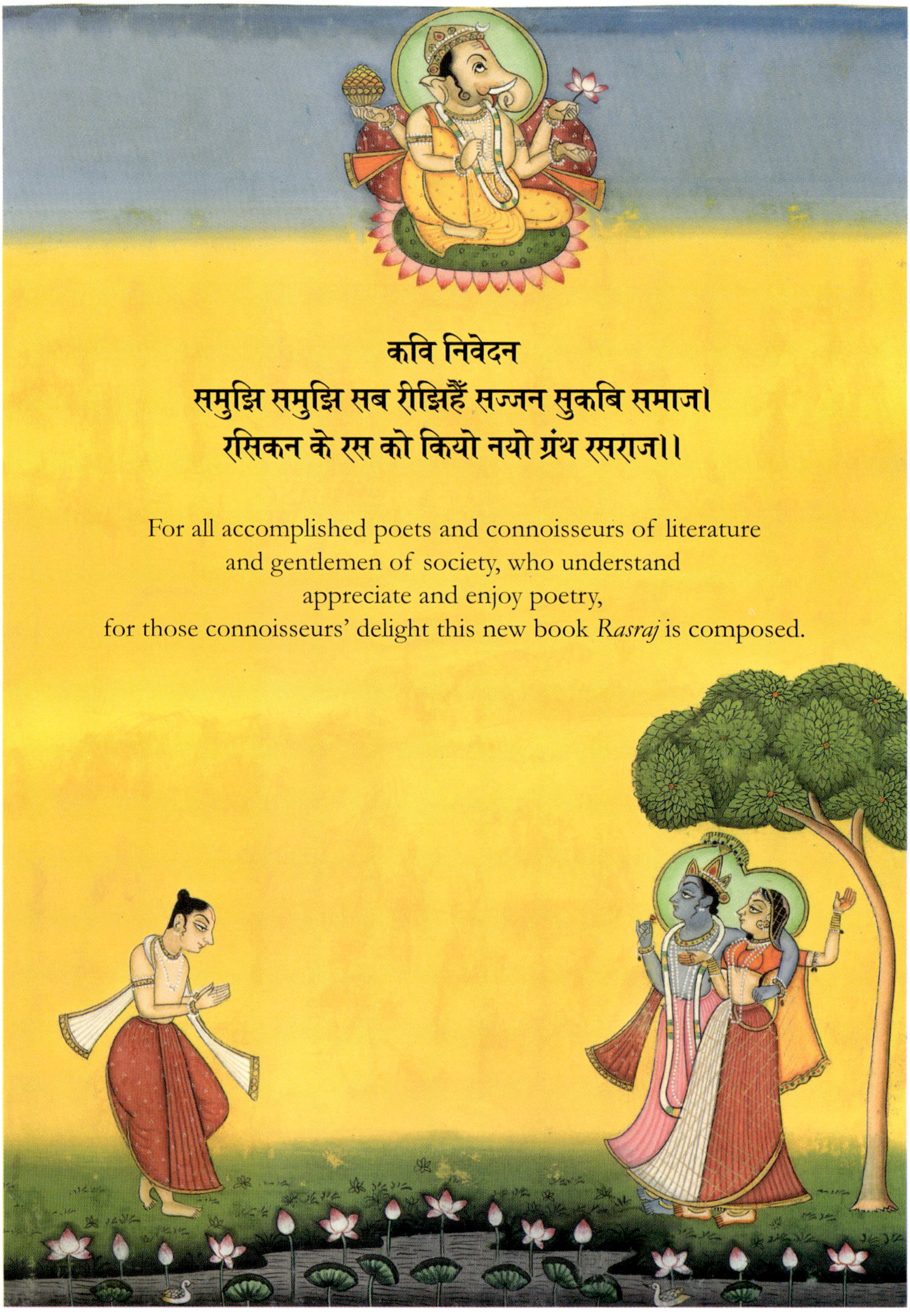

कवि निवेदन

समुझि समुझि सब रीझिहैं सज्जन सुकबि समाज।
रसिकन के रस को कियो नयो ग्रंथ रसराज।।

For all accomplished poets and connoisseurs of literature
and gentlemen of society, who understand
appreciate and enjoy poetry,
for those connoisseurs' delight this new book *Rasraj* is composed.